BUILDING CLASSROOM DISCIPLINE

Sixth Edition

C. M. Charles
San Diego State University

Collaboration by
Gail W. Senter
Karen Blaine Barr

 **LONGMAN**

An imprint of Addison Wesley Longman, Inc.

New York • Reading, Massachusetts • Menlo Park, California • Harlow, England
Don Mills, Ontario • Sydney • Mexico City • Madrid • Amsterdam

Acquisitions Editor: Virginia L. Blanford
Development Manager: Arlene Bessenoff
Associate Editor: Arianne J. Weber
Marketing Manager: Renée Ortbals
Project Coordination and Text Design: Electronic Publishing Services Inc., NYC
Cover Designer: Kay Petronio
Cover Design Manager: Nancy Danahy
Cover Photo: © PhotoDisc
Full Service Production Manager: Valerie L. Zaborski
Photo Researcher: Sandy Schneider
Publishing Services Manager: Al Dorsey
Electronic Page Makeup: Electronic Publishing Services Inc., NYC
Printer and Binder: The Maple-Vail Book Manufacturing Group
Cover Printer: The Lehigh Press, Inc.

For permission to use copyrighted material, grateful acknowledgment is made to the
copyright holders on pp. 150, 152, 154, and 156, which are hereby made part of this
copyright page.

Library of Congress Cataloging-in-Publication Data
Charles, C. M.
    Building classroom discipline / C. M. Charles [with] collaboration
by Gail W. Senter, Karen Blaine Barr. — 6th ed.
        p.   cm.
    Includes bibliographical references (p. 303) and index.
    ISBN 0-8013-3004-1 (pbk.)
    1. School discipline.   2. Classroom management.   I. Senter,
Gail W.   II. Barr, Karen Blaine.   III. Title.
LB3012.C46   1998
371.5—dc21   97-49873
                                                                  CIP

Please visit our website at http://longman.awl.com

ISBN 0-8013-3004-1

1 2 3 4 5 6 7 8 9 10—MA—01009998

Contents

CHAPTER 2   **INSTRUCTIONAL MANAGEMENT
AND DEMOCRATIC TEACHING**
*The Contributions of Jacob Kounin
and Rudolf Dreikurs*   *34*

Ali

CHAPTER 6 LINDA ALBERT'S *COOPERATIVE DISCIPLINE* 123

CHAPTER 7 THOMAS GORDON'S *DISCIPLINE AS SELF-CONTROL* 143

CHAPTER 8 JANE NELSEN, LYNN LOTT, AND H. STEPHEN GLENN'S *POSITIVE DISCIPLINE IN THE CLASSROOM* 163

Preface

Teachers are keenly concerned with maintaining pleasant, well-mannered behavior in their classrooms, and there are times when they must use some form of discipline in order for class time to remain interesting and productive. *Building Classroom Discipline,* Sixth Edition, presents the suggestions of leading authorities for reducing the types of student misbehavior that stifle learning and produce stress for both teachers and students.

Building Classroom Discipline, Sixth Edition, is appropriate for pre-service courses in discipline and classroom management, learning and instruction, methods of teaching, and educational psychology. It is equally appropriate for teachers already in service who are experiencing difficulty with classroom discipline. Instructors in school district training programs and teacher institutes will also find the book useful.

In keeping with previous editions, *Building Classroom Discipline,* Sixth Edition, takes an eminently practical approach to classroom discipline. Comprehensive enough to serve as a single or primary text, yet compact enough for use with other texts, it describes for analysis models of discipline developed by some of the most influential educational thinkers of the past half century. Five of these models, called Foundational Models, explain early scholarship in discipline that has helped form present-day thinking, whereas seven later models, called Application Models, present carefully constructed and complete plans for establishing positive discipline in today's classrooms. Information presented in the models is later augmented with material on related topics, such as organizing classrooms to reduce misbehavior and tailoring systems of discipline to teacher preferences, the realities of school, and the special needs of students. Application exercises, including review of terminology, analysis of concept cases, and questions and activities, are included to help users refine new knowledge and skills.

NEW TO THIS EDITION

The sixth edition features several important additions and modifications.

- Two new models of discipline have been added: Linda Albert's *Cooperative Discipline* and Jane Nelsen, Lynn Lott, and H. Stephen Glenn's *Positive Discipline in the Classroom.* Albert's model uses principles of discipline set forth earlier by Rudolf Dreikurs but amplifies them in scope and meaning, so that teachers can help all students feel they are capable, connected with others, and contributors to the well-being of class and school—Albert's "three C's." Nelsen, Lott, and Glenn's *Positive Discipline in the Classroom* shows teachers how to use class meetings to establish codes of classroom conduct and resolve behavior problems in a student-centered forum. Both *Cooperative Discipline* and *Positive Discipline in the Classroom* exemplify the trend toward involving students as full partners in establishing and maintaining suitable classroom behavior.

- Two new thrusts in classroom discipline are explored: Barbara Coloroso's *Inner Discipline* and Alfie Kohn's *Beyond Discipline.* These new ideas, just beginning to impact scholarship in classroom discipline, are presented as "emerging views" that seem likely to take their place among established models of discipline in the next few years. Coloroso's contention is that teachers can help students develop inner discipline that enables them to interact successfully with others. This ability is developed apart from typical systems of reward and punishment and will serve individuals for the rest of their lives. Kohn's contention is that existing approaches to discipline do more harm than good. Because present approaches are based on reward and punishment, they teach students short-term expediency rather than the desired ability to control themselves in a responsible fashion. Kohn would do away with classroom discipline altogether and in its place have teachers work to develop a sense of community in their classrooms.

- To keep the book from growing too large, the first five chapters of the previous edition have been reduced to three chapters that detail the work of earlier contributors to scholarship in classroom discipline.

- The book has been organized into three parts, such that each leads progressively into the next. Part I, Foundational Work in Classroom Discipline, explains the highly important work of earlier contributors to knowledge about classroom discipline. The models they set forth are no longer used as complete discipline systems, but each has contributed importantly to models now in use. Part II, Application Models of Classroom Discipline, presents seven models of discipline that are widely used today and ends with an examination of Coloroso's and Kohn's intriguing views on discipline. Part III, Toward Building a Personal System of Discipline, presents additional information about the characteristics of teachers and classrooms where good discipline prevails and culminates with guidance for helping readers build personal systems of discipline attuned to their philosophies and personalities and to the realities of students and settings where they teach.

- Review and feedback have been solicited from the developers of all seven of the application models. This ensures that the essence of their thought is captured and presented accurately in the chapters.

- A comprehensive glossary of terms important in the foundational and application models is new to this edition. Over 230 key terms are defined, and the names of authorities who used the terms in special ways are identified. Each of these terms, when first introduced in the text, is presented in boldface type.

- A comprehensive bibliography is presented in this edition, consisting of approximately 220 references cited in the text and/or recommended for reading.
- Chapter formats have been changed to facilitate reading and comprehension. Each chapter begins with a one-page Preview of the chapter contents. Where foundational and application models of discipline are described, the chapters are organized as follows: (1) Preview, consisting of focus, logic, contributions, and suggestions of the model, (2) Information about the model's author or authors, (3) Contributions the authors have made to discipline, (4) Central focus of the authors, (5) Principal teachings of the authors, (6) Analysis of the model, (7) Strengths of the model, (8) Initiating the model in classroom practice, (9) Application exercises, including review of terminology, consideration of concept cases, and questions and activities, and (10) References and recommended readings.

ACKNOWLEDGMENTS

The author gratefully acknowledges the valuable contributions to this edition made by the following people:

Teachers

Roy Allen	Leslie Hays
Constance Bauer	Elaine Maltz
Linda Blacklock	Colleen Meagher
Tom Bolz	Nancy Natale
Michael Brus	Linda Pohlenz
Gail Charles	David Sisk
Ruth Charles	Deborah Sund
Diana Cordero	Mike Straus
Keith Correll	Deborah Trivoli
Barbara Gallegos	Virginia Villalpando
Kris Halverson	

Critical Reviewers

Linda Albert, Cooperative Discipline Institute
Dale Allee, Southwest Missouri State University
Lee Canter, Lee Canter & Associates, Inc.
Barbara Coloroso, *Kids Are Worth It!*
Richard Curwin, Discipline Associates

Philip DiMattia, Boston College

Karen M. Dutt, Indiana State University

Carolyn Eichenberger, St. Louis University

Sara S. Garcia, Santa Clara University

William Glasser, Institute for Reality Therapy

Thomas Gordon, Effectiveness Training International

Marci Greene, University of South Florida at Ft. Myers

C. Bobbi Hansen, University of San Diego

Fredric Jones, Fredric H. Jones and Associates, Inc.

David I. Joyner, Old Dominion University

Alfie Kohn, Author and Critic

Thomas J. Lasley, The University of Dayton

Bernice Magnus-Brown, University of Maine

Janey L. Montgomery, University of Northern Iowa

Janice L. Nath, University of Houston

Jane Nelsen, Lynn Lott, and H. Steven Glenn, Empowering People

Merrill M. Oaks, Washington State University

Jack Vaughan Powell, University of Georgia

Mary C. Shake, University of Kentucky

Alma A. Shearin, University of Central Arkansas

Terry R. Shepherd, Southern Illinois University at Carbondale

JoAnne Smatlan, Seattle Pacific University

Kay Stickle, Ball State University

Sylvia Tinling, University of California, Riverside

Bill Weldon, Arizona State University

Kathleen Whittier, State University of New York at Plattsburgh

Introduction

Classroom Discipline: Myriad Problems and Multiple Prospects

PREVIEW

Misbehavior

■ Student misbehavior is one of the most serious problems teachers have to face.

■ Student misbehavior consists of acts students know they should not do while at school.

■ Teachers must deal with five types of student misbehavior. In order from most serious to least serious they are:

    aggression
    immorality
    defiance
    disruption
    goofing off

■ Of these types of misbehavior, goofing off is the greatest thief of teaching-learning time.

Classroom Discipline

■ Discipline refers to teachers' attempts to prevent, suppress, and redirect student misbehavior.

■ Traditionally, discipline was forceful and authoritarian; newer approaches are more humane.

■ The first "modern" approach to discipline appeared in 1951. Several have appeared since 1970.

The scene is an inner-city school. Classroom 314 is quiet as students listen attentively to the teacher's questions about a recent lesson. Suddenly, eager hands begin to wave and bodies twist out of their seats amidst shouts of "ooh me," "I know," "ooh-oh." Quiet returns when one student is chosen to answer. As soon as she has responded, others begin to yell out refutations or additions and compete again for teacher recognition. As they participate wholeheartedly in class, several students are simultaneously but secretly passing notes and candy and signaling to each other in sign and face language. When the questions end and seat work begins, some students offer to help others who are unsure of how to proceed.

But across the hall in room 315, chaos reigns. The room is noisy with the shouting, laughter, and movement of many children. Though most students are seated, many are walking or running aimlessly around the classroom. Some stop at others' desks, provoke them briefly, and move on. Several students who are lining up textbooks as "race courses" for toy cars laugh when the teacher demands their attention. As the teacher struggles to ask a question over the noise, few if any students volunteer to answer. When one student does respond correctly, others yell out, "You think you're so smart." (Schwartz 1981, 99)

By most teachers' standards, the discipline in Room 314 is good, while that in Room 315 is poor. But what is the difference? In both rooms, students are making noise and behaving in ways usually considered unacceptable. Yet the teacher in Room 314 is probably quite satisfied with the lesson, while the teacher in Room 315 is probably frustrated and laboring under stress. Why? Simply because in the teachers' eyes, students in Room 314 are behaving acceptably, while those in Room 315 are not.

BEHAVIOR AND MISBEHAVIOR

Behavior is whatever one does, whether good or bad, right or wrong, helpful or useless, productive or wasteful. **Misbehavior** is behavior that is considered inappropriate for the setting or situation in which it occurs. Generally speaking, classroom misbehavior occurs intentionally, not inadvertently—that is, students purposely do something they know they should not do. An accidental hiccup during quiet work time is not misbehavior, but when feigned for the purpose of disrupting a lesson, the same behavior is justifiably recognized as misbehavior.

Five Types of Misbehavior

Teachers contend with five broad **types of misbehavior.** In descending order of seriousness, as judged by social scientists, they are as follows:

1. Aggression: physical and verbal attacks on the teacher or other students.
2. Immorality: acts such as cheating, lying, and stealing.
3. Defiance of authority: refusal, sometimes hostile, to do as the teacher requests.

4. Class disruptions: talking loudly, calling out, walking about the room, clowning, tossing objects.
5. Goofing off: fooling around, out of seat, not doing assigned tasks, dawdling, daydreaming.

Teachers generally concur with social scientists' judgments concerning the levels of social seriousness of the five categories of misbehavior, and indeed they dread having to deal with aggression, immorality, and defiance. But in practice they seldom have to do so. The misbehavior that troubles their classrooms is usually much less serious—goofing off, talking, and inattention, for example—relatively innocuous behaviors that nevertheless waste much instructional time and interfere with learning. Lee Canter (Canter and Canter 1992), whose Assertive Discipline is one of the most widely used discipline systems, was asked how he could justify taking disciplinary action against a student for misbehavior as benign as inappropriate laughter or talking without permission. He replied that it was precisely such behaviors, which no one considers serious, that drive teachers to distraction and ruin learning for everyone.

DISCIPLINE AND MISBEHAVIOR

The word **discipline** has several different definitions, but in this book it means what teachers do to help students behave acceptably in school. You can see that discipline is tied directly to misbehavior—where there is no misbehavior, no discipline is required.

Discipline is intended to prevent, suppress, and redirect misbehavior. All teachers know that students sometimes behave with sweetness, kindness, gentility, consideration, helpfulness, and honesty. Their doing so makes teaching one of the most satisfying of all professions. But students also behave at times with hostility, abusiveness, disrespect, disinterest, and cruelty, all of which can devastate personal feelings and severely damage the learning climate of the classroom. Ideally, the goal of discipline is to reduce the need for teacher intervention over time by helping students learn to control their own behavior. When teachers apply various discipline techniques, they hope not only that misbehavior will cease but that students will internalize self-discipline and display it in the classroom and elsewhere.

IS DISCIPLINE A SERIOUS MATTER?

Phi Delta Kappa, a professional organization for educators, sponsors a Gallup Poll of the public's attitudes toward education. One question on the survey asks: "What do you think are the biggest problems with which the public schools of this community must contend?" In 18 of the first 26 polls, which began in 1969, lack of discipline was listed as the top problem, a position it has held with little interruption in recent years. For example, the 27th Annual Poll (Elam, Rose, and Gallup 1995) named discipline the top concern, followed in order by lack of proper financial support for education, fighting/violence/gangs, and drug abuse.

Of course, public opinion can be suspect because it is influenced by the sensational, such as physical attacks on teachers and wanton vandalism of schools. In the case of discipline, however, little disagreement exists between educators and the public. Administrators perceive a widespread increase in school violence, and for years teachers have maintained that misbehavior interferes significantly with their teaching (Elam 1989). The resultant frustration produces stress that affects some teachers as severely as does battle fatigue experienced by soldiers in combat, symptoms of which include lethargy, exhaustion, tension, depression, and high blood pressure.

The concern about discipline is not declining, but is growing year by year. Numerous studies list discipline among the most serious problems with which teachers must contend and a significant factor in their leaving the profession—it is largely responsible for the teacher dropout rate of around 40 percent after three years on the job ("Study backs" 1987; Curwin 1992). Adding to the problem is the fact that experienced teachers try to transfer away from schools that have high levels of misbehavior, leaving those schools in the hands of teachers not yet skilled in discipline.

The Decline in Humane Behavior

Why is student behavior becoming steadily worse? The cause is easy to pinpoint, but very difficult to correct. Schools always reflect the nature of the society they serve. When society is humane, gentle, and caring, so are students in the schools. When society is hostile and uncaring, students behave in accordance. At present, societies around the world are showing a progressive decline in humane behavior—that is, in individuals' willingness to help, rather than do harm to each other. That same change is evident among students in schools. The fundamental proposition of mass education is that schooling improves society, and who would argue that democratic societies would be better off uneducated? But many have believed, and still do, that schools can make right, on a large scale, what has gone wrong in society. That belief, unfortunately, has little foundation.

How is this decline in humane behavior being manifested in schools? Thirty years ago, the vast majority of schools were barely touched by serious student misbehavior. Occasionally one would hear of expulsions for violations of dress code, but rarely for violently antisocial behavior. Today, it is a rare school, even in best neighborhoods, that escapes the stigma of aggressive, sometimes criminal behavior by school students, ranging from vandalism to physical violence, sometimes against teachers. Much of this change in behavior is related to the scourge of drugs in society, but much of it can also be attributed to an increased societal penchant for violence, me-first-ism, and general disdain for authority. Instead of tolerance and willingness to help others, we see among our young a surprisingly callous disregard, and even intentional belittlement, of others.

One must take care not to tar all students with this brush. The truth is, the majority of students remain well-intentioned, willing to learn, and inclined to cooperate. But that does not negate the fact that misbehavior, even if it does come from relatively few students, presents an increasingly serious problem for teachers and parents alike (Shen 1995). Students bringing weapons to school has increased to such proportions that schools have had to implement stringent measures to detect and remove weapons from students. This phenomenon is not limited to secondary schools; guns are being brought into elementary schools as well (Collins 1995).

How are teachers contending with these realities? We have already alluded to teachers' preoccupation with misbehavior, the serious psychological effects it has on them, and the astonishing number of young teachers who admit leaving the profession because so much effort has to be expended on controlling student misbehavior. The concern about misbehavior, rather than diminishing, is growing. Greenlee and Ogletree (1993) surveyed 50 elementary and secondary teachers. Of the respondents, 41 said they needed more training in handling disruptive behavior, and 39 said they were suffering undue stress because of the difficulties in dealing with misbehavior. It is important to note that these teachers were not referring to criminal or violent behavior. They identified the behaviors that most seriously interfered with their work as student disrespect for others, disinterest in school, lack of attention, and excessive talking. It is not just older students whose behavior troubles teachers. Micklo (1993) found discipline to be a major concern among prekindergarten teachers.

Misbehavior, as we have seen, does more than merely disrupt learning—it also has a harmful effect on teachers. Rancifer (1993) when proposing discipline strategies, reported that teachers who lack control experience little job satisfaction and become increasingly ineffective in their work. This ineffectiveness becomes clearly evident to colleagues and administrators. Shreeve (1993) surveyed 91 school districts in Washington State and found that between 1984 and 1987, 153 teachers were placed on probation. Sixty-nine percent of that group were then dismissed or else retired or were reassigned to other duties. Most of them failed as teachers because of their inability to control their classes.

In a similar vein, (Ehrgott et al. 1993) explored "marginal teachers" in 518 elementary and secondary schools in California. They concluded that somewhere between 5 and 20 percent of all teachers in those schools were considered marginal, not because they were failing, but because they functioned at substandard levels, being especially poor at maintaining discipline, establishing adequate relations with students, and conveying subject matter. Generally speaking, novice teachers seem not to anticipate the difficulties they will encounter with misbehavior. At first their teaching concerns are primarily content oriented, but later misbehavior and discipline become overriding concerns (Gibbons and Jones 1994; Richardson 1993). There is evidence, however, that special programs provided in the schools for new teachers—programs that emphasize discipline expectations, classroom management, and peer support—can improve new teachers' chances of success (Loucks 1993; Rancifer 1995).

Schools' Efforts to Make Adjustments

Schools and community agencies have begun taking action to curb violently disruptive behavior. Some urban schools are merging the school police force with that of the city, for increased training and authority (Dowdy 1995). To help allay teacher fear of violence, some schools are implementing "zero tolerance" policies against weapons and violence, that bring immediate suspension against violators ("Teachers fear . . ." 1995). New York State has put into law automatic one-year suspensions for students caught bringing weapons to school (Dao 1995).

Schools' efforts are not being limited to sanctions against students, but are being extended to programmatical provisions as well. Most are implementing special programs and many are designating special schools for students prone to serious misbehavior ("A place for . . ." 1994). In 1995 the New York City Schools Chancellor took over direct control of 16 city schools especially troubled with misbehavior and chronic low achievement (Newman 1995). In many schools where misbehavior has not reached serious levels, school boards are re-implementing programs that teach values and ethics, including self-discipline, respect, honesty, responsibility and integrity ("Classroom discipline . . ." 1990; "Fighting violence . . . 1993; Weirs 1995; Woo 1995; Harrow 1995; Shen 1995; Schmidt 1996).

But it is still behavior in the classroom itself that troubles teachers most. For years teachers have felt they were fighting a lonely and losing battle over misbehavior, but now parents and even other students are raising voices against classroom behavior that damages learning (Nealon 1995). It remains to be seen whether schoolwide measures such as those listed here will have a positive affect on disruptive (or more frequently, non-cooperative) classroom behavior that interferes strongly with teaching and learning.

Improving Discipline in the Classroom

All teachers want to teach well and help students learn. Misbehavior often prevents their doing so. Thus, the fundamental question for teachers is: "What can I do to promote attention, cooperation, and civil behavior among the students under my direction?" Happily, answers to this question are available, and new suggestions appear regularly for helping teachers, novice and experienced, understand misbehavior and deal with it more effectively.

But if teachers need a better understanding of the causes of misbehavior, they also need effective countermeasures they can apply. Weinstein, Woolfolk, and Dittmeier (1994) found that while student teachers seemed to conceptualize discipline as preventive and nonpunitive, they were more comfortable when assuming an authoritarian role in the classroom. Johnson (1994) discovered that when student teachers were asked to judge the comparative merits of dominance, rule-based, and nurturing styles of discipline, they indicated preference for rule-based, suggesting they needed practice in that approach. Differences have been found between the discipline preferences of elementary and secondary teachers. Eccles, Wigfield, and Midgley (1993) discovered that middle school math teachers, when compared to sixth-grade math teachers, controlled students more, gave students fewer decision-making opportunities, and felt less effective in their work. It is interesting to note that, in contrast, teachers designated as outstanding may be more nurturing than other teachers in dealing with students. Agne, Greenwood, and Miller (1994) compared "teachers of the year" against matched inservice teachers and explored the effects of gender, years of service, grade levels taught, and highest degrees earned. They found teachers of the year to be significantly more humanistic than others in their dealings with students. What does it mean to be "humanistic?" Curwin (1995) seems to refer to it in his suggestions that schools reduce cynicism, welcome all students, replace reward and punishment with strong values, and ask students to contribute their own ideas about problems encountered. These ideas are carried forward by Kohn (1996) who advises moving beyond discipline entirely in favor of developing a sense of community in the classroom.

It is clear that being humanistic does not imply that schools should abandon standards of order. To the contrary, Blendinger (1996) maintains that an orderly classroom is a primary determinant of teaching success. He advocates clearly communicated approaches to discipline that include the following steps: (1) develop a discipline plan, (2) establish classroom rules, (3) determine consequences for violating rules, (4) recognize and celebrate good behavior, and (5) involve parents in helping children behave well. Martens and Kelly (1993) advocate instructional practices that reduce misbehavior by emphasizing learning. Castle and Rogers (1993) found that student participation in rule making encourages active involvement, respect for rules, cooperation, and sense of ownership in the classroom. Similar results were found when eight middle schools implemented a program to improve adolescent conduct through clarity of rules, school–home communication, and reinforcement of positive behavior (Gottfredson, Gottfredson, and Hybl 1993).

Conflict resolution has been a fairly recent, and widely acclaimed, addition to efforts in classroom discipline. When students learn and practice skills of conflict resolution, they become more inclined to work out problems among themselves before the problems escalate (Bozzone 1994; Castle and Rogers 1994; Johnson, Acikogz, and Johnson 1994).

More than any other single thrust, the past few years have witnessed a movement toward the teaching of values, ethical behavior, and decision making. Stone (1993) recommends patiently teaching social and moral understanding. Black (1994) surveyed 40 classroom management studies and found that in most of them teachers were being asked to design lessons that helped students make ethical judgments and decisions, and Fuhr (1993) stresses the importance in discipline of helping students distinguish between right and wrong. Teachers were also being asked to use discipline procedures that promoted children's sense of self-worth ("La Disciplina Positiva" 1994), and that focused on students' personal growth and academic progress (Hindle 1994; Powell and Taylor 1994). Moreover, the desirability of teachers giving up part of their traditional control in favor of student decision making is an ongoing topic in discipline (Blank and Kershaw 1993; Kohn 1996).

FORMAL APPROACHES TO CLASSROOM DISCIPLINE

It has been less than 50 years since educators began looking seriously for ways to promote good student behavior by means other than intimidation and punishment, and it has been less than three decades since discipline rose to the top of teacher concerns. Fortunately, a few earlier educators saw the problem emerging, and occasional scholars began identifying and clarifying new nonpunitive approaches that teachers could use to lessen the impact of misbehavior.

The first approach that was sufficiently organized and complete to be used as a discipline plan was set forth in 1951 by Wayne State University professors Fritz Redl, a psychotherapist, and William Wattenberg, an educational psychologist. Their pioneering efforts identified special characteristics of group behavior and explained how individual behavior within groups could be understood and controlled. Around 1965, behavior modification came into wide use in the classroom. Developed out of the findings of psychologist B. F. Skinner, behavior modification has helped teachers shape desired student behavior through benign application of principles of reinforcement. In

1971, Jacob Kounin's landmark studies on behavior control through lesson management appeared, as did Haim Ginott's 1971 commentaries on controlling misbehavior through congruent communication. In 1972, Rudolf Dreikurs presented his prescriptions for democratic (collaborative) decision making in the classroom as a means of helping students achieve a sense of belonging. Those works, highly important though rarely used as complete systems today, are shown in Figure I.1, and are presented as chapters in Part I of this book. They comprise the major foundational efforts out of which newer and more complete models of discipline have been built.

As concern about discipline continued to grow, other educators, psychologists, and psychiatrists developed still more effective and workable approaches to school discipline. The best known and most widely used is Lee and Marlene Canter's *Assertive Discipline,* the preeminent application model since 1976. Fredric Jones's *Positive Discipline,* which has been in use since 1979, continues to attract a wide following, as does William Glasser's *Noncoercive Discipline.* Glasser's first work related to discipline appeared in 1969, was reformulated in 1985, and continues to be modified for effectiveness in accordance with realities of schools, teachers, and students. Thomas Gordon has acquired a considerable following for his *Discipline As Self-Control* approach, which appeared in 1989 as an outgrowth of his earlier *Effectiveness Training* work, and Richard Curwin and Allen Mendler have struck a resonant chord among teachers through their *Discipline with Dignity,* set forth in 1988 and amplified in 1992. More recently, two new application models have gained a substantial following—Linda Albert's *Cooperative Discipline,* which appeared in 1989 (expanded in 1996), and Jane Nelsen, Lynn Lott, and H. Stephen Glenn's *Positive Discipline in the*

Fritz Redl and William Wattenberg
1951, 1959

Control through understanding group dynamics
Dealing with behavior of the group
Identifying student roles in the group
Using influence against misbehavior

Jacob Kounin **1971**	**Rudolf Dreikurs** **1972**
Control through lesson management Showing withitness Using group alerting and accountability Delaying the onset of satiation	*Control through providing sense of belonging* Teaching in a democratic fashion Identifying students' mistaken goals Confronting mistaken-goal behavior
Haim Ginott **1971**	**B.F. Skinner** **1953 through 1973**
Control through congruent communication Using sane messages Inviting student cooperation Correcting misbehavior through redirection	*Control through shaping of proper behavior* Identifying desired behaviors Shaping behavior through reinforcement Using behavior modification systematically

Figure I.1
Foundational work in classroom discipline

Lee and Marlene Canter 1976, 1992, 1993	Fredric Jones 1979, 1987
Assertive discipline Recognizing classroom rights Teaching desired behavior Establishing consequences	*Positive discipline* Using effective body language Providing efficient help Using incentive systems

Linda Albert 1989, 1996	Thomas Gordon 1974, 1989	Jane Nelsen, Lynn Lott, and H. Stephen Glenn 1993
Cooperative discipline Establishing sense of belonging Avoiding/defusing confrontations Teaching conflict resolution	*Discipline as self-control* Identifying problem ownership Using the power of influence Maximizing communication	*Positive classroom discipline* Students controlling own lives Caring and communicating Using class meetings effectively

William Glasser 1969, 1985, 1992	Richard Curwin and Allen Mendler 1988
Noncoercive discipline Meeting students' basic needs Providing quality education Teaching by leading	*Discipline with dignity* Helping the behaviorally at risk Working to restore student hope Establishing the social contract

Figure I.2
Application models of classroom discipline

Classroom (1993). The efforts of these seven innovators are noted in Figure I.2 and appear in Part II as application models of discipline.

Part II ends with an examination of two emerging views of discipline that urge involving students more closely in developing self-discipline and responsibility. Shown in Figure I.3, they are Barbara Coloroso's *Inner Discipline* (1994), which attempts to enable students to take control of their academic lives, and Alfie Kohn's *Beyond Discipline* (1996), which urges educators to develop caring, self-directed students by moving away from discipline based on compliance and toward developing a sense of community in the classroom.

As you examine the application models presented in Chapters 4–10, note how each is built on work done by earlier thinkers whose work is presented in Chapters 1–3, and how each introduces its own new concepts and techniques. Note also how

Barbara Coloroso 1994	Alfie Kohn 1996
Developing inner discipline Students taking control of their lives Developing care and acceptance Using classroom meetings effectively	*Moving from discipline to community* Involving students in all decisions Building teacher-student trust Developing a caring community

Figure I.3
Two emerging views on classroom discipline

some of the application models have been modified over time—especially those of Canter and Glasser—and how thinking has evolved into the suggestions of Coloroso and Kohn.

GOAL: BUILDING YOUR PERSONAL SYSTEM OF DISCIPLINE

A wealth of information about discipline is contained in the chapters that follow, as well as in the Appendix and Glossary, but if this information is to serve you best, you must organize it in your own mind so that it meshes with your outlook and personality and, of course, with the realities of the students you teach. Part III, entitled Toward Building a Personal System of Discipline, is presented for that express purpose. It consists of two chapters: Classrooms That Encourage Good Behavior, and Building a Personal System of Discipline.

REFERENCES AND RECOMMENDED READINGS

A handbook of alternatives to corporal punishment. 4th ed. 1994. Oklahoma City: Oklahoma State Department of Education.

A place for problem students: Separate school proposed for disruptive teenagers. 1994. *Washington Post,* VAW, 1:5, January 13.

Agne, J., G. Greenwood, and L. Miller. 1994. Relationships between teacher belief systems and teacher effectiveness. *Journal of Research and Development in Education, 27*(3), 141–152.

Black, S. 1994. Throw away the hickory stick. *Executive Educator, 16*(4), 44–47.

Blank, M., and C. Kershaw. 1993. Perceptions of educators about classroom management demands when using interactive strategies. Paper presented at the annual meeting of the American Educational Research Association, Atlanta, April 12–16.

Blendinger, J. 1996. *QLM: Quality leading & managing: A practical guide for improving schools.* Dubuque, Iowa: Kendall Hunt.

Boothe, J., L. Bradley, and T. Flick. 1993. The violence at your door. *Executive Educator, 15* (1), 16–22.

Bozzone, M. 1994. Spend less time refereeing and more time teaching. *Instructor, 104*(1), 88–93.

Canter, L., and M. Canter. 1992. *Assertive discipline: Positive behavior management for today's classroom.* 2d ed. Santa Monica, Calif.: Lee Canter & Associates.

Castle, K., and K. Rogers. 1993. Rule-creating in a constructivist classroom community. *Childhood Education, 70*(2), 77–80.

Clawson, P. 1995. Hispanic parents demonstrate to protest students' expulsions. *Chicago Tribune,* 2NW, 2:4, October 24.

Classroom discipline and lessons in social values. 1990. *New York Times,* B, 7:3, January 31.

Collins, R. 1995. Dover takes action. *Boston Globe,* NH, 1:1, November 12.

Coloroso, B. 1994. *Kids are worth it! Giving your child the gift of inner discipline.* New York: William Morrow.

Curwin, R. 1992. *Rediscovering hope: Our greatest teaching strategy.* Bloomington, Ind.: National Educational Service.

———. 1995. A humane approach to reducing violence in schools. *Educational Leadership, 52*(5), 72-75.

Dao, J. 1995. Suspension now required for taking gun to school. *New York Times,* B, 4:5, August 1.

Dowdy, Z. 1995. School officers to merge with Boston police force. *Boston Globe,* 33:4, March 16.

Eccles, J., A. Wigfield, and C. Midgley. 1993. Negative effects of traditional middle schools on students' motivation. *Elementary School Journal, 93*(5), 553-574.

Ehrgott, et al. 1992. A study of the marginal teacher in California. Paper presented at the annual meeting of the California Educational Research Association, San Francisco, November.

Elam, S. 1989. The second Gallup/Phi Delta Kappa Poll of teachers' attitudes toward the public schools. *Phi Delta Kappan 70*(10), 785-798.

Elam, S., L. Rose, and A. Gallup. 1995. The 27th annual Phi Delta Kappa/Gallup Poll of the public's attitudes toward the public schools. *Phi Delta Kappan, 76*(1), 41-56.

Ellis, D., and P. Karr-Kidwell. 1995. A study of assertive discipline and recommendations for effective classroom management methods. Paper 26 p. Washington, D.C.: U.S. Department of Education. ERIC Clearinghouse #35596.

Feldman, D. 1994. The effect of assertive discipline procedures on preschool children in segregated and integrated settings: A longitudinal study. *Education and Training in Mental Retardation and Developmental Disabilities, 29*(4), 291-306.

Fighting violence with values. 1993. *Atlanta Journal,* A, 12:1, December 23.

Fuhr, D. 1993. Effective classroom discipline: Advice for educators. *NASSP Bulletin, 76*(549), 82-86.

Gibbons, L., and L. Jones. 1994. Novice teachers' reflectivity upon their classroom management. Paper, 13 p. Washington, D.C.: U.S. Department of Education. ERIC Clearinghouse #SPO36198.

Gottfredson, D., G. Gottfredson, and L. Hybl. 1993. Managing adolescent behavior: A multiyear, multischool study. *American Educational Research Journal, 30*(1), 179-215.

Greenlee, A., and E. Ogletree. 1993. Teachers' attitudes toward student discipline problems and classroom management strategies. Washington, D.C.: U.S. Department of Education. ERIC Clearinghouse #PSO21851.

Hindle, D. 1994. Coping proactively with middle years students. *Middle School Journal, 25*(3), 31-34.

Horne, A. 1994. Teaching children with behavior problems takes understanding, tools, and courage. *Contemporary Education, 65*(3), 122-127.

Hughes, H. 1994. From fistfights to gunfights: Preparing teachers and administrators to cope with violence in school. Paper presented at the annual meeting of the American Association of Colleges for Teacher Education, Chicago, February.

Johnson, D., K. Acikogz, and R. Johnson. 1994. Effects of conflict resolution training on elementary school students. *Journal of Social Psychology, 134*(6), 803-817.

Johnson, V. 1994. Student teachers' conceptions of classroom control. *Journal of Educational Research, 88*(2), 109-117.

Kohn, A. 1996. *Beyond discipline: From compliance to community.* Alexandria, Va.: Association for Supervision and Curriculum Development.

La disciplina positiva. 1994. ERIC Digest. Urbana, Ill.: ERIC Clearinghouse on Elementary and Early Childhood Education.

Landen, W. 1992. Violence and our schools: What can we do? *Updating School Board Policies, 23,* 1-5.

Loucks, H. 1993. Teacher education: A success story. *Principal, 73*(1), 27-29.

Martens, B., and S. Kelly. 1993. A behavioral analysis of effective teaching. *School Psychology Quarterly, 8*(1), 10-26.

Micklo, S. 1993. Perceived problems of public school prekindergarten teachers. *Journal of Research in Childhood Education, 8*(1), 57-68.

N.H. schools begin program to teach ethics, values. 1989. *Boston Globe,* 67:1, August 31.

Nealon, P. 1995. *Boston Globe,* 17:2, March 14.

Nelsen, J., L. Lott, and H. Glenn. 1993. *Positive discipline in the classroom.* Rocklin, Calif.: Prima Publishing.

Newman, M. 1995. Sixteen city schools are taken over by chancellor. *New York Times,* A, 1:2, October 20.

O Harrow, R. 1995. Reading, writing, right and wrong. *Washington Post,* D, 1:1, September 8.

Paradise, R. 1994. Spontaneous cultural compatibility: Mazahua students and their teachers constructing trusting relationships. *Peabody Journal of Education, 69*(2), 60-70.

Peng, S. 1993. Fostering student discipline and effort: Approaches used in Chinese schools. Paper presented at the annual meeting of the American Educational Research Association, Atlanta, April 12-16.

Powell, T., and S. Taylor. 1994. Taking care of risky business. *South Carolina Middle School Journal, (Spring)* 5-6.

Rancifer, J. 1993. Effective classroom management: A teaching strategy for a maturing profession. Paper presented at the annual conference of the Southeastern Regional Association of Teacher Educators, Nashville, October 27-30.

———. 1995. Revolving classroom door: Management strategies to eliminate the quick spin. Paper presented at the annual meeting of the Southern Regional Association of Teacher Educators, Lake Charles, La. November 2-4.

Rich, J. 1992. Predicting and controlling school violence. *Contemporary Education, 64*(1) 35-39.

Richardson, G. 1993. Student teacher journals: Reflective and nonreflective. Paper presented at the annual Mid-South Educational Research Association, New Orleans, November 10-12.

Richardson, R., D. Wilcox, and J. Dunne. 1994. Corporal punishment in schools: Initial progress in the bible belt. *Journal of Humanistic Education and Development, 32*(4), 173-182.

Ryan, F. 1994. From rod to reason: Historical perspectives on corporal punishment in the public schools. *Educational Horizons, 72*(2), 70-77.

Schwartz, F. (1981). Supporting or subverting learning: Peer group patterns in four tracked schools. *Anthropology and Education Quarterly, 12*(2), 99-120.

Schmidt, S. 1996. Character in the classroom. *The San Diego Union,* 1:22, May 19.

Shen, F. 1995. Educators get tough on violence. *Washington Post,* MDP, 1:1, August 24.

Shreeve, W. 1993. Evaluating teacher evaluation: Who is responsible for teacher probation? *NAASP Bulletin,* 77(551), 8-19.

Stone, S. (1993). Issues in education: Taking time to teach social skills. *Childhood Education,* 69(4), 194-195.

Study backs induction schools to help new teachers stay teachers. 1987. *ASCD Update, 29*(4), 1.

Taking action against violence. *Instructor, 103*(6), 41-43.

Teachers fear violence in schools. 1994. *Atlanta Journal Constitution,* E, 12:1, March 20.

Weinstein, C., A. Woolfolk, and L. Dittmeier. 1994. Protector or prison guard? Using metaphors and media to explore student teachers' thinking about classroom management. *Action in Teacher Education, 16*(1), 41-54.

Weirs, M. 1995. Clayton County adds boot camp to school program. *Atlanta Constitution,* XJI, 1:5, October 19.

Woo, E. 1995. New math: Dividing school day differently. *Los Angeles Times,* A, 1:1, September 29.

Zeller, N., and M. Gutierrez. 1995. Speaking of discipline, . . . : An international perspective. *Thresholds in Education, 21*(2), 60-66.

PART I Foundational Work in Classroom Discipline

The next three chapters describe the works of outstanding pioneers in the development of modern classroom discipline. As mentioned in the Introduction, these early contributions are rarely employed as complete discipline systems in themselves. Yet in every case they set forth fundamental propositions about discipline that have been incorporated into the more elaborate systems currently in use. We would be remiss if we failed to comprehend these contributions and see the roles they play in today's classroom discipline. This foundational work is presented in the following chapters:

Chapter 1. Group Dynamics and Classroom Discipline: The Pioneering Work of Fritz Redl and William Wattenberg

Chapter 2. Instructional Management and Democratic Teaching: The Contributions of Jacob Kounin and Rudolf Dreikurs

Chapter 3. Shaping Behavior through Communication and Reinforcement: The Contributions of Haim Ginott and B. F. Skinner.

Group Dynamics and Classroom Discipline

The Pioneering Work of Fritz Redl and William Wattenberg

Fritz Redl

William Wattenberg

PREVIEW OF REDL AND WATTENBERG'S WORK

Focus

- Group behavior in the classroom and how it differs from individual behavior.
- The nature of group dynamics and the roles played by students and teacher.
- Effective strategies that help teachers improve classroom discipline.

Logic

- Classroom discipline depends on understanding of student misbehavior and its causes.
- Classroom discipline requires knowledge of student roles and how to deal with them effectively.
- Alternatives to punishment are needed; punishment is counterproductive in classroom discipline.
- Teachers become better at discipline as they learn how to use procedures of diagnostic thinking.

Contributions

- Provided insight into group dynamics, group behavior, and roles of students and teachers.
- Furnished the first widely used set of "modern" discipline techniques for teachers.
- Devised procedures of "diagnostic thinking" to help teachers deal better with misbehavior.
- Championed involving students, eschewing punishment, and maintaining positive feelings.

Redl and Wattenberg's Suggestions

- Recognize the causes of student misbehavior, in order to deal with it more effectively.
- Use a diagnostic thinking procedure when assessing misbehavior and applying consequences.
- Do everything possible to assist students in developing their own self-control.
- At all times be helpful and respectful to students, while paying attention to their feelings.

ABOUT FRITZ REDL AND WILLIAM WATTENBERG

Fritz Redl, born in Austria, immigrated to the United States in 1936 and devoted his career to research, therapy, and teaching, principally as professor of behavioral science at Wayne State University. He is also recognized for contributions made while a member of the department of criminal justice at the State University of New York at Albany, where he worked with deviant juveniles. Redl's numerous writings in the field of education and psychology include *Mental Hygiene in Teaching* (1951, revised 1959), coauthored with William Wattenberg; *Controls from Within* (1952), coauthored with David Wineman; *Discipline for Today's Children* (1956), coauthored with George Sheviakov; and *When We Deal with Children* (1972).

William Wattenberg, born in 1911, received his doctorate from Columbia University in 1936. He specialized in educational psychology and held professorships at Northwestern University, Chicago Teacher's College, and Wayne State University. Wattenberg's writings include *Mental Hygiene in Teaching,* coauthored with Redl; *The Adolescent Years* (1955); and *All Men Are Created Equal* (1967).

REDL AND WATTENBERG'S CONTRIBUTIONS TO DISCIPLINE

In *Mental Hygiene in Teaching* (1951), Redl and Wattenberg presented the first set of theory-based suggestions designed specifically to help teachers understand and deal with misbehavior in the classroom. Prior to Redl and Wattenberg's contributions, classroom discipline was thought of as teachers' strong efforts to impose behavior requirements upon resistant students, the view held of discipline virtually since the beginning of teaching. Although many fine teachers had historically been humane and considerate of students, the common practice was to apply discipline requirements autocratically and somewhat harshly.

Redl and Wattenberg's investigations led them to believe that a markedly different approach to classroom discipline could maintain control and at the same time help students develop their own self-discipline. Redl and Wattenberg were the first to describe how students behave differently in groups than as individuals and the first to identify social and psychological forces that affect classroom behavior. Out of those ideas came specific disciplinary techniques that not only helped teachers maintain control but, according to Redl and Wattenberg, also strengthened students' emotional growth and ability to work effectively with others. Redl and Wattenberg's efforts established a beginning point for newer views of discipline to come later and provided insights into behavior that teachers still find useful today.

REDL AND WATTENBERG'S CENTRAL FOCUS

Redl and Wattenberg focused on group behavior, its manifestations, causes, and control. Their purpose was to help teachers understand and deal with group behavior in the classroom. They showed how group behavior differs from individual behavior, pinpointed some of the causes of those differences, and set forth specific techniques for helping teachers deal with the undesirable aspects of group behavior.

REDL AND WATTENBERG'S PRINCIPAL TEACHINGS

People in groups behave differently than they do individually. Group pressures influence individual behavior. Students in classrooms do things they would not do if by themselves, and will not do certain things they would do if by themselves.

Students adopt identifiable roles in the classroom. Within any group, students adopt roles such as leaders, instigators, and fall guys. Teachers should be aware of the emergence of such roles, be prepared to deal with them, and be ready to limit the detrimental effects that some of them might have on behavior and learning.

Group dynamics—a term used for the generation of forces by and within groups—strongly affect behavior. If teachers are to deal effectively with group behavior, they must understand group dynamics, how the forces develop, and how they affect behavior in the classroom.

Teachers play many different roles that affect student behavior. Students perceive teachers filling a number of roles such as sources of knowledge, judges, and surrogate parents. Teachers must be aware of those potential roles and what students expect of them.

Diagnostic thinking helps teachers solve behavior problems effectively. The diagnostic thinking process involves (1) forming a first hunch, (2) gathering facts, (3) exploring hidden factors (background information about students), (4) taking action, and (5) remaining flexible.

Teachers can correct student misbehavior and maintain class control by using influence techniques such as (1) supporting student self-control, (2) offering situational assistance, (3) appraising reality, and (4) invoking the pleasure–pain principle (reward and punishment).

Supporting student self-control is a low-key influence technique that enables teachers to address emerging problems before they become serious. In it, teachers use eye contact, move closer to misbehaving students, provide encouragement, make use of humor, and in some cases simply ignore minor misbehavior.

Providing situational assistance is also a low-key influence technique. When students have difficulty regaining self-control, teachers can provide situational assistance by helping students over a hurdle, restructuring the time schedule, establishing new routines, removing seductive objects, and occasionally removing a student from the situation.

Appraising reality is an influence technique that helps students understand the underlying causes of their misbehavior and foresee the consequences if they continue. Teachers speak openly and frankly about the situation and reemphasize existing limits on behavior, but at the same time they offer encouragement. In more severe cases, this is done in individual conferences with students.

Invoking the pleasure–pain principle is an influence technique that entails rewarding good behavior and punishing bad behavior. Punishment should be used only as a last resort, however, because it is frequently counterproductive.

ANALYSIS OF REDL AND WATTENBERG'S VIEWS ON DISCIPLINE

Redl and Wattenberg's contentions can be understood more fully by examining student roles and behaviors in the classroom, group dynamics, psychological roles of teachers, diagnostic thinking, and influence techniques.

Student Roles and Behaviors in the Classroom

Redl and Wattenberg believe that if teachers can learn to identify the basic causes underlying behavior and conflict, they can correct most of those causes and thus maintain desirable classroom control. They suggest that outward behavior has roots in identifiable needs, and they recognize that students are continually torn between personal desires and the expectations of society.

Redl and Wattenberg emphasize that students behave differently in groups than when alone, and further, that teachers seldom deal with students on a purely individual basis, since the entire class is usually affected by the behavior of each member. This does not mean that teachers can never use insights into individual behavior but only that they must come to understand group behavior as well. Redl and Wattenberg (1959) view the group as an organism. As they put it,

> A group creates conditions such that its members will behave in certain ways because they belong to it; at the same time, the manner in which the parts function affects the whole. (p. 267)

In other words, group expectations strongly influence individual behavior, and individual behavior in turn affects the group.

Redl and Wattenberg identify several **student roles** that are likely to be adopted when students function within groups. The roles serve to fill personal needs and are usually reinforced in some manner by other members of the group. The following are some of the roles that teachers regularly encounter.

Leaders

A leadership role is available in almost every group. This role varies according to the group's purpose, makeup, and activities. Within the same group, different individuals may act as leaders in different activities. For example, a student who is a leader in physical education may fill a different role in music.

Group leaders tend to share certain qualities. They usually show above-average intelligence, responsibility, and social skills. They generally have a highly developed understanding of others, and they embody and reflect group ideals.

Teachers should recognize that the leaders they appoint for various activities are not necessarily the group's natural leaders. When such mismatches are made, they often lead to conflict within the group.

Clowns

Clowns are individuals who assume the role of entertainer. Students sometimes adopt this role as a way to mask feelings of inferiority, making fun of situations and of themselves before others do so. Clowning can be beneficial to both the teacher and the group, especially when the group is anxious or frustrated. At times, however, clowning hinders group progress, and group members may support the disruptive antics of the clown as a way of expressing hostility toward the teacher.

Fall Guys

A fall guy is an individual who takes blame and punishment in order to gain favor with the group. Fall guys give members of the group latitude to misbehave, since the group can set them up to suffer the penalties that might result. Teachers need to be alert for this kind of manipulation and make sure to focus their corrective actions on the true instigators of misbehavior.

Instigators

Instigators are individuals who cause trouble but make it appear they are not involved. They often solve their inner conflicts by getting others to act them out. They may even feel that they are benefiting the victim in some way. Teachers need to look into recurring conflicts carefully to see if there is an unnoticed instigator. It may be necessary to point out this role to the group, as they are often unaware of it. The group may need help in recognizing and discouraging this role.

Group Dynamics

Previous paragraphs have described some of the roles and role expectations that influence behavior. Membership in groups affects individuals in other ways, too. Groups create their own psychological forces that bring strong pressure to bear on individuals. The process that produces these forces is called **group dynamics.**

Group dynamics help produce unwritten codes of classroom conduct. When these codes run counter to the teacher's expectations, misbehavior is said to occur. Because teachers are powerful, they seem to win out in conflicts with students. However, the group code usually prevails under the surface, contributing to lasting attitudes that may be the opposite of what the teacher desired.

The following are some of the effects of group dynamics that, according to Redl and Wattenberg, often lead to behavior problems in the classroom.

Contagious Behavior

Undesirable behavior becomes **contagious behavior** when it spreads quickly in the classroom, as occurs frequently. One student's misbehavior may be a good indication of what other students are also itching to do. Once the ice is broken, others may join the misbehavior, especially if the perpetrator has high status.

Therefore, before reacting to misbehavior, the teacher should evaluate the misbehavior's potential for spread. If the potential is high, the teacher should squelch the misbehavior at once. If the potential is low, it may be safe to ignore the behavior or use a low-pressure technique such as reminding students that more appropriate behavior is expected.

Teachers can reduce incipient contagion by attending to negative factors that foster it, such as poor seating arrangements, boredom, fatigue, lack of purpose in lessons, and poor student manners.

On the positive side, desirable behavior can also be contagious, though this effect is rarely so rampant as it is with misbehavior. Teachers can encourage positive behavior through approval, reinforcement, and giving status to those who display it.

Scapegoating

Scapegoating is a phenomenon in which the group seeks to displace its hostility onto an unpopular individual or subgroup. The target person or subgroup is usually weak or outcast, unable to cope well with normal occurrences in the classroom. Scapegoating has undesirable consequences for everyone concerned, and teachers must be alert to thwart it. When so doing, however, they should take care that their approach does not produce even more hostility toward the target.

Teachers' Pets

When a group believes that a teacher is playing favorites, it reacts with jealousy and resentment. These emotions may be manifested as hostile behavior toward the favored individual or group, who are referred to as teachers' pets. Hostility may also be directed at the teacher. When it is necessary to give individual students extra help, teachers should make sure that their actions never suggest favoritism but are seen as impartial, necessary, and professional.

Reactions to Strangers

It is common in most schools for strangers to enter the classroom occasionally. Reactions to strangers provide teachers with a key to group emotions. When a stranger enters the classroom, tension increases for teachers and students alike, and a marked change in student behavior usually occurs. If the stranger is a new student, the group code may become exaggerated to show the newcomer how to act. For example, if the group prizes cooperation, they might go to great lengths to be helpful to the newcomer and each other. On the other hand, the group may test the new student. They may withhold acceptance, vie for friendship, or even taunt the new student or each other.

If the stranger is an adult, the students may rally to support their teacher, provided the teacher is liked and respected. If they do not respect their teacher, the students may misbehave rudely and boisterously.

Teachers should note class reactions when a stranger enters the room. Extreme behaviors provide clues to underlying motivations and feelings that are operating within the group.

Group Disintegration

Groups serve many purposes, and good group behavior is highly desirable. Teachers hope to establish groups that will prosper, grow in maturity, and help meet everyone's needs. Even the strongest groups, however, show strain as time passes. **Group disintegration** can occur when a group loses its cohesiveness.

Consider Mrs. Brown's discouragement when her group began to disintegrate. Early in the year her class worked strongly together, helpfully and cooperatively. But as the weeks passed, cohesion began to decline. Increasingly, students dawdled, looked out the window instead of paying attention, and talked during Mrs. Brown's lessons. Cliques developed, and jealousies surfaced. Mrs. Brown did not know how to get her students to work together as before, which left her frustrated and dismayed.

Teachers frequently encounter such situations and do not know how to correct them. Redl and Wattenberg suggest that when a formerly effective group begins to disintegrate, teachers should ask themselves the following questions:

1. Are class activities becoming boring to the students?
2. Is there too much emphasis on competition among groups?
3. Have unexpected changes occurred in leadership roles, environment, or schedules?
4. Are new class activities needed to stimulate and provoke thought?
5. Are students given ample opportunity to experience success, or are too many experiencing frustration and failure?
6. Has the classroom climate become threatening rather than supportive?

Conditions such as these can create emotional changes within the group, which can cause class members, especially the weaker ones, to feel insecure concerning their places and expected roles. An increase in deviant behavior is likely at such times, with a lessening of mutual support within the group.

Disintegration is not inevitable, however, nor necessarily permanent. New activities, new purposes, and new working relationships all can help provide a new sense of group cohesiveness.

Psychological Roles of Teachers

Group and individual classroom behavior is greatly influenced by how students perceive the teacher. Students assign many different roles to teachers and expect teachers to present many different images. Sometimes teachers have little choice about those roles, but normally they have some control over which they will accept and how they will carry them out. These **teacher roles** and images include the following:

Representatives of Society
Teachers are seen to reflect values, moral attitudes, and thinking patterns typical of the community.

Judges
Teachers are supposed to judge students' behavior, character, work, and progress.

Sources of Knowledge
Teachers are seen as the primary source of knowledge, a resource from which students can obtain information.

Helpers in Learning
Teachers are expected to help students learn by giving directions, furnishing information, removing obstacles to learning, facilitating problem solving, and requiring that work be done.

Referees
Students expect teachers to arbitrate and make decisions when class disputes arise.

Detectives
Teachers are to oversee security in the classroom, discover wrongdoing, identify guilty students, and impose penalties.

Models
Teachers are to model the best in customs, manners, values, and beliefs, which students may or may not elect to imitate.

Caretakers
Teachers are to reduce anxiety by maintaining standards of behavior, regular schedules, and safe environments.

Ego Supporters
Teachers are to support student egos by building student self-confidence and bettering student self-images.

Group Leaders
Teachers are expected to lead the class in such a way that harmony and efficiency prevail.

Surrogate Parents
Teachers are to be like parents in providing protection, approval, advice, correction, and affection.

Targets for Hostility
When student hostility cannot be appropriately expressed to other adults, it can be displaced with relative safety onto teachers.

Friends and Confidants
Teachers can be talked with and confided in.

Objects of Affection
Teachers are to be ideal people, worthy of esteem, affection, and hero worship.

Control Techniques for Misbehavior
So far we have examined several of Redl and Wattenberg's teachings about how groups function, how they are affected by group dynamics, and how group behavior is influenced by the roles assumed by students and teachers. Now we switch attention to Redl and Wattenberg's suggestions concerning how teachers should control misbehavior. Redl and Wattenberg offer two groups of specific suggestions. The first has to do with *diagnostic thinking* in the classroom and the second with *applying influence techniques.* Let us see what is involved in each.

Diagnostic Thinking

Redl and Wattenberg suggest that teachers employ a procedure of **diagnostic thinking** when faced with incidents of student misbehavior. Their diagnostic thinking approach seems at first laborious, but with practice one can make it seem second nature. The process includes forming a first hunch, gathering facts, exploring hidden factors, taking action, and remaining flexible.

Forming a First Hunch

When a problem first becomes apparent, teachers should form a preliminary hunch about its underlying cause. This hunch is based on a general feeling about the incident.

Gathering Facts

Next, the teacher quickly reviews obvious facts. Are students inattentive? Is someone breaking a rule? Are students arguing angrily? Is the group paying attention to something irrelevant to the lesson?

Exploring Hidden Factors

Teachers should add to the obvious facts hidden factors of which they might be aware, such as background information on students involved and general knowledge of human psychological and moral development.

Taking Action

Once teachers have quickly considered facts, background information, and possible motivations behind the misbehavior, they should take action to resolve the situation. Their first efforts may be successful; if not, they need to revise their appraisal of the situation and make new efforts to resolve it.

Remaining Flexible

When teachers take action (or fail to take action) to resolve a conflict, they may, by their action or inaction, alter classroom dynamics, thus creating a situation that requires further attention. A single action is often not enough. Teachers may need to employ a series of steps that lead ultimately to a resolution of the situation, and they may have to change their minds or approaches while doing so.

Redl and Wattenberg offer an additional word of advice concerning diagnostic thinking in resolving problem situations: student feelings are very important. Teachers should therefore try to put themselves in the students' place, both those students who commit offenses and those who are victimized. By understanding the feelings of everyone involved, more suitable resolutions can usually be found.

Applying Influence Techniques

Redl and Wattenberg give considerable attention to the actions that teachers use when attempting to resolve problem behavior. They call these actions **influence techniques.**

Every teacher uses several different influence techniques to maintain class control. Some of those techniques may be embedded in the overall school discipline policy, and some may have grown from years of effective use. Some work well, some work in certain situations and not in others, and some almost never produce positive results.

What do teachers normally do when students misbehave? Redl and Wattenberg found that some shouted at students, some removed students from the class, some invoked punishment, and some simply ignored the misbehavior. Some of these actions were taken consistently, others inconsistently. In order that teachers might acquire a consistently effective procedure for dealing with misbehavior, Redl and Wattenberg urge that teachers ask themselves a rapid series of questions before taking action.

1. What is the motivation behind the misbehavior?
2. How is the class reacting?
3. Is the misbehavior related to interaction with me?
4. How will the student react when corrected?
5. How will the correction affect future behavior?

The answers to these questions help teachers select a **corrective technique** that is likely to produce positive results overall. Four categories of corrective techniques Redl and Wattenberg suggest are (1) supporting self-control, (2) providing situational assistance, (3) appraising reality, and (4) invoking the pleasure–pain principle. These four categories are discussed in the following paragraphs. It should be remembered that for any of these techniques to be effective, students must know exactly what the issues are, know how they are expected to behave, and understand the consequences of breaking or following the rules.

1. Supporting Self-Control

The majority of students, most of the time, want to behave correctly and thus enjoy the teacher's approval. Only occasionally do they misbehave simply because they want to be unpleasant. Therefore, when misbehavior does occur, teachers should first assume that the misbehavior is not ill-intentioned and that it may represent nothing more than a momentary lapse in student self-control, which can easily be corrected.

Techniques for **supporting self-control** are *low-key,* which means they are not forceful, aggressive, or punitive but instead aim at helping students help themselves. Such techniques are very useful. They often eliminate the need to confront students and dole out penalties, and they give students much needed opportunities to work on controlling their own behavior. But it should not be expected that supportive techniques can correct all misbehavior. They work only when misbehavior is mild or just beginning. If they don't get the message across, firmer, more direct techniques are required. Redl and Wattenberg describe five ways to support student self-control.

Sending Signals. Teachers use **signals** that show students they know what is going on and that they do not approve. Examples are making eye contact, frowning, and shaking the head. These signals are most effective when given during the first indications of misbehavior.

Physical Proximity. If students do not respond to signals, teachers can move into closer **physical proximity** of the offenders. By doing so, teachers communicate that they are aware of the misbehavior and want to help students regain control, which allows students to draw strength from the nearness of the teacher. It is usually enough simply to move closer to the offender, but sometimes a friendly touch on the shoulder or head—*if appropriate for the students being taught*—might be needed.

Showing Interest. Even students who normally have good self-control may begin to misbehave when they lose interest in an assignment. Teachers can help by going to such students and showing interest in their work. A teacher might say, "I see you've completed the first five problems correctly. I bet you can finish all of them before the end of the period." This technique is only effective, of course, if the student feels able to do the assignment.

Humor. Using humor is a pleasant way of making students aware of lapses in self-control. It is important that this humor be gentle and accompanied by a smile. An example might be, "My, there is so much chattering, I thought for a minute I was in the cafeteria." Teachers must be careful that they do not use sarcasm or ridicule in their attempts at humor, for students usually interpret sarcasm as punishment, not support.

Ignoring. Occasionally, simply ignoring misbehavior is appropriate, especially in classes that are normally well behaved. Ignoring sends a signal to other students that they should do the same; the misbehaving student therefore receives no reinforcing attention.

2. Providing Situational Assistance

When misbehavior reaches the point that students cannot regain self-control, the teacher must step in with **situational assistance** to guide students back onto the proper course. Punitive measures are not needed. Instead, the teacher should provide only the assistance needed to help students regain control. In their second set of influence techniques, Redl and Wattenberg describe several things that teachers can do.

Provide Hurdle Help. Suppose an algebra assignment has been made. Susana begins work as expected but soon realizes she does not understand the procedure involved. She begins to talk to another student. In this case, the teacher need only provide **hurdle help** to assist Susana in understanding what to do rather than berate her for talking instead of working.

Restructure or Reschedule. Mr. James's sixth-grade students have returned to class after participating in a hotly contested game of volleyball. He knows it will be difficult for the students to get to work on their math lesson, so instead of the regular assignment, he improvises by using the game's scores to construct a number of computational problems.

Mr. James's appraisal of the situation suggested that overexcitement would almost certainly interfere with the regular lesson. He therefore restructured the lesson so he could use the students' interest to his advantage. Other ways of **restructuring activities** involve giving a brief time for rest, changing the nature of the activities, or rescheduling the work for a more appropriate time.

Establish Routines. Often students misbehave when they do not know exactly what they should be doing or when. Teachers can forestall such problems by establishing routines that make expectations predictable. Routines are especially valuable in helping students get to work quickly and complete work expeditiously.

Remove Seductive Objects. Attractive objects that students have in their possession, such as photographs, toys, and the like, can often overpower self-control. When that happens, removing the object is all that is required. This is a temporary measure and should be explained as such to the student. The object is returned at the end of the period or day.

Remove the Student from the Situation. When a student has lost self-control and is disturbing the rest of the class, the teacher needs to do something immediately so that the class can continue the lesson. A lengthy confrontation with the offending student will be of little value to either student or teacher, so simply removing the student from the situation is often the best alternative. For example, third-grader Travis is upset and disrupts the lesson by continually blurting out negative comments. The teacher, in accordance with consequences anticipated by the class, tells Travis to take a seat at a table in the far corner of the room, saying, "When you decide you can help us, you may return to the group."

This should be done in a nonpunitive way. The teacher should emphasize that Travis is only exiled until he regains his self-control. It is important, too, that the incident be followed up with a private talk, in which both student and teacher can discuss their feelings.

Use Physical Restraint. Very occasionally, students who lapse in self-control may become a danger to themselves or others. When this happens, the teacher may have to use physical restraint. Restraint should be used only in dire circumstances, and then with caution. Teachers may get injured themselves, and if a student is injured, the threat of a lawsuit is a distinct possibility. The guiding principle is that the teacher should always try to safeguard the student in a reasonable and prudent manner and get help as quickly as possible.

3. Appraising Reality

By **appraising reality** Redl and Wattenberg mean having students examine a behavior situation, note its underlying causes, and foresee its probable consequences. This knowledge helps students develop their own values so they behave more appropriately in future situations.

For incidents that disturb the class, it is usually advisable to postpone reality appraisal discussions until a later time. Emotions may be running strong, and both teacher and students are apt to say things that make it doubly hard for parties to listen to each other. After emotions have cooled down, causes and feelings can be sorted out without lecturing or scolding. It is important that the teacher understand why students felt and behaved as they did, and it is equally important for students to understand the teacher's feelings and behaviors. When these matters are aired, it becomes easier to handle similar situations in the future.

Because student misbehavior often escalates for reasons that are not clear, Redl and Wattenberg suggest that teachers do the following to help illuminate and defuse situations involving misbehavior.

Clearly Make a Frank Appraisal. Too often teachers overlook the simplest method for dealing with students, which is to make a frank appraisal by explaining exactly why behavior is inappropriate and to outline clear connections between conduct and consequences. Teachers should not underestimate students' ability to comprehend statements such as, "Let's raise our hands, please. If everyone talks at once, no one gets heard" or "These assignments have to be completed. If you don't keep up with them, you aren't going to learn what you should." Students respect reasonable rules whose purposes they understand, and they appreciate teachers who insist that they learn.

Show Encouragement. When using reality appraisal, teachers may seem to be critical of students. Few people respond well to criticism. Teachers therefore should express themselves in ways that show encouragement rather than criticism. They should stress that students are capable of the best behavior, and they should urge students to do the best they can. In making frank appraisals, teachers must guard against humiliating students, attacking their personal values, or frustrating them with impossible expectations. The teacher's primary role is always to support and encourage, not to attack or blame.

Set Clear, Enforceable Limits. Students often misbehave just to see how much they can get away with, which is their means of determining where the limits of permissible behavior actually lie. Teachers can prevent such misbehavior by **setting limits** that are clear and enforceable. They discuss with the class exactly what is expected and what constitutes acceptable and unacceptable behavior. They clearly explain the reasons for those limits and the rules associated with them. Students usually respond positively, appreciating the security provided by knowledge of limits and rules. Redl and Wattenberg caution teachers about making threats when explaining limits, contending that threats imply that the teacher expects the rules to be broken. Students should know in advance about consequences of breaking rules, but those consequences should be stated in a matter-of-fact manner, never as threats.

4. Invoking the Pleasure-Pain Principle

When behavior problems persist despite a teacher's attempts to support student self-control, provide situational assistance, and appraise reality, it becomes necessary to move to the strongest influence technique suggested by Redl and Wattenberg: invoking the **pleasure-pain principle.** In describing this principle, Redl and Wattenberg refer to rewards and punishments but give relatively little attention to the reward (pleasure) aspect, while having much to say about the punishment (pain) aspect.

With regard to pleasure, they limit their discussions to acknowledgments that praise, rewards, and teacher promises can influence behavior for the better, but they provide no specific suggestions as to how these elements can be used systematically.

With regard to pain, Redl and Wattenberg emphasize that pain, when used to control misbehavior, must not be harsh punishment but rather simply consequences that are somewhat unpleasant to the student. It is important to recognize the benign nature of the suggested unpleasant consequences.

Punishment. Redl and Wattenberg say that **punishment** should consist of planned, unpleasant consequences, the purpose of which is to change behavior in positive directions. Punishment should not be physical, nor should it involve angry outbursts that indicate lack of self-control on the part of the teacher. Neither should it consist of actions taken to get back at misbehaving students or to "teach them a lesson." Instead, it should require students to make amends for breaking rules, to do correctly what was done incorrectly, or to forgo enjoyable activities in which they would otherwise participate.

Even when punishing in this manner, teachers should communicate that they are not angry at the students but are truly trying to help. Students should see punishment as a natural and understandable consequence of unacceptable behavior. If students sense good intentions from the teacher, they will be at least partly upset with themselves for losing self-control and will not focus anger or hostility on the teacher.

Overall, punishment should be used only as a last resort when other approaches have failed. That is because there are many things that can go wrong when punishment is used, as follows:

1. Punishment takes the form of revenge or release from tension.
2. Punishment has detrimental effects on student self-concept and on relations with the teacher.
3. Over time, punishment reduces the likelihood that students will maintain self-control.
4. Students may endure punishment in order to elevate their status among peers.
5. Punishment presents an undesirable model for solving problems.

Threats versus Promises. The pain component of Redl and Wattenberg's plea-sure–pain principle should be communicated to students not as threats, but as promises. **Promises** are assurances that unpleasant consequences will be invoked when rules are broken. Promises can be made without negative connotations, and they do not promote undue fear or other negative reactions.

Threats, on the other hand, are emotional statements that make students anxious and fearful. They often interfere with learning and damage the classroom climate. Threats tend to be harsh and negative, taking the form of, "If you don't . . . I will . . . !" Teachers who make dire threats almost never carry them out, and that is all too often their undoing; because of their inconsistency, teachers' ability to control misbehavior consequently erodes, as does their ability to relate positively with the class.

Instead of making threats, Redl and Wattenberg would have teachers explain to students the kinds of behaviors that are unacceptable and identify the consequences associated with those misbehaviors. Unlike threats, these calm assertions lend security to the classroom and help students maintain their own self-control.

ADDITIONAL REMINDERS FROM REDL

Redl, in his 1972 book *When We Deal with Children,* reminds teachers of several principles to keep in mind with regard to student misbehavior:

1. Give students a say in setting standards and deciding consequences. Let them tell how they think you should handle situations that call for punishment.

2. Keep students' emotional health in mind at all times. Punished students must feel that the teacher likes them. Talk to students about their feelings once they have calmed down.
3. Be helpful, not hurtful. Show students you want to support their best behavior.
4. Punishment does not work well. Use it as a last resort. Try other approaches first.
5. Don't be hesitant to change your course of action if you get new insights into a situation.
6. Mistakes in discipline need not be considered disastrous unless they are repeated.
7. Be objective, maintain humor, and remember that we are all human.

STRENGTHS OF REDL AND WATTENBERG'S WORK

Redl and Wattenberg made four landmark contributions toward helping teachers work more effectively with students. First, they described how humans behave differently in groups than they do individually, thus helping teachers understand classroom behaviors that might otherwise seem perplexing. Second, they provided the first well-organized, systematic approach to improving student behavior in the classroom. Prior to their contributions, teachers relied mostly on aversive techniques that intimidated students and caused them to be fearful and experience other emotions counterproductive to long-term working relationships. Third, they devised for their system a procedure for diagnosing the causes of student misbehavior, in the belief that by dealing with causes, teachers could eliminate most misbehavior. And fourth, they established the value of involving students in discipline decisions and maintaining positive feelings.

The Redl and Wattenberg model not only provided teachers with a better way of dealing with classroom misbehavior but set the stage for other discipline models to come. In virtually all the application models presented later in this book, you will see frequent inclusion of elements that Redl and Wattenberg championed, such as supporting student self-control, providing situational assistance, establishing consistent consequences for misbehavior, and being wary of punishment.

Although Redl and Wattenberg's suggestions for identifying student and teacher roles seemed viable, in practice they have provided limited benefits in classroom discipline. Once teachers identified roles, they remained unclear as to what to do about them to help student behavior become more acceptable. It is probable, too, that Redl and Wattenberg were overly optimistic that teachers, within the harried context of classroom misbehavior, could either find the time or develop the necessary skills to do diagnostic thinking as suggested. Thus, while Redl and Wattenberg's work represented the state of the art in discipline when published, and while teachers found it interesting and in many ways helpful, it was in its totality too cumbersome and difficult to implement efficiently. It remained for later innovators to build its valuable components into discipline systems that could be used effectively.

REVIEW OF SELECTED TERMINOLOGY

The following terms are central to the Redl and Wattenberg model of discipline.

appraising reality	punishment
contagious behavior	restructuring activities
diagnostic thinking	scapegoating
group disintegration	setting limits
group dynamics	signals
hurdle help	situational assistance
influence techniques	student roles
pleasure–pain principle	supporting self-control
physical proximity	teacher roles
promises	threats

APPLICATION EXERCISES

CONCEPT CASES

For each of the organized approaches to discipline that are explored in this book, four concept cases—nonworking Kristina, talkative Sara, show-off Joshua, and hostile Tom—are provided so that you may practice and compare various authorities' advice on dealing with misbehavior.

Case 1: Kristina Will Not Work

There is a behavior common to all grade levels that continually frustrates teachers: One or more students fail to participate willingly in classroom activities. The students are often neither disruptive nor confrontive; the problem is simply that they will not complete assignments or participate in classroom happenings.

Kristina, in Mr. Jake's class, behaves in that manner. She is docile, never disrupts, and does little socializing with other students. She rarely completes an assignment. She is simply there, putting forth almost no effort.

How would Redl and Wattenberg deal with Kristina? They would suggest that teachers take the following steps in attempting to improve her classroom behavior.

1. Use diagnostic thinking—develop a hunch, gather facts, try to discover hidden factors, apply a tentative solution, and try out another solution if the first does not work. That might lead to questions such as, Does Kristina have emotional problems? Are things terribly difficult for her at home? Does she try to escape into a fantasy life? Will a warm, caring approach help her?
2. Depending on the conclusions reached in diagnostic thinking, try one or more solutions such as the following:

- Send signals to Kristina: "I know you are not working."
- Move closer to Kristina to prompt her into action.
- Show special interest in Kristina's work.
- Employ humor: "I know you want to finish this work sometime during my lifetime!"
- Offer assistance to Kristina.
- Appraise reality: "Kristina, each incomplete assignment only causes you to fall farther behind, and it hurts your grade!"
- Remove Kristina from the situation: "You can return to the group when you show you can complete your work."

Case 2: Sara Cannot Stop Talking

Sara is a pleasant girl who participates in class activities and does most of the assigned work, though she often fails to complete it. She cannot seem to refrain from talking to classmates during lessons. Her teacher, Mr. Gonzales, has to speak to her repeatedly during lessons, which sometimes exasperates him and causes him to lose his temper.

What suggestions would Redl and Wattenberg give Mr. Gonzales for dealing with Sara?

Case 3: Joshua Clowns and Intimidates

Joshua, larger and louder than his classmates, always wants to be the center of attention, which he accomplishes through a combination of clowning and intimidation. He makes wise remarks, talks back (smilingly) to the teacher, utters a variety of sound-effect noises such as gunshots and automobile crashes, and makes limitless sarcastic comments and other put-downs of classmates. Other students will not stand up to him, apparently fearing his size and verbal and (perhaps) physical aggression. Joshua's antics have brought his teacher, Miss Pearl, almost to her wit's end.

Using Redl and Wattenberg's suggestions, how would you deal with Joshua?

Case 4: Tom Is Hostile and Defiant

Tom has appeared to be in his usual sour mood all morning. On his way to sharpen his pencil, he bumps into Frank, who complains. Tom tells him loudly to shut up. Miss Baines, the teacher, says, "Tom, go back to your seat." Tom turns to face her and loudly says, "I'll go when I'm damned good and ready!"

How would Redl and Wattenberg have Miss Baines deal with Tom?

QUESTIONS

1. Were Kristina, Sara, Joshua, and Tom playing any of the roles identified by Redl and Wattenberg?
2. What psychological roles might the four students expect their teachers to fill?

3. What roles are the following students playing?
   a. Cheryl strolls into Spanish class five minutes late. "¿Qué pasa?" she says nonchalantly to the teacher. The class laughs.
   b. The auto shop teacher notices a group of boys squirting oil at one another. The boys point to Shaun, who is watching from the sidelines. "He started it," they all agree. Although their contention is not true, Shaun grins and does not deny it.
4. How do you think Redl and Wattenberg would suggest dealing with Cheryl's and Shaun's situations?
5. Based on Redl and Wattenberg's suggestions, how do you think Mr. Bryant should handle the following situation?

> Three girls come into the classroom. Alejandra seems very distracted. Susan appears to be crying. Patricia has an angrily hateful look on her face. The class becomes uneasy, and Mr. Bryant is hesitant to proceed with the lesson. There have been similar previous incidents involving the three girls, though none so severe.
>
> Mr. Bryant has a hunch that Patricia has been attempting to drive a wedge between the other two girls, who have been close friends. He examines the facts: Alejandra and Susan are upset; Patricia glares at Susan; these behaviors have occurred before. From their exchanges Mr. Bryant suspects that Patricia has this time been trying to entice Alejandra into doing something only with her, leaving Susan out.

What should Mr. Bryant do?
6. Examine Scenario 1 in the Appendix. What advice from Redl and Wattenberg would best help Mrs. Miller provide a better learning environment for her students?

REFERENCES AND RECOMMENDED READINGS

Redl, F. 1972. *When we deal with children.* New York: Free Press.

Redl, F., and W. Wattenberg. 1959. *Mental hygiene in teaching.* Rev. ed. New York: Harcourt, Brace & World. (Original work published 1951)

Redl, F., and D. Wineman. 1952. *Controls from within.* Glencoe, Ill.: Free Press.

Sheviakov, G., and F. Redl. 1956. *Discipline for today's children.* Washington, D.C.: Association for Supervision and Curriculum Development.

Wattenberg, W. 1955. *The adolescent years.* New York: Harcourt Brace.

———. 1967. *All men are created equal.* Detroit: Wayne State University Press.

CHAPTER 2

Instructional Management and Democratic Teaching

The Contributions of Jacob Kounin and Rudolf Dreikurs

Jacob Kounin

Rudolf Dreikurs

PART 1. KOUNIN'S INSTRUCTIONAL MANAGEMENT

PREVIEW OF KOUNIN'S WORK

Focus

- Classroom management as the key factor in good classroom discipline.
- Techniques that engage students and keep them on track, thereby reducing misbehavior.

Logic

- Management techniques, more than anything else, promote desirable classroom behavior.
- Quality management techniques are evident in the behavior of outstanding teachers.
- Misbehavior is best controlled by teachers' keeping students actively engaged in activities.

Contributions

- Demonstrated the positive effects of classroom management on student behavior.
- Identified specific teaching techniques that help, and hinder, classroom discipline.
- Showed that technique, not teacher personality, is most crucial to classroom control.

Kounin's Suggestions

- Control misbehavior by keeping students actively engaged in classroom activities.
- Rely on teaching techniques rather than verbal desists to control student behavior.
- Use withitness, alerting, accountability, challenge, enthusiasm, and variety to delay satiation.

ABOUT JACOB KOUNIN

Jacob Kounin was born in Cleveland, Ohio, in 1912, and earned his doctorate at Iowa State University in 1939. In 1946 he was appointed to a professorship in educational psychology at Wayne State University, where he spent most of his academic career. Kounin made numerous presentations to the American Psychological Association, the American Educational Research Association, and many other professional organizations. He served often as a consultant and visiting professor at other universities.

Kounin is best known for his detailed investigations into how instructional management affects student behavior. Reports of those investigations are presented in his book *Discipline and Group Management in Classrooms* (1971, revised 1977). His work is cited in most writings about classroom discipline, and his discoveries have been made part of most of the application models presented later in this book.

KOUNIN'S CONTRIBUTIONS TO DISCIPLINE

Kounin was the first researcher to present a detailed analysis of the effect that certain teaching behaviors have on the behavior of students in classrooms. Using videotapes made in hundreds of classrooms, Kounin was able to identify a number of teacher strategies that engaged students in lessons and thus greatly reduced misbehavior. His work led to several conclusions about what teachers should and should not do in order to ensure better student behavior and learning.

KOUNIN'S CENTRAL FOCUS

Kounin's central focus was on classroom management—on how teachers organized and presented lessons, arranged the classroom, provided for movement in the room, gave attention to all students simultaneously, and made transitions from one lesson to another. His studies showed significant correlations between what teachers did in these areas and the resultant student behavior and learning.

KOUNIN'S PRINCIPAL TEACHINGS

Teachers need to know what is going on in all parts of the classroom at all times. Kounin verified that teachers good in discipline displayed this trait, which he called "withitness."

Good lesson momentum helps keep students on track. Kounin used the term "momentum" to refer to teachers' starting lessons with dispatch, keeping those lessons moving ahead, bringing them to a satisfactory close, and making transitions efficiently.

Smoothness in lesson presentation helps keep students involved. The term "smoothness" refers to steady progression of lessons, without abrupt changes or disturbing incidents.

Effective teachers have systems for gaining student attention and clarifying expectations. Kounin called this tactic "group alerting."

Effective teachers keep students attentive and actively involved. Such "student accountability" is maintained by regularly calling on students to respond, demonstrate, or explain.

Teachers good in behavior management are able to attend to two or more events simultaneously. This skill, which Kounin called "overlapping," is shown, for example, when teachers answer questions for students doing independent work while at the same time instructing a small group of students.

Teachers must see to it that students are not given over-exposure to a particular topic. Over-exposure produces "satiation," evidenced in boredom, resistance, and misbehavior.

Teachers should make instructional activities enjoyable and challenging. Kounin described how fun and challenge delay satiation.

ANALYSIS OF KOUNIN'S WORK

The Ripple Effect

Kounin's research grew out of an accidental observation he made while teaching his own university class, in which he noticed that when he reprimanded one of his students, other students were affected by the reprimand and changed their behavior as well.

Intrigued by this observation, Kounin proceeded to investigate the nature of **desists** (remarks and reprimands to stop misbehavior) and the spread of their effects, a phenomenon he called the **ripple effect.** He arranged experiments at different grade levels and settings, in which he tried to determine whether and to what extent the nature of a desist influenced the degree of conforming behavior not only among students who received the desist, but among those who witnessed it. He found, contrary to his expectations, that the ripple effect was powerful only at the early primary level. At the university level, a mild ripple effect was discernible, but at the secondary level, desists neither decreased nor increased the amount of misbehavior among students other than the offender. Kounin did find that secondary school students' behavior was strongly affected by their liking for the teacher.

Kounin's investigations produced 300 different statistical correlations involving desists and behavior. Only 2 were marginally significant (meaning they were probably real), while the other 298 were statistically insignificant (meaning that there was an unacceptable probability that the findings were not real, but only the result of chance). That caused Kounin to conclude that there is no relationship between teachers' desist techniques and the degree of success in handling unacceptable behavior. He also wrote that

> the techniques of dealing with misbehavior, as such, are not significant determinants of how well or poorly children behave in classrooms, or with how successful a teacher is in preventing one child's misbehavior from contaging others. (p. 70)

Those conclusions caused Kounin to change his research focus away from desists and toward identification of teacher traits and behaviors that seemed to influence student involvement in class activities, thus resulting in a reduction in misbehavior.

Kounin subsequently found several factors that are influential in classroom control. They include *withitness, momentum and smoothness, group alerting and accountability, overlapping,* and *satiation and challenge arousal.*

Withitness

Kounin discovered that teachers very good in classroom control seem to have the proverbial eyes in the back of the head and know what is going on in all areas of the classroom at all times. He called this awareness phenomenon **withitness** and considered it the factor that most clearly differentiated between effective and ineffective teachers.

However, withitness depends on students' being convinced that the teacher does in fact know what is occurring everywhere in the room. Teachers therefore need to communicate their awareness through behaviors and words. If Bob is not working, the teacher's eye contact will show she is aware. If necessary, the teacher may say, "This work must be done today."

Kounin identified several aspects of withitness that contribute to its effectiveness. One is the ability to *select the proper student for correction.* Suppose that Bob and Bill are teasing Shawanna while the teacher is working elsewhere with a small group. Shawanna protests aloud. Withitness permits the teacher to correctly identify the boys and tells them to get to work. But a teacher not fully aware of the situation may only hear Shawanna and thus incorrectly tell her to stop talking and get to work. By failing to attend to the instigators of the situation, the teacher communicates to the class a lack of awareness of what is really going on.

A second aspect of withitness is the ability to *attend first to the more serious deviancy* when two or more misbehaviors are occurring simultaneously. To illustrate: Janille is playing with something at her desk and is not doing the assigned work. Meanwhile, Carlos and Eric are angrily pushing each other in a corner of the room. The teacher looks up and says, "Janille, put that away and get to work." The teacher failed to identify the more serious misbehavior. If this occurs often, students begin to realize that their teacher is not truly aware of events in the classroom.

A third aspect of withitness has to do with *timing.* Teachers possessing withitness do not allow misbehavior to spread to other students before taking action. Consider this scene: Markus crumples his paper and throws it at the wastebasket. Ian sees him and decides to try it, too. Before long, several other boys have happily joined in. The situation should never have been allowed to progress to that point. The teacher should have noted and corrected the misbehavior when it first occurred.

A similar timing mistake is to allow misbehavior to increase in seriousness before taking action. Consider the following: The second-grade teacher has given two boys permission to go to the drinking fountain. Michael was there first, but Justin rushed around and pushed in ahead of him. Michael pushed Justin in return. The two glared at each other, exchanged words, and postured for a while before beginning to scuffle.

Only then did the teacher intervene, but it was too late. This suggested to the class that the teacher was not aware of the situation until it got out of hand. By speaking to the boys earlier, the teacher could have prevented the confrontation and at the same time communicated withitness.

Momentum and Smoothness

Kounin observed that all teachers have to manage a great deal of what he called **activity movement.** By activity movement, he meant both psychological and physical progression of lessons. Kounin drew special attention to two phenomena within activity movement: (1) **momentum,** which refers to teachers' getting activities started promptly, keeping them moving ahead, and bringing them to efficient closure or transition, and (2) **smoothness,** which avoids abrupt changes that interfere with students' activities or thought processes. Kounin found that momentum and smoothness, which he ultimately investigated as a single combined factor, correlate highly with desired student behavior. Momentum and smoothness were found to be especially important during lesson presentations and during transitions from one lesson or activity to another, for it is at those times that student misbehavior is most likely to occur. Consider the following episodes: High school students are working on an art project. Unexpectedly, Miss Montoni says, "Put your supplies away and get ready for a visitor." Half the class does not hear the directions and the other half starts to move around in confusion. An elementary class has just begun a math lesson. Mr. Contreras calls on three students to go to the board. On their way up, he suddenly asks, "Just a minute. Class, how many of you brought your money for the field trip?" The teacher counts the raised hands, goes to the desk, and writes down the number. In a middle school class, Mrs. Anderson is teaching a composition lesson. She directs students to begin writing, but stops them frequently with comments such as "Make sure you leave space at the margins," "Remember the sequence we spoke of," "Don't forget to number each paragraph," "Keep your paragraphs fairly short," and "Be sure each paragraph contains a topic sentence." Her comments, intended to be helpful, break student concentration and slow their progress. In all three cases unnecessary noise and confusion occur while the likelihood of misbehavior increases.

These matters may seem inconsequential in the larger context of the school day, but Kounin's investigations led him to conclude that the teacher's ability to manage smooth transitions and maintain momentum is *more important to work involvement and classroom control than any other behavior-management technique.*

Group Alerting and Accountability

Teachers do not have many opportunities to work exclusively with one student. Mostly they work with groups or with the entire class. Kounin found that the ability to maintain a concerted group focus—by which he meant the ability to keep students alert, attentive, and actively involved in appropriate activities—is essential to a productive, efficient classroom. Group focus is most easily obtained through *alerting and accountability.*

Alerting

By **group alerting,** Kounin meant (1) getting students' attention and (2) quickly letting students know what they are supposed to do. Kounin reported that teachers adept in alerting tend to use such attention-getting approaches as looking around the group in a suspenseful manner and perhaps making statements as the following:

> "I wonder who can . . ."
>
> "Class, look at this odd illustration. What do you think it might mean? If you can guess, raise your hand."
>
> "We are now going to have a timed test with thirty problems to solve. Let's see if we can set a new record this morning."

Such tactics draw the attention of all group members. Kounin contrasted them with ineffective practices that lead to inattention, such as the following:

1. The teacher focuses on one student at a time and fails to include other students in the discussion.
2. The teacher chooses the person who is to respond before asking the question.
3. The teacher begins a lesson without attempting to get students' minds engaged in the central question, topic, or skill to be learned.

Accountability

By **accountability,** Kounin meant holding each student in the group responsible for active involvement in learning the facts, concepts, or procedures being taught. To encourage accountability, he said, teachers need to know what each student is doing and how each is responding and progressing. Kounin recommends several techniques for holding students accountable, including the following:

1. All students hold up response cards for the teacher to see.
2. The teacher asks all students to observe and check accuracy while one group member performs.
3. The teacher asks all students to write an answer and then, at random, calls on various students to respond aloud.
4. The teacher circulates and observes the responses of nonreciters.

These approaches enable teachers to work with the entire group and still obtain individual evidence of involvement and progress. When students see that the teacher intends to hold them definitely and immediately accountable for the content of the lesson, they pay better attention, involve themselves in the activities, and find fewer reasons to misbehave.

Overlapping

In his studies of classroom practices, Kounin became aware of a group-management technique that skilled teachers used, a technique that he called **overlapping.**

Overlapping refers to attending to two or more issues at the same time. For example, a teacher is meeting with a small group and notices that two students at their seats are playing cards instead of doing their assignment. The teacher could correct the behavior by either of the following methods:

1. Stopping the small-group activity, walking over to the cardplayers and getting them back on task, and then attempting to reestablish the small-group work; or
2. Having the small group continue their activity while addressing the cardplayers from a distance, then monitoring the students at their desks while continuing with the small-group activity.

As you can see, the second approach involves overlapping. Teachers are continually interrupted while working with groups or individuals. If a student approaches with a paper that must be reviewed before the student can continue, teachers adroit in overlapping can check the paper while glancing at the small group and making encouraging remarks to them such as "Go on" or "That's correct." In that manner, the teacher attends to various issues simultaneously.

Kounin found that teachers adept in overlapping are also aware of the broader scope of happenings in the classroom. They are more "with-it," as Kounin would say. Overlapping, in fact, cannot be done effectively if the teacher does not demonstrate withitness.

Satiation and Challenge Arousal

Kounin found that misbehavior is more likely to occur as students become bored and restless, or "satiated," as he called it. He therefore investigated what teachers do that contributes to **satiation,** and conversely what they do to avoid it. Students become tired and bored with anything if given too much of it, as becomes evident when they look elsewhere, make more frequent mistakes, disengage from the lesson, and turn to less acceptable behaviors such as sharpening pencils, talking, annoying each other, or getting up and moving about the room.

But Kounin found that satiation can be delayed. He saw that many teachers used techniques that rekindled student interest when it lagged, thereby avoiding the misbehavior that would otherwise occur. He classified the delaying techniques as *routine, positive,* and *negative.* Routine techniques are familiar classroom and instructional practices, such as having students take turns, providing regular explanations, calling on reciters, and the like. Positive techniques are extra things teachers do, perhaps a bit out of the ordinary, to excite student interest or involvement. Negative techniques are such things as using instructional activities that are clearly uninspiring or giving explanations, demonstrations, or directions well beyond what is necessary.

Challenge

Kounin noticed that teachers who offer **challenge** throughout a lesson hold off satiation for a long while. To keep students alert and eager they say things like "You are going to need your thinking caps for this one; it's tricky" or "I'm going to predict that nobody in the room can figure this one out. Anybody want to try?" or "This is something I bet your parents have never done; if you can do this, you can do anything."

Enthusiasm

Kounin found that students respond well to **teacher enthusiasm** shown in statements from the teacher such as "This is going to be a magical day for us!" or "This has been my favorite story ever since I was a child" or "You will remember this experience the rest of your life!" Comments of this sort must, of course, reflect the teacher's genuine feelings. Teachers quickly lose their credibility if they carry on about how exciting dull activities are going to be.

Instructional Variety

Kounin found that effective teachers offer a **variety** of instructional activities. He found that elementary teachers varied activities so that quiet activities, noisy activities, seated activities, and movement activities were interspersed, thus providing pleasant changes in thought, movement, and use of the senses. Secondary teachers made similar variations within instructional periods, or from day to day, varying reading and analysis with skill practice, discussion, creative production, and purposeful problem solving. He also noted that teachers built variety into lesson presentations, by demonstrating, directing activities, asking questions, leading discussions, and having students solve problems on their own.

Student Progress

Kounin found students' sense of progress to be helpful in delaying satiation. Students are often unclear about whether they are making progress. Teachers can reassure them verbally, but it is more helpful if progress is depicted numerically or graphically.

KOUNIN'S REFLECTIONS ON HIS INVESTIGATIONS

In commenting on what he had learned from his studies, Kounin explained that he was forced to reconsider the original intentions of his research. He had expected to find a relationship between student behavior and the quality of the desists that teachers use to curb misbehavior. But no such findings emerged, either for immediate effect on students or for the overall amount of misbehavior in the classroom. Kounin stated:

> That unexpected fact required unlearning on my part, in the sense of having to replace the original question by other questions. Questions about disciplinary techniques were eliminated and replaced by questions about classroom management in general [and] preventing misbehavior was given higher investigative priority than handling misbehavior. (p. 143)

Thereafter, Kounin looked carefully at two kinds of student behavior—work involvement and misbehavior—and tried to identify teacher behaviors associated with both. He identified the elements considered to this point: withitness, momentum, smoothness, group alerting, group accountability, overlapping, challenge, enthusiasm, and instructional variety. He asserted:

> These techniques of classroom management apply to emotionally disturbed children in regular classrooms as well as to nondisturbed children. They apply to boys as well as to girls. [They] apply to the group and not merely to individual children. They are techniques of creating an effective classroom

ecology and learning milieu. One might note that none of them necessitate punitiveness or restrictiveness. (p. 144)

He went on to say that

> the business of running a classroom is a complicated technology having to do with developing a nonsatiating learning program; programming for progress, challenge, and variety in learning activities; initiating and maintaining movement in classroom tasks with smoothness and momentum; coping with more than one event simultaneously; observing and emitting feedback for many different events; directing actions at appropriate targets; maintaining a focus upon a group; and doubtless other techniques not measured in these researches. (pp. 144–145)

STRENGTHS OF KOUNIN'S WORK

The management techniques Kounin clarified are without question helpful in creating and maintaining a classroom atmosphere conducive to learning. By keeping students busily and willingly engaged in learning activities, teachers cut down markedly on the number of behavior problems with which they would otherwise have to contend. The techniques are also rather easily learned and performed by teachers.

It is interesting to note that Kounin judged that teachers' personality traits had little to do with classroom control. In reference to teacher traits such as friendliness, helpfulness, rapport, warmth, patience, and the like, he declared that (contrary to popular opinion) such traits are of no value in managing a classroom. Management, he insisted, is a complicated technology consisting of specific techniques applied at the appropriate times and in the appropriate manner so as to provide learning experiences that are nonsatiating.

Kounin's ideas have been widely acknowledged and well received. His clarification of the role of management in maintaining good behavior has made a powerful contribution to school discipline and is incorporated into almost all application models. But while there is no doubt about the value of Kounin's suggestions, his proposals fail to provide teachers a complete program of discipline that can both prevent student misbehavior and correct it expeditiously when necessary. Teachers accept Kounin's advice concerning the prevention of misbehavior but find little help in his work when classroom misbehavior must be stopped, dealt with, and redirected.

REVIEW OF SELECTED TERMINOLOGY

The following terms are central to understanding Kounin's work.

accountability	group alerting
activity movement	momentum
challenge	overlapping
desists	ripple effect

satiation   variety

smoothness   withitness

teacher enthusiasm

PART 2. DREIKURS'S DEMOCRATIC TEACHING

PREVIEW OF DREIKURS'S WORK

Focus

- Discipline as self-generated respectfulness developed as an outgrowth of Social Interest.
- Attaining the genuine goal of belonging versus mistaken goals that lead to misbehavior.
- The teacher's role in helping students develop Social Interest for good classroom behavior.

Logic

- Genuine discipline is internal and comes from respectfulness developed within each student.
- Most misbehavior occurs when students are unable to reach the genuine goal of belonging.
- Teachers, with proper technique, can redirect mistaken-goal behavior toward the genuine goal.

Contributions

- Provided teachers help in building genuine internal self-direction in students.
- Showed teachers how to function democratically, rather than authoritarianly or permissively.
- Offered techniques for giving positive redirection to students' mistaken-goal behavior.

Dreikurs's Suggestions

- Do the best possible to give every student a sense of belonging in the classroom.
- When misbehavior occurs, identify the mistaken goal of that behavior.
- Confront mistaken-goal behavior and help students redirect it in positive ways.

ABOUT RUDOLF DREIKURS

Rudolf Dreikurs (1897–1972) was born in Vienna, Austria. After receiving his medical degree from the University of Vienna, he entered into a long association with the renowned psychiatrist Alfred Adler, with whom he worked in family and child counseling. Dreikurs immigrated to the United States in 1937 and eventually became director of the Alfred Adler Institute in Chicago. He also served as professor of psychiatry at the Chicago Medical School. Throughout his career, he focused on family and child counseling. He became a recognized authority in the area of classroom behavior through his books *Psychology in the Classroom* (1968), *Discipline without Tears* (1972, 1995), coauthored with Pearl Cassel, *Logical Consequences* (reissued in 1995), coauthored with Loren Grey, and *Maintaining Sanity in the Classroom* (1982, 1988), coauthored with Bernice Grunwald and Floy Pepper and published posthumously. Basic principles are also presented in Eva Dreikurs Ferguson's *Adlerian Theory: An Introduction* (1995).

DREIKURS'S CONTRIBUTIONS TO DISCIPLINE

Dreikurs was among the first to explore the underlying causes of student misbehavior in the classroom. He concluded that virtually all human beings have a primary need to belong, to feel that they have an important place in the group. He insisted that all school students desire more than anything else to feel that they have value, that they belong in the classroom, and that they can contribute. Dreikurs called the need for belonging the **genuine goal** of human social behavior. Belonging is tied to a feeling of equality and to contribution, based on concern for the welfare of the group. Dreikurs maintained that students who have gained that genuine sense of belonging rarely misbehave seriously.

But the sense of belonging does not come easily to all students, he explained. When unable to attain their genuine goal, students turn to a series of **mistaken goals** in an attempt to gain a sense of importance. Dreikurs identified those mistaken goals as **attention, power, revenge,** and **inadequacy.** When students pursue those goals, they often disrupt learning and cause other problems for teachers and themselves.

Dreikurs maintained that teachers could ensure acceptable classroom behavior by helping all students reach their genuine goal of belonging. He believed they could best do so by functioning as what he called **democratic teachers,** involving students in decisions that affected their lives in school. But he also recognized that even in the best classrooms, some students will inevitably pursue mistaken goals. To help teachers deal with that eventuality, Dreikurs presented a set of tactics for teachers to use in confronting mistaken goals while reorienting students to the genuine goal of belonging.

DREIKURS'S CENTRAL FOCUS

Dreikurs focused on constructive behavior rather than on coercive discipline. He followed two primary focuses. The first focus was on helping teachers establish a **democratic classroom and teaching style,** intended to help students acquire social interest and a sense of belonging. **Social interest** is a condition in which students come to see that it is to their advantage to contribute to the welfare of the group. Dreikurs's second focus was on identifying and dealing with mistaken goals that students pursue when unable to attain their genuine goal of belonging. Dreikurs labeled those mistaken goals, described the misbehaviors associated with them, and provided directions for how to recognize and redirect the attendant misbehaviors.

DREIKURS'S PRINCIPAL TEACHINGS

Discipline is based on mutual respect, which motivates students to behave constructively out of a heightened sense of social interest. Social interest means concern with the welfare of others as well as with oneself. This developmental process is facilitated by the skill of the teacher.

An autocratic teacher is one who lays down the law in the classroom, feels a strong need to be always in charge, and doles out harsh consequences when rules are broken. Autocratic teachers are relatively ineffective in helping students develop self-discipline.

A permissive teacher is one who fails to insist that students comply with reasonable expectations and consequences. Permissive teachers do not help students realize that freedom must be linked to responsibility; they therefore do little to foster student self-discipline.

A democratic teacher is one who tries to motivate students from within, helps students develop rules of conduct that will enable the class to prosper, and allows students to exercise freedom coupled with responsibility. Democratic teachers have better success than do autocratic or permissive teachers in helping students develop genuine self-discipline.

A democratic classroom is a classroom in which teacher and students cooperate in making joint decisions about class procedures, rules, and consequences for misbehavior. Democratic classrooms are more effective than others in fostering student self-discipline.

Virtually all students have a compelling desire to feel a sense of belonging in the classroom. Belonging is achieved when the student feels equal with others and is concerned with everyone's welfare. The need to belong is the "genuine goal" that all students strive for.

When students are unable to attain the genuine goal of belonging, they turn to mistaken goals. Mistaken goals are those of attention, power, revenge, and inadequacy. When students pursue mistaken goals, their actions often result in classroom misbehavior.

The first mistaken goal is that of trying to get attention. Students who are not gaining a sense of belonging usually attempt to get attention from peers and teacher.

The second mistaken goal is that of seeking power. When students are not satisfied in their attempts to get attention, they often seek a sense of power, usually manifest in their refusing to do what the teacher requests.

The third mistaken goal is that of seeking revenge. When students are thwarted in their attempts to display power over teachers, they sometimes try to gain a sense of importance by exacting revenge on the teacher. They most often do so by defacing property, subverting the class, cheating, or spreading lies.

The fourth mistaken goal is that of displaying inadequacy. When all else has failed, students attempt to shield themselves from further damage by withdrawing and making no attempt to participate in class activities.

Encouragement is words or actions teachers use to convey respect for students and belief in their abilities. It is differentiated from *praise,* which is counterproductive since praise comes only when a task is done well.

When teachers see a student pursuing a mistaken goal, they should point out that fact to the student. They do this calmly by asking "Do you need me to pay more attention to you?" or "Could it be that you want to show that I can't make you do the assignment?"

Logical consequences are reasonable results that follow behavior, desirable or undesirable. Good behavior brings pleasant consequences, such as enjoyment of learning. Misbehavior brings unpleasant consequences such as having to complete work at home that was supposed to be completed in class.

Punishment is action taken by the teacher to get back at students and show them who is boss, usually by humiliating or isolating the offending students. Punishment has many pitfalls; it should be replaced by logical consequences.

ANALYSIS OF DREIKURS'S WORK

The Nature of Discipline

Discipline at its best encourages a sense of belonging and promotes student contribution to the group. This kind of discipline, helpful and liberating, assists smooth, productive functioning in schools and elsewhere. It contrasts strongly with **aversive discipline,** based on threat and punishment, which stifles initiative. Aversive discipline does little to help students develop self-control. Instead, it is more likely to make students want to subvert the controls and do whatever they feel capable of getting away with. Many teachers believe that in order to prevent students' taking advantage of them, it is necessary to retain the threat of punishment and be willing to use it. But students see this kind of discipline as arbitrary, set up by the teacher to show who is in charge. Teachers who hold this view of discipline find that they cannot always enforce their rules. Over time they tend to become autocratic in demeanor while permissive in enforcement. That is, they tend to shout and make threats, but seldom carry out the threats.

Good discipline, Dreikurs maintained, makes no use of punishment. Good discipline is an outcome of the understanding of the needs of the situation. It involves respect for orderly processes and for recognizing that actions lead to natural or logical consequences, both of which are emphasized by Dreikurs. **Natural consequences** are results that naturally occur following behavior, and they can bring pleasure or discomfort or can be neutral. For example, Jonathan tips his chair backward during a lesson and as a result falls, leaving him hurt or embarrassed. **Logical consequences** ordinarily require students to make right what they have done wrong. If Marisa does not complete her work during class, she is required to complete it as homework. The consequence of having to complete work is "logically" related to the failure to comply with class expectations. In democratic classrooms, students know in advance what the logical consequences of misbehavior are likely to be—they will have helped formulate the consequences. When they behave as the class has agreed, they enjoy pleasant consequences; when they break agreed-upon rules, they must accept the unpleasant consequences they helped formulate. Students come to see this type of discipline not as dreadful punishment from teachers, but as logical extensions of the behavior choices they are free to make.

Discipline is best accomplished when students and teachers jointly set limits on behavior until students become able to set such limits for themselves. It is important for students to participate in clarifying the behavior that will best promote the interests of the class. They should also take part in deciding what the consequences should be when behavior agreements are broken. This gives them an understanding of the reasons behind rules and consequences and helps them see that behavior produces consequences that may be desirable or undesirable.

Discipline and Types of Teachers

Dreikurs believed that teachers he defined as "democratic" are more likely than others to help students become self-disciplined. In explaining his views, he contrasted democratic teachers with teachers he called autocratic or permissive, depending on how they handled the classroom.

Autocratic teachers are teachers who exhibit the following traits (Dreikurs, Grunwald, & Pepper 1982, p. 76): They boss, use a sharp voice, command, exercise power, exert pressure, demand cooperation, tell you what you should do, impose ideas, dominate, criticize, find fault, punish, and unilaterally establish all procedures, rules, and consequences.

Permissive teachers put few if any limits on student behavior, nor do they invoke logical consequences when misbehavior disrupts the class. Their demeanor is wishy-washy, and they make excuses, such as "bad background," for students who misbehave.

Democratic teachers stand in marked contrast to autocratic and permissive teachers. Democratic teachers exhibit the following traits of democratic teaching: leadership, friendliness, inviting nature, stimulation, ideas, cooperation, guidance, encouragement, acknowledgment, helpfulness, and shared responsibility. Democratic teachers' classrooms reflect the following (Dreikurs, Grunwald, and Pepper 1982):

- Order necessary for required work is present.
- Rules, responsibilities, and consequences students have helped frame are in place.
- Mutual trust exists between students and teacher.
- The teacher solicits student help rather than demands it.
- Cooperation is more evident than competition.
- The classroom atmosphere is warm and friendly.
- Group discussions of class concerns are routine.
- The teacher is more concerned with class progress than with personal prestige.
- Students are encouraged and helped to learn from their mistakes.

Discipline and Mistaken Goals

Dreikurs makes three important points in his writings. The first is that students are social beings who want to feel they belong to the groups in which they participate—family, peer, school, class, and other groups. Dreikurs calls this desire a **genuine goal of belonging** that strongly motivates student behavior.

Dreikurs's second point is that students **choose their behavior** based on their understanding of a situation. Nature does not compel them to behave in any particular way.

Dreikurs's third point is that when students fail to achieve their genuine goal of belonging, they tend to choose other (undesirable) behaviors in the mistaken belief that those behaviors will get them the recognition they seek. Dreikurs calls these erroneous beliefs **mistaken goals.**

It is Dreikurs's contention that all people want to belong, to have a place. They try many kinds of behavior to obtain status and recognition. If they do not receive recognition through socially acceptable means, they turn to mistaken goals, which prompt antisocial behavior.

Dreikurs identifies four mistaken goals to which students turn when unable to satisfy the genuine goal of belonging: (1) getting attention, (2) seeking power, (3) seeking revenge, and (4) displaying inadequacy. Let's examine each of these mistaken goals more closely.

Getting Attention

When students are not receiving the recognition they desire, they may resort to **getting attention** through misbehavior. They feel important if the teacher pays attention to them and provides them extra services. They may disrupt, ask special favors, raise irrelevant questions, continually call for help with assignments, and refuse to work unless the teacher hovers over them. Good students, as well as poor students, make bids for attention. They function well so long as they have the teacher's approval, but if approval is not forthcoming, they sometimes resort to less acceptable ways of getting attention.

Teachers should understand that giving attention to misbehaving students does not improve the improper behavior; rather, it increases those students' desire for attention and causes them to look for external sources of motivation. If attention-getting behavior does not provide students the recognition they seek, they turn to the next mistaken goal: **seeking power.**

Seeking Power

At times students feel that the only way they can get the recognition they desire is through defying the teacher. They may seek power by arguing, contradicting, lying, having temper tantrums, refusing to follow directions, or behaving hostilely. If students can get the teacher to fight with them, they feel they have won whether or not they actually got their way, because they have succeeded in showing they have the power to disrupt the class and put the teacher on the defensive. Even when the teacher wins the contest of wills, the student comes to believe that power is what matters in life. If students fail to obtain the recognition they desire through power seeking, they move to the next, more severe, misbehavior: **seeking revenge.**

Seeking Revenge

Students who move on to seeking revenge have failed to gain status through attention or power. The reasoning for their next mistaken goal is "I can only feel significant if I have the ability to hurt others. Hurting others makes up for my being hurt."

Students who seek revenge set themselves up to be punished. They may behave cruelly and, when punished, feel they have renewed cause for vengeful action. The more trouble they cause for themselves, the more justified they feel. They consider it a victory to be disliked.

But underneath their bravado these individuals are deeply discouraged. Their behavior only brings more hurt from others, causing them to feel even more worthless. Finally, they pursue the one mistaken goal left available: **displaying inadequacy.**

Displaying Inadequacy

Students who resort to displaying inadequacy see themselves as failures. There is no need to try further. They withdraw from situations that might add to their feeling of worthlessness. They guard what little self-esteem they have left by removing themselves from social tests. Their mistaken belief is "If I appear inadequate, others will leave me alone." Students who seek this goal do so by pretending to be stupid. They are unresponsive to teacher urgings and passively refuse to participate in class activities. They sit silently and engage in no interaction. The behavior associated with this mistaken goal is serious and difficult to overcome. Worse, because withdrawn students do not disrupt classes, teachers may not see the depth of the problem and take steps to correct it.

What Should Teachers Do Regarding Mistaken Goals?

Students seek the four mistaken goals in hopes of gaining status. But instead of leading to success, those goals lead to failure. What can the teacher do to redirect students? Dreikurs makes the following suggestions:

1. Identify the Mistaken Goal

The easiest way to **identify the mistaken goal** is to note the teacher's own response to the misbehavior. If the teacher feels

- *annoyed,* the student is probably seeking attention
- *threatened,* the student is probably seeking power
- *hurt,* the student is probably seeking revenge
- *powerless,* the student is displaying inadequacy.

Another way to identify mistaken goals is to observe students' reactions to being corrected.

If Students	Then Their Goal Is
stop the misbehavior and then repeat it	attention
refuse to stop or increase the misbehavior	power
become violent or hostile	revenge
refuse to cooperate, participate, or interact	inadequacy

2. Confront the Mistaken Goal

After the teacher has identified mistaken goals, the second step is to **confront the mistaken goal** and provide an explanation of it together with a discussion of the faulty logic involved. By doing this in a friendly, nonthreatening manner, teachers can usually get students to examine and change their behavior. Dreikurs would have teachers ask students the following questions, in order, and observe reactions that might indicate a mistaken goal:

- "Could it be that you want me to pay attention to you?"
- "Could it be that you want to prove that nobody can make you do anything?"

- "Could it be that you want to hurt me (or others)?"
- "Could it be that you want me to believe you are not capable?"

These questions, when non-threatening, can improve misbehavior by removing the fun of provoking the teacher. And they take the initiative away from the student, allowing the teacher to implement actions to change the misbehavior.

3. Avoid Power Struggles with Students

When students engage teachers in power struggles, it is natural for teachers to feel threatened and want to fight back. But by participating in power struggles, teachers only cause students to become more rebellious and hostile and to think about getting revenge. Teachers can avoid power struggles simply by withdrawing as an authority figure. The student cannot exert power if there is no one with whom to fight. Teachers may wish to state to the student and the class that they recognize the offending student's need for power. They may decide to stop the entire class and wait for the disruptive behavior to cease, in which case the offending student may receive pressure from peers rather than from the teacher.

Teachers can also redirect students' ambitions for power by inviting them to participate in making decisions or by giving them positions of responsibility. A teacher might take a student aside and say, "The language I am hearing is very offensive to me. The other students look up to you. Do you think you could help out by setting an example?" Or in the same situation the teacher might say, "I have a problem. It concerns the language I am hearing. What do you think I should do?" In this way, teachers admit that the student has power but refuse to be engaged in conflicts.

4. Take Positive Steps against Revenge-Seeking Behavior

Students seeking revenge may want to hurt others because they have been hurt themselves. What they need most is not retaliation but understanding and acceptance. The teacher may be able to set up situations that allow vengeful students to exhibit talents or strengths, thus helping the students see that they can behave in ways that bring acceptance and status. But it must be understood that students who seek revenge at first reject efforts to help them. Persistence and patience are required.

5. Encourage Students Who Display Inadequacy

Students who have been unable to gain belonging, attention, power, or revenge usually withdraw and want to be left alone. They want the teacher to believe that they are not worth dealing with. Teachers must never give up on these students, but offer encouragement and support for even the smallest efforts. They should also be very sensitive to their own reactions to these students. Any indication of defeat or frustration reinforces a student's sense of worthlessness and desire to appear inadequate.

The Distinction between Encouragement and Praise

Dreikurs believed **encouragement** to be a crucial element in establishing good behavior. Through encouragement teachers make learning seem worthwhile and help students develop self-esteem. Encouragement consists of words or actions that convey the teacher's respect and belief in students' abilities. It recognizes effort, not achievement, and promotes feelings of being a contributing member of the group. Teachers should always be alert for opportunities to recognize effort, regardless of the quality of work.

Praise is very different from encouragement. Praise is given when a task is done well. It promotes the idea that a product is worthless unless it receives praise. Students who receive steady praise fail to learn to work for self-satisfaction. Praise encourages the attitude "What am I going to get out of it?" These examples show the differences between praise and encouragement:

> **Praise:** "You are such a good girl for finishing your assignment."
> **Encouragement:** "I can tell that you have been working hard."
> **Praise:** "You play the guitar so well!"
> **Encouragement:** "I can see that you really enjoy playing the guitar."

Dreikurs (Dreikurs and Cassel 1972, pp. 51-54) makes the following suggestions for encouraging students:

1. Always be positive; avoid negative comments.
2. Encourage students to strive for improvement, not perfection.
3. Encourage effort. Results don't matter very much so long as students try hard.
4. Emphasize strengths and minimize weaknesses.
5. Teach students to learn from mistakes. Emphasize that mistakes are not failures.
6. Stimulate motivation from within. Do not exert pressure from without.
7. Encourage independence.
8. Let students know that you have faith in their abilities.
9. Offer to help overcome obstacles.
10. Encourage students to help classmates who are having difficulties. This helps them appreciate their own strengths.
11. Send positive notes home, especially concerning effort.
12. Show pride in students' work. Display the work and invite others to see it.
13. Be optimistic and enthusiastic—it is catching.
14. Try to set up situations that guarantee success for all.
15. Use encouraging remarks often, such as:
    You have improved!
    Can I help you?
    What did you learn from that mistake?

Logical Consequences versus Punishment

No matter how much encouragement teachers give, they still encounter behavior problems. Dreikurs advises setting up logical consequences to help deter misbehavior and motivate appropriate behavior. As noted earlier, logical consequences are results that the teacher consistently applies following certain behaviors; they are arranged jointly by teacher and students.

Logical consequences are clearly different from **punishment.** Punishment is action taken by the teacher to get back at misbehaving students and show them who is boss. It prompts retaliation and makes students feel they have the right to punish in return. Logical consequences, on the other hand, are not weapons used by the teacher. They teach students that all behavior produces a corresponding result. Appropriate behavior brings rewards, while unacceptable behavior brings unpleasant consequences.

Logical consequences must be explained, understood, and agreed to by students. If they are sprung on students at the time of conflict, they will be considered punishment. When applying consequences, teachers should not act as self-appointed authorities. They should simply represent the order required by society and enforce the rules agreed to by the students.

To be effective, consequences must be applied consistently. If teachers apply them only when in a bad mood or only to certain students, students will not learn that misbehavior always carries unpleasant consequences. They will misbehave and gamble that they can get away with it. Students must be convinced that consequences will be applied each and every time they choose to misbehave. They will have to consider carefully whether misbehaving is worth it. It takes time to break old behavior habits, but teachers should never become discouraged and give up on implementing consequences. Applying consequences encourages students to make careful choices about how they behave and helps them rely on their own inner discipline to control their actions. They learn that poor choices invariably result in unpleasant consequences through nobody's fault but their own. Students also learn that the teacher respects their ability to make their own decisions.

STRENGTHS OF DREIKURS'S WORK

Dreikurs's teachings have potential for bringing about attitudinal changes that cause students to behave better because they see the value of doing so. These results are produced by teachers treating students as social equals and involving them in making decisions about their life in the classroom. Toward that end, Dreikurs would have teachers spend considerable time talking with students about how their actions, efforts, and results affect themselves and others. Dreikurs's emphasis on mutual respect, encouragement, student effort, and general responsibility sits well with teachers, who appreciate his suggestions for instilling in students an inner sense of responsibility and respect for others.

REVIEW OF SELECTED TERMINOLOGY

The following terms are central to Dreikurs's work. See if you can explain their meanings.

autocratic teacher	democratic discipline
aversive discipline	democratic classroom
choosing behavior	democratic teacher
confronting mistaken goals	displaying inadequacy

encouragement	permissive teacher
genuine goal of belonging	praise
getting attention	punishment
identifying mistaken goals	seeking revenge
logical consequences	seeking power
mistaken goals	self-discipline
natural consequences	social interest

APPLICATION EXERCISES

CONCEPT CASES

Case 1: Kristina Will Not Work

Kristina, a student in Mr. Jake's class, is quite docile. She socializes little with other students and never disrupts the class. But despite Mr. Jake's best efforts, Kristina will not do her work. She rarely completes an assignment. She is simply there, putting forth no effort.

How would Jacob Kounin deal with Kristina? Kounin would use these interventions, hoping to find one that is effective with Kristina.

1. Provide interesting learning activities with variety and challenge. Observe and talk with Kristina about what she most likes to do in school and incorporate some of her favorite activities into the lessons.
2. Call on Kristina in discussions preceding independent work as a means of involving her. If she is reluctant to speak, ask questions that she can at first answer by saying yes or no or by holding her thumb up or down. As she responds, involve her more.
3. When Kristina does some work, acknowledge her progress: "Good for you! Now you are on to it! I can see you are trying hard." Challenge her to do more: "I want to see if you can answer two more problems before the end of the period. What do you think?"
4. Hold Kristina accountable in group activities. Be persistent. Do not ignore her simply because she refuses to work.

How would Rudolf Dreikurs deal with Kristina? Dreikurs would follow these steps:

1. Identify Kristina's mistaken goal. Mr. Jake can check his own reaction to Kristina's lethargy and note the reactions of other students when he attempts to correct her.
2. If Kristina's mistaken goal is getting attention, ignore her when she misbehaves and ask for her help or contribution at other times.
3. If Kristina's mistaken goal is seeking power, admit that Kristina has power: "I can't make you do your work. What do you think I should do?"

4. If Kristina's goal is seeking revenge, ask other members of the class to be especially encouraging to her.
5. If Kristina's goal is displaying inadequacy, encourage her frequently and give her continual support.
6. Confront Kristina with her mistaken goal and draw her into a discussion about the goal and her behavior.

Case 2: Sara Cannot Stop Talking

Sara is a pleasant girl who participates in class activities and does most, though not all, of her assigned work. She cannot seem to refrain from talking to classmates, however. Her teacher, Mr. Gonzales, has to speak to her repeatedly during lessons, to the point that he often becomes exasperated and loses his temper.

What suggestions would Kounin give Mr. Gonzales for dealing with Sara? What suggestions would Dreikurs make?

Case 3: Joshua Clowns and Intimidates

Joshua, larger and louder than his classmates, always wants to be the center of attention, which he accomplishes through a combination of clowning and intimidation. He makes wise remarks, talks back (smilingly) to the teacher, utters a variety of sound-effect noises such as automobile crashes and gunshots, and makes limitless sarcastic comments and put-downs of his classmates. Other students will not stand up to him, apparently fearing his size and verbal aggression. His teacher, Miss Pearl, has come to her wit's end.

What is Joshua's mistaken goal, and how would Dreikurs have you deal with it? How would Kounin suggest dealing with Joshua?

Case 4: Tom Is Hostile and Defiant

Tom has appeared to be in his usual foul mood ever since arriving in class. On his way to sharpen his pencil, he bumps into Frank, who complains. Tom tells him loudly to shut up. Miss Baines, the teacher, says, "Tom, go back to your seat." Tom wheels around, swears loudly, and says heatedly, "I'll go when I'm damned good and ready!"

What can you find in Dreikurs's work that might help you in this instance? Does Kounin offer any suggestions of value?

QUESTIONS AND ACTIVITIES

1. Evaluate the following to determine where, and to what extent, satiation (Kounin) might become a problem. Explain your conclusions.
   a. Mrs. Ames does not allow her class to move ahead into a new unit of work until all students have completed the old unit with grades of C or

better. Those who pass early are given review and worksheets for further practice until the others catch up.

b. Mr. Grant has developed a systematic procedure in which all of his lessons are delivered in the same way—lecture followed by reading followed by worksheets. Mr. Grant contends that this routine helps students feel comfortable in that they know what to do and how to use the materials.

2. One of the things Ms. Alletto's students like best about her is that she never pressures them to move quickly from one activity to the next. She seems to understand their need to talk with each other about nonschool matters. She always waits until all the class gets ready before beginning a new lesson or activity. What would Kounin say about Ms. Alletto's style?

3. Examine Scenario 4 or 5 in the Appendix. Which of Kounin's suggestions would be helpful to Mrs. Desmond or Mrs. Reed in establishing a more productive and pleasant learning environment?

4. For the following cases, first identify the student's mistaken goal and then explain how Dreikurs would have the teacher deal with it.

a. Maria sits in the back of the classroom. She stares at her desk. She has never turned in an assignment. She replies only perfunctorily when the teacher speaks to her.

b. Teresa likes to enter the classroom five minutes late, making enough noise to distract the class. When asked to explain her tardiness, she accuses the teacher of picking on her.

5. Examine Scenario 1 or 2 in the Appendix. Indicate how Dreikurs would advise Mr. Platt or Mrs. Miller to deal with attention-seeking students.

REFERENCES AND RECOMMENDED READINGS

Albert, L. 1996. *A teacher's guide to cooperative discipline.* Rev. ed. Circle Pines, Minn.: American Guidance Service. (Original work published 1989)

Dreikurs, R. 1968. *Psychology in the classroom.* 2d ed. New York: Harper & Row.

Dreikurs, R., and P. Cassel. 1972. *Discipline without tears.* Reissued in 1995. New York: Penguin-NAL.

Dreikurs, R., and L. Grey. 1995. *Logical consequences.* New York: Penguin-NAL.

Dreikurs, R., B. Grunwald, and F. Pepper. 1982. *Maintaining sanity in the classroom.* Reissued in 1998. New York: Taylor & Francis.

Ferguson, E. 1995. *Adlerian theory: An introduction.* Chicago: Adler School of Professional Psychology.

Kounin, J. 1977. *Discipline and group management in classrooms.* Rev. ed. New York: Holt, Rinehart & Winston. (Original work published 1971)

CHAPTER 3

Shaping Behavior through Communication and Reinforcement

The Contributions of Haim Ginott and B. F. Skinner

Haim Ginott

B.F. Skinner

PART 1. HAIM GINOTT'S CONGRUENT COMMUNICATION

PREVIEW OF GINOTT'S WORK

Focus

- Communication between teacher and students and how it affects behavior.
- The nature and techniques of congruent (sane) communication to address problems.
- How teachers at their best behave and communicate with students.
- What teachers should, and should not, say when talking with students about behavior.

Logic

- Classroom behavior is powerfully affected by how teachers speak to and with students.
- Problems are best dealt with by addressing the situation, not the student's character.
- The best discipline is student self-discipline, brought about by self-disciplined teachers.

Contributions

- Provided the first coherent strategies for building classroom discipline through communication.
- Explained the nature of congruent communication and detailed the techniques for its use.
- Showed how effective discipline is gained through small gentle steps rather than strong tactics.
- Explained how teachers can show genuine emotion without hurting relations with students.

Ginott's Suggestions

- When dealing with problem behavior, address the situation, not the character of the student.
- Invite cooperation by focusing on what needs to be done, rather than what was done wrong.
- Speak to misbehaving students as you would like to be spoken to yourself, in the situation.
- Maintain this attitude: What can I do that will best help my students right now?

ABOUT HAIM GINOTT

Haim Ginott was born in 1922 in Tel Aviv, Israel. A classroom teacher early in his career, he earned his doctorate at Columbia University and went on to hold professorships in psychology at Adelphi University and at New York University Graduate School. Ginott also served as a UNESCO consultant in Israel, was resident psychologist on the "Today" show, and wrote a weekly syndicated column entitled *Between Us* that dealt with interpersonal communication. He became familiar to teachers through his best-selling books that described how parents and teachers could communicate most effectively with children and teenagers. Ginott's career was cut short by his death in 1973.

GINOTT'S CONTRIBUTIONS TO DISCIPLINE

Ginott was the first to champion the role of communication skills in building sound classroom discipline. He set forth a strong case for what he called "congruent communication," a style of speaking that does not attack others, but instead remains harmonious with feelings being experienced. Ginott carried his messages to parents and educators by means of three extremely popular books. In the first two, *Between Parent and Child* (1965) and *Between Parent and Teenager* (1969), Ginott focused on communication breakdowns that drive wedges between parents and their offspring and described means of avoiding those breakdowns. He believed that adults, whether parents, teachers, or others, vitally impact children's self-esteem through the messages they send. That impact can be either negatively destructive or positively constructive.

Ginott endeavored to show how communication can foster desirable relationships between adults and the young, and he developed specific skills to help parents resolve conflicts they might encounter with their children. The fundamental principle Ginott emphasized was that when adults speak to children they must always address the *situation,* not the character of the child. It was Ginott who popularized the notion of parents showing their children that they still love them even when strongly disapproving of their behavior.

In 1971, Ginott published *Teacher and Child,* a book that carried his ideas on communicating with the young into school settings. In that book he wrote that as a young teacher he came to the frightening conclusion that

> I am the decisive element in the classroom. It is my personal approach that creates the climate. It is my daily mood that makes the weather. As a teacher I possess tremendous power to make a child's life miserable or joyous. I can be a tool of torture or an instrument of inspiration. I can humiliate or humor, hurt or heal. In all situations it is my response that decides whether a crisis will be escalated or de-escalated, and a child humanized or de-humanized. (p. 13)

Ginott was certain that teachers hold the power to make or break a child's self-concept, just as do the child's parents, and that teachers' power is wielded primarily through communication. In *Teacher and Child,* Ginott explained how proper communication in the classroom helps establish and maintain a secure, humane, productive environment for learning.

GINOTT'S CENTRAL FOCUS

Ginott's focus regarding classroom discipline remained always on what he called *congruent communication*—communication that addresses the teacher's and student's situations rather than the student's character and personality. Ginott referred to congruent messages as "sane messages," and he showed how such messages could be used to guide students away from self-defeating behavior and toward behavior that is appropriate and lasting. He cautioned educators that his suggestions would not produce instantaneous results, that guidance through communication had to be used repeatedly over time for its power to take effect. Ginott's discipline system, therefore, was never intended to be one that reached full effectiveness in a single day. True discipline (by which Ginott meant self-discipline) never occurs in that manner, he explained. True discipline occurs over time, in a series of small steps that produce genuine changes within the hearts of students.

GINOTT'S PRINCIPAL TEACHINGS

Learning always takes place in the present tense, meaning teachers do not pre-judge students or hold grudges.

Learning is always a personal matter to the student. Large classes often make teachers forget that each student-learner is an individual who must be treated as such.

Teachers should always endeavor to use congruent communication, which is communication that is harmonious with students' feelings about situations and themselves.

The cardinal principle of congruent communication is that it addresses situations. It never addresses students' character or personality.

Teachers at their best, using congruent communication, do not preach or moralize, nor impose guilt or demand promises. Instead, they confer dignity on their students.

Teachers at their worst label students, belittle them, and denigrate their character. They usually do these things inadvertently.

Sane messages are communications from adults that encourage the young to trust their own perceptions and feelings.

Effective teachers invite cooperation of their students by describing the situation and indicating what needs to be done. They do not dictate to students or boss them around, which provokes resistance.

The Ten Commands is a term Ginott uses to refer to the unnecessarily detailed work directions that many teachers give their students. Superfluous directions slow work and provoke annoyance.

Acceptance and acknowledgment are behaviors that Ginott would like to see in all teachers—the acceptance and acknowledgment of genuine student comments or behaviors without denying, disputing, deriding, denigrating, derogating, degrading, or arguing. (This does not mean that the teacher must appear to agree with the comments or behaviors or let them go past without comment.)

Teachers have a hidden asset upon which they should always call, namely, "How can I be helpful to my students right now?" Most classroom difficulties are avoided when teachers remember to call upon that asset.

Teachers should feel free to express their anger, but in doing so should use I-messages rather than you-messages. Teachers have a right to be genuinely angry when provoked by student misbehavior. Their anger, however, should not be leveled at a student's character. Instead of saying, "You are incredibly inconsiderate!" teachers should tell how they feel: "I am so angry right now that I feel I had better not say anything."

It is wise to use laconic language when responding to or redirecting student misbehavior. Laconic means short, concise, and brief, which describes the sort of responses Ginott advocates.

Yet at times it is useful to use long or difficult words that students are not accustomed to hearing, such as "I am aghast!" or "I am appalled!" or "I am dismayed!"

Evaluative praise is worse than none at all and should never be used. An example of evaluative praise is "Good boy for raising your hand."

Teachers should use appreciative praise when responding to effort or improvement. This is praise in which the teacher shows appreciation for what the student has done, without evaluating the student's character (e.g., "I can almost smell those pine trees in your drawing").

Labeling is disabling, Ginott contends, a saying he used to emphasize the harm done to students by labeling them derogatorily. Students tend to live up to the labels they are given.

Always respect students' privacy. Teachers should never pry when students do not wish to discuss personal matters, but should show they are available should students need to talk.

Correcting by directing describes how misbehaving students should be dealt with. Instead of reprimanding students, teachers should (re)direct them into appropriate behavior.

Teachers' "why" questions do not prompt inquiry but are used to make students feel guilty. An example of a teacher "why" question is, "Why are you so disorganized?"

Sarcasm is almost always dangerous and should not be used when talking with students.

Classroom discipline is attained gradually, as a series of little victories in which the teacher, through self-discipline and helpfulness, promotes humaneness within students.

Punishment should not be used with students. Punishment only produces hostility, rancor, and vengefulness, while never making students really desire to improve.

Teachers should strive continually for self-discipline in their work with students. They must be careful not to display the very behaviors they are trying to eradicate in their students, such as raising their voice to end noise, using force to break up fighting, showing rudeness to students who are impolite, and berating students who have used bad language.

ANALYSIS OF GINOTT'S WORK

Teachers Are the Decisive Element

Ginott depicts teachers as the most powerful, most decisive element in setting and maintaining an effective climate in the classroom. As he puts it, teachers create and maintain the environment. Depending on what they do, teachers can humanize or dehumanize their students. Dehumanized students are kept in constant emotional turmoil and, in that condition, find it difficult to learn. It is the responsibility of teachers to reduce this turmoil. It can be done by consistently using what Ginott calls **congruent communication,** a style of speaking that acknowledges and accepts students' feelings about situations and themselves. To illustrate what teachers do that promotes positive or negative climates, Ginott contrasts teachers *at their best* with teachers *at their worst.*

Teachers at Their Best

Teachers at their best use congruent communication, in which they

- address the situation rather than a student's character
- invite student cooperation
- accept and acknowledge students' feelings
- confer dignity upon students
- express anger appropriately
- use brevity in correcting misbehavior
- use appreciative praise rather than evaluative praise

Teachers at Their Worst

In contrast with teachers at their best, **teachers at their worst** make little if any use of congruent communication, as shown in their inclination to

- name-call and label students as slow, unmotivated, or troublesome
- ask rhetorical "why" questions and give long moralistic lectures
- invade students' privacy
- make caustic and sarcastic remarks to students

- attack students' character
- demand, rather than invite, cooperation
- deny students' feelings
- lose their tempers and self-control
- use evaluative praise to manipulate students
- show themselves to be poor models of humane behavior

Congruent Communication

Congruent communication is the cornerstone of the Ginott model of discipline. Congruent communication has been defined as communication that is harmonious with students' feelings about situations and themselves. What it entails in actual practice is shown in the following paragraphs.

Sane Messages

Sane messages is a term Ginott uses for teacher messages that address situations rather than students' character. Such messages communicate that teachers accept and acknowledge how students feel. Ginott explains his use of the word *sane* by pointing out that sanity depends on people's ability to trust their own perceptions of reality. All too often, adults send insane messages, which tell the young to distrust or deny their feelings or perceptions. Adults use insane messages when they blame, preach, command, accuse, belittle, and threaten. Doing these things tells children to deny their feelings about themselves and to base their sense of self-worth upon judgments others make of them.

Ginott (1973) repeatedly reiterated his fundamental principle of the sane message. When a student gets in trouble, the teacher should always address the situation but never judge the student's character or personality. The following is an example of what Ginott means:

Two students are talking during a quiet study time, in violation of class rules. The teacher says, "This is quiet time. It needs to be absolutely silent." By simply describing the concern, teachers allow students to appraise the situation, consider what is right and wrong, and decide how they feel about the situation and themselves.

An "insane teacher message," by contrast, might be the following:

"Stop that talking. You two are not only breaking rules, you are being very rude. You evidently have no consideration for others who are trying to work."

Ginott continually maintained that teacher communication has the power to build or destroy student self-concept and personal relationships. Poor teacher communication causes students to doubt their own perceptions of themselves. Good teacher communication simply states the facts and lets students decide whether their behavior is in keeping with what they expect of themselves.

Inviting Student Cooperation

Ginott urged teachers to learn to **invite cooperation** from students rather than demand it. One of the ways he suggests is to decide with the class before an activity what kinds of personal behavior will be needed during the activity. Another is to stop an activity that has gotten out of control and say, "We can watch the film in silence, or we can do another math worksheet. You decide." If the students continue to disrupt, the teacher must follow through with the alternative, making it clear that such was the students' decision.

Teachers who do not invite cooperation usually resort to demanding it by ordering, bossing, and commanding. Ginott urges teachers to avoid direct commands, which tend to provoke student resistance. Once again, Ginott says to describe the situation and let students decide what their course of action should be. Too often, teachers use long, drawn-out directions or explanations. Ginott called such directions the Ten Commands. Rather than have teachers spend so much time on needless directions, Ginott would have them simply say, "It is now math time. The assignment is on page 60." With that kind of message, teachers show that they respect students' ability to behave autonomously.

Acceptance and Acknowledgment

Students' perceptions are often quite different from those of adults. Ginott suggested that teachers accept and acknowledge students' feelings, primarily by acting as sounding boards when students give opinions or voice concerns. For example:

> Juan comes running in from the playground crying, "José threw a ball at me and hit me in the head on purpose! Everyone is laughing at me! Nobody likes me!" The teacher could argue with the child's perception, saying, "That's silly. I'm sure it was an accident. The others were laughing at something else." But the teacher would do better to respond with sympathy and understanding, offering no judgment on the situation, saying, "I can see how upset you are. You feel that nobody likes you. It hurts our feelings when others laugh at us." These accepting responses acknowledge and show understanding of Juan's feelings. They don't tell him how he should think or feel.

Ginott suggested that teachers add another comment to such situations: "How can I help you?" When asked sincerely, this question provides an opportunity for the student to come up with a solution to the problem and reveals the teacher's confidence in the student's ability to cope. Ginott calls this question the teacher's **hidden asset** and suggests they use it frequently.

Conferring Dignity upon Students

Teachers wise in the use of congruent communication look for opportunities to **confer dignity** on their students. Such opportunities often occur when a student is in distress. At such times, teachers should put aside the student's past history and concern themselves only with the immediate situation. Ginott (1972) provided the following example of a situation in which a teacher successfully conferred dignity upon a distressed student:

> Twelve-year-old Susan had volunteered to help catalog library books on Saturday. But when the weekend came, she realized with dismay that she was overwhelmed with homework. Knowing that she would receive poor grades for delinquent homework, she went to the library anyway but was so obviously distracted that the librarian asked her what was wrong. Susan began to cry as she told her story of overwork and regret. The librarian might have responded, "I was counting on you. Why did you volunteer if you had so much homework?" That would have made Susan feel even more guilty. Instead, the librarian listened attentively and said, "Feeling so disheartened, you still came to work. That's discipline. That's character. That's integrity." The librarian's words showed respect and conferred dignity upon Susan. (p. 44)

Teachers' Expressing Anger: I-Messages versus You-Messages

Teaching is a demanding job. Fatigue, frustration, and conflict make it inevitable that teachers become angry from time to time. Many people, adults and students alike, do not believe that teachers should allow themselves to show anger. Ginott disagrees. Such expectations, he argues, are wrong and even damaging to teachers. Teachers are bound to become angry at times, and when they do, they should be afforded the same opportunity as anyone else to express that anger. Congruent communication, however, places restrictions on how teacher anger should be expressed, as shown in the following:

> Mrs. Abel, the art teacher, has obtained prints of several of the most famous Grecian sculptures of human figures, which she has displayed in the room. During class she is called from the room. She asks students to work on drawings in progress. When she returns, she finds that someone has used a felt-tip marker to draw genitalia on one of the pictures. She is flabbergasted and her anger surges. She could say, "Class, how could you let this happen? Are you barbarians? Have you lost all sense of decency?" But better, she might say, "I am appalled! I am so angry I could cry! I am so disappointed about this I can't say anything more."

The first response would only make an unfortunate situation worse, as it attacks students' character and made it difficult to resolve the situation gracefully. But Mrs. Abel's

I-messages have a good chance of causing students to think about the right and wrong of the situation. I-messages express the effect on the person sending the message (e.g., "I am so disappointed . . ."), as contrasted with the character attacks inherent in **you-messages** (e.g., "You are barbarians").

Using Laconic Language

Ginott advised teachers to speak succinctly when working with students. Students tend to close their minds to overtalkative teachers. Whenever a problem occurs, teachers should assume what Ginott calls a *solution-oriented focus;* that is, they should be interested only in solving the problem, not in dwelling on philosophies and responsibilities. The following is an example that illustrates the point:

> During a lesson, several students begin talking when they shouldn't. The teacher could say the following and even more: "Some of you are cooperating and some aren't. Now you all know this is not a playground. Good citizens don't bother others who are trying to learn."

Ginott claimed that all a teacher needs to say in such a case is "It's hard to learn when there's a lot of noise." The other statements only waste time and keep students from learning. Teachers should talk as reporters write: give headlines, main points, and specific details as briefly as possible. Brevity and succinctness are what Ginott means by **laconic language.** Teacher strength, he wrote, is not conveyed by arguing or making long explanations; it is much conveyed by brevity.

Providing Appreciative Praise

Ginott urged teachers to be positive with their students, rather than negative. Most attempt to do so, and their stock-in-trade is the use of praise. Praise is ubiquitous, and certain adjectives are so overworked that they have lost their meaning. Every few minutes classroom teachers, when reacting to student responses, are heard to say, "Great!" or "Terrific!" or "Super!" Ginott said teachers should not use praise of this type because it is evaluative. **Evaluative praise** is worse than no praise at all, for it produces anxiety ("Can I live up to this?") and creates dependency ("I'm no good unless the teacher praises me"). Ginott's position on praise is supported strongly by present-day authorities (see Gordon 1989; Kohn 1993).

Ginott admits that praise has its place, but it should not be used to evaluate students. Instead, praise should show teacher appreciation for student effort. The distinction between evaluative and appreciative praise is akin to that between you-messages and I-messages. The teacher who says, "Great!" or "Super!" is in effect saying, "You are great! You are super!" Evaluative praise can make students feel good—temporarily. But it does not help them, because it creates dependency upon the teacher. In contrast, **appreciative praise** does not describe the student but instead directs attention to the students' efforts. The following are examples of appreciative praise that a teacher might make after reading a student's poem: "I thought the alliteration was delightful." "I found the descriptive words especially effective." "It was a pleasure to read this work."

This kind of praise does not describe the character of the student but instead indicates that the teacher appreciates the student's work or effort. Ginott stressed this point: Avoid praise that attaches adjectives to a child's character. Use praise that shows your appreciation of specific student acts.

Noncongruent Communication

To this point we have considered congruent communication. Now let us take a moment to consider some instances of communication that, while common in classrooms, is **noncongruent communication;** that is, it is not harmonious with students' feelings about situations and themselves and, further, attacks students' character rather than dealing with the situation at hand.

Name-Calling and Labeling

Teachers sometimes make statements to students such as "You're lazy. Your work is sloppy and you are showing no responsibility. Don't you want to amount to anything?" Ginott claims that such labeling is damaging. "He says, **labeling is disabling**" because it tells students how to think of themselves. If they hear such messages often enough, they begin to believe and live up to them. Teaching should open up vistas for students, not close them off. Labeling another's character never provides enlightenment or encourages growth and achievement.

Teachers' Why Questions

Teachers effective in discipline are careful not to do or say anything that makes a student look foolish or feel guilty, angry, or resentful. They have learned that such emotions breed resistance and encourage misbehavior. For that reason, Ginott asks teachers to avoid **why questions,** which are in reality hostile inquiries into students' character traits. Ginott (1972) gives the following examples of why questions:

Why do you have to fight with everybody?

Why must you interrupt everybody?

Why are you so slow?

These questions, Ginott argues, don't call for answers, but are instead ways of criticizing students. A better approach is shown in the following (Ginott 1972):

A student informs the teacher: "I'm not prepared to take the test." The teacher wants to know why, but resists the temptation to use the damaging *why.* In its place, the teacher says, "We have a problem. What do you see as the solution?" (p. 89)

Ginott says that this type of response has the opposite effect of why questions. Instead of doing damage, it conveys respect and encourages the student to take corrective steps.

Invasion of Privacy

We all hear frequently that, when burdened with a problem, it is better to talk the problem out than to keep it bottled up inside. Teachers want to be helpful to students and so sometimes, when they see a student who is uncharacteristically quiet, take the student aside and probe with questions such as "What's the matter today? What's bothering you."

If the student feels like talking about the matter, fine. But if not, the teacher should do nothing more than say, for that student's ears only, "If I can help, let me know." Anything more, says Ginott, is an **invasion of privacy.** None of us should be urged to discuss personal matters when we are uncomfortable in doing so; it produces embarrassment and resentment.

Correcting by Directing

Throughout every day, mistakes and misbehaviors occur in the classroom that must be corrected by the teacher. Brian may be working on the wrong page in his workbook. A group of girls may be discussing a favorite soap opera instead of working as directed. Given such situations, teachers' natural inclinations are to say hurtful things to the offending students: "Oh, good grief, Brian. Well, all that work was certainly for nothing." Or, "Girls, let's not have any more of that. No wonder your work has been so poor."

Such noncongruent comments are likely to sting students and produce resentment. Ginott says that instead of correcting with negative comments, teachers should respond by describing the situation and suggesting an acceptable alternative. Usually, students only need be reminded of what they are supposed to be doing. The teacher would do better to respond as follows:

To Brian (quietly): "Oh, I'm sorry, Brian. The assignment is on page 34. You certainly worked hard on this one, though."

To the girls: "Let's finish this assignment now; there will be time for talking later."

This approach is what Ginott calls **correcting by directing.** To correct misbehavior, he says, one needs to tell students respectfully what they should be doing instead of the inappropriate behavior.

Overdwelling

Ginott observed that students react much better to teachers who get to the point quickly than to those who pontificate endlessly. The opposite of brevity is **overdwelling,** in which teachers spend long and needless time in explaining, warning, or reacting to misbehavior. Especially when dealing with minor misbehavior, Ginott says, teachers should learn economical responses for correcting the situation. Even if the student has talked without permission, forgotten a book, or lost a homework assignment, it is better to leave the misdeed in the past and suggest a better behavior, thus inviting the student to assume responsibility for behaving appropriately.

Sarcasm

Sarcasm is a chief contributor to teachers' communication breakdowns. Many teachers use sarcasm as a form of humor, but all too frequently sarcasm only hurts feelings and damages self-esteem. Ginott had a strong word of advice for teachers inclined to use sarcasm: *don't.*

GINOTT'S SPECIAL VIEWS ON DISCIPLINE

Ginott described discipline as a **series of little victories** that over time helps students acquire self-direction, responsibility, and concern for others. He believed that true discipline (that is, student self-discipline) cannot be brought about overnight, but is a process that grows gradually as teachers treat students humanely and considerately.

Ginott did acknowledge that teachers can influence student behavior with threats and punishment, but he insisted that aversive techniques inevitably make students resentful toward the teacher and less willing to cooperate. The essence of discipline, Ginott said, lies in finding effective alternatives to punishment. By using those alternatives, teachers achieve the series of little victories.

Ginott maintained that the most important factor in improving classroom behavior is the **teacher's self-discipline.** Self-disciplined teachers only rarely lose their temper, and they never behave rudely. They model the courtesy and language they want to see in their students. They are polite, helpful, and respectful. They handle crises calmly and reasonably. In times of conflict, they show civilized behavior. Meanwhile, students, even those who are poorly behaved, keep watch to see how teachers handle difficult situations. Given repeated exposure to civil behavior, students begin to display it themselves.

STRENGTHS OF GINOTT'S WORK

Ginott was the first authority to emphasize the strong linkage between the way teachers talk to students and the way students behave in return. He stressed that teachers must provide an environment conducive to learning, and that nothing is more important to quality learning than the socio-emotional atmosphere that pervades the classroom. Discipline problems diminish, Ginott insisted, when teachers show concern for students' feelings and recognize that their comments have strong impact on feelings and self-image.

Ginott reminds teachers that students are very sensitive. Being bossed or labeled gives students justification for distrusting adults and behaving rebelliously. Teachers therefore should treat students as they themselves want to be treated. By following Ginott's suggestions, most teachers can bring about better student behavior, while adding enjoyment to the educational experience. While virtually all teachers agree with what Ginott has to say, most do not find his techniques adequate for dealing with the hard-to-manage.

REVIEW OF SELECTED TERMINOLOGY

The following terms are central to your understanding of Ginott's work.

congruent communication	correcting by directing
noncongruent communication	you-messages
sane messages	laconic language
invasion of privacy	overdwelling
conferring dignity	teachers at their best
I-messages	labeling is disabling
evaluative praise	inviting cooperation
appreciative praise	hidden asset
teachers at their worst	series of little victories
why questions	teacher self-discipline

PART 2. B. F. SKINNER'S BEHAVIOR SHAPING THROUGH REINFORCEMENT

PREVIEW OF SKINNER'S WORK

Focus

- How learned behavior in humans and other animals is affected by reinforcing stimuli.
- The nature of reinforcing stimuli and the processes of intentional reinforcement.
- Schedules of reinforcement and their respective effects on learning.

Logic

- Learning is powerfully affected by reinforcing stimuli, received just after an act is performed.
- Behavior can be shaped in desired directions by applying reinforcement systematically.
- Human learned behavior is explainable in terms of behaviors reinforced and not reinforced.

Contributions

- Formulated principles of learning based on scientific knowledge about reinforcement.
- Showed how to teach complex behavior through application of reinforcement.
- Provided the scientific principles upon which behavior modification was developed.

Skinner's Suggestions

- Strengthen desired behavior by providing reinforcement immediately when it is noted.
- Extinguish undesired behavior by seeing that it is followed by no reinforcement at all.
- Shape complex behavior gradually, through successive approximations.

ABOUT B. F. SKINNER

B. F. Skinner (1904–1990) is considered by many to have been the greatest behavioral psychologist of all time. Born in Susquehanna, Pennsylvania, he earned a doctorate in psychology at Harvard in 1931 and spent most of his academic career researching and teaching there.

Skinner's work in the 1930s consisted primarily of laboratory experiments in learning, in which he used rats and pigeons as subjects. Later, he drew world attention to his ideas about rearing and teaching human beings. Among other things, he proposed raising infants in glass enclosures he called air cribs, where the child was kept dry, warm, and comfortable, with all needs satisfied. He raised his own daughter in an air crib.

In 1948 he published a novel, *Walden Two*, in which he described the workings of a utopian community based on systematic application of principles of reinforcement to everyday life. That novel, still widely read, served as a model for communes established in the late 1960s. In 1971 Skinner published his controversial book *Beyond Freedom and Dignity*, which again attracted world attention. In that book he challenged traditional concepts of freedom and dignity, explaining why he considered them outmoded, useless, and incorrect. He claimed that we are not really acting freely in most of our decisions but that our choices are made instead on the basis of what has happened to us in the past; that is, our present behavior depends on which of our previous behaviors has been reinforced (rewarded). He urged that rather than debating the concept of free choice, humans should turn their efforts to providing conditions that reinforce desired behavior, thus improving human behavior in general.

SKINNER'S CONTRIBUTIONS TO DISCIPLINE

Skinner did not concern himself with the topic of classroom discipline per se, but his discoveries about shaping behavior through reinforcement have led to "behavior modification" and have been assigned major roles in several of today's systems of discipline.

SKINNER'S CENTRAL FOCUS

Skinner explored how behavior is affected by stimuli received by an organism *after* it has performed an act. Voluntary acts (which Skinner called *operants* rather than responses) can be affected by stimuli ocurring immediately after the operant. Sometimes the stimulus can make the organism more likely than before to repeat the operant behavior; Skinner called such stimuli *reinforcing stimuli*. Skinner's lifework dealt largely with discovering how animal and human behavior is affected by patterns and frequencies of reinforcing stimuli.

SKINNER'S PRINCIPAL TEACHINGS

Behavior is often shaped (influenced in some way) by reinforcing stimuli received immediately after an organism performs an act.

Operant behavior, which can be influenced by reinforcement, is a voluntary action performed by an organism. It is not a response, reaction, or reflex.

A reinforcing stimulus is anything that happens to the organism after it performs an operant that increases the likelihood it will repeat the operant. Reinforcing stimuli common in classrooms include knowledge of results, peer approval, awards and free time, and smiles, nods, and praise from the teacher.

Most stimuli, if they are to have a reinforcing effect, must be received within two or three seconds after the operant is performed.

Reinforcement refers to the process of supplying reinforcing stimuli to individuals after they have performed a particular behavior.

Positive reinforcement is the technical name for the process of supplying a stimulus that reinforces behavior. In classrooms, positive reinforcement is intentionally accomplished when teachers provide something the class desires after they have behaved appropriately. Such reinforcers are typically comments ("Good job," "Nice work"), points, or tangible objects such as stickers.

Negative reinforcement is the technical name for the process of removing something following an operant; the absence of whatever was removed then reinforces behavior—makes it more likely to recur. This term is widely misunderstood and misused. Most teachers think that negative reinforcement means punishment that stifles misbehavior. The opposite is true. Negative reinforcement *increases* the likelihood of a given behavior's being repeated, just as does positive reinforcement. Negative means taking away something that the student doesn't like rather than adding something that the student does like, for example, "Because you scored higher than 80 percent on the exam, you will not have to turn in a final paper." (The final paper is taken away as a reward for scoring well on the exam.)

Schedules of reinforcement describe when and how often reinforcement is provided when someone (e.g., a teacher) attempts to shape an individual's behavior. Different schedules of reinforcement produce different effects on behavior.

Constant reinforcement, provided every time a desired act is seen, is most effective in establishing new learnings.

Once new learning is acquired, it can be maintained indefinitely by using intermittent reinforcement, in which reinforcing stimuli are supplied only occasionally. Individuals anticipate receiving the "reward" sooner or later and so continue trying.

Successive approximation refers to a behavior-shaping progression in which actions (operants) come closer and closer to a preset goal. Most complex behaviors are gradually shaped, rather than acquired immediately.

Extinction is the disappearance of a particular behavior. Skinner believed that behaviors become extinguished over time if they are never reinforced.

Behavior modification (not a term used by Skinner) refers to the overall procedure of shaping behavior intentionally through reinforcement. The procedure is widely used in educational settings and other training efforts.

ANALYSIS OF SKINNER'S WORK

In the 1930s, Burrhus Frederic Skinner, a young psychologist at Harvard, began conducting experiments dealing with **operant behavior**—any behavior that an organism produces voluntarily. He found that one could often provide a stimulus to the organism just *after* it performed an operant, with the result that the organism became more likely to repeat the operant. Skinner discovered that by skillfully providing appropriate stimuli at the proper time, one could **shape behavior,** causing the organism to behave in ways it had never behaved before. Skinner's approach became known as **operant conditioning.** It is depicted as follows, using pigeon behavior to illustrate:

1. The pigeon performs an operant (e.g., stretches its wings).
2. A stimulus (e.g., pellet of food) is provided to the pigeon immediately after the operant.
3. When the pigeon stretches its wings again, another pellet of food is supplied.
4. After a few trials, the pigeon learns to stretch its wings, then look for food.
5. Gradually, the pigeon's behavior can be shaped—it may be caused, through this procedure, to stretch its wings, flap them, turn in a circle, bob its head, and so forth.

Skinner believed that most if not all learned human behavior occurs through this process. We behave in various ways, he said, and repeat the behaviors that are rewarded while dropping those that are not rewarded. Complex human behavior is built up through behavior shaping.

Reinforcers and Reinforcement

Reinforcers, called **reinforcing stimuli** by Skinner, can consist of anything individuals experience or receive, following a behavior, that serves to *increase the likelihood* that the behavior will be repeated. In human life experience, reinforcers can be anything the individual likes or wants. In popular terminology, we think of reinforcers as synonymous with rewards, but for scientific precision Skinner avoided terms such as reward, punishment, pleasant, and unpleasant.

    Reinforcement refers to the organism's receiving reinforcing stimuli. **Positive reinforcement** involves *providing* a reinforcing stimulus to an organism. **Negative reinforcement** involves *removing* something from the organism (e.g., discomfort) that makes it more likely to repeat the behavior. Negative reinforcement is not the same as punishment; in fact, it is the opposite. Both positive and negative reinforcement increase the likelihood that the organism will repeat a given act. In order to cause an organism to *stop* performing a given act, Skinner would simply withhold reinforcement. After a time the behavior would disappear. Skinner called this process of removing a behavior through lack of reinforcement **extinction.**

In life, reinforcement occurs regularly, but in random fashion. In education and other training efforts, reinforcement is done purposefully, in an attempt to shape desirable behavior. For initial learning *continuous reinforcement* is most effective. Every time kindergartner Juan raises his hand, the teacher says, "Thank you, Juan, for raising your hand." This continuous reinforcement promotes a high rate of appropriate responses and strengthens learning quickly.

Once the behavior is learned, only *intermittent reinforcement* is needed to maintain it. When the kindergartners have learned to raise their hands before speaking out, the teacher may occasionally say "Thank you, Juan, for remembering to raise your hand."

Behavior Modification

The procedure called **behavior modification** uses Skinnerian principles to shape behavior in educational settings. Systems of behavior modification all function in the same essential way:

1. The teacher observes one or more students displaying desired behavior.
2. The teacher immediately supplies some kind of reinforcement to those students.
3. The reinforced students tend to repeat or improve their behavior.

Behavior modification has been found valuable for speeding the learning of academic material as well as improving personal behavior. It allows the teacher to work with students in a supportive rather than adversarial manner. When using behavior modification, teachers need not be cold, harsh, and punitive but can accomplish their intentions in a warm, supportive, and positive manner, a demeanor greatly preferred by teachers and students alike.

Why Punishment Is Not Used in Behavior Modification

Punishment can promote motivation and proper behavior, but it often produces highly undesirable side effects of fear, dislike, and desire for revenge. Skinner discovered that animals and humans alike work harder and learn more quickly when rewarded for doing something right than when punished for doing something wrong. Therefore, punishment has no part in behavior modification except in rare instances where individuals are exceedingly difficult to teach. Teachers are advised to use a positive approach instead and to resort to punishment only when everything else fails.

Reinforcers in Behavior Modification

Educators use a wide variety of reinforcers in interactions with students. For the most part, those reinforcers are categorized as *social, graphic,* and *activity.*

   Social reinforcers consist of words and behaviors such as comments, gestures, and facial expressions. Teachers know that a great many students will work diligently just to obtain a smile, pat, or kind word. Social reinforcers can be verbal or nonverbal. Some examples are:

Verbal—"Okay." "Wow!" "Excellent." "Nice going." "Exactly." "Right." "Thank you." "I like that." "Would you share that with the class?"
   Nonverbal—Smiles, winks, eye contact, nods, thumbs up, touches, pats, handshakes, walking beside, standing near.

Graphic reinforcers are marks such as numerals, check marks, stars, and happy faces. Teachers make these marks with pens and rubber stamps and may enter them on charts or use a paper punch to make holes in cards kept by the students. They often use stickers that are commercially available in large quantities and varieties.

Activity reinforcers include those activities that students prefer in school. Any school activity can be used as a reinforcer if students prefer it to what they would otherwise be doing. Examples of activities that usually reinforce academic learning are:

For Younger Students—Being a monitor. Sitting near the teacher. Choosing the song. Caring for the pet. Sharing a pet or toy.

For Middle School Students—Playing a game. Free reading. Decorating the classroom. Having extra recess time. Going to an assembly. Watching a class videotape.

For Older Students—Working or talking with a friend. Being excused from a test. Working on a special project. Being excused from homework.

Tangible reinforcers are real objects students can earn for desired behavior. They are widely used with students who have special behavior problems. Many elementary teachers make regular use of tangible reinforcers such as popcorn, raisins, chalk, crayons, felt pens, pencils, badges, decals, pennants, used books, magazines, stationery, posters, rubber stamps, certificates, notes, letters, and plastic disks.

Systems of Behavior Modification

Behavior modification produces results even when used sporadically, but it works best when applied in a regular, systematic manner. Organized systems of behavior modification can be grouped roughly into five categories: (1) "catch 'em being good," (2) rules-ignore-praise (RIP), (3) rules-reward-punishment (RRP), (4) token economies, and (5) behavior contracts.

Catch 'Em Being Good
Catch 'em being good involves rewarding students who are seen to be doing what is expected.

The second-grade teacher says, "Class, take out your math books." Several students get their books at once. Others waste time talking. The teacher picks out students who behaved as directed and says, "Thank you, Heather, for being ready. Thank you, Shaun. I like the way Ramón got his book out and is paying attention."

The "catch 'em being good" system is especially effective in primary grades, and teachers up through third grade use it extensively, regardless of the overall discipline system they employ. By fourth grade the approach begins to lose effectiveness, and middle school students react to it with a certain disdain. However, even older students tend to respond positively when reinforced privately or as a group rather than singled out publicly.

Rules-Ignore-Praise (RIP)

The **rules-ignore-praise (RIP)** approach is described by its label. The teacher, with student involvement, formulates a set of rules for class behavior, such as:

1. Be courteous to others.
2. Keep hands, feet, and objects to yourself.
3. Follow all directions.

Once the rules are established, understood, and practiced, the teacher watches for students who comply with them. The teacher might say, "Row one is doing an excellent job of following directions." Students who break the rules are ignored; that is, no direct attention at all is given to them or their behavior. Instead, the teacher finds a student who is complying with the rules and praises that student. When Mrs. Jennet sees Tim poke his neighbor, she goes to an adjacent student, Samantha, who is following the rules, gives Samantha a sticker, and says, "Thank you, Samantha, for working without bothering others." This system serves well at the elementary school level, provided that the class is fairly well behaved to begin with. But generally speaking, it is not effective with older students.

Rules-Reward-Punishment (RRP)

The **rules-reward-punishment (RRP)** approach builds limits and consequences into behavior modification. As with RIP, this approach begins with rules and emphasizes rewards, but it does not ignore improper behavior. The added factor of consequences for misbehavior makes this approach effective with older students and with students who chronically misbehave.

In RRP, the rules phase is the same as described earlier. The teacher explains that compliance with the rules is expected: Students who follow the rules will be rewarded in various ways—they will receive praise if appropriate, laudatory notes to take home to parents, or earn points that count toward a larger reward, either for the individual or for the class. Students are also clearly informed about what will happen if the rules are broken. They realize it is their prerogative to break the rules but that if they do so, they simultaneously choose the consequences (mild punishments) attached to rule breaking, which will be invoked immediately in accordance with procedures that have been described fully and carefully. When Jane refuses to begin her work, Mr. Trammel tells her that, in accordance with class rules and consequences, she must sit at the table in the rear of the room until she completes her assignment.

This system is effective with students at all grade levels. Students generally consider it to be fair and recognize they have the power to choose good or bad consequences through their behavior.

Token Economies

Token economies are elaborate behavior modification systems that involve student accumulation of graphic or tangible reinforcers that can be saved and traded for other items. Token economies work as follows: As students comply with class rules, they are rewarded systematically with tally marks, stamps on a card, or tokens such as plastic chips. The marks or tokens can be accumulated and later exchanged for other activities or tangible rewards such as toys, comic books, or magazines. Some teachers do nothing at all when students break rules (in other words, they ignore the infraction). Other teachers direct the offending student to return a chip or remove a sticker previously earned. While the plan involves exchanging tokens and marks for presumably more desirable rewards, in actual practice teachers find that the tokens often become sufficiently rewarding in themselves.

Teachers who use token economies must be sure to award the tokens fairly and consistently and to treat rule transgressions with equal consistency. To implement the program, they must have an adequate supply of tokens, provide a manageable way for students to keep the tokens, and be sure that counterfeiting and extortion do not occur. They must set aside a time every couple of weeks for students to cash in their tokens. For larger prizes, students enjoy buying white elephants that other students have brought from home. Teachers can also obtain free materials from shops and stores, and vouchers can be made for special activities and privileges. Each object and voucher is assigned a price in tokens. Some teachers hold auctions in which students bid for available items. This plan should be explained carefully to school principal, students, and parents before being put into practice. This will ensure that everyone understands and approves what is taking place. While token economy behavior modification was once popular, teachers have largely abandoned it because it is cumbersome and because they feel students concentrate too much on the rewards and not enough on personal responsibility.

Behavior Contracts

Behavior contracts are sometimes used with individual students who are difficult to manage. Contracts specify work to be done or behavior to be established and deadlines for completion. They also state what the payoff to students will be for successful accomplishment, and they indicate input the teacher will give. The agreements are signed by teacher and student and sometimes by parents and principal as well, which lends an air of formality.

Mr. Lex's contract with Jesse is an example. Jesse has a history of never completing assigned homework. Mr. Lex prepares a contract in which Jesse agrees to do his homework properly. If he does so five days in a row, Mr. Lex will assign him five points. When Jesse has accumulated 15 points, he can exchange them for a pen bearing his favorite sport team's logo.

Contract forms can be prepared so as to appear very official. Quasi-legal terminology adds a pleasing touch for older children, as do filigree and official stamps of gold-colored foil. While contracts may be fun to use, they must be treated as serious commitments, the terms of which must be complied with by all who have signed.

STRENGTHS OF SKINNER'S WORK

Skinner's discoveries have led to behavior modification, until recently a favored control strategy for many teachers, and his ideas about reinforcement have been incorporated into many models of discipline. But despite their power, behavior modification and reinforcement in general have received much criticism. A major point of dispute concerns rewards. Some authorities contend that rewards are counterproductive in that they reduce intrinsic motivation (that is, students work only to get the reward) while supplanting genuine desire to learn with extrinsic motivation and tight behavior control (Hill 1990; Kohn 1993). Nevertheless, many teachers believe behavior modification makes teaching easier and more enjoyable, especially at the primary grade level, and teachers at all levels make extensive use of reinforcement techniques.

REVIEW OF SELECTED TERMINOLOGY

The following terms are central to understanding Skinnerian principles.

activity reinforcers	punishment
behavior modification	reinforcement
behavior contracts	reinforcing stimuli
catch 'em being good	rules-reward-punishment (RRP)
extinction	rules-ignore-praise (RIP)
graphic reinforcers	shaping behavior
negative reinforcement	social reinforcers
operant behavior	tangible reinforcers
operant conditioning	token economy
positive reinforcement	

APPLICATION EXERCISES

CONCEPT CASES

Case 1: Kristina Will Not Work

Kristina, in Mr. Jake's class, is quite docile. She never disrupts class and does little socializing with other students. But despite all his efforts, Mr. Jake cannot get Kristina to participate in class activities. She rarely makes progress on assignments and never completes one. She is simply there, putting forth no effort.

How would Ginott deal with Kristina? Ginott would use a number of gentle tactics to encourage Kristina to do her work. These would include the following:

Using sane messages: "Students in my class are expected to complete all assignments."

Inviting cooperation: "All students who finish their work can then choose to play a game with a friend."

Accepting and acknowledging Kristina's feelings: "Kristina, I can tell that you find it difficult to begin work on your assignment. How can I help you?"

Correcting by directing: "You need to finish ten problems within the next thirty minutes."

Focusing on solutions: "This cannot continue. What do you think we might be able to do about it?"

How would followers of Skinner's teachings deal with Kristina? Skinnerians would suggest that Mr. Jake try the following approaches with Kristina:

1. Try to discover a social reinforcer to which Kristina responds, such as physical proximity, a pat, a smile, or a kind word. Catch her being good (doing anything appropriate) and apply the reinforcer at that time.
2. Reiterate the class rules regarding work and completion of assignments. Praise Kristina publicly or privately, or use any effective reinforcer whenever she follows the rules.
3. If Kristina does not respond to social reinforcers, look for stronger ones. Try using points, tokens, or tangible objects to reinforce and shape Kristina's improvement.
4. Set up a contract with Kristina and her parent, whose help you request. Identify a reward that is especially attractive to Kristina. Outline what she must do in order to earn the reward. Reinforce every improvement she makes.

Case 2: Sara Cannot Stop Talking

Sara is a pleasant girl who participates in class activities and does most, though not all, of the work assigned to her. She could do much better but cannot seem to refrain from talking to classmates. Mr. Gonzales, her teacher, has to speak to her repeatedly during lessons, to the point that he often becomes exasperated and loses his temper.

What could Mr. Gonzales learn from Ginott that would make it easier to deal with Sara? What techniques of behavior modification might help Mr. Gonzales in dealing with Sara?

Case 3: Joshua Clowns and Intimidates

Joshua, larger and louder than his classmates, always wants to be the center of attention, which he accomplishes through a combination of clowning and intimidation. He makes wise remarks, talks back (smilingly) to the teacher, utters a variety of sound-effect noises such as automobile crashes and gunshots, and makes limitless sarcastic comments and put-downs of his classmates. Other students will not stand up to him, apparently fearing his size and verbal aggressiveness. His teacher, Miss Pearl, has come to her wit's end.

How, according to Ginott, should Miss Pearl speak with Joshua? What behavior modification system would work best with Joshua?

Case 4: Tom Is Hostile and Defiant

Tom has appeared to be in his usual foul mood ever since arriving in class. On his way to sharpen his pencil, he bumps into Frank, who complains. Tom tells him loudly to shut up. Miss Baines, the teacher, says, "Tom, go back to your seat." Tom wheels around and says heatedly, "I'll go when I'm damned good and ready!"

How do you think Skinner would suggest that Miss Baines deal with Tom? What do you think Ginott would suggest?

QUESTIONS AND ACTIVITIES

1. The following statements illustrate some of Ginott's main points about talking with students. Identify the main point with which each statement is associated.
   a. You boys head the list of my all-time laziest students.
   b. Yes, I'm just sure you didn't do your assignment because your mother was sick last night.
   c. I am so disappointed and angry I don't know what to do!
   d. Alicia, you are the most intelligent kid I have ever known!
2. Peggy and June are each accusing the other of taking personal items without permission. What would Ginott have the teacher say to the girls?
3. Examine Scenario 6 in the Appendix. What specifically would Ginott have Mr. Carnett say to his misbehaving students?
4. Describe how an effective system of behavior modification for use at the primary grade level would differ from an effective system for use at the high school level.
5. Examine Scenario 7 or 8 in the Appendix. Explain how principles of behavior modification might be used to improve the behaviors of specific students in Mrs. Bates's or Mr. Jaramillo's class.

REFERENCES AND RECOMMENDED READINGS

Firth, G. 1985. *Behavior management in the schools: A primer for parents.* New York: Charles C. Thomas.

Ginott, H. 1965. *Between parent and child.* New York: Avon.

———. 1969. *Between parent and teenager.* New York: Macmillan.

———. 1971. *Teacher and child.* New York: Macmillan.

——. 1972. I am angry! I am appalled! I am furious! *Today's Education, 61,* 23-24.

——. 1973. Driving children sane. *Today's Education, 62,* 20-25.

Gordon, T. (1989). *Discipline that works: Promoting self-discipline in children.* New York: Random House.

Hill, D. 1990. Order in the classroom. *Teacher, 1*(7), 70-77.

Kohn, A. 1993. *Punished by rewards: The trouble with gold stars, incentive plans, A's, praise, and other bribes.* Boston: Houghton Mifflin.

Kounin, J. 1977. *Discipline and group management in classrooms.* Rev. ed. New York: Holt, Rinehart & Winston. (Original work published 1971)

Ladoucer, R., and J. Armstrong. 1983. Evaluation of a behavioral program for the improvement of grades among high school students. *Journal of Counseling Psychology, 30,* 100-103.

Macht, J. 1989. *Managing classroom behavior: An ecological approach to academic and social learning.* White Plains, N.Y.: Longman.

McIntyre, T. 1989. *The behavior management handbook: Setting up effective behavior management systems.* Boston: Allyn & Bacon.

Milhollan, F., and B. Forisha. 1972. *From Skinner to Rogers: Contrasting approaches to education.* Lincoln, Nebr.: Professional Educators Publications, Inc.

Precision teaching in perspective: An interview with Ogden R. Lindsley. 1971. *Teaching Exceptional Children, 3,* 114-119.

Sharpley, C. 1985. Implicit rewards in the classroom. *Contemporary Educational Psychology, 10,* 349-368.

Skinner, B. F. 1948. *Walden two.* New York: Macmillan.

——. 1953. *Science and human behavior.* New York: Macmillan.

——. 1954. The science of learning and the art of teaching. *Harvard Educational Review, 24,* 86-97.

——. 1958. Teaching machines. *Science, 128,* 969-977.

——. 1968. *The technology of teaching.* New York: Appleton-Century-Crofts.

——. 1971. *Beyond freedom and dignity.* New York: Knopf.

——. 1973. The free and happy student. *Phi Delta Kappan, 55,* 13-16.

Tauber, R. 1982. Negative reinforcement: A positive strategy in classroom management. *Clearing House, 56,* 64-67.

Zirpoli, T., and K. Mellow. 1997. *Behavior management: Applications for teachers and parents.* 2d ed. Upper Saddle River, N.J.: Prentice-Hall.

PART II Application Models of Classroom Discipline

Seven models of classroom discipline are presented in Part II. They are called *application models* because they are sufficiently complete in themselves to serve as discipline systems in most classrooms at most grade levels. The qualifier "sufficiently complete" means that the models give adequate attention to all three dimensions of discipline—prevention, support, and positive redirection of misbehavior. These seven models, widely used in schools today, are described in the following chapters:

CHAPTER 4

Lee and Marlene Canter's *Assertive Discipline*

Lee Canter  Marlene Canter

PREVIEW OF LEE AND MARLENE CANTER'S WORK

Focus

- Maintaining a calm, productive classroom environment.
- Meeting students' needs for learning and ensuring that students' rights are attended to.
- Helping the teacher remain calmly, nonstressfully in charge in the classroom.

Logic

- Teachers have a right to teach as they see best, without disruption.
- Students have a right to learn in a safe, calm environment, with full teacher support.
- These ends are best met by in-charge teachers who do not violate students' best interests.
- Trust, respect, and perseverance enable teachers to earn student cooperation.

Contributions

- A classroom control strategy that places teachers humanely in charge in the classroom.
- A system that allows teachers to invoke positive and negative consequences calmly and fairly.
- Techniques for teaching students how to behave and for dealing with difficult students.

Canters' Suggestions

- Remain always in charge in the classroom, but not in a hostile or authoritarian manner.
- Take specific steps to teach students how to behave acceptably in the classroom.
- Identify students' personal needs and show your understanding and willingness to help.
- Continually strive to build trust between yourself and your students.

ABOUT LEE AND MARLENE CANTER

Lee Canter is founder of Lee Canter & Associates, an organization that provides training in classroom discipline and publishes related materials for educators and parents. Marlene Canter collaborates in the work. Although the two Canters work together, they are seldom referred to as Canter and Canter, but instead merely as Canter. Thus one sees "Canter says . . ." and "Canter's views are . . ." In this chapter, both individuals are recognized equally and are referred to as the Canters.

For many years the Canters have been refining their system of discipline, which they call *Assertive Discipline,* to better help teachers interact with students in a calm, helpful, and consistent manner. The goal of their program is to maintain order in the classroom so that students may learn and teachers may teach effectively. Through workshops and graduate courses, the Canters have brought *Assertive Discipline* to well over a million teachers and administrators, making their program the most widely used of all discipline systems.

In addition to offering books, tapes, and training programs in discipline, the Canters produce materials and graduate level courses on topics such as motivation, instructional strategies, homework, dealing with severe behavior problems, and activities for positive reinforcement. For more information on *Assertive Discipline,* contact Lee Canter & Associates, P.O. Box 2113, Santa Monica, CA 90406; telephone 310-395-3221.

THE CANTERS' CONTRIBUTIONS TO DISCIPLINE

The Canters have made several major contributions to classroom discipline. They popularized the concept of rights in the classroom—the rights of students to have teachers who help them learn in a calm, safe environment and the rights of teachers to teach without disruption. They explained that students need, and want, limits that assist their proper conduct and that it is the teacher's responsibility to set and enforce those limits. The Canters were the first to insist that teachers have a right to backing from administrators and cooperation from parents in helping students behave acceptably, and also the first to provide teachers with a workable procedure for correcting misbehavior efficiently through a system of easily administered consequences, positive and negative. The Canters continually modify their approach to ensure that it remains effective as social realities change. Earlier they focused on teachers being strong leaders in the classroom, while now they emphasize the building of a trusting and helpful relationship between teachers and students.

THE CANTERS' CENTRAL FOCUS

The central focus of the Canters' model is on showing teachers how to establish a classroom climate in which needs are met, behavior is managed humanely, and learning occurs as intended. This end is accomplished by attending closely to student needs, establishing good class rules of behavior, teaching students how to behave properly, regularly giving students positive attention, talking helpfully with students who misbehave, and establishing a climate of mutual trust and respect.

THE CANTERS' PRINCIPAL TEACHINGS

Today's students have clear rights and needs that must be met if they are to be taught effectively. These student rights and needs include a caring teacher who persistently works to foster the best interests of students.

Teachers have rights and needs in the classroom as well. Teachers' rights include teaching in a classroom that is free from disruption, with support from parents and administrators as they work to help students.

The most effective teachers are those who remain in control of the class while always remembering that their principal duty is to help students learn and behave responsibly.

Teachers must continually model through their own behavior the kind of trust and respect for students that they want students to show toward others.

A good discipline plan, built upon trust and respect, is necessary for helping students limit their own counterproductive behavior. Such a discipline plan contains rules and consequences, and it must be fully understood and supported by students and their parents.

Most teachers need practice in making positive repetitions. Positive repetitions involve repeating directions as positive statements to students who are complying with class rules, for example, "Fred remembered to raise his hand. Good job."

Negative consequences are penalties teachers invoke when students violate class expectations. They are brought to bear only when all else fails. Negative consequences must be something students dislike (staying in after class, being isolated from the group) but must never be physically or psychologically harmful.

Positive consequences are rewards, usually words or facial expressions, that teachers offer when students comply with class expectations. The Canters consider positive consequences to be very powerful.

Today's teachers must both model and directly teach proper behavior. It is not enough for teachers simply to set limits and apply consequences. They must go well beyond that to actually teaching students how to behave responsibly in the classroom.

Teachers can have success with a majority of students deemed difficult-to-manage. They can accomplish this by reaching out to those students, learning about their needs, interacting with them personally, and showing a constant willingness to help.

ANALYSIS OF THE CANTERS' *ASSERTIVE DISCIPLINE*

In 1976, the Canters first set forth the basic premises and practices of *Assertive Discipline,* designed to bring relief to teachers for whom classroom misbehavior caused great concern. They have progressively modified their approach over the years. As societal conditions have worsened, teachers have felt increasingly insecure about dealing with misbehavior. They know they must retain control of their classes, but want to do so in positive ways without harming or antagonizing their students. The Canters have provided help by developing and explaining several new concepts and techniques, such as those described in the following paragraphs.

Needs and Rights in the Classroom

Canter and Canter (1992, pp. 12–13) explain that students have a need for and the right to a warm, supportive classroom environment in which to learn, where teachers do all in their power to help students be successful. Teachers have needs and rights in the classroom as well, which include the need and right to teach as they believe correct without interruption, with support from their administrators.

Types of Teachers and Their Effects on Students

The Canters (1992, pp. 26–27) describe three types of teachers, differentiated on the basis of how they respond, proactively and reactively, to students. They call the three types *hostile teachers, nonassertive teachers,* and *assertive teachers.*

Hostile teachers seem to view students as adversaries. They feel if they are to maintain order and teach properly, they must keep the upper hand over students, which they attempt to do by laying down the law, accepting no nonsense, and using loud commands and stern facial expressions. They make needlessly strong statements such as: "Sit down, shut up, and listen!"

> This approach is exemplified in Mr. Carmody's seeing Alonso and Shawn talking instead of paying attention. He yells, "All right, you two! That's it for you! Either you pay attention or I guarantee you are going to regret it!"

A hostile stance prohibits the development of trust and cooperation between teacher and students. Hostile teachers' messages indicate a dislike for students, and cause students to feel they are being unjustly controlled. Students show little willingness to cooperate with hostile teachers. No sense of joy is experienced by either the teacher or the students in such classrooms.

Nonassertive teachers take a passive approach to students. They seem unable to state their expectations clearly and are inconsistent in their dealings with students, allowing certain behaviors one day while trying to prevent them the next. They come across as wishy-washy, making statements such as "For heaven's sake, please try to behave like ladies and gentlemen" or "How many times do I have to tell you no talking?"

> This is exemplified in Terry and Rick's laughing and engaging in horseplay that has almost ruined the lesson. Miss Jenkins, who has not established behavior standards, looks up and says, "For the tenth time, would you two please stop that?" She continues the lesson, but within a few minutes the two boys are disrupting again. She resignedly accepts whatever they do.

After a time students learn not to take these teachers seriously. Yet, the same teachers, once they finally get fed up, come down hard on students. This inconsistency leaves students confused about expectations and enforcement.

Assertive teachers clearly, confidently, and consistently express class expectations to students. They attempt to build trust, they teach students how to behave so learning can progress, and they implement a discipline plan that encourages student cooperation. Such teachers help students understand exactly what is acceptable and unacceptable, and they make plain the consequences that will follow student behavior. Assertive teachers are not harsh taskmasters. They recognize students' needs for consistent limits on behavior, but at the same time are ever mindful of students' needs for warmth and encouragement. They also know that students may require direct instruction in how to behave acceptably in the classroom. An assertive teacher might be heard to say "Our rule is no talking without raising your hand. Please raise your hand and wait for me to call on you."

This style is evident in Miss Berard. Terry and Rick are now in Miss Berard's class. They have continued the horseplay they began in Miss Jenkins's room. Miss Berard looks directly at them and says, "It is against the rules to talk without permission during the lesson. This is a warning." The boys know that, if they continue, Miss Berard will take further steps. The lesson resumes and so does their misbehavior. Miss Berard separates the boys and tells them they have chosen to remain for two minutes after class. Miss Berard has shown through her **assertive response style** that she follows through on enforcing class rules.

The Canters (1992, pp. 28–37) contrast the hostile, the nonassertive, and the assertive teacher in the following examples.

Example: Third Grade Class Lining Up for Recess. Three boys leap up from their desks and race to the door, pushing and shoving.

Hostile Style: I've had it with you boys. You are staying in after school.

Nonassertive Style: Boys, how many times do I have to ask you not to run in the room?

Assertive Style: Boys, the rule is no running in the classroom. I want the three of you to stand at the end of the line—quietly and quickly.

Example: Seventh Grade Lecture. Students in back of room are gazing out the window and doodling.

Hostile Style: You kids in the back—wake up and pay attention, or else you can stay after class and stare out the window all you want.

Nonassertive Style: (The teacher tries to ignore the inattention, thinking that nothing can be done anyhow.)

Assertive Style: (Continuing the lecture, the teacher walks to the back of the room and stands near the inattentive students.)

Example: Ninth Grade Cooperative Learning. Immature student who is usually disruptive is seen working productively in his group.

Hostile Style: I'm glad to see you finally started working as a ninth-grader should.

Nonassertive Style: (Teacher thinks "He's showing some real progress," but doesn't say anything supportive to the boy.)

Assertive Style: (Teacher catches student's eye and gives nod of approval. Later, the teacher says privately, "Your contribution in the group really helped everyone.")

Effects of Response Styles on Teachers and Students

Each of the response styles produces its own effects on teachers and students. The **hostile response style** takes away most of the pleasure teachers and students might otherwise enjoy. Teachers do not like to be cross and negative, but do so because they fear they will lose control of the class. This fear, together with resultant sense of guilt, curtails the possibility of developing a trusting cooperative relationship between teacher and student, and after a time it produces a negative teacher attitude toward students, who quickly come to dislike teacher and school.

The **nonassertive response style** leads to feelings of frustration and inadequacy. Nonassertive teachers cannot get their needs met in the classroom. This results in their experiencing symptoms of undue stress. These teachers frequently develop hostility toward chronically misbehaving students, a hostility they ordinarily keep suppressed but occasionally release explosively. Students of nonassertive teachers often come to feel frustrated, manipulated, and angry. They do not know exactly what limits the teacher is putting on their behavior, nor do they know how the teacher is likely to react, whether with threats, supplication, or ignoring. They tend not to believe what the teacher says and invariably test the teacher to see how much they can get away with. Students develop little respect for nonassertive teachers.

The **assertive response style** provides numerous benefits that are absent in the other styles. Assertive teachers create a classroom atmosphere that helps both teacher and students to meet their needs. They involve students in establishing expectations and limits on classroom behavior. They help students practice acceptable behavior and treat them with consideration and respect. This produces a climate that allows teachers to teach effectively, with cooperation from students, which meets the teacher's needs and leaves a feeling of pleasure and accomplishment. Students learn to trust assertive teachers because they provide clear knowledge of expectations, limits, and consequences. They know the teacher will work hard to help them learn in an atmosphere of warmth and support, while curtailing students' self-defeating behaviors. They know they will be recognized for effort and accomplishment. This increases their motivation and willingness to cooperate.

Moving toward Good Discipline

The Canters (Canter 1996) stress that good discipline does not depend on ever more rules and harsher consequences, which have no effect on students who see rules as meaningless and have no fear of the teacher's consequences. Instead, good discipline must grow out of mutual trust and respect between teachers and students. The Canters provide abundant advice to help teachers develop good discipline in their classrooms, summarized in the paragraphs that follow.

Developing a Solid Basis of Trust and Respect

In order to develop trust and respect in the classroom, teachers must always model the trust and respect they wish to see in their students. The Canters specifically suggest that teachers

- listen carefully to students, with complete attention
- speak respectfully to students
- treat everyone fairly

Further, teachers should get to know their students as individuals and acknowledge them as such. Toward this end the Canters suggest that teachers

- greet students by name, with a smile
- acknowledge birthdays and other important events in students' lives
- learn about students' interests and what motivates them
- chat with students individually in and out of the classroom

Also important in building trust and respect is the establishment of strong ties between the classroom and the home, through communicating positively with parents or guardians. The Canters advise teachers to

- send positive notes home with students
- make occasional phone calls to parents with positive comments about the student

Teaching Students How They Are Expected to Behave in the Classroom

Students do not automatically know how to behave in all school settings. Therefore, teachers must make sure to teach acceptable behavior to students through modeling, explanation, and practice. The Canters devote considerable attention to this topic, especially concerning (1) teaching students how to follow directions, (2) using positive recognition to motivate good behavior, and (3) redirecting nondisruptive off-task behavior.

Teaching Students to Follow Specific Directions

The Canters say that the most important classroom rule is "Follow directions," but students can't be expected to know automatically how to do so in all the many classroom activities. Recognizing that different teachers have their own ways of doing things, the Canters (1992, p. 122) say "Your students need to follow your expectations, not another teacher's expectations." To prevent student difficulties in following directions, the Canters suggest that teachers identify the academic activities, routine procedures, and special procedures for which directions are needed and then determine the specific directions that students are to follow for each. The following are two examples, one for an academic activity and one for a routine procedure: (Canter and Canter 1992, 126–127)

> **Teacher conducting a directed lesson, teaches students how to follow these directions:**
> 1. Please clear your desks of everything but paper and pencil.
> 2. Eyes on me. No talking while I'm talking.
> 3. Raise hand and wait to be called on before speaking.

> **For routine procedure for entering the room, the teacher teaches students how to:**
> 1. Walk into the room.
> 2. Go directly to their seat and sit down.
> 3. Cease talking when the bell rings.

The best time for teaching directions is immediately prior to the first (or next) time the activity is to take place. For young children, give demonstrations and have children act them out. Frequent reteaching and reinforcement will be necessary.

For older students, explain the reasons behind the directions and the benefits they provide. The Canters (1992, 131–138) suggest the following procedure:

1. Explain the rationale for the direction.
2. Involve the students by asking questions.
3. Explain the specific directions.
4. Check for student understanding (by asking questions or having students role play).

Once taught, the specific directions should be reinforced regularly through **positive repetition.** This means that rather than identify and correct a student who is not following directions, the (primary grade) teacher notes one or more who are following directions and says, "Joshua has remembered to raise his hand. So has Elsa." Directions should be reviewed each time the activity is repeated during the first two weeks. For the next month the directions should be reviewed each Monday as a refresher, and for the remainder of the year they should be reviewed after vacations and before special events such as holidays and field trips.

Establishing a Discipline Plan That Provides Structure and Identifies Behavior Limits

Since they first introduced Assertive Discipline, the Canters have advocated a formalized, written discipline plan that includes rules, positive recognition, and consequences.

Rules

Rules state exactly how students are to behave. The rules should indicate observable behaviors such as "Keep your hands to yourself" rather than vague ideas such as "Show respect to other students." Rules remain always in effect, in contrast to **directions** which only last for a given activity. Rules should be limited in number (three to five) and refer only to behavior, not to academic issues. In accordance with those guidelines, the Canters (1992, p. 53) suggest the following rules for different grade levels:

Grades K–6
- Follow directions.
- Keep hands, feet, and objects to yourself.
- Do not leave the room without permission.
- No swearing or teasing.
- No yelling or screaming.

Grades 7–12
- Follow directions.
- No swearing or teasing.
- Be in your seat when the bell rings.

Positive Recognition

Positive recognition refers to giving sincere personal attention to students who behave in keeping with class expectations. The Canters say recognition should be used frequently because it increases self-esteem, encourages good behavior, and helps build a positive classroom climate. Teachers should make special efforts such as the following in giving positive recognition:

- Praise students for behaving appropriately.
- Send positive notes and make positive phone calls to parents.
- Give awards for good behavior.
- Assign special privileges to students who earn them through good behavior.
- Use classwide positive recognition, in which all students work together to earn a reward for the entire class.
- Give tangible awards such as stickers, trinkets, and treats, *but do so only if other positive recognition has been ineffective.*

Consequences

Consequences are penalties invoked by teachers when students interfere with others' right to learn. Consequences must be unpleasant to students, but never harmful physically or psychologically. The Canters stress that it is not severity that makes consequences effective, but rather the teacher's consistency in applying consequences. Students have full knowledge of the consequences in advance. When consequences must be invoked, students are reminded that, by their behavior, they have chosen the consequence. Teachers usually don't like to invoke consequences, but the Canters (1992, p. 79) write:

> There is perhaps nothing more harmful we can do to children than allow them to disrupt or misbehave without showing them we care enough to let them know their behavior is not acceptable.

With advance preparation, misbehavior can be dealt with calmly and quickly. The Canters advise making what they call a **discipline hierarchy** that lists consequences and the order in which they will be imposed within the day. (Each day or secondary class period begins afresh.) Each consequence in the hierarchy is a bit more unpleasant than its predecessor. The Canters (1992, p. 85) illustrate the discipline hierarchy as follows:

> *First time a student disrupts.* Consequence: "Bobby, our rule is no shouting out. That's a warning."
>
> *Second or third time the same student disrupts.* Consequence: "Bobby, our rule is no shouting out. You have chosen 5 minutes time out at the back table."
>
> *Fourth time the same student disrupts.* Consequence: "Bobby, you know our rules about shouting out. You have chosen to have your parents called." The teacher informs Bobby's parents. This is best done by phone and is especially effective if Bobby is required to place the call and explain what has happened.
>
> *Fifth time the same student disrupts.* Consequence: "Bobby, our rule is no shouting out. You have chosen to go to the office to talk with the principal about your behavior."
>
> *Severe clause.* Sometimes behavior is so severe that the hierarchy is disregarded and the *severe clause*—being sent to the principal—is invoked on the first offense. Consequence: "Bobby, fighting is not allowed in this class. You have chosen to go to the principal immediately. We will talk about this later."

Teachers are advised to organize hierarchies of rules and consequences in accordance with their needs. For guidance, the Canters (1992, p. 88) provide the following illustrations:

Grades K–3

Rule Is Broken	Consequence
first	warning
second	5 minutes working away from the group
third	10 minutes working away from the group
fourth	call parents
fifth	send to principal
severe clause	send to principal

Grades 4–6

Rule Is Broken	Consequence
first	warning
second	10 minutes working away from group
third	15 minutes working away from group, plus write in the behavior journal
fourth	call parents
fifth	send to principal
severe clause	send to principal

Grades 7–12

Rule Is Broken	Consequence
first	warning
second	stay in class 1 minute after the bell
third	stay in class 2 minutes after the bell, plus write in the behavior journal
fourth	call parents
fifth	send to principal
severe clause	send to principal

The **behavior journal** referred to in the foregoing suggestions is a log book in which students write accounts of their own misbehavior, including why they broke the rule and what alternative action might have been better to have taken. To employ the discipline hierarchy effectively, teachers must keep track of offenses that students commit. This is easily done by recording on a clipboard students' names and the number of violations. Other options include recording this information in the plan book or, in primary grades, using a system of colored cards that students "turn" or change after each violation. The Canters advise that names of offending students not be written on the board.

The Canters stress this point: In order to make a discipline plan work effectively, teachers must actually teach the discipline plan to their students. It is not enough just to read it aloud or display it on a poster. The Canters provide a number of sample lessons showing how the plan can be taught at different grade levels (see Canter and Canter 1992, pp. 98–115). All the plans they suggest follow this sequence:

1. Explain why rules are needed.
2. Teach the specific rules.
3. Check for understanding.
4. Explain how you will reward students who follow rules.
5. Explain why you have consequences.
6. Teach the consequences.
7. Check again for understanding.

Providing Positive Recognition

The Canters (1992, p. 146) say that the best way to build responsible behavior is to "continually provide frequent positive recognition to those students who are on task." By positive recognition, they mean praise and support, both of which should be integrated naturally into lessons being taught. They go on to say (1992, pp. 148–150) that **praise** is the most effective technique teachers have for encouraging responsible behavior, and they provide guidelines for its use:

- Effective praise is personal. The student's name is mentioned along with the desired behavior: "Jack, thank you for working quietly back there."
- Effective praise is genuine. It must be related to the situation and behavior, and the teacher's demeanor should show that it is sincere.
- Effective praise is descriptive and specific. It lets students know when and why they are behaving appropriately: "Good, Susan. You went right to work on your essay."
- Effective praise is age appropriate. Young children like to be praised publicly. Older students like praise but usually prefer to receive it privately.

The Canters make several recommendations concerning how to go about providing positive praise and support, including the following:

- Scanning—looking around the classroom regularly to find students who are working appropriately.
- Circulating around the classroom to give one-on-one attention.
- Writing names on the board of students who are behaving responsibly. Set a goal with the class for getting at least 20 names on the board each day.

Redirecting Nondisruptive Off-Task Behavior

Often students fail to behave responsibly, but not in a way that disrupts the class. They may look out the window instead of working, read a book instead of doing their assignment, doodle instead of completing their work, do work for another class, or daydream or sleep. Instead of applying consequences for these benign misbehaviors, teachers should redirect students back to the assigned task. The Canters (1992, pp. 164–166) describe four techniques teachers can use in these circumstances:

1. Use "the look": Make eye contact and use an expression that shows awareness and disapproval.
2. Use **physical proximity:** Move beside the student. Usually there is no need to do more.
3. Mention the offending student's name. The teacher says, "I want all of you, including Tanya and Michael, to come up with the answer to this problem."
4. Use **proximity praise:** Jason is not working, but Alicia and Maria, seated nearby, are. The teacher says, "Alicia and Maria are doing a good job of completing their work."

Normally, these redirecting techniques are quite effective. If they do not produce the needed results, the teacher should assume that the offending student needs more help for self-control and should turn to the discipline hierarchy and issue a warning.

Invoking Consequences

Consequences are unpleasant (but not harmful) penalties students must suffer when they disruptively violate class rules. Students will have been clearly informed of both positive recognition and consequences associated with class rules, and they may have role-played situations involving both. They realize that consequences naturally follow misbehavior. The Canters (1992, pp. 170–186) make these suggestions for invoking consequences:

1. Provide consequences calmly in a matter-of-fact manner: "Nathan, speaking like that to others is against our rules. You have chosen to stay after class."
2. Be consistent: Provide a consequence every time students choose to disrupt.
3. After a student receives a consequence, find the first opportunity to recognize that student's positive behavior: "Nathan, I appreciate how you are working. You are making a good choice."
4. Provide an escape mechanism for students who are upset and want to talk about what happened: Allow the student to describe feelings or the situation in a journal or log.
5. When a younger student continues to disrupt—move in: Nathan again speaks hurtfully to another student. The teacher moves close to Nathan and quietly and firmly tells him his behavior is inappropriate. She reminds him of the consequences he has already received and of the next consequence in the hierarchy.
6. When an older student continues to disrupt—move out: Marta once again talks during work time. The teacher asks Marta to step outside the classroom, where she reminds Marta of the inappropriate behavior and its consequences. All the while, the teacher stays calm, shows respect for Marta's feelings, and refrains from arguing.

WORKING WITH DIFFICULT STUDENTS

The Canters have found that the techniques described to this point help almost all students behave in a responsible manner, but they recognize that a few students may require additional consideration. Those are the difficult-to-handle students the Canters (1993, p. 6) describe as:

students who are continually disruptive, persistently defiant, demanding of attention or unmotivated. They are the students who defy your authority and cause you stress, frustration and anger. Many of these students have severe emotional or behavioral problems. They may have been physically or psychologically abused, or born substance-addicted to alcohol, crack or other drugs. Many of them come from home environments where parents have minimal, if any, influence or control over their behavior.

Difficult students are *not* the students in your class who act up occasionally. They're not the ones who once in a while may cause you to lose your temper. Difficult students are those who engage in disruptive, off-task behavior with great intensity and frequency.

Teachers detest having to contend with these students, but they are the students most in need of attention and adult guidance.

The Canters acknowledge that "You can't 'cure' or change these students, but you can create an environment that will help (them) achieve." (1993, p. 11). This is accomplished in three phases, which the Canters call (1) Reaching out to difficult students, (2) Meeting the special needs of difficult students, and (3) Communicating with difficult students.

Reaching Out to Difficult Students

Teachers must take the initiative. Instead of continually reacting to the misbehavior of difficult students, teachers will have to reach out to them and try to gain their trust. The Canters (1993, p. 13) remind us that most students arrive in the classroom feeling they can trust the teacher, and they therefore accept teacher guidance. But difficult students are different. For a number of reasons, they do not see teachers as positive, caring role models. They do not trust teachers, do not like school, and do not see any point in their behaving nicely in school. They find satisfaction in ignoring teacher requests and behaving impudently. A teacher's first priority in working with such students is, therefore, to build a sense of trust.

The process is not an easy one. Teachers can begin by trying to put themselves in the student's place, trying to see teachers and schools from the student's point of view. Then they can change the ways they *respond* to the difficult student. They need to know beforehand what they will do when the student behaves defiantly or confrontationally. This tactic involves anticipation and practice. The Canters contrast **reactive teacher behavior** with **proactive teacher behavior.** When responding reactively to a difficult student, teachers usually lose their tempers, fail to impose their will on the student, and end up sending the student to the principal's office. This accomplishes nothing positive. The teacher feels bad, stress is increased, and sense of frustration and failure remain. The student does not become more willing to comply with teacher requests, but rather more resistant and untrusting, and the class is left feeling uneasy.

By preparing proactive responses, teachers can avoid much of the uneasiness and begin building a sense of trust. The Canters (1993, pp. 32–34) advise teachers as follows:

1. Anticipate what the difficult student will do and say. Think through how you will respond.
2. Remember that you have a choice in your responses. You can choose *not* to respond angrily or defensively. You can choose *not* to let your feelings get hurt.
3. Do not give up on difficult students. They need to see that you care about them.

Building Trust with Difficult Students

Teachers can show that they care about students as individuals by treating every student as they would want their own child to be treated. Further, they can reach out to students in ways such as the following:

1. Take a student interest inventory. Find out about brothers and sisters, friends, preferred activities, hobbies, favorite books and TV shows, future hopes, and what students like their teachers to do.
2. Greet students individually at the door. Say something special to each, personally.
3. Spend some individual time with students. Give one-on-one attention when possible.
4. Make a phone call to the student after school and express appreciation, emphathy, or regret, as appropriate.
5. When a student is ill, send a get-well card or use the phone to convey best wishes.

Meeting Difficult Students' Needs

Although all students have similar needs, certain strongly felt needs of difficult students are not being adequately met at school. In order to be successful with these students, teachers need to help them meet those needs. But what are they?

The Canters explain that three kinds of special needs underlie the behavior of difficult students: (1) a need for extra attention, (2) a need for firmer limits, and (3) a need for motivation. You can see a parallel with Rudolf Dreikurs's contentions, explained earlier in Chapter 2. The Canters say that when a difficult student is disruptive or noncompliant, he or she is attempting to fulfill a need for either extra attention, firmer limits, or extra motivation.

Identifying Students' Needs

How does a teacher identify the particular need that a student seems to be striving to satisfy? By doing three things, the Canters say: (1) Look at the student's behavior, (2) look at your own response to the student's behavior, and (3) look at the student's reaction to your response. Suppose fourth-grader Jonathan continually makes silly noises, gets out of his seat, makes irrelevant comments, shouts out, and grins at others. His behavior annoys you greatly, and after days of it you feel like he is driving you crazy. Every time you reprimand Jonathan, he gets quiet for a little while, then begins disrupting again. Jonathan is annoying you (a sign of persistent attention-seeking behavior) and is satisfied temporarily when you give him attention. It is clear that Jonathan has a **need for extra attention.**

Suppose that ninth-grader Alicia talks back to you, argues with others, and refuses to do what you ask of her. She doesn't want you or anyone else telling her what to do. Alicia's behavior makes you angry, and after a time you feel threatened. You want to put her in her place. When you reprimand and redirect her, she is unwilling to comply with your reasonable requests. Alicia shows a **need for firmer limits.**

Suppose that eleventh-grader Arthur is always reluctant to begin an assignment, never completes one, continually makes excuses, and has an "I-can't" attitude. Arthur's behavior over time frustrates you; you try everything you know to get him going. He doesn't fight back, but nothing works. Arthur, the Canters would say, has a **need for extra motivation.**

Fulfilling the Student's Primary Need

Once a difficult student's predominant need is identified, the teacher can address it in a beneficial manner (Canter and Canter 1993, pp. 68–73):

If the student needs *attention,* provide the maximum amount of attention in the shortest amount of time. Plan some proactive steps, such as greeting the student at the door, taking him or her aside for occasional brief chats, giving personal attention during directions and work time, and providing positive recognition for effort and attentiveness. Through the process, help the student see how to obtain recognition through appropriate, rather than inappropriate, behavior.

If the student needs *firmer limits,* enforce class rules in a nonconfrontational way. Do not give these students occasion to show how tough and defiant they can be. Quietly and privately remind them of rules and show appreciation when they comply.

If the student needs *greater motivation,* let him or her know you have faith in their ability. Make sure the assignment is within the student's capability. Break the task down into small parts if possible. Compliment the student on any effort or progress he or she makes.

Teaching Appropriate Behavior

Once you have identified a difficult student's special needs, you can help the student enjoy more success by directly teaching appropriate behavior. Many students simply don't seem to know how to behave, even when told. They require direct practice, but on what? The Canters (1993, pp. 77–92) provide detailed instruction on how to establish exactly what behaviors you want your difficult students to practice. They suggest making and filling in a table such as shown in Figure 4.1.

The Canters say that, once you have identified exactly what behaviors you want from a particular *primary grade* student, you should meet the student when no one

When is the student most often noncompliant?	What behaviors does the student usually show?	What specific behaviors do I want from this student?
1.	1.	1.
2.	2.	2.
3.	3.	3.

Figure 4.1. Guide for Analyzing the Behavior of Difficult Students

else is around. Speaking calmly and with care,

- indicate how you want to help the student;
- model the behavior you want the student to show;
- ask the student to emulate that behavior;
- reinforce the student for trying, now and in the actual classroom situation.

For a *middle level student,*

- explain the rationale for engaging in the behavior;
- describe the exact behavior you want the student to exhibit;
- have the student repeat or write down the desired behavior;
- reinforce as appropriate.

For a *secondary level student,*

- in a matter-of-fact manner, specify the exact behaviors you expect; and
- show appreciation privately when the student behaves as desired.

Be sure to remind the students privately of what you expect each time just before the activity takes place.

Providing Positive Support

Positive interactions with difficult students are one of the keys to success, but most teachers find this an especially difficult task, since they are so often provoked by the students' misbehavior. The Canters (1993, pp. 100–116) provide a number of suggestions, including:

1. In the plan book, enter reminders of whom you wish to praise, what for, and when.
2. Post reminders at strategic points in the classroom, such as beside the clock.
3. Put a sticker on your watch face, so that every time you look at your watch you will be reminded to provide positive recognition to someone in need of it.
4. Walk around the room and look for positive behavior, then supply recognition.

Positive support is best provided in the form of *praise.* It can also be given effectively in positive notes and phone calls home, special privileges, behavior awards, and tangible rewards.

Redirecting Nondisruptive Misbehavior

Difficult students often misbehave in ways that do not disrupt the class, such as daydreaming, doodling, looking out the window, and withdrawing. Teachers usually react to this kind of misbehavior by either ignoring it or giving an immediate consequence.

The Canters suggest, however, that nondisruptive misbehavior offers a good opportunity to build positive relationships with the student. The strategy proceeds this way (Canter and Canter 1993, pp. 120–124): The teacher says quietly to the student, "Your behavior is inappropriate, but I care about you and I'm going to give you the chance to choose more appropriate behavior." This gives the student an opportunity to meet the teacher's expectations. Probably further help will be needed, which the teacher provides by establishing eye contact, moving into physical proximity, or softly calling the student's name. If this is not sufficient, the student can be reminded of the rules and seated near the teacher. Teachers must remember to give plenty of encouragement as the student shows signs of complying with the rules.

Interacting with Difficult Students

The Canters make a number of suggestions about how to interact with difficult-to-manage students, including how to handle oneself, how to defuse confrontations, and how to use one-to-one problem solving. They begin by cautioning against "reactive responses" which usually make relationships worse, not better. They remind us that:

> When a student becomes increasingly upset or defiant, *you can* stay calm and deescalate the situation.

> When meeting in a problem-solving conference with a student, *you can* communicate both firmness and caring.

> Effective communication skills will enable you to continue to build trust with a student even in difficult circumstances. (1993, p. 190)

Defusing Confrontations

Teachers intensely dislike confrontations with students, which put teachers on the defensive and stir up heated emotions. The Canters point out that when you set limits and hold difficult students accountable, there will be confrontations. How do you deal with them? The Canters (1993, pp. 162–175) make suggestions that include the following:

1. Tell yourself to stay calm. Do not speak for a moment or two. Take a slow deep breath and count to three, four, or five. This will help you relax.
2. Depersonalize the situation. Realize that the student is not attacking you personally, but rather the situation. Think of it as a scene in a movie. The calmer you remain, the harder it is for the student to remain upset.
3. Differentiate between covert and overt confrontations. In covert confrontations, the student mumbles or sneers but does not attack you verbally. In this case, step away from the student, but later speak to him or her privately. Overt confrontations are treated differently. Here, the student reacts defiantly to the teacher's requests, drawing other students' attention. In this case, remain calm and refuse to engage the student hostilely. Instead, acknowledge the student's emotion and restate what the student needs to do. If the student remains hostile, take him or her apart from the class, acknowledge the student's feelings, and renew your request for cooperation.

4. If the student is especially hostile, you should back off. Drop the matter temporarily so the class may continue. But make sure later to talk with the student privately.

Difficult though it may be, teachers should not view confrontations as setbacks, but rather as new opportunities to show commitment to the student. A calm, caring attitude will do much toward building trust between teacher and student.

One-to-One Problem Solving

Students who continue to misbehave seriously require more in-depth, personal guidance from the teacher. This can be provided in what the Canters call one-to-one problem-solving conferences, useful when the student's misbehavior is chronic, or when there is a sudden change in behavior, or when there is a serious problem (such as fighting) that cannot be overlooked. The Canters (1993, pp. 180–189) provide these guidelines for personal conferences:

1. Meet privately with the student and keep the meeting brief.
2. Show empathy and concern. The meeting is about the student's behavior, not your classroom and not about you.
3. Focus on helping the student gain insight into the misbehavior and into more appropriate behavior that will meet the student's needs. Try to find out why the problem behavior persists—is there a problem at home, with other students, with the difficulty of assignments? Listen and show respect for the student.
4. Help the student determine how his or her behavior can be improved.
5. Disarm the student's criticism of you. Ask for specific examples of what you are doing that bothers the student. Show empathy. Focus on the student's needs.
6. State your expectations about how the student is to behave. Make it clear (in a calm, friendly manner) that you will not allow the student to continue disruptive behavior.

INITIATING THE CANTERS' *ASSERTIVE DISCIPLINE*

Assertive Discipline can be introduced in the class at any time, although the first few days of a new school year or semester are especially appropriate. Decide on behaviors you want from students, what you will do to build trust, and what positive recognitions you will provide and consequences you will invoke. Meet with your class and discuss the kinds of behavior that will make the classroom pleasant, safe, and productive. Solicit student ideas. Using their input, jointly formulate three to five rules to govern behavior. Sincerely ask all students if they can agree to abide by the rules. Discuss with students the positive recognitions you will provide and the hierarchy of consequences, associated with the rules, that you will invoke. Make sure students realize that the rules apply to every member of the class all the time. Take your plan to the principal for approval and administrative support. Send a copy of the discipline plan home for parents to read. Ask parents to sign and return a slip indicating their approval and support. With students, role-play rules, recognitions, and consequences, and emphasize repeatedly that the plan helps everyone enjoy a safe, positive environment.

STRENGTHS OF THE CANTERS' *ASSERTIVE DISCIPLINE*

The Canters have developed and refined a system of discipline for helping promote a pleasant, supportive classroom environment that frees teachers to teach and students to learn. Their approach has broken new ground in several ways—ease of implementation, meeting teachers' and students' needs, teaching students how to behave responsibly, and insistence on support from administrators and parents. A great many teachers are very enthusiastic about *Assertive Discipline* because it helps them deal with students positively and teach with little interruption. It also helps relieve the annoyance of verbal confrontations and preserves instructional time.

Does *Assertive Discipline* have shortcomings? In the past it was criticized for being unnecessarily harsh and too focused on suppressing unwanted behavior rather than on helping students learn to control their own behavior. The Canters have been sensitive to those concerns and have taken pains to make sure that teachers understand this central point: Students must be taught, in an atmosphere of respect, trust, and support, how to behave responsibly.

Assertive Discipline is now criticized mainly for its extensive use of praise and other rewards, which some authorities believe reduce intrinsic motivation. Debate continues, too, concerning whether research supports the effectiveness of *Assertive Discipline.* Some writers present evidence that it does (Canter 1988; McCormack 1989), while others claim the opposite (Curwin and Mendler 1989; Render, Padilla, and Krank 1989; Kohn 1993). Perhaps most telling is the continued widespread popularity of *Assertive Discipline,* which suggests that it provides educators effective skills they have not been able to find elsewhere.

REVIEW OF SELECTED TERMINOLOGY

The following terms are central to an understanding of the Canter model.

assertive response style	nonassertive teachers
assertive teacher	nonassertive response style
behavior journal	physical proximity
consequences	positive recognition
directions	positive repetitions
discipline hierarchy	praise
hostile response style	proactive teacher behavior
hostile teacher	proximity praise
need for firmer limits	reactive teacher behavior
need for extra motivation	rules
need for extra attention	setting limits

severe clause

students' rights

teachers' rights

teaching the discipline plan

teaching proper behavior

APPLICATION EXERCISES

CONCEPT CASES

Case 1: Kristina Will Not Work

Kristina, a student in Mr. Jake's class, is quite docile. She socializes little with other students and never disrupts lessons. However, despite Mr. Jake's best efforts, Kristina will not do her work. She rarely completes an assignment. She is simply there, putting forth no effort at all.

How would the Canters deal with Kristina? They would advise Mr. Jake to do the following: Quietly and clearly communicate class expectations to Kristina. Redirect her to on-task behavior. Have private talks with her to determine why she is not doing her work and what Mr. Jake might do to help. Provide personal recognition regularly and try to build a bond of care and trust with Kristina. Contact Kristina's parents about her behavior. See if they can provide insights that will help Mr. Jake work with Kristina. If necessary, make an individualized behavior plan for helping Kristina do her work.

Case 2: Sara Cannot Stop Talking

Sara is a pleasant girl who participates in class activities and does most, though not all, of her assigned work. She cannot seem to refrain from talking to classmates, however. Her teacher, Mr. Gonzales, has to speak to her repeatedly during lessons, to the point that he often becomes exasperated and loses his temper.

What suggestions would the Canters give Mr. Gonzales for dealing with Sara?

Case 3: Joshua Clowns and Intimidates

Joshua, larger and louder than his classmates, always wants to be the center of attention, which he accomplishes through a combination of clowning and intimidation. He makes wise remarks, talks back (smilingly) to the teacher, utters a variety of sound-effect noises such as automobile crashes and gunshots, and makes limitless sarcastic comments and put-downs of his classmates. Other students will not stand up to him, apparently fearing his size and verbal aggression. His teacher, Miss Pearl, has come to her wit's end.

Would Joshua's behavior be likely to improve if the Canters' techniques were used in Miss Pearl's classroom? Explain.

Case 4: Tom Is Hostile and Defiant

Tom has appeared to be in his usual foul mood ever since arriving in class. On his way to sharpen his pencil, he bumps into Frank, who complains. Tom tells him loudly to shut up. Miss Baines, the teacher, says, "Tom, go back to your seat." Tom wheels around, swears loudly, and says heatedly, "I'll go when I'm damned good and ready!"

How would the Canters have Miss Baines deal with Tom?

QUESTIONS AND ACTIVITIES

1. Each of the following exemplifies an important point in the Canter model of discipline. Identify the point illustrated by each.
   a. Miss Hatcher, on seeing her class list for the coming year, exclaims, "Oh no! Billy Smythe in my class! Nobody can do a thing with him! There goes my sanity!"
   b. "If I catch you talking again during the class, you will have to stay an extra five minutes."
   c. "I wish you would try your best not to curse in this room."
   d. Students who receive a fourth check mark must go to the office and call their parents to explain what has happened.
   e. If the class is especially attentive and hardworking, students earn five minutes they can use for talking quietly at the end of the period.
2. For a grade level and/or subject you select, outline an *Assertive Discipline* plan that includes the following:
   • four rules,
   • positive recognition and consequences associated with the rules, and
   • the people you will inform about your system, and how you will inform them.
3. Examine Scenario 3 or 4 in the Appendix. How could *Assertive Discipline* be used to improve behavior in Mrs. Daniels's library or Mrs. Desmond's second grade?

REFERENCES AND RECOMMENDED READINGS

Canter, L. 1976. *Assertive Discipline: A take-charge approach for today's educator.* Seal Beach, Calif.: Lee Canter & Associates.

———. 1978. Be an assertive teacher. *Instructor, 88*(1), 60.

———. 1988. Let the educator beware: A response to Curwin and Mendler. *Educational Leadership, 46*(2), 71-73.

———. 1996. First, the rapport—then, the rules. *Learning, 24*(5), 12,14.

Canter, L., and M. Canter. 1986. *Assertive Discipline Phase 2 in-service media package* [videotapes and manuals]. Santa Monica, Calif.: Lee Canter & Associates.

———. 1989. *Assertive Discipline for secondary school educators: In-service video package and leader's manual.* Santa Monica, Calif.: Lee Canter & Associates.

———. 1992. *Assertive Discipline: Positive behavior management for today's classrooms.* 2d ed. Santa Monica, Calif.: Lee Canter & Associates.

———. 1993. *Succeeding with difficult students: New strategies for reaching your most challenging students.* Santa Monica, Calif.: Lee Canter & Associates.

Curwin, R., and A. Mendler. 1988. Packaged discipline programs: Let the buyer beware. *Educational Leadership, 46*(2), 68-71.

————. 1989. We repeat, let the buyer beware: A response to Canter. *Educational Leadership, 46*(6), 83.

Hill, D. 1990. Order in the classroom. *Teacher Magazine, 1*(7), 70–77.

Kohn, A. 1993. *Punished by rewards: The trouble with gold stars, incentive plans, A's, praise, and other bribes.* Boston: Houghton Mifflin.

McCormack, S. 1989. Response to Render, Padilla, and Krank: But practitioners say it works! *Educational Leadership, 46*(6), 77–79.

Render, G., J. Padilla, and H. Krank. 1989. What research really shows about Assertive Discipline. *Educational Leadership, 46*(6), 72–75.

CHAPTER **5**

Fredric Jones's
Positive Classroom Discipline

Fredric Jones

PREVIEW OF JONES'S WORK

Focus

- Organizing the classroom environment to reduce the amount of inappropriate behavior.
- Using body effective body language to help students pay attention and remain on task.
- Using incentive systems to motivate responsibility, good behavior, and productive work.
- Providing help efficiently to students needing teacher guidance during independent work.

Logic

- The easiest and best way to deal with behavior problems is to prevent their occurrence.
- Teachers are most effective in managing behavior when they remain calm and poised.
- Good body language is the single most effective control strategy available to teachers.

Contributions

- Renewed emphasis on the importance of classroom structure in maintaining discipline.
- Clarification of the value and techniques of effective body language.
- The use of incentive systems to motivate responsible behavior.
- Clear suggestions for providing help efficiently to students during independent work.

Jones's Suggestions

- Make it a priority to eliminate the vast time wasting that is evident in most classrooms.
- Use good classroom organization and efficient help to forestall most behavior problems.
- Use effective body language and incentive systems to deal with incipient misbehavior.
- Teach students responsibility; don't do for them what they are capable of doing for themselves.

ABOUT FREDRIC JONES

Fredric H. Jones is the developer of Positive Classroom Management, based in Santa Cruz, California. Jones, a clinical psychologist, has worked for many years to develop training procedures for improving teacher effectiveness in motivating, managing, and instructing school students. His procedures have grown from his extensive field observations of effective teachers that he conducted while on the faculties of the UCLA Medical Center and the University of Rochester School of Medicine and Dentistry. An independent consultant since 1978, Jones now devotes full efforts to his training programs, which are widely used for staff development in school districts. Teachers receive his ideas with a good deal of enthusiasm, recognizing in them refinements of practices with which they are already familiar but which they have not seen organized into a systematic approach.

Jones did not publish a book describing his management system until 1987, several years after full development of his "pyramid" training system, which trains teachers to teach fellow teachers. Jones's behavior management book, *Positive Classroom Discipline,* was published in 1987, together with its companion volume, *Positive Classroom Instruction.* Jones also makes available two video courses of study called *Positive Classroom Discipline* (1996) and *Positive Classroom Instruction* (1996). The manuals for both are authored by JoLynne Talbott Jones. These materials and others for Jones's programs are available from Fredric H. Jones & Associates, Inc., 103 Quarry Lane, Santa Cruz, CA 95060; telephone 408-425-8222; fax 408-426-8222; e-mail FHJ123@aol.com

JONES'S CONTRIBUTIONS TO DISCIPLINE

While other authorities have devoted much attention to the role of verbal communication in promoting classroom discipline, Jones was the first to place major emphasis on the importance of nonverbal communication such as teachers' body language, facial expressions, gestures, eye contact, and physical proximity. He was also the first to note how teachers reinforce learned helplessness as they give feedback to students he calls "helpless handraisers," and the first to prescribe the cure. Recently, he has reemphasized the value of good classroom organization and management, and is stressing the importance of teaching students to behave responsibly. Jones's contributions to dealing with such nondramatic yet troublesome classroom matters have earned him a wide following among teachers.

JONES'S CENTRAL FOCUS

The main focus of Jones's efforts is on helping students support their own self-control so that they behave properly and maintain a positive attitude (Jones 1987a). Toward that end he emphasizes the importance of good classroom management, describes the effective use of body language, reveals how to provide incentives that motivate desired behavior, explains how to help students assume personal responsibility, and details procedures for providing efficient help to students during independent work time.

JONES'S PRINCIPAL TEACHINGS

Approximately 99 percent of all student misbehavior consists of talking without permission and generally goofing off, such as daydreaming, making noise, and being out of one's seat. But it is this behavior that disrupts teaching and learning.

On the average, teachers in typical classrooms lose approximately 50 percent of their teaching time because students are off task or otherwise disrupting learning. This amounts to massive time wasting.

Most teaching time that is otherwise lost can be recouped when teachers provide efficient help to students, use effective body language, and use incentive systems.

Discipline is the process of enforcing standards and building cooperation so that disruptions are minimized and learning is maximized.

Efficient arrangement of the classroom improves the likelihood of successful teaching and learning. This includes seating arrangements that permit the teacher to "work the crowd" as they supervise student work and provide help.

Proper use of body language is one of the most effective discipline skills available to teachers. Body language refers to a group of physical mannerisms that include eye contact, physical proximity, body carriage, facial expressions, and gestures.

Physical proximity of the teacher helps students maintain self-control. This involves teachers stationing themselves near students who show an inclination to misbehave.

Body carriage is very effective in communicating teacher authority. Body carriage refers to teacher posture and movement.

Teachers set limits on student behavior not so much through rules as through subtle interpersonal skills. These are the skills which convey that teachers mean business.

Students will work hard and behave well when given incentives to do so. These incentives are teachers' promises that students will receive, in return for proper behavior, rewards in the form of favorite activities that can be earned by all members of the group for the enjoyment of all members of the group.

Incentives are cost-effective when they motivate __all__ students to remain on task and behave properly. Jones emphasizes the difference between group incentives and traditional behavior management programs that affect only a few behaviors at great cost, in time and effort, to the teacher.

To be effective, an incentive must be attractive to the entire group and be available equally to all. Incentives that are available only to certain members of the class will affect only the behavior of those few individuals and leave the class as a whole little changed.

Students must learn to do their work without the teacher hovering over them. Jones calls students' reliance on teacher presence the "dependency syndrome." He devised a method of providing help very efficiently to students who call for teacher assistance during independent work. He says efficient help should include (1) mention of anything the student has done correctly, (2) direct suggestion of what needs to be done next, and (3) immediate teacher departure. All this is to be accomplished in 20 seconds or less. Jones says to "be positive, be brief, and be gone."

The goal of discipline is for students to assume responsibility for their actions. All aspects of learning are improved when students do so.

ANALYSIS OF JONES'S *POSITIVE CLASSROOM DISCIPLINE*

Misbehavior and Loss of Teaching-Learning Time

Since the early 1970s, Jones and his associates have spent thousands of hours observing and recording in hundreds of elementary and secondary classrooms across the country. Jones's main interest has been in identifying the methods of classroom management used by highly successful teachers, especially those methods concerned with keeping students working on task, providing individual help when needed, and dealing with misbehavior.

Those observations led Jones to several important conclusions. Principal among them was that classroom discipline problems are generally quite different from the way they are depicted in the media and perceived by the public. Even though many of the classrooms studied were located in inner-city schools and alternative schools for students with behavior problems, Jones found very little hostile defiance—the behavior that teachers fear and that many people believe predominates in schools. Instead, Jones found what he called **massive time wasting,** in which students talked when they shouldn't, goofed off, and moved about the room without permission. Jones found that in well-managed classrooms, one of those disruptions occurred about every two minutes. In loud, unruly classes the disruptions averaged about 2.5 per minute. In attempting to deal with those misbehaviors, teachers lost almost 50 percent of the time available for teaching and learning (Jones 1987a).

Jones also discovered a critical time during lessons in which misbehavior was most likely to occur. He found that most lessons go along fairly well until students are asked to work on their own. That is when, Jones (1987b) says, "the chickens come home to roost" (p. 14). Until that point, students seem to pay attention and give the impression they are learning perfectly. But when directed to continue work on their own, hands go up, talking begins, students rummage around or stare out the window, and some get out of their seats. The teacher doesn't know what to do except nag and admonish. This, Jones says, is "another day in the life of a typical classroom" (1987b, p. 14) where the teacher ends up reteaching the lesson to a group of "helpless hand-raisers" during time that should be devoted to supervising independent work.

Teachers everywhere relate to that scenario as one that repeatedly leaves them feeling frustrated and defeated. When discussing the phenomenon, many express bitterness over never having received training in how to deal effectively with such misbehavior. New teachers say they expected that they would quickly learn to maintain order in their classrooms but were only partially successful and found themselves resorting to punitive measures.

Jones concluded that teachers were correct in their contentions that they had not received training in behavior management and, further, that many, if not most, were unable to develop needed skills while working on the job. Jones decided to observe and document the methods used by the relatively few teachers who were notably successful with discipline. It was out of those observations that the Jones model of discipline took form.

Skill Clusters in Jones's Model

Jones (1993, p. 55) says that the purpose of **discipline** is to engage students in learning in the most positive, unobtrusive fashion possible. His analysis of the numerous classroom observations uncovered four clusters of teacher skills that keep students engaged in learning by forestalling misbehavior or dealing with it efficiently. Those skill clusters have to do with (1) classroom structure to discourage misbehavior, (2) limit-setting through body language, (3) responsibility training through incentive systems, and (4) providing efficient help to individual students. Let us explore these skill clusters further.

Skill Cluster #1: Classroom Structure to Discourage Misbehavior

Jones emphasizes that the best way to manage behavior problems is to prevent their occurrence. In turn, the best way to prevent their occurrence is by providing a **classroom structure** that gives specific attention to room arrangement, class rules, classroom chores, and routines to begin class.

Room Arrangement

An effective way to prevent students' fooling around and goofing off is to minimize the physical distance between teacher and students, so that the teacher can "work the crowd." Through movement and proximity with an occasional pause, look, or slow turn, teachers cause most students most of the time simply to rule out "goofing off" before they even begin.

Teachers with minimum discipline problems constantly move among students during seat work, group discussions, and cooperative learning. This calls for room arrangements with generous walkways that allow teachers to move quickly and easily among the students. Jones suggests the "interior loop" as ideal: There, desks or tables are set with two wide aisles from front to back and enough distance between side-to-side rows for teachers to walk easily among the students.

Classroom Rules

Classroom rules should be both general and specific. **General rules,** fairly few in number, define the teacher's broad guidelines, standards, and expectations for work and behavior. They can be reviewed and posted. **Specific rules** describe procedures and routines, detailing specifically what students are to do and how they are to do it. These rules must be taught and rehearsed to mastery just like any academic skill. Jones advocates spending the first two weeks making sure students understand the specific rules.

Classroom Chores

Jones believes in assigning as many classroom chores to students as possible. This gives them a sense of "buy-in" to the class and program and helps develop a sense of responsibility.

Opening Routines

Typically, classes begin in a fragmented way, with announcements, taking attendance, handling tardies, and the like. This produces delays that give students opportunity to waste time and misbehave. Jones says that, on average, about five to eight minutes are wasted in most classrooms after the bell rings. It is much preferable that teachers begin lessons promptly. Jones suggests beginning the class with **bell work,** work that does not require active instruction from the teacher, that engages and focuses students to the day's lesson, and that the students can begin upon entering the room. Examples of bell work are review questions, warm-up problems, brain teasers, sustained silent reading, and journal writing.

Skill Cluster #2: Limit-Setting through Body Language

Jones maintains that good discipline depends mostly—90 percent, he says—on effective **body language.** Therefore, his training program concentrates on helping teachers learn to use physical mannerisms in setting limits on behavior and in enforcing those limits. Body language, he says, is excellent for revealing thoughts, feelings, and intentions, and it can show that the teacher is calmly in control. The body language that Jones emphasizes includes (1) proper breathing, (2) eye contact, (3) physical proximity, (4) body carriage, (5) facial expressions, and (6) gestures.

Proper Breathing

Teachers do well to remain calm in all situations, as calm conveys strength. Calm is attained in part through proper breathing. The way teachers breathe when under pressure signals how they feel and what they are likely to do next. Skilled teachers breathe slowly and deliberately before responding to situations. Jones noted that some take two deep breaths before turning to a misbehaving student, enabling them to maintain self-control.

Eye Contact

Miss Remy is demonstrating and explaining the process of multiplying fractions. She sees that Jacob has stopped paying attention. She pauses in her explanation. The sudden quiet causes Jacob to look at Miss Remy and find that she is looking directly into his eyes. He straightens up and waits attentively. Few physical acts are more effective than **eye contact** for conveying the impression of being in control. Skilled teachers allow their eyes to sweep the room continually and engage the eyes of individual students. Locking eyes makes many people uncomfortable, teachers and students alike, and students often avert their eyes when teachers look directly at them. The effect is not lost, however, for the students realize that the teacher, in looking directly at them, takes continual note of their behavior, both good and bad.

Making eye contact does not seem to be a natural behavior for most beginning teachers and must therefore be practiced before it can be used effectively.

Inexperienced teachers tend to look over students' heads or between students or dart their eyes rapidly without locking on to individuals. Sometimes while teaching, they stare more or less directly ahead, losing track of students who are at the back and sides of the group, or they find comfort in looking only at the faces of two or three well-behaved, actively responding students, blocking out others who are not so attuned to the lesson.

These tendencies are persistent, and it is common to encounter experienced teachers who do not make good use of eye contact. With practice, however, any teacher can learn to focus the eyes directly on the face of each individual student. This in itself sends a message that the teacher is aware and in control. It further serves to inhibit students who are on the verge of misbehaving and provides an opportunity to send facial expressions of approval or disapproval.

Physical Proximity

Miss Remy has completed her demonstration of the multiplication of fractions. She has directed students to complete certain exercises on their own. After a time she sees from the back of the room that Jacob has stopped working and has begun talking to Jerry. She moves toward him. Jacob unexpectedly finds Miss Remy's shadow at his side. He immediately gets back to work, without Miss Remy having to say anything.

In his classroom observations, Jones noted that most misbehavior occurs some distance away from the teacher. Students near the teacher rarely misbehave. This phenomenon has long been recognized by experienced teachers, who have learned to move nearer to students who are prone to misbehave or to seat such students near them. Jones observed that teachers who use **physical proximity** rarely need to say anything to the offending students to get them to behave. He concluded that verbalization is not needed and that in fact it sometimes weakens the effect, due possibly to defensive reactions engendered in students when they are reprimanded. Teachers who need to deal with minor misbehavior are instructed to move near the offending student, establish brief eye contact, and say nothing. The student will usually return immediately to proper behavior.

Body Carriage

Jones also found that posture and **body carriage** are quite effective in communicating authority. Students quickly read body language and are able to tell whether the teacher is in charge, tired, disinterested, or intimidated. Good posture and confident carriage suggest strong leadership; a drooping posture and lethargic movements suggest resignation or fearfulness. Effective teachers, even when tired or troubled, tend to hold themselves erect and move assertively. One should note here that on those infrequent occasions when the teacher is feeling ill, it is good to inform the students and ask for their assistance and tolerance. Students usually behave with unexpected consideration at such times, provided the strategy is used sincerely and not too often.

Facial Expressions

Like body carriage, teachers' **facial expressions** communicate much to students. Facial expressions can show enthusiasm, seriousness, enjoyment, and appreciation, all of which tend to encourage good behavior; or they can reveal boredom, annoyance, and resignation, which may encourage misbehavior. Perhaps more than anything else, facial expressions such as winks and smiles demonstrate a sense of humor, the trait that students most enjoy in teachers.

The face can be put to good use in sending other types of nonverbal signals as well. Eye contact has been discussed as a prime example. Very slight shakes of the head can stop much misbehavior before it gets under way. Frowns show unmistakable disapproval. A firm lip line and flashing eyes can indicate powerfully that limits are being strained. These facial expressions are used instead of words whenever possible and are as effective as words in showing approval. For control and disapproval, they have the advantage over verbal rebuffs in that they seldom belittle, antagonize, or provoke counterattacks from students.

Jones (1993) says that effectively **setting limits** involves learning to "do nothing when under pressure" (p. 55). By that he means that teachers are usually most effective in controlling misbehavior when they use their bodies correctly but say nothing and take no other action. He reminds teachers that they cannot discipline with their mouths—that if they could do so, ". . . nagging would have fixed every kid a million years ago" (p. 77). When you open your mouth, he says, you run the risk of slitting your own throat.

Skill Cluster #3: Responsibility Training through Incentive Systems

Jones observed that teachers have three different management styles: (1) Some teach well and reward well; (2) Some nag, threaten, and punish, and; (3) Some lower their standards and accept whatever they can get from students. These management styles definitely affect teacher success in the classroom. To illustrate: Mr. Sharpe tells his class that if all of them complete their work in 45 minutes or less, they can have the last 10 minutes of class time to talk quietly with a friend. Mr. Dulle tells his class that if they promise to work very hard later on, he will allow them to begin the period by discussing their work with a friend. Which teacher is likely to get the best work from his students? This question has to do with responsibility and the use of incentives.

Why would a student ever give up the joys of goofing off and take on instead the burden of responsibility? Some would do it because they thought they were supposed to. Others would do it to please the teacher. Others would do it to avoid punishment or reprimand. But many, especially older students, would do it only if they thought it would bring them something worthwhile in return. To help provide that sense of worthwhileness, Jones suggests using incentives.

An **incentive** is something outside of the individual that prompts the individual to act. It is something that is promised as a consequence for desired behavior but is held in abeyance to occur or be provided later. It might be popcorn, a preferred activity, an unspecified surprise, or the like. It is an effective incentive if students behave as desired in order to obtain it later.

Jones gives a prominent place in his classroom management program to incentives as a means of motivating students. He found that some of the most effective teachers use incentives systematically but that most teachers use them ineffectively or not at all. The ineffective teachers typically made use of giving grades, marks, or stars; having work displayed; being dismissed first; and so forth. Jones points out that the problem with incentives of this type is that they go only to the top achievers; the less able students, once out of contention for the prize, have nothing left for which to work. Moreover, for many students, receiving a badge or being first in line does not compete strongly with the joys of talking or daydreaming.

What, then, are characteristics of effective incentives, and how should they be used? Responsibility training gains most of its strength, Jones says, from the "bonus" portion of the incentive. Bonuses encourage students to save time they would normally waste in order to get it back in the form of preferred activity time. It gives members of the class a shared vested interest in cooperating to save time rather than wasting it in small snippets throughout the period or day. Jones states or implies that teachers should carefully think through (1) Grandma's rule, (2) student responsibility, (3) genuine incentives, (4) preferred activities, (5) educational value, (6) group concern, (7) ease of implementation, (8) when incentives do not work, (9) omission training, and (10) back-up systems. Let us see what is involved in each.

Grandma's Rule

Grandma's rule states: "First eat your vegetables, and then you can have your dessert." Applied to the classroom, this rule requires that students first do what they are supposed to do, and then for a while they can do what they want to do. The incentive is the end product of the proposition. In order to obtain it, students must complete designated work while behaving acceptably.

Just as children (and many adults) ask to have their dessert first, promising to eat their vegetables afterward, students ask to have their incentive first, pledging on their honor to work feverishly afterward. As we all know, even the best intentions are hard to remember once the reason for doing so is gone. Thus, teachers who wish to use effective incentive systems must, despite student urging, delay the rewards until last and make the reward contingent on the students' doing required work acceptably. In other words, if they don't eat their broccoli, they don't get their pudding.

Student Responsibility

Jones strongly believes that effective incentives can help everyone to feel responsible for their actions. For example, cooperation may be one way to show responsibility. However, cooperation is voluntary; no one can force someone to cooperate. Students who enjoy goofing off and daydreaming, when asked to cooperate, can legitimately ask themselves, "Why should I?" Jones believes that if students show responsibility by doing what teachers ask them to do, it is because teachers have used encouragement and incentives, rather than nagging, bribing, threatening, or punishing.

Genuine Incentives

There is a wide difference between what many teachers hope will be incentives (e.g., "Let's all work in such a way that we will later be proud of what we do") and what students consider **genuine incentives** (e.g., "If you complete your work on time, you can have five minutes of preferred activity time.)" Jones cautions against allowing students to earn "free time" to do whatever they wish: He says students won't work for long to earn free time. Teachers often fail to take into account that what they believe to be an incentive for students may, in actuality, not work for most students in the class. For example, a teacher may say, "The first person to complete a perfect paper will receive two bonus points." This may motivate a few of the most able students, but most know they have little chance to win so they barely try. Or the teacher may say, "If you really work hard, you can be the best class I have ever had." This usually sounds better to the teacher than to the students. Although the students might like to think of themselves as the best, that thought will not be strong enough to keep them hard at work.

What, then, are some genuine incentives that can be used in the classroom? Generally, students respond well to the anticipation of preferred group activities such as art, viewing a film, or having time to pursue personal interests or talk with friends. Such group activities are genuine incentives in that, first, almost all students desire them sufficiently to make extra effort to obtain them and, second, they are available to all students, not just a few. Many teachers use tangible objects, awards, and certificates as incentives. Jones does not recommend them because they may be costly or difficult to dispense or, worse, because they have little educational value.

Preferred Activity Time

Preferred activity time is time allotted for any activity that can be used as an incentive. "Preferred activity" means that the activity is one students enjoy, one that they prefer to most other class activities, such as talking with fellow students or viewing a videotape. Jones calls the activities PAT and advises that when selecting and introducing PAT, teachers must consider three things: (1) Students must want the activity, (2) they must earn the time, through showing responsibility, that will go to the PAT, and (3) the teacher must be able to live with the PAT.

PAT may be earned in a number of different ways. Mr. Jorgensen gives his fourth graders three minutes to put away their language arts materials and prepare for math: Any time left over from the three minutes goes to later PAT. In Mrs. Nguyen's room, if everyone is seated and ready when the bell rings, the class earns two additional minutes of PAT. However, if a group continues to be noisy, the class loses the amount of PAT that they have wasted. Some PAT may be used immediately, while other time may be for a future activity. Ms. Connelly's class saves some of their PAT for a spring field trip. In some instances, PAT may be earned as individual bonuses. When Mickey continues to be unprepared and consequently loses PAT for the class, Mr. Duncan decides to work with him individually. As he improves, he earns PAT for the entire class.

Educational Value

To the extent feasible, every class period should be devoted to activities that have **educational value.** Work that keeps students occupied but teaches them nothing can seldom be justified. This principle applies equally to incentive systems. While few educators would be loath never to allow a moment of innocent frivolity, the opposite extreme of throwing daily or weekly classroom parties as incentives for work and behavior is difficult to condone from an educational standpoint. What then should one use at PAT?

There are many activities with educational value that students enjoy greatly, both individually and in groups. For individual students, the activities fall into two classes—

enrichment activities and team learning games. Students are not left to do just anything, nor do they proceed without rules of guidance. The freedom is that of choosing from a variety of approved activities. For the total group, activities can be chosen by vote, and all students engage in the same activity during the time allotted. Elementary school students often select physical education, art, music, drama, or construction activities. Frequently, they want the teacher to read to them from a favorite book. Secondary students often choose to watch a film, hold class discussions on special topics, watch performances by class members, or work together on such projects as producing a class magazine. JoLynne Talbott Jones (1993) gives directions for a large number of educationally sound class activities that students of various grade levels enjoy greatly and that therefore serve as excellent preferred activities.

Group Concern

Jones emphasizes the importance of making sure every student has a stake in earning the incentive for the entire class. This **group concern** motivates all students to keep on task, behave well, and complete assigned work. Here is how it is done.

The teacher agrees to set aside a period of time in which students might be allowed to engage in a preferred activity. In keeping with Grandma's rule, this time period must come after a significant amount of work time has been devoted to the standard curriculum. The time can be at the end of the school day for self-contained classes—perhaps 15 to 20 minutes. For departmentalized classes, the time can be set aside at the end of the week—perhaps 30 minutes on Friday. The students can decide on the activity for their dessert time, and to earn it they have only to work and behave as expected.

The teacher manages the system by keeping track of the time students gain, through their behavior, for PAT. Of course, it is possible that a single student, by misbehaving, can prevent the class from earning full PAT. Teachers often think it unfair to penalize the entire class for the sins of a few. In practice this is rarely a problem, because the class quickly understands that this is a group, not an individual, effort. The group is rewarded together and punished together regardless of who might transgress. A strength of this approach is that it brings peer pressure to bear against misbehavior. Ordinarily a misbehaving student obtains reinforcement from the group in the form of attention, laughter, or admiration. With proper PAT, the opposite is true. The class is likely to discourage individual misbehavior, because it takes away something the class members want.

Ease of Implementation

Unlike other incentive systems, that advocated by Jones is notable for two important features that work hand in hand: (1) its effectiveness for all students in that all are brought into the picture, and (2) its ease of implementation. To implement Jones's incentive system, teachers need do only four things.

1. Establish and explain the system.
2. Allow the class to vote from time to time on the teacher-approved activities they wish to enjoy during incentive time.
3. Keep track of the bonus time students have earned for PAT.

4. Be prepared when necessary to conduct the class in low-preference activities for the amount of time that students might have lost from the time allotted to their preferred activity.

When Incentives Do Not Work

If an incentive system loses effectiveness, it is likely for one of the following reasons:

1. The preferred activities might have grown stale. This is cured by allowing the class to discuss the matter and decide on new preferences.
2. The class may temporarily be overexcited by unsettling occurrences such as unusual weather, a holiday, special events at school, or an accident. In such cases the teacher may suspend the incentive program for a time, giving explanation and allowing discussion.
3. Individual students may occasionally lose self-control or decide to defy the teacher. In this case the teacher can resort to omission training and backup systems, as explained in the following paragraphs.

Omission Training

Generally speaking, incentives and PAT bonuses are earned by the entire class. Teachers cannot possibly monitor incentives for all students individually. The exception lies in the occasional student whose misbehavior repeatedly ruins PAT for the rest of the class. For those few students Jones describes **omission training,** a plan that allows a student to earn PAT time for the entire class by omitting a certain misbehavior.

Kevin is one such student. In Ms. VanEtten's class he simply does not seem to care about PAT, and consequently is late, loud, and unprepared, thus ruining PAT for the others. Ms. VanEtten privately explains to Kevin that he doesn't have to participate in PAT, particularly since he doesn't care about it, but she does want him to be successful with his own work and behavior. She explains that she will use a timer, and when Kevin behaves in accordance with class rules, he will earn time for himself, and also PAT for the class. When he misbehaves, he loses time for himself but not for the class.

Backup Systems

As a last option for students like Kevin, Jones suggests **backup systems,** which are hierarchical arrangements of negative sanctions intended to put a stop to unacceptable student behavior. Jones identifies three levels of backup:

1. Small backup responses, said privately or semiprivately to the student: "I expect you to stop talking so we can get on with our work." For these responses the teacher can lean down close enough so that only the student hears the message. With such low-keyed messages the student knows the teacher means business. Jones points out that the small backup responses gain their power not from the size of the negative sanction but, rather, from the students' perception of the teacher as "meaning business." The teacher's messages to the student in such cases are always given privately and, typically, at very close range. Whispering privately to students is a constructive way of protecting their dignity.

2. Medium backup responses, delivered publicly in the classroom: "Emily, sit in the thinking chair for three minutes and consider how you are acting that causes me to send you there." Or, "Brian, you are late again. You'll have detention with me tomorrow after school." Other medium backup responses include warnings, reprimands, loss of privilege, and parent conferences. Because these are public, they are risky. Students may try to get even with teachers who humiliate them in front of their peers.

3. Large backup responses require at least two professionals, usually the teacher and an administrator. They are given in response to outrageous, intolerable behavior or for chronic repeated disruptions. Large backup responses include trips to the office, in- or out-of-school suspension, special class, and special school.

Skill Cluster #4: Providing Efficient Help to Individual Students

One of the most interesting, important, and useful findings in Jones's research has to do with the way teachers provide individual help to students who are stuck during seatwork. Suppose that a grammar lesson is in progress. The teacher introduces the topic, explains the concept on the board, asks a couple of questions to determine whether the students are understanding, and then assigns 10 exercises for students to complete at their desks. Very soon a hand is raised to signal that a student needs help. If only three or four hands are raised during work time, the teacher has no problem. But if 20 students fill the air with waving arms, most of them sit for several minutes doing nothing while awaiting attention from the teacher. For each student needing help, this waiting time is pure waste and an invitation to misbehave.

Jones asked teachers how much time they thought they spent on the average when providing help to individuals who signaled. The teachers felt that they spent from one to two minutes with each student, but when Jones's researchers timed the episodes, they found that teachers actually spent around four minutes with each student. This consumed much time and made it impossible for the teacher to attend to more than a few students during the work period. Even if the amount of time were only one minute per contact, several minutes would pass while some students sat and did nothing.

Jones noted an additional phenomenon that compounded the problem. He described it as a **dependency syndrome** wherein some students routinely raised their hands for teacher help even when they did not need it. To have the teacher unfailingly come to their side and give personal attention proved rewarding indeed, and the constant reinforcement strengthened the dependency.

Based on those observations, Jones concluded that independent seatwork is prone to four inherent problems: (1) insufficient time for teachers to answer all requests for help; (2) wasted student time; (3) the high potential for misbehavior; and (4) the perpetuation of dependency. Consequently, he gives this matter high priority in his training program.

Jones determined that all four problems can be solved through teaching teachers how to give **efficient help,** which is accomplished as follows:

Step 1

Organize the classroom seating so that students are within easy reach of the teacher. The interior loop seating arrangement previously described is suggested. Without quick, easy passage, the teacher uses too much time and energy dashing from one part of the room to another.

Step 2

Use graphic reminders, such as models or charts, that provide clear examples and instructions. These reminders might show steps in algorithms, proper form for business letters, or written directions for the lesson. The reminders are posted and can be consulted by students before they call for teacher help.

Step 3

This step is a hallmark of the Jones model. It involves learning how to cut to a bare minimum the time used for individual help. To see how the process is accomplished, consider that teachers normally give help very inefficiently through a questioning tutorial that proceeds something like this:

> "What's the problem?"
>
> "All right, what did we say was the first thing to do?" *[Waits; repeats question.]*
>
> "No, that was the second. You are forgetting the first step. What was it? Think again." *[Waits until student finally makes a guess.]*
>
> "No, let me help you with another example. Suppose . . ."

Often, in this helping mode, the teacher reteaches the concept or process to each student who requests help. Thus, four minutes can be unexpectedly spent in each interaction. If help is to be provided more quickly, this questioning method must be reconsidered. Jones trains teachers to give help in a very different way, and he insists that it be done in 20 seconds or less for each student, with an optimal goal of about 10 seconds. To reach this level of efficiency, the teacher should do the following when arriving beside the student:

1. (Optional). Quickly find anything that the student has done correctly and mention it favorably: "Your work is very neat" or "Good job up to here."
2. Give a straightforward prompt that will get the student going: "Follow step two on the chart" or "Regroup here." Jones says to teach students to ask themselves "What do I do next?" instead of tutoring them through the whole task—minimize verbiage.
3. Leave immediately. As Jones says, "Be positive, be brief, and be gone."

Help provided in this way solves the major problems that teachers encounter during instructional work time. Every student who needs help can be attended to. Students waste little time waiting for the teacher. Misbehavior is much less likely to occur. The dependency syndrome is broken, especially if the teacher gives attention to students who work without calling for assistance. Rapid circulation by the teacher also permits better monitoring of work being done by students who do not raise their hands. When errors are noted in those students' work, the teacher should help them in the efficient manner Jones suggests for dependent students.

INITIATING JONES'S *POSITIVE CLASSROOM DISCIPLINE*

Jones (1987a, p. 321) suggests that his model of discipline be initiated as a four-tiered system of closely related management methodologies: (1) classroom structure, (2) limit setting, (3) incentives, and (4) backup systems. All four tiers are planned in advance and introduced simultaneously. It is important to understand that *Positive Classroom Discipline* is a system in which the parts interrelate. For example, if prevention is done poorly through inadequate classroom structure, all the unmanaged behavior will surface as overt misbehavior which requires the teacher to stop teaching in order to take action. If this happens often, the cost in time and effort skyrockets. Further, any discipline management that is not handled successfully at the prevention level gets forwarded to responsibility training by default. If the load is too great, teachers may begin using limit setting in a punitive fashion, which is contrary to the overall strategy of the program.

To introduce *Positive Classroom Discipline* to students, one begins with a discussion of limit setting, which leads to the formulation of agreements (rules) about what students may and may not do in the classroom. It is explained to students that when rules are violated, their behavior will be corrected with body language that does nothing more than make the misbehaving student feel uncomfortable. Examples such as eye contact, stares, and physical proximity are given and demonstrated.

To make limit setting work effectively, mild discomfort is counterbalanced with incentives and social rewards, such as acknowledgment and approval, in return for students' observing rules and agreements. Desirable incentives are discussed, and procedures for managing incentives are described. Students are reminded that the incentives they select are to have instructional value.

Teachers will also need to discuss with students the **backup systems** they will employ when students misbehave seriously and refuse to comply with positive teacher requests. Such backup sanctions receive relatively little attention in Jones's system, which attempts to move teachers away from reliance on admonition and threat, yet Jones acknowledges that at times the teacher may be unable to get misbehaving students to comply with the rules. At those times, teachers may tell the student, "If you are not going to do your work, sit there quietly and don't bother others." And for yet more serious situations of defiance or aggression, teachers must have a plan by which they isolate the student or call for help if needed.

STRENGTHS OF JONES'S *POSITIVE CLASSROOM DISCIPLINE*

The Jones model provides strong help in preventive and supportive discipline and does so in a balanced way. Jones has been successful in identifying and compiling discipline techniques used by teachers who are often called "naturals." That is why teachers' heads nod in agreement with his suggestions. Jones has found that the strategies he advocates are all teachable, though many teachers do not learn them well within the pressures of day-to-day teaching. Through specific training episodes, most teachers can acquire the techniques that are usually seen only in their most effective colleagues.

But it is unrealistic to expect that teachers can read Jones's work and then walk into the classroom the next day transformed. The acts he describes must be understood and then practiced repeatedly, which is accomplished best through Jones's training seminars. Fortunately, motivated teachers can assess their classroom behavior in light of Jones's suggestions and isolate certain control tactics on which they would like to improve. They can practice what Jones suggests and then take their new learnings into the classroom to be tested. That is one of the most appealing qualities of Jones's suggestions: They do not have to be put into place as a full-blown total system but can instead be practiced, perfected, and added incrementally.

REVIEW OF SELECTED TERMINOLOGY

The following terms are central to the Jones model of discipline. Check yourself to make sure you can explain their meanings.

backup systems	Grandma's rule
bell work	group concern
body language	incentive
body carriage	interior loop
dependency syndrome	massive time wasting
discipline	omission training
efficient help	physical proximity
eye contact	preferred activity time
facial expressions	proper breathing
general rules	setting limits
genuine incentives	specific rules
gestures	

APPLICATION EXERCISES

CONCEPT CASES

Case 1: Kristina Will Not Work

Kristina, a student in Mr. Jake's class, is quite docile. She socializes little with other students and never disrupts the class. However, Mr. Jake cannot get Kristina to do any work. She rarely completes an assignment. She is simply there, putting forth almost no effort at all.

How would Jones deal with Kristina? Jones would suggest that Mr. Jake take the following steps to improve Kristina's behavior:

1. Make frequent eye contact with her. Even when she looks down, Mr. Jake should make sure to look directly at her. She will be aware of it, and it may make her uncomfortable enough that she will begin work.
2. Move close to Kristina. Stand beside her while presenting the lesson.
3. Give Kristina frequent help during seatwork. Check on her progress several times during the lesson. Give specific suggestions and then move quickly on.
4. Set up a personal incentive system with Kristina; for example, a certain amount of work earns an activity she especially enjoys.
5. Set up a system in which Kristina's working can earn rewards for the entire class. This brings her peer attention and support.

Case 2: Sara Cannot Stop Talking

Sara is a pleasant girl who participates in class activities and does most, though not all, of her assigned work. She cannot seem to refrain from talking to classmates, however. Her teacher, Mr. Gonzales, has to speak to her repeatedly during lessons, to the point that he often becomes exasperated and loses his temper.

What suggestions would Jones give Mr. Gonzales for dealing with Sara?

Case 3: Joshua Clowns and Intimidates

Joshua, larger and louder than his classmates, always wants to be the center of attention, which he accomplishes through a combination of clowning and intimidation. He makes wise remarks, talks back (smilingly) to the teacher, utters a variety of sound-effect noises such as automobile crashes and gunshots, and makes limitless sarcastic comments and put-downs of his classmates. Other students will not stand up to him, apparently fearing his size and verbal aggression. His teacher, Miss Pearl, has come to her wit's end.

What specifically do you find in Jones's suggestions that would help Miss Pearl with Joshua?

Case 4: Tom Is Hostile and Defiant

Tom has appeared to be in his usual foul mood ever since arriving in class. On his way to sharpen his pencil, he bumps into Frank, who complains. Tom tells him loudly to shut up. Miss Baines, the teacher, says, "Tom, go back to your seat." Tom wheels around, swears loudly, and says heatedly, "I'll go when I'm damned good and ready!"

How effective do you believe Jones's suggestions would be in dealing with Tom?

QUESTIONS AND ACTIVITIES

1. For each of the following scenarios, first identify the problem that underlies the undesired behavior, then describe how Jones would have the teacher deal with it.
   a. Mr. Anton tries to help all of his students during independent work time but finds himself unable to get around to all who have their hands raised.
   b. Ms. Sevier wants to show trust for her class. She accepts their promise to work hard if they can first listen to a few favorite recorded songs. After listening to the songs, the students talk so much that they fail to get their work done.
   c. Mr. Gregory wears himself out every day dealing ceaselessly with three class clowns who disrupt his lessons. The other students always laugh at the clowns' antics.
2. Examine Scenario 2 or 10 in the Appendix. What changes would Jones suggest that Mr. Platt or Miss Thorpe make in order to provide a more efficient and satisfactory learning environment?

REFERENCES AND RECOMMENDED READINGS

Jones, F. 1979. The gentle art of classroom discipline. *National Elementary Principal, 58,* 26–32.

———. 1987a. *Positive classroom discipline.* New York: McGraw-Hill.

———. 1987b. *Positive classroom instruction.* New York: McGraw-Hill.

———. 1996. Did not! Did, too! *Learning, 24*(6), 24–26.

———. 1996. *Positive Classroom Discipline—a video course of study.* Santa Cruz, Calif.: Fredric H. Jones & Associates.

———. 1996. *Positive classroom instruction—a video course of study.* Santa Cruz, Calif.: Fredric H. Jones & Associates.

Jones, J. 1993. *Instructor's guide: Positive classroom discipline—a video course of study.* Santa Cruz, Calif.: Fredric H. Jones & Associates.

———. 1996. *Instructor's guide: Positive classroom discipline—a video course of study.* Santa Cruz, Calif.: Fredric H. Jones & Associates.

———. 1996. *Instructor's guide: Positive classroom instruction—a video course of study.* Santa Cruz, Calif.: Fredric H. Jones & Associates.

CHAPTER 6

Linda Albert's
Cooperative Discipline

Linda Albert

PREVIEW OF ALBERT'S WORK

Focus

■ A cooperative approach to help students connect, contribute, and feel capable.

■ A class code of conduct that fosters an optimal climate for learning and teaching.

■ A plan for student–parent partnership in sustaining an optimal learning environment.

Logic

■ Behavior is based on choice: Students choose to behave the way they do.

■ Teachers are in a powerful position to influence the choices students make.

■ Teachers best influence students through encouragement, intervention, and collaboration.

■ Students behave better when they and their parents help establish the class behavior code.

Contributions

■ Explained teacher-student-parent cooperation as the key to positive classroom behavior.

■ Extended Rudolf Dreikurs's discipline concepts to the classroom in a more useful form.

■ Devised the Three C's—capable, connect, contribute—to help students feel they belong.

Albert's Suggestions

■ Strive to help every student feel they belong in the class, that they have a place and are valued.

■ Find ways to help every student connect with others, contribute to the class, and feel capable.

■ Involve students in planning the class code of conduct and the consequences for misbehavior.

■ Turn every classroom misbehavior into an opportunity to help students learn better behavior.

ABOUT LINDA ALBERT

Linda Albert, author and disseminator of *Cooperative Discipline,* is an educator, counselor, syndicated columnist, and former classroom teacher who works nationally and internationally with educators and parents. She has authored regular columns in *Working Mother* and *Family* magazines and has made featured appearances on NBC's "Today Show," CBS's "This Morning," and CNN's "Cable News."

Dr. Albert has produced a quantity of materials and programs for educators and parents, including the books, *Coping with Kids and School* (1985), *Strengthening Stepfamilies* (1986), *Quality Parenting* (with Michael Popkin, 1987), *An Administrator's Guide to Cooperative Discipline* (1992), *Coping with Kids* (1993), *Cooperative Discipline* (1996), *A Teacher's Guide to Cooperative Discipline* (1996), and *Cooperative Discipline Implementation Guide: Resources for Staff Development* (1996). She has produced two video series, *Responsible Kids in School and at Home: The Cooperative Discipline Way* (1994), and *Cooperative Discipline Staff Development Videos* (1996), with separate materials for elementary and secondary teachers.

Dr. Albert is married, has three children, and several grandchildren. She lives in Tampa, Florida, and can be reached at 3405 Ellenwood Lane, Tampa, FL 33618. Fax 813-265-3399; e-mail LindAlbert@aol.com

ALBERT'S CONTRIBUTIONS TO DISCIPLINE

Albert first published *Cooperative Discipline* in 1989. Since that time her work has attracted a growing following in the United States and abroad. Influenced by Adlerian psychology and the work of Rudolf Dreikurs, Albert became convinced that students' behavior—and misbehavior—is a consequence of students' attempts to meet certain needs. By attending to those needs and providing much encouragement, teachers can reduce misbehavior greatly and establish classrooms where students participate cooperatively with the teacher and each other. Albert details how this is accomplished and provides clear techniques and strategies for classroom use.

ALBERT'S CENTRAL FOCUS

Albert's main focus is on helping teachers meet student needs so that students will choose to cooperate with the teacher and each other. This obviates the adversarial roles so often evident between teacher and student. Albert believes cooperation is made likely when students truly feel they belong to and in the class. To ensure that students acquire that feeling, she gives heavy attention to what she calls the Three C's— helping all students feel capable, helping them connect with others, and helping them make contributions to the class and elsewhere. Albert also shows how parental support can be solicited and obtained. Although Albert gives major emphasis to developing a classroom climate that significantly diminishes misbehavior, she acknowledges that some misbehavior will occur in even the best circumstances. Therefore, she explains carefully how to intervene effectively when misbehavior occurs. Beyond that, she provides strategies that minimize classroom conflict and permit teachers to deal with it in a positive manner.

ALBERT'S PRINCIPAL TEACHINGS

Students choose their behavior. How they behave is not outside their control. Albert acknowledges that heredity, environment, innate needs, happy and unhappy experiences, and conditioned responses all affect how students behave. But she maintains that most students, under most circumstances, choose to behave the way they do, and that virtually all can behave properly when they see the need to do so. Once teachers understand that behavior is based on choice, they begin to see that they can influence how students choose to behave.

Students need to feel that they belong in the classroom, which means they must perceive themselves to be important, worthwhile, and valued. Their behavior is reflective of that desire. Teachers can defuse incipient misbehavior by using appropriate intervention techniques and encouragement to help students attain a sense of belonging.

When students misbehave, their goal is usually either to gain attention, gain power, exact revenge, or avoid failure. At times, misbehavior can also occur because of exuberance or simply not knowing the proper way to behave.

Teachers can only influence student behavior; they cannot directly control it. This is because students can always choose their behavior, even when it is contrary to teacher demands. But by knowing which goal students hope to achieve through misbehavior, and by employing an intervention strategy tailored to that goal, teachers can exert positive influence on behavior choices that students make.

Teachers in general reflect three styles of classroom management: permissive, autocratic, and democratic. Of the three, the democratic style best promotes good discipline. Albert refers to these three styles as the **hands-off, hands-on,** and **hands-joined** styles. The hands-off style fails to help students make responsible decisions about their learning. The hands-on style attempts to force behavior change, with the result that students rebel and come to dislike their teachers and their classes. The cooperative hands-joined style works to gain student trust and allow students to participate in making choices about their education, which invites them to be more cooperative and more motivated to achieve.

The Three C's—capable, connect, and contribute—are essential in helping students feel a sense of belonging. When students feel capable, are able to connect personally with peers and teachers, and able to make contributions to the class and elsewhere, the incidence of misbehavior drops dramatically.

Teachers should work cooperatively with students to develop a classroom code of conduct. This code of conduct stipulates the kind of behavior expected of everyone in the class. It replaces the sets of rules seen in other systems of discipline and defines the operating principles of the class.

Teachers should also work cooperatively with students to develop a set of consequences to be invoked when the classroom code of conduct is transgressed. When students participate in developing consequences, they are more likely to accept them as fair and reasonable.

*One of a teacher's greatest assets is good **self-control.*** While teachers cannot control students by making them do as they are told, they can control themselves and their actions.

When conflicts occur between teacher and students, the teacher should remain cool and relaxed. Teachers should adopt a businesslike attitude and use a calm yet firm tone of voice. It is a losing proposition to engage in power struggles with students, where students are forced to back down. Instead, teachers should use any of *Cooperative Discipline's* "graceful exit" strategies that give teachers specific responses to confrontive student behavior.

Encouragement is the most powerful teaching tool available to teachers. Rudolf Dreikurs, Haim Ginott, and others have made clear distinctions between praise and encouragement, pointing out the danger of praise and the value of encouragement. Albert contends that "Perhaps no factor that influences how students choose to behave is as important as the amount of encouragement students receive from a teacher." (1996b, p. 15)

Teachers should remember that in order to develop a good system of discipline, they require the cooperation of students and parents. Both should be valued as partners and their contributions brought meaningfully into cooperative discipline.

ANALYSIS OF ALBERT'S *COOPERATIVE DISCIPLINE*

In her work with teachers throughout the world, Linda Albert has found a recurring theme: Teachers everywhere are feeling overwhelmed by the unacceptable behavior of their students. They feel incapable of dealing effectively with special-needs students, are dismayed by the number of severe classroom disruptions, and are increasingly frightened by violence against teachers. These conditions are ruining the quality of teaching for many teachers and are wiping away job satisfaction. Teachers are crying for an effective approach to discipline that will allow them to regain control of their classrooms and, at the same time, work happily and productively with students.

Albert has concluded that existing systems of discipline, whether based on principles of reinforcement or strong teacher assertions, are not the answer to beleaguered teachers' problems. Instead, teachers require a strategy that enables them to work in a cooperative fashion with students and parents. She judges that when a true cooperative understanding is reached, two prized results can be attained: First, the classroom can be transformed into a safe, orderly, inviting place for teaching and learning, and second, students have a good chance of learning to behave responsibly while achieving more academically.

The Goal of Classroom Discipline

Albert says that the goal of classroom discipline is the same everywhere—helping students learn to choose responsible behavior. Developing a positive relationship between teachers and students that extends to include parents, other teachers, and administrators helps that goal become a reality. It is the combination of intervention strategies to deal with the moment of misbehavior, encouragement strategies to build self-esteem, and collaboration strategies that involve students as partners that enables teachers to reach the goal of influencing students to choose positive behavior.

Why Students Misbehave

In agreement with Rudolf Dreikurs, Albert contends that most misbehavior occurs as students attempt unsuccessfully to meet a universal psychological need—the **need to belong.** We all need to see ourselves as belonging to family, peer group, social group, school, and elsewhere. Students desire this very strongly for the classes of which they are members. They want to feel secure, wanted, and valued, and fortunately most can acquire sense of belonging through acceptable behavior.

But when they are unable, for whatever reason, to experience the desired sense of belonging, many students, though certainly not all, direct their behavior toward **mistaken goals,** so-called because students have the mistaken idea that through misbehavior they can somehow fulfill this need to belong. Dreikurs identified four mistaken goals, which he called attention, power, revenge, and assumed disability. Albert calls behavior that students direct at those mistaken goals **attention-seeking, power-seeking, revenge-seeking,** and **avoidance-of-failure.**

Attention-seeking Behavior

Most students receive enough attention in the classroom to satisfy them. Some, however, require still more, and they seek it both actively and passively. Active attention seeking involves what Albert calls **AGMs**—attention-getting mechanisms. The variety of AGMs is enormous—pencil tapping, showing off, calling out, asking irrelevant questions. Passive attention-seeking is evident in students who dawdle, lag behind, and are slow to comply. They behave in this way to get attention from the teacher.

Attention-seeking behavior disrupts the class and annoys the teacher, but Albert says there is a silver lining to attention seeking: It shows that the offending student desires a positive relationship with the teacher, but does not know how to connect in appropriate ways. For such students, Albert suggests providing abundant recognition when they behave properly. For misbehavior that becomes excessive, Albert provides 31 intervention techniques for dealing with attention seeking. Two examples are standing beside the offending student, and using I-messages such as "I find it difficult to keep my train of thought when talking is occurring."

Power-seeking Behavior

When they do not receive enough attention to feel they belong in the classroom, some students resort to power-seeking behavior. Through words and actions they try to show that they cannot be controlled by the teacher, that they will do as they please. They may mutter replies, disregard instructions, comply insolently, or directly challenge the teacher. Active power-seeking may take the form of temper tantrums, back talk, disrespect, and defiance. Passive power seeking may take the form of quiet noncompliance with directions, with the student willing to hide behind labels such as lazy, forgetful, and inattentive.

Power-seeking behavior makes teachers angry and frustrated. They worry they will lose face or even lose control of the class. Albert says that power seeking has its silver lining, too, in that many students who display this behavior show good verbal skills and leadership ability, as well as assertiveness and independent thinking. Keeping the silver lining in mind, teachers can prevent much power-seeking behavior by giving students options from which they can choose, delegating them responsibilities, and granting them legitimate power when appropriate. For dealing with power struggles that have begun, Albert advises teachers to use graceful exit, time out, and consequence strategies.

Revenge-seeking Behavior

When students suffer real or imagined hurts in the class, a few may set out to retaliate against teachers and classmates. This is likely when teachers have dealt forcefully with students, and sometimes happens when students are angry at parents or others, people too risky to rebel against. The teacher is a convenient, relatively nonthreatening target. Revenge seeking usually takes the form of verbal attacks on the teacher, for example, "You really stink as a teacher!" or in destruction of materials or room environment or, most frightening of all, in direct physical attacks on teachers or other students. Revenge seeking makes the teacher feel hurt and disappointed and can damage the relationship between teacher and student.

Albert suggests two tactics for decreasing revenge-seeking behavior. The first is to work at building caring relationships with all students. This includes students whose behavior is often unacceptable. The second tactic is to teach students to express hostility in acceptable ways, such as through talking about their problems or developing a personal anger management plan.

Avoidance-of-failure Behavior

Many students have an intense fear of failure. A few, especially when assignments are difficult, withdraw and quit trying, preferring to appear lazy rather than stupid. Albert advises teachers not to allow students to withdraw; altering assignments and providing plentiful encouragement can help prevent it. Specifically suggested are (1) using concrete learning materials that students can see, feel, and manipulate, (2) using computer-based instruction, taking advantages of the latest technology and many students' natural interest in computers, (3) teaching students to accomplish one step at a time so they enjoy small successes, and (4) teaching to the various intelligences described by Howard Gardner (1983). This last strategy encourages students to use particular talents they might have—linguistic, mathematical, visual, kinesthetic, rhythmic, intra-personal, and interpersonal. In addition, special help can be provided by the teacher or by remedial programs, adult volunteers, peer tutoring, or commercial learning centers. It is important that withdrawn students be constantly encouraged to try. The teacher must show belief in them and help remove negative thoughts about ability to succeed.

Albert's Plethora of Strategies

Albert puts great stock in strategies that serve to prevent misbehavior, but she is equally concerned with strategies teachers can employ at what she calls "the moment of misbehavior." She states that her intention is to give teachers so many specific strategies that they are never at a loss for what to do next when a student misbehaves. Space within this chapter does not permit presentation of the numerous strategies she describes. Readers are directed to the Appendixes of *Cooperative Discipline* (1996b), especially Appendix C which provides a summary chart of the numerous effective interventions she advocates.

The First C—Helping Students Feel Capable

Albert contends that one of the most important factors in school success is what she calls students' **I-can level.** The I-can level refers to the degree to which students believe they are capable of accomplishing work given them in school. Albert suggests teachers consider the following approaches to increase students' sense of capability.

1. Make Mistakes Okay. The fear of failure, of making mistakes, undermines students' sense of capability, and when fearful, many will not try. To minimize this fear, Albert would have teachers talk with students about mistakes, explain that mistakes always occur when one is learning something new, and minimize the effect of mistakes.

Students are keenly aware of their own mistakes, but not so aware of the mistakes others make. This causes many to believe that other students are more capable than they. Albert suggests that teachers discuss with students what mistakes are and help them understand that everyone makes mistakes. Students need to see that mistakes are a natural part of learning. The more an individual does, the more mistakes he or she will make. Mistakes are often an indicator of how hard one is trying. Albert also urges teachers to be careful how they correct students' mistakes. Too many corrections are overwhelming, especially so when papers come back covered with red ink. While teachers should correct learners' mistakes, they should do so in small steps, focusing on only one or two mistakes at a time.

2. Build Confidence. In order to feel capable, students must have confidence that success is possible. To raise student confidence, Albert says teachers should think of learning as a process of improvement, not as an end product, and when improvement occurs it should be acknowledged. The student's work is compared only to his or her own past efforts, not against other students or grade level expectations. It should be remembered that people can be successful in a number of ways that do not involve written work. Students may show neatness, good handwriting, persistence, and any number of other special talents. Teachers can capitalize on these qualities and provide activities that bring them into play. This helps reluctant students feel more able and willing to participate.

Teachers should hold high learning expectations for everyone, but may need to tailor activities to students' ability to make success possible. New tasks seem difficult to practically everyone, so there is little point in calling a task "easy" or saying "Oh, anybody can do this." It is better to tell students, "I know this may seem difficult at first, but keep at it. Let's see how you do." When students succeed in tasks they consider difficult, their sense of capability rises.

3. Focus on Past Successes. Very few people are motivated by having their mistakes pointed out. When they know they are being successful, however, they like to proceed. Albert cites Bernard Weiner's (1984) contention that people generally attribute success to five factors: belief in their own ability, effort expended, help from others, task difficulty, and luck. She points out that school students have control over two of those factors—belief in their ability and effort they expend. Teachers should help student realize that success grows out of these two components. Albert says teachers should ask students why they think they were successful in assigned tasks. If they say it was because the task was easy, teachers can say "It seemed easy because you had developed the skills to do it." If they say it was because they tried hard, teachers can say "You surely did. That is one of the main reasons you were successful."

4. Make Learning Tangible. Teachers should provide tangible evidence of student progress. Grades such as "B" and "satisfactory" are ineffective because they tell little about specific accomplishments. Albert suggests more effective devices such as I-can cans, accomplishment albums and portfolios, checklists of skills, flowcharts of concepts, and talks about yesterday, today, and tomorrow. She describes these devices as follows:

I-can cans are empty coffee cans, decorated and used by primary grade students, in which students place strips of paper indicating skills they have mastered, books they have read, and so forth. As the cans fill, they show how learnings are accumulating. These cans are useful for sharing in parent–teacher conferences.

Accomplishment albums and portfolios are better for older students. There, students can place evidence of accomplishments, such as papers written, books read, projects completed, special skills attained, and the like. Students should not be allowed to compare their accomplishment albums against each other. The emphasis is solely on personal growth, drawing attention to what individuals can do now that they couldn't do before.

Some classes use lists of specific skills as objectives. As students attain the skills, their progress is shown by check marks. Graphs and charts can also be used to indicate progress. Most commercially prepared academic programs contain flowcharts that show where new skills are introduced in the program. These flowcharts can be duplicated and kept with individual students' records, to show where the student began academically, where he or she is going, and how much progress has been made.

In addition, teachers should regularly discuss with their classes the progress that is being made, contrasting where students were earlier in the year, where they are now, and where they are headed. Helpful comments include "Remember when you couldn't spell these words? Look how easy they are now. You are learning fast. By the end of the year you will be able to . . ." Or, "Remember three weeks ago when you couldn't even read these Spanish verbs? Now you can conjugate all of them in the present tense. By next month, you'll be able to conjugate them in both future and past tense."

5. Recognize Achievement. Albert believes that sense of capability increases when students receive attention from others for what they've accomplished. She suggests having the class acknowledge each other's accomplishments, recognize students at awards assemblies, set up exhibits, and make presentations for parents and other classes. Other suggestions include positive time out in which students are sent to administrators, counselors, or librarians for a few minutes of personal attention, and giving self-approval for achievements.

The Second C—Helping Students Connect

Albert considers it essential that all students **connect,** meaning that they initiate and maintain positive relationships with peers and teachers. As students make these connections, they become more cooperative and helpful with each other and more receptive to teachers. In discussing making connections, Albert uses the term **the Five A's,** which are acceptance, attention, appreciation, affirmation, and affection.

Acceptance means communicating that it is all right for each student to be as he or she is, regarding culture, abilities, disabilities, and personal style. Teachers need not pretend that whatever students do is all right, but should always indicate that the student is a person of potential, worthy of care.

Attention means making oneself available to students, by sharing time and energy with them. Most students desire attention, and many misbehave as they try to obtain it. Albert suggests that some of the best ways for teachers to give personal attention are greeting students by name, listening to what they say, chatting with them individually, eating in the cafeteria with them occasionally, scheduling personal conferences, recognizing birthdays, making bulletin boards with students' baby pictures on them, sending cards and messages to absent students, and showing real interest in students' work and hobbies.

Appreciation involves showing students that we are proud of their accomplishments or pleased by their behavior. It is made evident when we give compliments, express gratitude, and describe how students have helped the class. Appreciation can be expressed orally, in writing, or behaviorally in how we treat others. In showing appreciation, it is important to focus on the deed, not the doer. Albert suggests making statements of appreciation that include three parts—the action, how we feel about it, and the action's positive effect. For example, a teacher might say "Carlos, when you complete your assignment as you did today, it makes me very pleased because we can get all our work done on time."

Affirmation refers to making positive statements about students, statements that recognize desirable traits, such as bravery, cheerfulness, dedication, enthusiasm, friendliness, helpfulness, kindness, loyalty, originality, persistence, sensitivity, and thoughtfulness. By consciously looking for such traits, teachers can find something positive to say about every student, even those with difficult behavior problems. Albert suggests phrasing affirmations as follows: "I have noticed your thoughtfulness" and "Your kindness is always evident."

Affection refers to displays of kindness and caring that people show each other. Albert points out that affection differs from reward, where kindness is shown only when the student behaves as desired. Affection is freely given, with nothing required in return. As Albert (1996b, p. 117) puts it: "[affection] is a gift with no strings attached. It is not 'I like you when' or 'I'd like you if.' Instead, it is simply 'I like you because I like you.'" Unlike appreciation, affection is always addressed to the doer, regardless of the deed. It helps students believe that their teacher likes them even when they make mistakes.

The Third C—Helping Students Contribute

Albert quotes H. Stephen Glenn and Jane Nelsen, who in their book *Raising Children for Success* (1987) contend that the need to be needed is often stronger than the need to survive. People who do not feel they are needed often see life as purposeless, with no need to try or progress. Albert suggests that one of the best ways to help students feel they are needed is to help them to contribute to the class. Some of the ways she suggests to do this are:

1. *Encourage students' contributions in the class.* This is done by asking students to state their opinions and preferences about class requirements, routines, and other matters. This gives them some legitimate power and helps prevent power struggles between teacher and students. Students can also furnish ideas about improving the classroom environment. Ask for their help with daily tasks such as taking attendance, inventorying books and supplies, operating audiovisual equipment, and distributing and collecting materials. Sincerely indicate you need their help and appreciate it.

2. *Encourage students' contributions to the school.* Albert suggests creating **Three C Committees** whose purpose is to think of ways to help all students feel more capable, connecting, and contributing. Teachers and administrators can assign school service time, in which students perform such tasks as dusting shelves, beautifying classrooms, and cleaning the grounds, all of which help build a sense of pride in the school.

3. *Encourage students' contributions to the community.* Albert makes a number of suggestions in this regard, including the following:
   - adopting a health care center and providing services such as reading, singing, and running errands for residents of the center
   - contributing to community drives such Meals on Wheels, Toys for Tots, and disaster relief funds
   - promoting volunteerism in which students volunteer their services to local institutions
   - encouraging random acts of kindness, such as opening doors for people and providing help with their packages.

4. *Encourage students to work to protect the environment.* One of Albert's suggestions is for the class to adopt a street or area of the community and keep it litter free.

5. *Encourage students to help other students.* Albert's suggestions include:
   - establishing a **circle of friends** who make sure that everyone has a partner to talk with, to sit with during lunch, and to walk with between classes
   - doing peer tutoring, in which adept students help students who are having difficulty

- doing peer counseling, in which students talk with other students who are experiencing certain difficulties in their lives
- providing peer mediation where students mediate disputes between other students
- giving peer recognition, in which students recognize efforts and contributions made by fellow students.

The Classroom Code of Conduct

Albert strongly advises teachers to work together with their classes to establish a **classroom code of conduct** which specifies how everyone is supposed to behave and interact, including the teacher. In accordance with the code of conduct, every person is held accountable for his or her behavior all the time. Albert would have this code of conduct replace the sets of rules that teachers normally use. Rules, she says, cause difficulty because students interpret the word *rule* as meaning what teachers do to control students. Moreover, rules are limited in scope, while classroom code of conduct covers a wider variety of behavior. The code of conduct is developed as follows:

1. *Envision the ideal.* Spend time thinking about how you would like your classroom to be, if everything were as you wanted. What would it look and sound like? How would the students behave toward each other? This vision helps specify goals for classroom behavior.
2. *Ask students for their vision of how they would like the room to be.* It is important to involve students at all levels in this process. Usually, students want the same conditions that teachers want. It will be easy to merge the two visions.
3. *Ask for parents' input.* Albert suggests involving parents by sending them a letter summarizing the ideas students have expressed and asking for comments and suggestions. This increases parental support for the code of conduct.

Albert presents several examples of codes of conduct developed in elementary, middle, and secondary schools. They are quite similar at the various grade levels. This is one such example for the secondary level: (Albert 1996b, p. 131)

I am respectful.

I am responsible.

I am safe.

I am prepared.

Because "Excellence in Education" is our motto, I will:

- do nothing to prevent the teacher from teaching and anyone, myself included, from participating in educational endeavors
- cooperate with all members of the school community
- respect myself, others, and the environment.

Teaching the Code of Conduct

The code of conduct can be taught in three steps:

1. *Identify appropriate and inappropriate behaviors.* Begin by asking students to identify specific behaviors that are appropriate for each operating principle. For example, in discussing what one does when "treating everyone with courtesy and respect," students might suggest:
   - Use a pleasant tone of voice.
   - Listen when others are speaking.
   - Use proper language.
   - Respond politely to requests from teachers and classmates.

   Behaviors that these same students might list as inappropriate could be:
   - making obscene gestures
   - putting-down others
   - pushing and shoving
   - ridiculing others
   - making ethnic jokes

   Albert says it doesn't matter if these lists become long. They are not for memorizing. Their purpose is to help students develop the judgment and understanding needed for evaluating their own behavior choices and for accepting responsibility for all their behavior all the time.

2. *Clarify appropriate and inappropriate behaviors.* It is not enough simply to list student suggestions. They must be clarified so that every student knows exactly what each suggestion means. This is accomplished through explanation, modeling, and role playing.

3. *Involve parents.* Students can write a letter to parents explaining the code of conduct and listing the appropriate and inappropriate behaviors they have identified. The teacher can add a postscript to the letter asking parents to save the letter for discussions with their children.

Enforcing the Code of Conduct

Albert advises teachers to do the following when misbehavior occurs:

1. *Check for understanding.* Ask questions to make sure students grasp that their behavior is inappropriate as relates to the code. Examples of questions are:
   - What behavior are you choosing at the moment?
   - Is the behavior you are choosing right now appropriate to our code of conduct?
   - Is this behavior on our *appropriate list* or *inappropriate list* of behaviors?
   - Can you help me understand why you are violating our code of conduct at this moment?
   - Given our code of conduct, what should I say to you right now?

These questions are asked in a businesslike manner, without implying accusation.

2. *Problem-solve when disagreements occur.* Students may at times disagree with the teacher about whether a behavior is appropriate or inappropriate. These disagreements should be resolved in one of three ways:
   - with a student–teacher conference;
   - in a class meeting dealing with the behavior; or
   - by any other mediation or conflict resolution process.

3. *Post the code of conduct.* It is a good idea to keep the code of conduct displayed in the classroom. When prominently displayed, the teacher can:
   - walk to the display, point to the operating principle being violated, and make eye contact with the offending student;
   - write the number of the principle being violated on an adhesive note and put it on the student's desk;
   - point to the operating principle and say, "Class, notice principle number three, please.";
   - point to the operating principle being violated and say, "Tell me in your own words, Clarissa, what this principle means."

Reinforcing the Code of Conduct

Regular repetition and review are needed in helping students become proficient in monitoring and judging their behavior. Albert makes these suggestions:

- Publicize the code of conduct by reviewing it daily or weekly.
- Model self-correction. When the teacher makes a mistake, such as yelling at the students, the violation should be admitted, with a description of how it will be done correctly the next time.
- Encourage student self-evaluation. Ask students to make lists of their own behavior that show how they are complying with or violating the code of behavior.

Involving Students and Parents as Partners

The effectiveness of *Cooperative Discipline* is increased when supported by students and parents. That support is made possible by bringing students and parents into the plan as partners. Albert makes many suggestions for accomplishing this important task.

For enlisting students as partners, Albert suggests:

1. *Teach students about the fundamental concepts in cooperative discipline, which are as follows:*
   - Behavior is based on choice. Students choose to behave as they do.
   - Everyone needs to feel they belong in the class, and will be helped to do so.
   - The four goals of misbehavior are attention, power, revenge, and avoidance of failure.

- The Three C's help everyone feel capable, connected, and contributing.
2. *Involve students in formulating the classroom code of conduct.* This is the blueprint for the kind of classroom climate that teacher and students desire.
3. *Involve students in establishing consequences for misbehavior.* Teacher and students make mutual decisions about what ought to happen when students violate the code of conduct.
4. *Involve students in decision making about classroom and curriculum.* Use class meetings for this purpose.

For enlisting parents as partners, Albert makes the following suggestions:

1. *Inform parents about cooperative discipline and the class code of conduct that teacher and students have been discussing. Ask for parents' comments.* This is best done through newsletters sent home to parents and may be reinforced through parent group presentations.
2. *Establish guidelines for the style of communicating with parents.* Teachers should
   - use objective terms when referring to students and their behavior;
   - limit the number of complaints made to parents; and
   - anticipate student success because every parent needs hope for their child.
3. *Notify parents when behavior problems occur.* Begin with a positive statement about the student, then identify the problem, and end with another positive statement about the student.
4. *Structure parent-teacher conferences for success.* When it is necessary to conference with a parent, Albert suggests using the **Five A**'s strategy:
   - Accept the parent without prejudice.
   - Attend carefully to what the parent says.
   - Appreciate the parent's efforts and support.
   - Affirm the child's strengths and qualities.
   - Affection for the child is made evident to the parent.

Avoiding and Defusing Confrontations

Teachers greatly fear having to deal with situations in which students defy them. It is important to think through, and practice, how you want to conduct yourself when students exhibit power or revenge behaviors and defiantly challenge your authority. The situation can either be calmed or made worse by how you react. Albert suggests practicing how to:

1. *Focus on the behavior, not the student.* To do this, a teacher can
   - Describe the behavior that is occurring, but without evaluating it. Use objective terms to tell the student exactly what he or she is doing. Do not use subjective words such as bad, wrong, or stupid.
   - Deal with the moment. This means talking only about what is happening now, not what happened yesterday or last week.

- Be firm, but friendly. Being firm means indicating that the misbehavior must stop, but at the same time, we want to show the student that we have continuing care and interest.
2. *Take charge of negative emotions.* This means your own negative emotions, not those of the student. In confrontations, teachers feel angry, frustrated, or hurt, but acting on those emotions is counterproductive. One should therefore:
    - Control negative emotions. Teachers should practice responding in a calm, objective, noncombative manner. This blocks the student's intent to instigate conflict and helps everyone calm down so the problem can be resolved.
    - Release negative emotions. Emotions, though controlled, will remain after the confrontation. Albert suggests that teachers release those emotions as soon as possible by physical activity such as walking, playing tennis, or doing house or yard work.
3. *Avoid escalating the situation.* This recommendation dovetails with controlling negative emotions. Certain reactions make the situation worse, not better. Albert provides an extensive list of behaviors teachers should avoid. The following are examples: raising the voice, insisting on the last word, using tense body language, using sarcasm or put-downs, backing the student into a corner, holding a grudge, mimicking the student, making comparisons with siblings or other students, and commanding or demanding.
4. *Discuss the misbehavior later.* At the time of the confrontation, make a brief, direct, friendly intervention that will defuse tensions. When feelings are strong, the matter cannot be resolved instantly. Wait an hour or until the next day when both parties have cooled down.
5. *Allow students to save face.* Students know teachers have the ultimate power in confrontations, so eventually they comply with teacher expectations. However, to save face with their peers and make it seem they are not backing down completely, they often mutter, take their time complying, or repeat the misbehavior one more time before stopping. Albert advises teachers to overlook these behaviors rather than confront the student anew. When allowed to save face students are more willing to settle down and behave appropriately.

Dealing with More Severe Confrontations

Suppose that a very upset student is having a real tantrum, yelling and throwing things. What does the teacher do then? Albert offers a number of suggestions which she calls **graceful exits,** which allow teachers to distance themselves from the situation. These exits are made calmly, with poise, and without sarcasm.

- Acknowledge the student's power. Recognize that you can't make the offending student do anything and be willing to admit it to the student. But also state your expectation: "I can't make you write this essay, but it does need to be turned in by Friday. Let me know your plan for completing the assignment."

- Move away from the student and use fogging techniques. Albert suggests walking away from an irate student, putting distance between the two of you. One effective response is to state both viewpoints, such as: To *you* it seems I'm being unfair when I lower your grade for turning in an assignment after the due date. To *me* it's a logical consequence for not meeting an important deadline.

- Remove the audience. By this, Albert means removing the onlookers' attention when a confrontation arises. This can be done by making an announcement or raising an interesting topic for discussion.

- Table the matter. When emotions are running high or when the entire class is likely to become embroiled in a confrontation, say "You may be right. Let's talk about it later." Or "I am not willing to talk with you about this right now."

- Call the student's bluff and deliver a closing statement. "Let me get this straight. I asked you to _____ and you are refusing. Is this correct?" The teacher stands with pencil and clipboard, to write down what the student says. Albert also suggests using a closing statement, which she calls a one-liner to communicate that the confrontation has ended, for example, "You've mistaken me for someone who wants to fight. I don't."

- If you feel yourself losing control, take a teacher time-out. Say something like "What's happening right now is not okay with me. I need some teacher time-out to think about it. We'll talk later."

- If you see that the student will not calm down, have the student take time out in the classroom, principal's office, or designated room.

Implementing Consequences

When a student seriously or repeatedly violates the classroom code of conduct, particularly with power or revenge behavior, consequences are invoked in keeping with previous agreement. Consequences are a teaching tool, designed to help students learn to make better behavior choices in the future. They are usually unpleasant, but are not harmful physically or psychologically. Albert says consequences should be related, reasonable, respectful, and reliably enforced. By *related,* she means that the consequence should involve an act that has something to do with the misbehavior. For example, Betsy continues to talk disruptively; her consequence is isolation in the back of the room where she cannot talk to others. She should not be kept after class for talking, as the penalty has no logical connection with the offense. By *reasonable,* Albert means that the consequence is proportional to the misbehavior. She reminds us that consequences are used to teach students to behave properly, not to punish them. If Jonathan fails to turn in an assignment, the consequence should be to re-do the assignment. By *respectful,* Albert means that the consequence is invoked in a friendly but firm manner, with no blaming, shaming, or preaching. By *reliably enforced,* Albert means that teachers invariably follow through and invoke consequences. To invoke them one day and not the next leaves students unsure about behavior limits. Students will try to avoid consequences by buttering teachers up, apologizing, and promising not to misbehave again, but the teacher must regularly follow through.

Albert describes four categories of consequences for teachers to discuss with their class:

- loss or delay of privileges, such as loss or delay of a favorite activity
- loss of freedom of interaction, such as talking with other students
- restitution, such as return, repair, or replacement of objects, doing school service, or helping other students that one has offended
- reteaching appropriate behavior, such as practicing correct behavior and writing about how one should behave in a given situation

Resolution of more serious misbehaviors or repeated violations of the class code of conduct should be done in a conference with the student. The purpose of the conference is never to cast blame, but rather to work out ways for helping the student behave responsibly. Albert's **Six-D conflict resolution plan** is a useful tool for helping resolve matters under dispute, whether in conferences or between students in the classroom. The plan is comprised of six steps:

1. Define the problem objectively, without blaming or using emotional words.
2. Declare the need, that is, tell what makes the situation a problem.
3. Describe the feelings experienced by both sides.
4. Discuss possible solutions. Consider pros and cons of each.
5. Decide on a plan. Choose the solution with the most support from both sides. Be specific about when it will begin.
6. Determine the plan's effectiveness. A follow-up meeting is arranged after the plan has been in use for a time in order to evaluate its effectiveness.

INITIATING ALBERT'S *COOPERATIVE DISCIPLINE*

Cooperative Discipline can be put into effect at any time, through the procedures that Albert clearly outlines. Teacher and class, working together, envision the sort of environment that would best meet their needs. They identify specific behaviors that would contribute to such an environment as well as behaviors that would work against it. They clarify these behaviors through discussion, demonstration, and role playing. Teachers and students jointly decide on the consequences to be invoked for violations of the standards they have agreed to, remembering that consequences should be related to specific misbehaviors. They write out the agreement, which becomes known as the code of classroom conduct, and before it is finalized, the teacher sends copies to parents and asks for input and support. In final form, the code of conduct is posted in the room. The behaviors it calls for must be taught, not taken for granted, and the code should be discussed regularly. This keeps it in the foreground where it is useful in reminding students and in correcting misbehavior. When serious violations of the code occur, procedures of conflict resolution are applied.

Cooperative Discipline puts equal emphasis on preventing and correcting misbehavior. In-depth attention is given to helping students feel they belong in the classroom and can be successful there. This entails making on-going concerted efforts to help students feel capable, connect with others, and contribute to the class and elsewhere.

STRENGTHS OF ALBERT'S *COOPERATIVE DISCIPLINE*

Cooperative Discipline is designed to help students achieve their ultimate goal of belonging in the class. When they sense belonging, and when they find success, students show comparatively little misbehavior. Albert recognizes that students will misbehave, even in the best settings, and has therefore developed approximately 70 effective procedures for dealing with misbehavior, procedures that stress teaching proper behavior rather than punishing transgressions. She has provided a clear rationale for cooperative discipline and a detailed guide for implementing and maintaining the program. She recognizes the importance of strong support from administrators and parents and provides many suggestions for ensuring that support.

REVIEW OF SELECTED TERMINOLOGY

The following terms are important in Albert's *Cooperative Discipline.*

accomplishment albums and port-
    folios
attention-getting mechanisms (AGMs)
attention-seeking behavior
avoidance-of-failure behavior
capable
circle of friends
classroom code of conduct
connect
contribute
graceful exits
hands-joined teaching style
hands-off teaching style

hands-on teaching style
I-can cans
I-can level
mistaken goals
need to belong
power-seeking behavior
revenge-seeking behavior
self-control
Six-D conflict resolution plan
the Five A's
the Three C's
Three C Committee

APPLICATION EXERCISES

CONCEPT CASES

Case 1: Kristina Will Not Work

Kristina, a student in Mr. Jake's class, is quite docile. She socializes little with other students and never disrupts lessons. However, despite Mr. Jake's best efforts, Kristina will not do her work. She rarely completes an assignment. She is simply there, putting forth no effort at all.

How would Albert deal with Kristina? Albert would advise Mr. Jake to do the following: Work hard at the Three C's with Kristina. Give her work she can do easily so she begins to feel more capable, then gradually increase the difficulty, teaching one new step at a time. Help her connect through a buddy system with another student and through participation in small group work. Give her opportunities to contribute by sharing information with the class about hobbies, siblings, and the like. Perhaps she has a skill she could teach to another student. Encourage her at every opportunity. Talk with her; ask her if there is something that is preventing her from completing her work. Show that you will help her however you can.

Case 2: Sara Cannot Stop Talking

Sara is a pleasant girl who participates in class activities and does most, though not all, of her assigned work. She cannot seem to refrain from talking to classmates, however. Her teacher, Mr. Gonzales, has to speak to her repeatedly during lessons, to the point that he often becomes exasperated and loses his temper.

What suggestions would Albert give Mr. Gonzales for dealing with Sara?

Case 3: Joshua Clowns and Intimidates

Joshua, larger and louder than his classmates, always wants to be the center of attention, which he accomplishes through a combination of clowning and intimidation. He makes wise remarks, talks back (smilingly) to the teacher, utters a variety of sound-effect noises such as automobile crashes and gunshots, and makes limitless sarcastic comments and put-downs of his classmates. Other students will not stand up to him, apparently fearing his size and verbal aggression. His teacher, Miss Pearl, has come to her wit's end.

Would Joshua's behavior be likely to improve if Albert's techniques were used in Miss Pearl's classroom? Explain.

Case 4: Tom Is Hostile and Defiant

Tom has appeared to be in his usual foul mood ever since arriving in class. On his way to sharpen his pencil, he bumps into Frank, who complains. Tom tells him loudly to shut up. Miss Baines, the teacher, says, "Tom, go back to your seat." Tom wheels around, swears loudly, and says heatedly, "I'll go when I'm damned good and ready!"

How would Albert have Miss Baines deal with Tom?

QUESTIONS AND ACTIVITIES

1. How would you personally, as a student, react to a teacher's using Albert's suggestions about the Three C's and encouragement? Would those techniques be helpful to you?
2. For a grade level and/or subject you select, outline your vision of how you would prefer that teacher and students behave and interact.
3. Examine your choice of Scenario 4 or 8 in the Appendix. How could *Cooperative Discipline* be used to improve behavior in Mrs. Desmond's second grade or Mr. Jaramillo's World History class?

REFERENCES AND RECOMMENDED READINGS

Albert, L. 1985. *Coping with kids and school.* New York: Ballantine.

———. 1992. *An administrator's guide to cooperative discipline.* Circle Pines, Minn.: American Guidance Service.

———. 1993. *Coping with kids.* Tampa, Fla.: Alkorn House.

———. 1994. *Bringing home cooperative discipline.* Circle Pines, Minn.: American Guidance Service.

———. 1994. *Responsible kids in school and at home: The cooperative discipline way.* Videotape Series. Circle Pines, Minn.: American Guidance Service.

———. 1996a. *A teacher's guide to cooperative discipline.* Circle Pines, Minn.: American Guidance Service.

———. 1996b. *Cooperative discipline.* Circle Pines, Minn.: American Guidance Service.

———. 1996c. *Cooperative discipline implementation guide: Resources for staff development.* Circle Pines, Minn.: American Guidance Service.

Albert, L., and M. Popkin. 1989. *Quality parenting.* New York: Ballantine.

Berne, E. 1964. *Games people play.* New York: Grove Press.

Dreikurs, R. 1957. *Psychology in the classroom.* New York: Harper and Row.

Gardner, H. 1983. *Frames of mind: The theory of multiple intelligences.* New York: Harper and Row.

Glasser, W. 1969. *Schools without failure.* New York: Harper and Row.

Glenn, H., and J. Nelsen. 1987. *Raising children for success.* Fair Oaks, Calif.: Sunshine Press.

Weiner, B. 1984. Principles for a theory of student motivation and their application within an attributional framework. In *Research on Motivation in Education: Student Motivation.* R. Ames and C. Ames, eds., Vol. 1. New York: Academic Press.

CHAPTER 7

Thomas Gordon's
Discipline as Self-Control

Thomas Gordon

PREVIEW OF GORDON'S WORK

Focus

- Participative management in the classroom and how it contributes to student self-control.
- Identification and clarification of interpersonal problems and determining problem ownership.
- Helping teachers acquire positive influence with students and make the best use of it.

Logic

- The most desirable kind of classroom discipline comes from students' inner sense of self-control.
- Authority can be used to control others, but is best used when it influences rather than controls.
- Neither punishment nor reward is effective in promoting lasting change in behavior.

Contributions

- Championed participative management, with teachers and students sharing decision making.

- Popularized the no-lose method of conflict resolution, which preserves self-esteem.
- Identified roadblocks to communication which suppress students' willingness to discuss problems.
- Demonstrated how to clarify problems, determine ownership, and deal with the problems.

Gordon's Suggestions

- Involve students in problem solving and decision making about class rules and procedures.
- Use the behavior window to identify interpersonal problems and determine their ownership.
- Use helping skills when students own the problem, confrontive skills when teachers own it.
- Learn to see misbehavior simply as student action that the teacher considers to be undesirable.

143

ABOUT THOMAS GORDON

Thomas Gordon, a clinical psychologist, is founder and director of Gordon Training International, possibly the largest human relations training organization in the world. He is known for pioneering the teaching of communication skills and conflict resolution methods to parents, teachers, youth, and managers of organizations. More than one million persons have taken his training programs worldwide.

Gordon is the author of eight books, including *Parent Effectiveness Training: A Tested New Way to Raise Responsible Children* (1970), *T.E.T.: Teacher Effectiveness Training* (1974), *P.E.T. in Action* (1976), and *Discipline That Works: Promoting Self-Discipline in Children* (1989). His books have been published in 27 foreign countries and have sold more than five million copies. In his books and training programs, Gordon offers parents and teachers strategies for helping children become more self-reliant, self-controlled, responsible, and cooperative.

Gordon, a Fellow of the American Psychological Association, has received numerous honors and has been a guest on the "Today Show," the "Tonight Show," "Donahue," and many other TV and radio programs. Catalogs and information about his programs are available from Gordon Training International, 531 Stevens Avenue West, Solana Beach, CA 92075; telephone 619-481-8121; e-mail GordonTrng@aol.com

GORDON'S CONTRIBUTIONS TO DISCIPLINE

Gordon's views first began receiving public attention in 1962 following his work with parents in a new program he called Parent Effectiveness Training (P.E.T.). Published research and his own work as a clinical psychologist convinced him that traditional power-based methods of discipline were ineffective in the long run. He determined that punitive methods more often than not created new problems that ranged from rebellion to withdrawal. He concluded, too, that praise and reward were notably ineffective in managing and changing student behavior. Gordon's reputation grew as parents trained in P.E.T. experienced improved relationships with their children and as word spread about his teachings concerning the value of cooperation instead of power and punishment in working with the young.

In order to help parents and teachers with their management efforts, Gordon created a graphic device he called *the behavior window.* This device helps teachers visualize situations and student behavior so that they may determine whether a problem exists, who owns it, and which skills should be applied to handle the situation.

Gordon devised a series of confrontive skills for teachers to use when they own the problem, helping skills to use when students own the problem, and preventive skills that are used to prevent the occurrence of possible problems. Gordon also described a participative style of classroom management where teachers and students share in planning and decision making.

Gordon's approach has helped lead to the current trend in school discipline which seeks to improve interactions between teachers and students and develop student responsibility and self-control. He believes that participative management helps students become more self-reliant, responsible, cooperative, and in control of their own behavior.

GORDON'S CENTRAL FOCUS

Gordon has taken a leadership role in the recent trend in school discipline that places primary emphasis on development of student responsibility and self-control. Like Richard Curwin and Allen Mendler (1988), William Glasser (1990), Kay Burke (1992), Alfie Kohn (1993), and Barbara Coloroso (1994), Gordon believes that effective discipline cannot be achieved through either coercion or reward and punishment but rather must be developed within the character of each individual.

As noted earlier, Gordon's ideas concerning discipline grew from his work in *Parent Effectiveness Training.* Parents began spreading the word about the effectiveness of Gordon's ideas, and soon schools began offering effectiveness training to teachers. That led to Gordon's giving direct attention to how teachers could best work with students in their charge. Gordon described the techniques he advocated in a book and concomitant training program called *Teacher Effectiveness Training.*

Gordon's 1989 book, *Discipline That Works,* was the culmination of ideas and techniques that grew within P.E.T. and T.E.T. After examining school discipline policies, Gordon concluded that the punitive actions prevalent in discipline harmed children by leading to self-destructive and antisocial behavior. He became convinced that punishment doled out by authoritarian adults could never lead to truly effective classroom discipline. But he was quick to state that permissiveness in dealing with children is just as misguided as authoritarianism. In place of power or permissiveness, Gordon offers middle-ground strategies designed to help children make positive decisions, become more self-reliant, and control their own behavior. Gordon (1989) summed up his concerns about current discipline practices and their results as follows:

> As a society we must urgently adopt the goal of finding and teaching effective alternatives to authority and power in dealing with other persons—children or adults—alternatives that will produce human beings with sufficient courage, autonomy, and self-discipline to resist being controlled by authority when obedience to that authority would contradict their own sense of what is right and what is wrong. (p. 98)

Gordon maintains that the only truly effective discipline is self-control that occurs internally in each child. The development of such self-control, he says, can be strongly assisted by teachers. To help children control their own behavior and become self-reliant in making positive decisions, teachers must first give up their "controlling" power. As Gordon (1989) says,

> You acquire more influence with young people when you give up using your power to control them . . . and the more you use power to try to control people, the less real influence you'll have on their lives. (p. 7)

Precisely how teachers acquire influence with students, and how they can best use that influence, is the central focus of Gordon's work.

GORDON'S PRINCIPAL TEACHINGS

Authority is a condition that enables one to exert influence or control over others. There are at least four kinds of authority:

Authority E is recognized expertise in a given matter.

Authority J is based on job description.

Authority C comes from contracts and agreements.

Authority P is the power to control others.

The first three forms of authority are sources of influence (which teachers should use), while authority P is a source of control (which teachers should avoid).

Noncontrolling methods of behavior change are available for teachers to use in influencing students to behave properly. Teachers do not have to resort to authoritative power or rewards and punishments.

A problem is a condition, event, or situation that troubles someone. A problem exists only when someone is troubled.

When an individual is troubled by a condition, event, or situation, that individual is said to "own" the problem. How problems are resolved depends in part upon who owns the problem.

Primary feelings are fundamental feelings that one experiences after observing another person's unacceptable behavior. For example, a teacher feels extremely worried (primary feeling) when a child runs from the playground into the street.

Secondary feelings are manufactured feelings that one senses following the resolution of a difficulty. For example, the teacher is very worried (primary feeling) about the child who ran onto the street, but once the child is brought back safely, the teacher reacts angrily (secondary feeling) because the child violated playground rules.

I-messages are statements in which people tell what they personally think or feel about another's behavior and its consequences. For example, the teacher is using an I-message when saying, "I am having trouble concentrating because there is so much noise in the room."

You-messages are statements of blame leveled at someone's behavior. For example, the teacher is using a you-message when saying, "You girls are making too much noise. You know better than that."

Confrontive I-messages are messages that attempt to influence another to cease an unacceptable behavior. The teacher is using a confrontive I-message when saying, "I'm pleased so many of you have something to share about this, but when everyone tries to talk at once, I can't hear what anyone has to say."

Shifting gears is a tactic that involves changing from a confrontive to a listening posture. This strategy is helpful when students resist the teacher's I-messages or defend themselves.

Students' coping mechanisms are strategies that students use to deal with coercive power. The three coping mechanisms are:

fighting (combating the person with whom they have the conflict)

taking flight (trying to escape the situation)

submitting (giving in to the other person).

Win–lose conflict resolution is a way of ending disputes (temporarily) by producing a "winner" and a "loser." This usually has a detrimental effect on the loser. For example, Samuel and Justin scuffle and Samuel is made to apologize to Justin, which supposedly resolves the conflict.

No-lose conflict resolution is a way of ending disputes by enabling both sides to emerge as "winners." For example, when Samuel and Justin get in a scuffle, the teacher takes them aside and asks sincerely, "I wonder what we might do, so that you boys won't feel like fighting any more?"

Door openers are words and actions that invite others to speak about whatever is on their minds. The teacher is using a door opener when asking Sheri, who appears to be upset, "Do you feel like telling me if anything is troubling you?"

Active listening involves carefully attending to and demonstrating understanding of what another person says. The teacher is using active listening when nodding and reflecting back what Bobby is saying.

Communication roadblocks are comments by well-meaning teachers that shut down student willingness to communicate. Examples of roadblocks include moralizing and telling the student what he or she ought to do.

Preventive I-messages attempt to forestall future actions that may later constitute a problem. For example, the teacher might say, "I really hope we can have a quiet room when the principal visits. Can you help us all remember things we can do to help keep the room quiet?"

Preventive you-messages (to be avoided) are used to scold students for past behavior. For example, the teacher might say, "You were very rude the last time our principal visited. You made me feel ashamed. I certainly hope you do better this time."

Participative classroom management permits students to share in problem solving and decision making concerning the classroom and class rules. This participation makes students more inclined to abide by rules they have helped formulate.

Problem solving is a process that should be taught and practiced in all classrooms. In problem solving, students help clarify problems, put forth possible solutions, select solutions that are acceptable to all, implement the solutions, and evaluate the solutions in practice.

ANALYSIS OF GORDON'S *DISCIPLINE AS SELF-CONTROL*

As you have seen, Gordon believes that good classroom discipline ultimately involves students' developing their own inner sense of self-control. The techniques he teaches are designed to help teachers promote self-control in students. He rejects as counterproductive the traditional intervention techniques of power-based authority and win–lose conflict resolution. He also strongly urges teachers not to use rewards or punishments to control student behavior. In order to understand Gordon's overall position more fully, let us examine what he has to say about authority, rewards and punishment, misbehavior, problem ownership, the behavior window, and teacher skills, including confrontive skills, helping skills, and preventive skills.

Authority

Authority is a condition that allows one to exert influence or control over others. Gordon teaches that there are four different kinds of authority:

1. **Authority E** (expertise) is inherent in a person's special knowledge, experience, training, skill, wisdom, and education. For example, your expertise as an artist enables you to exert influence over others in matters having to do with art.
2. **Authority J** (job) comes with one's job description. As principal of the school, your position enables you to influence educational decisions made by teachers, parents, and others.
3. **Authority C** (commitments, agreements, or contracts) comes from the daily interactions and subsequent understandings, agreements, and contracts that people make. When students actively participate in setting classroom rules, it strongly influences them to comply.
4. **Authority P** (power) is evident in a person's ability to control as opposed to influence others. For example, because of the power you have to give students low grades, you can make them do assignments they would not otherwise do.

Teachers who use authority E, J, or C exert positive influence on students. But when they use authority P to control students rather than influence them, their effectiveness is diminished. Gordon urges teachers to use **noncontrolling methods** of behavior change that are derived from authority J, C, and E.

Rewards and Punishment

Gordon (1989) summarizes his concerns about discipline based on **rewards** as follows:

> Using rewards to try to control children's behavior is so common that its effectiveness is rarely questioned. . . . the fact that rewards are used so often and unsuccessfully by so many teachers and parents proves they don't work very well. . . . The ineffectiveness of using rewards to control children is

due in part to the fact that the method requires such a high level of technical competence on the part of the controller—a level few parents or teachers can ever attain. (pp. 34–35)

Considering all of the precise conditions that must be met to make this complex method work and the inordinate amount of time it takes, I am convinced that behavior modification with rewards could never be a method of any practical use for either parents or teachers. (pp. 37–38).

What does Gordon see as negative effects of behavior modification? He says the following are likely to occur when rewards are used to influence behavior:

- Students become concerned only with getting the rewards, not with learning or behaving desirably.
- When rewards are removed, students tend to revert at once to undesirable behavior.
- When students accustomed to receiving rewards are not rewarded, they may equate the lack of reward with punishment.
- Students may receive stronger rewards from classmates for behaving improperly than from the teacher for behaving properly.

And why is **punishment** ineffective in producing self-discipline? According to Gordon, punishment's long-term negative effects include the following:

- Punished students experience feelings of belittlement, rage, and hostility.
- Punished students have a decreased desire to cooperate willingly with the teacher.
- There is an increased likelihood that punished students will lie and cheat in order to avoid punishment.
- Punishment engenders a false notion that might makes right.

What Is Misbehavior, and Who Owns the Problem?

Gordon (1976) sees **misbehavior** as an *adult concept* in which "a specific action of the child is seen by the adult as producing an *undesirable consequence for the adult*" (p. 107, italics added). It is the teacher, he says, not the student, who experiences the sense of "badness" in student behavior.

If students are to develop self-control, teachers must shift away from their traditional concept of misbehavior. Gordon says that teachers should begin by learning to identify correctly who owns a particular problem, the teacher or the student. The following example illustrates what Gordon means by **problem ownership:** When Kyla becomes morose because she feels other girls have slighted her, she sulks but doesn't bother anyone else. Because no one else is affected, Kyla "owns" the problem; it bothers her but causes no difficulty for teacher or classmates. Her behavior may in fact be entirely acceptable to the teacher, since the class work continues normally. But if Kyla decides to confront the other girls angrily, the resultant squabble causes difficulties for the teacher. Because the teacher is now troubled by the situation (students become inattentive and the lesson is disrupted), the teacher is said to own the problem. When owning a problem of this sort, the teacher feels obliged to deal with it and may take corrective action against Kyla in order to stop the disruption that has ensued.

The Behavior Window

Gordon created a graphic device called the **behavior window** to help clarify the concept of problem ownership. Teachers are taught to visualize student behavior through the behavior window, which shows who owns the problem, depending on whether teachers see the behavior as acceptable or unacceptable. The behavior window is shown in Figure 7.1.

The behaviors found in the top section of the behavior window in Figure 7.1 are acceptable to the teacher, though they are troublesome for the student. The student's needs are not being met, or the student is unhappy or frustrated or in trouble, but these behaviors do not much affect the teacher or other students in the class. For example, Mark's failure to appear for his scheduled drama audition (because he is overly self-conscious) affects only Mark, so Mark owns the problem. The drama teacher, Ms. Aldrice, will take no action against Mark, but if she is aware of his feelings, she may decide to speak with him using a helping skill such as active listening.

Behaviors found in the bottom section of the behavior window are unacceptable to the teacher; that is, they cause a problem for the teacher. At the drama auditions Mark heckles when others read for their parts. His behavior interferes with the tryouts. This bothers Ms. Aldrice, who now owns the problem, and it is up to her to try to change Mark's problem-causing behavior.

In the middle section of the behavior window in Figure 7.1 are student behaviors that are problem-free. Here the teacher and student work together pleasantly. Mark does not want to try out for the play but does want to help with set construction and lighting, which leaves him on good terms with Ms. Aldrice.

Behavior Window	Acceptability to Teacher
Student's behavior causes a problem for the student only. **Student owns the problem.**	Acceptable behavior
Student's behavior does not cause a problem for either student or teacher. **No problem.**	Acceptable behavior
Student's behavior causes a problem for the teacher. **Teacher owns the problem.**	Unacceptable behavior

Figure 7.1

Source: Adapted from P.E.T. in Action (pp. 27, 174, 251) by T. Gordon, 1976. New York: Random House.

The behavior window helps teachers understand problem ownership, but it should be understood that the window is not static. As Gordon (1976) explains, "You inevitably will be inconsistent from day to day, with your different moods, with different children, and in different environments" (p. 18). The window lines that demarcate behavior move in accordance with teacher mood (teacher is rested or upset), student behavior (student is quiet or careful, or aggressive or noisy), and the environment (indoors or outdoors, quiet time or group activity).

By understanding the behavior window and correctly identifying problem ownership, teachers can increase the likelihood of having effective interactions with students. Gordon describes three groups of skills that teachers can use when working with students—skills that apply not only to problem behaviors but to ongoing communication and interactions. Those skills are clustered into three groups.

1. **Confrontive skills,** such as modifying the environment, recognizing and responding to primary feelings, sending I-messages that do not set off the coping mechanisms students use in response to power, shifting gears, and practicing the no-lose method of conflict resolution, are used when the teacher owns the problem.
2. **Helping skills,** such as passive listening, acknowledgment, door openers, active listening, and avoiding communication roadblocks, are used when the student owns the problem.
3. **Preventive skills,** such as rule setting, preventive I-messages, and participative problem solving and decision making, are used when neither the teacher nor the student has a problem with the behavior.

Put another way, confrontive skills help teachers meet their own needs, helping skills assist students in meeting their needs, and preventive skills help ensure mutual satisfaction for both teacher and student. Let us turn now to the relationship between the three sections of the behavior window and their pertinent skill clusters.

Skill Cluster 1: Confrontive Skills
This skill cluster pertains to the bottom section of the behavior window, as shown in Figure 7.2. Gordon explains that teachers are most likely to take action first at the point where they own the problem.

In this instance, teachers can meet their needs by confronting the misbehavior, provided they do so in a positive, nonadversarial manner. Five skills comprise this cluster: (1) modifying the environment, (2) recognizing and responding to primary feelings, (3) sending I-messages that do not trigger the student's coping mechanisms, (4) shifting gears, and (5) using a no-lose method of conflict resolution.

1. Modifying the Environment (Rather than the Student). By **modifying the environment** through enriching it or by limiting its distractors, teachers may be able to eliminate or minimize problem behavior. To encourage student curiosity and learning, teachers can enrich the room with learning centers and colorful posters, student murals, and displays on the topic being studied. If these effects are too distracting for

Behavior Window	Skill Clusters
Student's behavior causes a problem for the student only. **Student owns the problem.**	Helping skills
Student's behavior does not cause a problem for either student or teacher. **No problem.**	Preventive skills
Student's behavior causes a problem for the teacher. **Teacher owns the problem.**	*Confrontive skills*

Figure 7.2
Source: Adapted from P.E.T. in Action *(pp. 27, 174, 251) by T. Gordon, 1976. New York: Random House.*

some students, teachers can provide an area without displays or have study carrels for students who occasionally need a more subdued atmosphere. Teachers can play quiet background music during certain activities and set up areas in the classroom where students study independently or in groups. If the teacher is bothered by the amount of student movement around the room during an art project, sets of supplies can be placed on the students' desks.

2. Identifying and Responding to One's Own Primary Feelings. In intense situations, people often sense fear, worry, disappointment, or guilt; sometimes these **primary feelings** emerge later as anger. Gordon believes such anger is a manufactured **secondary feeling** that arises as a consequence of the primary feeling. When Maria and Susanna quarrel heatedly in class, Miss Maple feels like shouting at them in return. But by pausing, Miss Maple allows herself to realize that she is not so much angry at the girls as disappointed that they show no concern for all the time she has spent talking about this problem in class. So that her disappointment will not be expressed as a secondary feeling of anger, Miss Maple can use an I-message to let the girls know of her disappointment.

3. Sending I-Messages Regularly. When teachers own a problem because student behavior interferes with their needs or rights, instead of scolding students they should express their feelings through I-messages. Complete **I-messages** communicate three things: (1) the behavior that is presenting a problem for the teacher, (2) what the teacher is feeling about the behavior, and (3) why the behavior is causing a problem. Mrs. Watson's I-message is clear: "When class rules are broken as they are now, I feel upset because that keeps us from getting our work done and shows lack of consideration for others."

I-messages contrast with you-messages. I-messages describe situations and teacher feelings and are therefore relatively nonhurtful to students. **You-messages,** on the other hand, carry heavy judgments and put-downs, evident in statements such as "You've been very careless with this work" or "Shame on you for tattling" or "Can't you follow simple directions?"

A special kind of I-message—the **confrontive I-message** is used to ask students for help and suggestions. The teacher may say, "When I have to wait too long for quiet and readiness, I have to rush through the directions, and then I have to spend more time repeating myself because the directions are not clear. Do you have any suggestions that might help me with this problem?"

4. Shifting Gears. Sometimes the teacher's I-messages provoke defensive responses from students. When teachers see this happen, it is important that they listen sensitively to the resistance and change from a sending/assertive posture to a listening/understanding posture, a change that prompts students to react more positively. Gordon calls this change from assertion to listening **shifting gears.** The change usually improves the likelihood of reaching an acceptable solution, because students feel their needs are being considered and that the teacher understands how they feel. When Mr. Johnson sends a confrontive I-message to Marcos about his irregular attendance, Marcos heatedly responds, "School is not the only thing. I have responsibilities at home. I can't help missing class sometimes." Shifting gears, Mr. Johnson replies, "It sounds like you have some difficult things to deal with outside of school. Is there anything I can do to help?"

Sometimes when I-messages do not work, teachers resort to power to change the student's behavior. This is not likely to be effective because students will in turn resist the controlling power, using **coping mechanisms,** which Gordon identifies as fighting, taking flight, and submitting. For some individuals, the first inclination is one of *fighting* the person with whom they are in conflict. If, however, they see they are unlikely to win the fight, or if they perceive the consequences of fighting as too severe (i.e., harsh punishment or physical or psychological hurt), they will tend to avoid the conflict by *taking flight* from it altogether. If unwilling to fight and unable to escape (as is the case when teachers impose punitive discipline), students generally respond by *submitting.* But they do not do so acceptingly. Indeed, most students would rather lie, cheat, or place blame elsewhere than to accept punishment and loss of dignity. If punished, they are likely to harbor resentment for a long time.

5. Using the No-Lose Method of Conflict Resolution. When conflict occurs in the classroom, as it inevitably will, Gordon urges teachers to defuse the situation and bring about a solution acceptable to everyone. This can be done, Gordon says, by using a no-lose method to help resolve the conflict.

To see how the **no-lose method of conflict resolution** works, let us first consider the result of **win–lose conflict resolution.** Ego is on the line, and when the conflict is resolved, one person emerges as "winner" and the other as "loser." Suppose Mrs. Penny insists that Marta complete her assigned work before leaving the classroom. Marta complains that she cannot work fast enough to complete it and that it is unfair to make her stay longer than the other students. Mrs. Penny, who thinks Marta procrastinates, says, "You can either complete your work or take a grade of F on the assignment. It is your choice." Marta stays until she finishes but is seething with resentment. In this conflict, Mrs. Penny emerges as winner and Marta as loser, or so it would seem. In reality both may have lost, because their working relationship may have been ruined.

Instead of win–lose conflict resolution, Gordon advocates the no-lose method in resolving conflicts. This approach enables both sides to find a mutually acceptable solution to their disagreement. By avoiding use of power, egos are preserved, work continues, and personal relations are undamaged. In this approach, Marta and Mrs. Penny talk about what each feels and about what is causing them to get upset with each other. Then they seek a solution acceptable to both, such as allowing Marta extra time to complete her work in class. This same procedure works well when teachers mediate conflicts between students.

Skill Cluster 2: Helping Skills

This skill cluster applies to the top section of the behavior window, as shown in Figure 7.3, where the student owns the problem. Gordon's helping skills include (1) listening skills and (2) methods for avoiding communication roadblocks.

1. Using Listening Skills. Teachers should always listen carefully to students, especially to the problems they voice. But when doing so they should not attempt to solve students' problems for them. Instead of telling students what they ought to do, teachers should make use of four *listening skills,* which Gordon calls passive listening (silence), acknowledgment responses, door openers (invitations), and active listening.

Passive Listening. Often nothing but attentive silence is enough to encourage students to talk about what is bothering them. With passive listening, the teacher shows attention through posture, proximity, eye contact, and alertness as the student speaks. Mr. Aragon demonstrates this skill when he sits down beside Julian as the boy begins to speak of difficulties at home.

Acknowledgment Responses. Acknowledgment responses can be verbal ("uh-huh", "I see") or nonverbal (nods, smiles and frowns, and other body movements). They demonstrate the teacher's interest and attention. Mrs. Heck smiles and nods as Chris tells his story about his family's recent trip to Washington, D.C.

Door Openers. Door openers are invitations to students to discuss their problems. When the student needs encouragement, the teacher may say, "Would you like to talk about it?" or "It sounds like you have something to say about that." These comments are nonjudgmental and open-ended, and as they are nonthreatening, they invite

Behavior Window	Skill Clusters
Student's behavior causes a problem for the student only. **Student owns the problem.**	*Helping skills*
Student's behavior does not cause a problem for either student or teacher. **No problem.**	Preventive skills
Student's behavior causes a problem for the teacher. **Teacher owns the problem.**	Confrontive skills

Figure 7.3

Source: Adapted from P.E.T. in Action (pp. 27, 174, 251) by T. Gordon, 1976. New York: Random House.

the student to talk. Sensing that Eduardo is distressed about the math assignment, Mr. Sutton invites him to discuss his concerns: "I think there might be something bothering you about this assignment, Eduardo. Would you like to talk about it?"

Active Listening. Active listening involves teachers' mirroring back what students are saying. It confirms that the teacher is attentive and understands the student's message. No judgment or evaluation is made. The teacher simply helps the student verbalize problems and feelings clearly: "You've been late to class this week because you've been working the closing shift at the restaurant, and that makes you so tired you sleep through your alarm."

2. Avoiding Communication Roadblocks. Gordon points out that when teachers try to communicate with students, they often set up inadvertent roadblocks that shut off student willingness to talk. He goes to some lengths to help teachers learn to recognize and avoid setting up these **roadblocks to communication,** which are 12 in number: giving orders, warning, preaching, advising, lecturing, criticizing, name-calling, analyzing, praising, reassuring, questioning, and withdrawing. The following examples involving the 12 roadblocks show how a teacher might respond ineffectively or effectively. At student Del's middle school, all students are required to take physical education. Del, who is very self-conscious about his weight, detests physical education and has been offering various excuses in hopes that he won't be forced to participate.

When *giving orders,* the teacher tries to help by directing Del on what to do: "You might as well stop complaining about things you can't control. Go ahead and get ready now." A more effective response might be "Do you see any way I might be able to make this easier for you?"

When *warning,* the teacher threatens Del: "That's enough. Change into your PE clothes now, or I'll have you running laps." A more effective response might be "I can see this matter is bothering you a great deal. Would you like to discuss it after school?"

When *preaching,* the teacher reminds Del of "shoulds" and "oughts": "You ought to know that exercise is important. You should try to get yourself in shape." A more effective response might be "Some people like to exercise and others don't. How do you think we might help you get the exercise you need?"

When *advising,* the teacher tries to help by offering Del suggestions or giving solutions: "If you feel you can't keep up with the others, try setting your own personal goal and work to meet it." A more effective response might be "Sometimes even good athletes don't like PE classes. Have you heard any of them discuss their feelings?"

When *lecturing,* the teacher presents logical facts to counter Del's resistance: "I can assure you that if you develop a habit for exercise now, you will be pleased and will carry it with you for the rest of your life." A more effective response might be "Sometimes it is certainly tempting to stop exercising and just sit out the class. If you do, what effect do you think it might have on your health?"

When *criticizing,* the teacher points out Del's faults and inadequacies: "I can't believe you just said that. That kind of excuse-making is pitiful." A more effective response might be "I think I'm beginning to understand what you are saying. Could you tell me a bit more about that?"

When *name-calling,* the teacher labels or makes fun of Del: "I might expect third graders to argue about dressing out for PE. Aren't you a bit huge for third grade?"

A more effective response might be "Frankly, I haven't understood exactly why you are reluctant. Can you help me understand a bit better?"

When *analyzing,* the teacher diagnoses or interprets Del's behavior: "What you are really saying is that you are afraid others will laugh about your weight." A more effective response might be "Go ahead with that thought. Can you explain it further?"

When *praising,* the teacher uses positive statements and praise to encourage Del: "You have above-average coordination. You'll handle yourself real well out there." A more effective response might be "I understand your concern. What might I do to make physical education more enjoyable for you?"

When *reassuring,* the teacher tries to make Del feel better by offering sympathy and support: "I know how you feel. Remember, there are a lot of boys just like you. You will forget your concerns after a little while." A more effective response might be "Have you known other students with concerns like yours? How did they deal with them?"

When *questioning,* the teacher probes and questions Del for more facts: "What exactly are you afraid of? What do you think is going to happen?" A more effective response might be "We often anticipate the worst, don't we? Have you had other experiences like this that troubled you?"

When *withdrawing,* the teacher changes the subject in order to avoid Del's concerns: "Come on, now. Enough of that kind of talk. It's time to get ready and get out there." A more effective response might be "Do you think this matter might be bothering others, too? Do you think I should talk to the class about it, or would you rather keep it between us?"

Skill Cluster 3: Preventive Skills

This skill cluster is used in connection with the middle, or no problem, section of the behavior window as shown in Figure 7.4. Specific preventive skills addressed by Gordon include (1) preventive I-messages, (2) collaborative rule setting, and (3) participative classroom management, all of which contribute to maintaining harmonious relationships within the classroom.

1. Using Preventive I-Messages. **Preventive I-messages** influence students' future actions and thus help avoid problems. The teacher might say, "Next week we're going

Behavior Window	Skill Clusters
Student's behavior causes a problem for the student only. **Student owns the problem.**	Helping skills
Student's behavior does not cause a problem for either student or teacher. **No problem.**	*Preventive skills*
Student's behavior causes a problem for the teacher. **Teacher owns the problem.**	Confrontive skills

Figure 7.4

Source: Adapted from P.E.T. in Action (pp. 27, 174, 251) by T. Gordon, 1976. New York: Random House.

on our field trip. I need to make sure we all have a good time and don't have any problems. I'd like everyone to be sure to stay together so no one gets lost." By contrast, **preventive you-messages** such as "You behaved very badly on our last field trip, so I hope you can do better this time" are to be avoided.

2. Setting Rules Collaboratively. Gordon reminds us that rules are necessary in order to make classrooms safe, efficient, and harmonious. He believes those rules should be formulated collaboratively by teacher and students through discussions of what each wants and needs. In a democratic manner, everyone agrees to the rules mutually. **Collaborative rule setting** is similar to the no-lose method of conflict resolution in that students and teachers both win because everyone's needs receive attention.

3. Using Participative Classroom Management. Gordon believes that the most effective classrooms are those in which teachers share power and decision making with their students. He suggests **participative classroom management** in which teachers and students make joint decisions about class rules, room arrangement, seating, and preferred activities. That style of management motivates students, gives them greater confidence and self-esteem, and encourages them to take risks and behave more responsibly.

As part of participative management, Gordon (1989) recommends a process of **problem solving** through which teachers show students how to solve problems and make good decisions. The steps in the problem-solving process are as follows:

1. *Step 1. Identify and define the problem or situation.* Good solutions depend on accurate identification of the problem at hand. Questions that should be asked at the beginning include "What is really going on here?" "What problems are we having?" "What exactly do we need to solve or do?" and "Is there another deeper problem here?"
2. *Step 2. Generate alternatives.* Once the problem is clarified, a number of possible solutions should be generated. To help bring forth ideas, questions and statements such as the following are usually helpful: "What can we do differently to make our work easier or better?" "What rules or procedures do we need to follow?" "Let's see how many ideas we can come up with" and "Are there still more solutions we can think of?"
3. *Step 3. Evaluate the alternative suggestions.* When alternatives have been specified, participants are asked to comment on them. The goal is to choose a solution that is agreeable to all. Thus it is appropriate to ask for each proposal, "What do you think of this suggestion?" "What are its advantages and disadvantages?" "What problems does it leave unsolved?" and "If we try this idea, what do you think will happen?"
4. *Step 4. Make the decision.* Alternatives are examined. The one that seems to suit most people best is selected for trial.
5. *Step 5. Implement the solution or decision.* The trial solution is put into place with the understanding that it may or may not work as anticipated and that it can be changed if necessary.
6. *Step 6. Conduct a follow-up evaluation.* The results of the trial solution or decision are analyzed and evaluated. Helpful questions include "Was this a

good decision?" "Did it solve the problem?" "Is everyone happy with the decision?" and "How effective was our decision?" If the solution or decision is judged to be satisfactory, it is kept in place. If unsatisfactory, a modified or new solution is proposed and put to the test.

INITIATING GORDON'S *DISCIPLINE AS SELF-CONTROL*

Suppose it is the beginning of the school year. You like Gordon's ideas and want to use them in your discipline system. What exactly do you do during the first days to put the Gordon model into place? Gordon does not specify how his program should be introduced, but the following steps are implied. (You would use language and demonstrations appropriate for your students.)

1. *Step 1. Identify student behaviors that will help, and those that will hinder, learning in your classroom.* Are these behaviors most likely to occur during large group, small group, or individual activities? When is silence desirable? When is quiet talking helpful? When is group discussion and interaction needed? When is movement in the room necessary?

    It is also important to think about your own needs concerning student behavior. How much noise can you tolerate? What degree of formal respect do you want students to show to you and to each other? To what extent do you need to structure students' behavior? May they speak out, or should they raise their hands first? How do you expect them to enter and exit the classroom? How much neatness and order do you require?
2. *Step 2. Discuss your concerns with the class.* On the first day, describe the curriculum and general expectations concerning work and behavior, but make a point also of asking for student input, to which you give serious consideration as suggested in participative management. In this process, you involve students in clarifying the conditions and working relationships that will make the class profitable and enjoyable. It is important that you use active listening and keep communication open. When students disagree over certain points, you can implement the problem-solving process to help them reach agreement. To culminate this phase, make a written summary of class agreements and post a copy in the classroom.
3. *Step 3. Help students learn to function in keeping with the class agreements.* This requires frequent reminders and perhaps practice and role playing. You will need to use preventive, helping, and confrontive skills as suggested by problem ownership. As the weeks pass, you will help students become increasingly self-disciplined as you demonstrate, in daily practice, your own self-discipline, flexibility, and ability to communicate and solve problems.

STRENGTHS OF GORDON'S *DISCIPLINE AS SELF-CONTROL*

By identifying specific alternatives and strategies to promote self-discipline in children, Gordon gives teachers a new strategy for helping students become self-reliant decision makers who exercise control over their own behavior. He moves away from the punitive/permissive extremes of discipline. He shuns behavior management based on reward and punishment and in its place proposes noncontrolling alternatives for influencing, not forcing, student behavior.

But while Gordon's suggestions are well received, many teachers, especially those whose classes are hard to manage, do not picture students to be as well intentioned as Gordon seems to imply. Those teachers will be reluctant to abandon discipline techniques that, though controlling of students, nevertheless maintain order and allow instruction to occur.

A second concern has to do with whether teachers can easily acquire the skills that Gordon advocates. The Gordon model requires that teachers reconceptualize student behavior as "misbehavior" only when it presents a problem for the teacher. They must be able to examine problems and identify who owns them. They must be good listeners who can help students open up. They must be able to use clear I-messages that reveal their feelings in reaction to behavior. They must be able to shift gears from sending I-messages to listening in order to support successful problem solving. They must be willing to provide a participative classroom and share decision making with students. And they must continually model the decision-making process. Is it realistic to expect that the average, overburdened teacher can or will attempt the significant change of attitude that is needed and, moreover, acquire and implement such an array of new skills? Gordon feels that although the process may be difficult, it is essential. Increasingly, educators seem to agree with him.

REVIEW OF SELECTED TERMINOLOGY

The following terms are central to the Gordon model of discipline.

acknowledgment responses	modifying the environment
active listening	no-lose conflict resolution
authority	noncontrolling methods
authority C	participative management
authority E	passive listening
authority J	preventive skills
authority P	preventive I-messages
behavior window	preventive you-messages
collaborative rule setting	primary feelings
communication roadblocks	problem ownership
confrontive skills	problem solving
confrontive I-messages	punishment
coping mechanisms	rewards
door openers	secondary feelings
helping skills	shifting gears
I-messages	win–lose conflict resolution
misbehavior	you-messages

APPLICATION EXERCISES

CONCEPT CASES

Case 1: Kristina Will Not Work

Kristina, in Mr. Jake's class, is quite docile. She never disrupts class and does little socializing with other students. But despite Mr. Jake's best efforts, Kristina rarely completes an assignment. She doesn't seem to care. She is simply there, putting forth virtually no effort.

How would Gordon deal with Kristina? Gordon would suggest the following sequence of interventions:

> Recognize that it is the teacher who owns the problem, not Kristina.
>
> Don't try to force Kristina to complete the assignments.
>
> Use I-messages to convey teacher concern to Kristina.
>
> Encourage Kristina to communicate about the assignments. Use active listening skills as she does so. Ask her how you can help.
>
> Invite Kristina into a collaborative problem-solving exploration of why she doesn't work, and see if she has suggestions she wishes to make.
>
> Use I-messages to convey to the entire class how important it is that everyone, teacher and students alike, completes the work expected of them in school. But don't single out Kristina.

Case 2: Sara Cannot Stop Talking

Sara is a pleasant girl who participates in class activities and does most, though not all, of her assigned work. She cannot seem to refrain from talking to classmates, however. Her teacher, Mr. Gonzales, has to speak to her repeatedly during lessons, to the point that he often becomes exasperated and loses his temper.

What suggestions would Gordon give Mr. Gonzales to help with Sara's misbehavior?

Case 3: Joshua Clowns and Intimidates

Joshua, larger and louder than his classmates, always wants to be the center of attention, which he accomplishes through a combination of clowning and intimidation. He makes wise remarks, talks back (smilingly) to the teacher, utters a variety of sound-effect noises such as automobile crashes and gunshots, and makes limitless sarcastic comments and put-downs of his classmates. Other students will not stand up to him, apparently fearing his verbal and physical aggression. His teacher, Miss Pearl, has come to her wit's end.

What do you find in Gordon's work that might help Miss Pearl deal with Joshua?

Case 4: Tom Is Hostile and Defiant

Tom has appeared to be in his usual foul mood ever since arriving in class. On his way to sharpen his pencil, he bumps into Frank, who complains. Tom tells him loudly to shut up. Miss Baines, the teacher, says, "Tom, go back to your seat." Tom wheels around and says heatedly, "I'll go when I'm damned good and ready!"

How would Gordon have Miss Baines deal with Tom?

QUESTIONS AND ACTIVITIES

1. Describe how you would use the problem-solving process with your English class if they expressed concern about having too many projects, papers, and other assignments due at about the same time.

2. Refer to Scenario 2 in the Appendix. Which of Gordon's ideas do you think could best be used to improve Mr. Platt's interactions with student Arlene?

3. Refer to Scenario 4 in the Appendix. Explain how Gordon's ideas might be used to improve conditions in Mrs. Desmond's second-grade class.

4. Which type of authority is most evident in each of the following teacher statements?
   a. "Mr. Youngblood is a member of the Kiowa tribe. He is visiting our class today to share some of the legends of his people."
   b. "Class, I expect you to work quietly and finish before the bell. If not, you'll stay in for recess."
   c. "Officer Santos is with the police department. This morning she will talk to us about what you should do when a stranger tries to talk to you on the street.

5. Decide which of the following statements reflects 1) modifying the environment, 2) participative management, 3) confrontive I-message, or 4) preventive I-message.
   a. "Before we start our art project, let's talk about what we will need to do with the paints and brushes so we have enough time for cleanup before the bell rings."
   b. "Let's sit in our Jungle Hut today, and I'll turn down the lights while I read this story."
   c. "I am feeling tired, so let's all stand up. Is everyone ready? Good. Simon says . . ."
   d. "I feel so disappointed when I see one of my students being disrespectful to another."

REFERENCES AND RECOMMENDED READINGS

Burke, K. 1992. *What to do with the kid who . . . : Developing cooperation, self-discipline, and responsibility in the classroom.* Palatine, Ill.: IRI/Skylight.

Coloroso, B. 1994. *Kids are worth it! Giving your child the gift of inner discipline.* New York: William Morrow.

Curwin, R., and A. Mendler. 1988. *Discipline with dignity.* Alexandria, Va.: Association for Supervision and Curriculum Development.

Dewey, J. 1938. *Logic: The theory of inquiry.* New York: Holt, Rinehart & Winston.

Glasser, W. 1986. *Control theory in the classroom.* New York: Harper & Row.

———. 1990. *The quality school: Managing students without coercion.* New York: Perennial Library. (Reissued with additional material in 1992)

Gordon, T. 1970. *Parent Effectiveness Training: A tested new way to raise responsible children.* New York: New American Library.

———. 1974. *T.E.T.: Teacher Effectiveness Training.* New York: David McKay.

———. 1976. *P.E.T. in action.* New York: Bantam Books.

———. 1989. *Discipline that works: Promoting self-discipline in children.* New York: Random House.

Kohn, A. 1993. *Punished by rewards: The trouble with gold stars, incentive plans, A's, praise, and other bribes.* Boston: Houghton Mifflin.

CHAPTER 8

Jane Nelsen, Lynn Lott, and H. Stephen Glenn's *Positive Discipline in the Classroom*

Jane Nelsen

Lynn Lott

H. Stephen Glenn

PREVIEW OF NELSEN, LOTT, AND GLENN'S WORK

Focus

Joy for learning together with responsible student behavior that results from

- Acceptance of self and others;
- Humane, dignified regard for self and others; and
- A learning environment that encourages rather than discourages and humiliates.

Logic

- Students can and will learn to behave with dignity, self-control, and concern for others.
- These desirable traits develop in classrooms that are accepting, encouraging, and supportive.
- The vehicle that best promotes these conditions and learnings is the class meeting.

Contributions

- A strategic approach to positive classroom interaction, rather than a packaged system.
- Rationale for how teachers can stop directing students and begin working with them.

Nelsen, Lott, and Glenn's Suggestions

- Students must learn to see themselves as capable, significant, and able to control their own lives.
- Students need to develop important intrapersonal, interpersonal, strategic, and judgmental skills.
- These outcomes are best fostered by caring teachers who emphasize them in class meetings.
- Teachers must replace barriers to communication with builders of communication.

ABOUT JANE NELSEN, LYNN LOTT, AND H. STEPHEN GLENN

Jane Nelsen, Lynn Lott, and H. Stephen Glenn are educators who now do much of their work within a commercial organization called "Empowering People." The primary purpose of Empowering People is to help adults and children learn to accept themselves, accept others, behave responsibly, and contribute to the betterment of the groups of which they are members. The three have a total of more than 85 years of experience in teaching, lecturing, counseling, and writing. Their book *Positive Discipline in the Classroom* (1993, rev. ed. 1997) is intended to help teachers establish learning climates that foster responsibility, mutual respect, and cooperation. They believe that such climates do away with most of the discipline problems teachers otherwise encounter, since students learn the value, for themselves, of respect and helpfulness toward others.

Nelsen has authored a number of books, including her best-selling *Positive Discipline* (1987, 1996), *Raising Self-Reliant Children in a Self-Indulgent World* (coauthored with H. Stephen Glenn, 1989), and *Positive Discipline: A Teacher's A–Z Guide* (coauthored with several others). Lott has coauthored several works with Jane Nelsen, including *Positive Discipline for Teenagers* (1991) and *Positive Discipline for Parenting in Recovery* (1992, 1996). Glenn, in addition to his writings, has produced a number of video series with titles such as *Introduction to Developing Capable People* (1989), *Six Steps to Developing Responsibility* (1989), and *Teachers Who Make a Difference* (1989). Jane Nelsen, Lynn Lott, and H. Stephen Glenn can be contacted at Empowering People, P.O. Box 1926, Orem, UT 84059-1926. Tel. 1-800-879-0812. Internet page http://www.empoweringpeople.com

NELSEN, LOTT, AND GLENN'S CONTRIBUTIONS TO DISCIPLINE

Nelsen, Lott, and Glenn's main contribution is not a new set of techniques for controlling misbehavior, but rather an approach to discipline that puts faith in students' ability to control themselves, cooperate, assume responsibility, and behave in a dignified manner. They believe that these desirable traits grow especially well in groups that hold class meetings on a regular basis. Concerns of students or teacher are written regularly into a notebook and become agenda items for class meetings. In those meetings, everyone participates in attempting to resolve the problem in a manner that is satisfactory to all concerned, and in the process learns important life skills.

NELSEN, LOTT, AND GLENN'S CENTRAL FOCUS

Nelsen, Lott, and Glenn focus on developing classrooms where students are treated respectfully and are taught the skills needed for working with others. They stress the necessity of classrooms where students (1) never experience humiliation when they fail, but instead learn how to turn mistakes into successes, (2) learn how to cooperate with teachers and fellow students to find joint solutions to problems, and (3) are provided an environment that instills excitement for life and learning in place of fear, discouragement, and feelings of inadequacy.

NELSEN, LOTT, AND GLENN'S PRINCIPAL TEACHINGS

Discipline problems gradually become insignificant in classrooms where there is a climate of acceptance, dignity, respect, and encouragement.

Students need to perceive themselves as capable, significant, and in control of their own lives. These perceptions grow best in classes that hold regular class meetings.

Students need to develop skills of self-control, adaptability, cooperation, and judgment. These skills are also best developed in class meetings.

Teachers must show that they truly care about their students. This is necessary if the desired perceptions and skills are to develop properly.

Teachers demonstrate caring by showing personal interest, talking with students, offering encouragement, and providing opportunities to learn important life skills.

Teachers can greatly facilitate desirable student behavior by removing barriers to good relationships with students and replacing them with builders of good relationships. By simply avoiding certain barriers, teachers quickly realize great improvement in student behavior.

Class meetings should emphasize participation by everyone, group resolution of problems, and win/win solutions. They should also be a situation where everyone, teacher and students alike, practices communication, respect, support, encouragement, and cooperation.

ANALYSIS OF NELSEN, LOTT, AND GLENN'S *POSITIVE DISCIPLINE IN THE CLASSROOM*

Positive Discipline in the Classroom is intended to empower students at all levels to become more successful, not only in the classroom, but in all walks of life. The underlying belief in this approach is that discipline problems can be greatly diminished as students acquire the skills of accepting others, communicating effectively, showing respect, and maintaining a positive attitude.

The vehicle through which these skills and attitudes are best developed is the **class meeting.** The authors contend that class meetings are uniquely suited to teaching students social skills such as listening, taking turns, hearing different points of view, negotiating, communicating, helping one another, and taking responsibility for their own behavior. The authors believe that academic skills are strengthened in the process, as well, because students must practice language skills, attentiveness, critical thinking, decision making, and problem solving, all of which enhance academic performance.

Class meetings alter students' perception of teachers by helping students see teachers and other adults as people who need nurturing and encouragement just as much as they do. When teachers involve themselves as partners with students in class meetings, a climate of mutual respect is encouraged. Teachers and students listen to one another, take each other seriously, and work together to solve problems for the benefit of all. Antagonisms usually seen in the classroom tend to fade away.

The Significant Seven

Nelsen, Lott, and Glenn have identified three perceptions and four skills that, as they develop, comprise the special benefits of *Positive Discipline in the Classroom*. They call these perceptions and skills the **significant seven,** which they describe as follows:

The Three Empowering Perceptions
Class meetings help students develop **three perceptions** about themselves that lead to success in life. Those three perceptions are:

1. Perception of *personal capabilities.* (I have ability; I can do this.)
2. Perception of *significance in primary relationships.* (I am needed; I belong.)
3. Perception of *personal power* to influence one's life. (I have control over what happens to me.)

The Four Essential Skills
Class meetings help students develop **four essential skills** that contribute significantly to success in life:

1. Intrapersonal skill. (I understand my emotions and can control myself.)
2. Interpersonal skill. (I can communicate, cooperate, and work with others.)
3. Strategic skill. (I am flexible, adaptable, and responsible.)
4. Judgmental skill. (I can use my wisdom to evaluate situations.)

Developing the Significant Seven

Perception of Personal Capability
Being listened to and acknowledged for contributions builds a sense of personal capability. Class meetings provide a safe climate where students can express themselves and be listened to without concern about success or failure.

Perception of Significance in Primary Relationships
Primary relationships in the classroom refer to those between student and teacher and between student and student. The perception of personal significance develops when others listen to one's feelings, thoughts, and ideas and take them seriously. This occurs naturally in class meetings, where everyone has the opportunity to voice opinions and give suggestions.

Perception of Power and Influence over One's Own Life
Class meetings emphasize encouragement coupled with accountability. They permit students to make mistakes in a safe atmosphere, take responsibility for the mistakes, and learn from them without being judged negatively for what they say. This helps students give up a **victim mentality** in which they blame others ("The teacher has it in for me.") and accept an **accountability mentality** in which they accept personal responsibility ("I received an F because I didn't do the work."). They also learn that even when they can't control what happens, they *can* control their own responses and their resultant actions.

Intrapersonal Skills

Young people seem more willing to listen to one another than to adults. They gain understanding of their personal emotions and behavior by hearing feedback from their classmates. In a nonthreatening climate, young people are willing to be accountable for their actions. They learn to distinguish between their feelings and their actions, that is, that what they feel (anger) is separate from what they do (hit someone), and that while feelings are always acceptable, some actions are not.

Interpersonal Skills

Class meetings encourage students to develop **interpersonal skills** by means of dialogue, sharing, listening, empathizing, cooperating, negotiating, and resolving conflicts. Teachers, instead of stepping in and resolving problems for students, can suggest putting the problem on the class meeting agenda, where everyone can work to solve it together.

Strategic Skills

Students develop **strategic skills,** the ability to adapt to problems, by responding to the limits and consequences imposed by everyday life. Through the problem-solving process, they learn alternative ways to express or deal with their thoughts or feelings.

Judgmental Skills

Young people develop **judgmental skills,** the ability to evaluate situations and make good choices, when they have opportunity and encouragement to practice doing so. This process is fostered in class meetings which put emphasis on effort rather than on success or failure. There, students find themselves in a setting that allows them to make mistakes safely, learn, and try again.

The Importance of Caring

The approach to discipline advocated by Nelsen, Lott, and Glenn requires that teachers truly care about students' welfare and that such caring be made evident. Teachers show they care when they go out of their way to learn about students as individuals, encourage them to see mistakes as opportunities to learn and grow, and have faith in their ability to make meaningful contributions. Students know teachers care when they feel listened to and their thoughts and feelings are taken seriously.

Barriers to Relationships

Certain teacher behaviors act as barriers to developing caring relationships with students, while other behaviors help build such relationships. Nelsen, Lott, and Glenn identify five pairs of contrasting behaviors, which they call barriers and builders. **Barriers** are behaviors that are disrespectful and discouraging to students, whereas **builders** are behaviors that are respectful and encouraging, as explained in the following paragraphs.

***Barrier 1:* Assuming, *vs Builder 1:* Checking**

All too often teachers *assume* they know what students think and feel without asking them, what they can and cannot do, and how they should or shouldn't respond. Teachers then deal with students on the basis of those assumptions. When they do so, however, they prevent students' unique capabilities from becoming evident. It is greatly preferable that teachers determine what students actually think and feel, which is done by *checking* with them instead of assuming.

***Barrier 2:* Rescuing/Explaining, *vs Builder 2:* Exploring**

Teachers wish to be helpful to students. They usually think they are when they explain things, rescue students from difficulties, or do some of their work for them. Students progress better, however, when allowed to perceive situations for themselves and proceed accordingly. Elementary teachers explain and rescue, for example, when they say, "It's cold outside, so don't forget your jackets." They help explore when they say, "Take a look outside. What do you need to remember in order to take care of yourself?"

***Barrier 3:* Directing, *vs Builder 3:* Inviting/Encouraging**

Teachers do not realize they are being disrespectful to students when they say, "Pick that up." "Put that away." "Straighten up your desk before the bell rings." But such commands have many negative effects: They build dependency, eliminate initiative and cooperation, and encourage students to grudgingly do as little as possible. Directives of this type stand in contrast to *inviting and encouraging* students to become self-directed. Instead of commanding, the teacher might say, "The bell will ring soon. I would appreciate anything you might do to help get the room straightened up for the next class."

***Barrier 4:* Expecting, *vs Builder 4:* Celebrating**

It is important that teachers hold high expectations of students and believe in their potential. However, when students are judged for falling short of expectations, they become easily discouraged, as when teachers say, "I was expecting more maturity from you." "I thought you were more responsible than that." Students respond far better when teachers look for improvements to which they can call attention. This celebration of improvement is quite motivating to students.

***Barrier 5:* "Adult-isms," *vs Builder 5:* Respecting**

Nelsen, Lott, and Glenn use the term adult-ism for teacher statements that tell students what they *ought to do,* such as: "How come you never . . . ?" "Why can't you ever . . . ?" "I can't believe you would do such a thing!" These adult-isms produce guilt and shame rather than support and encouragement. Such statements can be eliminated in favor of helping students understand differences in how people perceive things. Instead of saying, "You knew what I wanted on this project!" a teacher could say, "What is your understanding of the requirements for this project?" Nelsen, Lott, and Glenn (1993, p. 18) flatly state:

> We guarantee 100% improvement in student–teacher relationships when teachers simply learn to recognize barrier behaviors and stop demonstrating

them. Where else can you get such a generous return for ceasing a behavior? And when the builders are added, the payoff is even greater.

In addition to concentrating on builders in lieu of barriers, teachers can do a number of other things to show that they care about their students, such as:

- Using a supportive tone of voice.
- Listening to students and taking them seriously.
- Acting as though they enjoy their jobs.
- Appreciating the uniqueness of individual students.
- Developing an appropriate attitude (e.g., eagerly looking forward to helping students).
- Showing a sense of humor.
- Showing interest in and respect for students' outside interests.
- Involving students in making decisions about the class and curriculum.
- Looking for improvement, not perfection in student work and behavior.

Eight Building Blocks to Effective Class Meetings

As you have seen, class meetings are the primary venue for identifying and implementing the caring, supportive, and cooperative climate that is the goal of *Positive Discipline in the Classroom*. Nelsen, Lott, and Glenn maintain that training in **eight building blocks** for effective class meetings is the surest route to the kind of classroom climate desired by both students and teachers. Each of the building blocks focuses on a particular skill. According to Nelsen, Lott, and Glenn, it takes about two hours to introduce the eight building blocks to students. After that, about four additional class meetings will be needed to give adequate attention to what they entail. The eight building blocks are:

1. Form a circle.
2. Practice compliments and appreciation.
3. Create an agenda.
4. Develop communication skills.
5. Learn about separate realities.
6. Recognize the four reasons people do what they do.
7. Practice role playing and brainstorming.
8. Focus on nonpunitive solutions.

Nelsen, Lott, and Glenn say that before beginning to explore the building blocks with the class, teachers should introduce the concept of class meetings to their students and get the students to buy into the idea. This can be approached by telling students you would like to begin holding class meetings where they can express their concerns and use their power and skills to help make decisions. Elementary students, they say, are usually eager to try class meetings, but middle school and high school students may need some persuading. If they don't buy into the plan, they may try to sabotage it. A way to begin is, using language appropriate for your grade level, initiate a discussion about power, about how problems are usually handled in school (with punishment and reward), and about how that method results in teachers telling kids what to do. The kids then either comply or rebel, without being brought into the decision-making process. To encourage discussion, Nelsen, Lott, and Glenn (1993, p. 33) suggest asking students:

> "Who has an example they would like to share about what happens when someone tries to control you? What do you feel? What do you do? What do you learn? How do you try to control or manipulate others, including teachers?" Kids will usually say that they feel angry or scared and manipulated. What they learn is to rebel or comply.

> Ask them if they would like to be more involved in the decisions that affect their lives. Would they be willing to do the work required to come up with win/win solutions? Point out that some students actually *prefer* having adults boss them around, so that they can rebel. Other students like having adults direct them, so they don't have to take responsibility themselves. It takes more time and personal responsibility from everyone to use class meetings effectively. Make it clear that you don't intend to waste time teaching and learning a respectful method if they prefer continuing with the usual disrespectful method in which the teacher has control and a student's only options are to comply, rebel, and/or spend time in detention. This kind of discussion is especially helpful and effective in classrooms where students have been taught with authoritarian methods.

Nelsen, Lott, and Glenn advise that once students indicate support for classroom meetings, the next step is to decide when the meetings will be held. Preferences vary from weekly half-hour meetings to three shorter meetings per week. A meeting every day is advisable for the first week, as students learn the eight building blocks.

Building Block 1: Form a Circle
The first step in implementing class meetings is to establish an atmosphere that allows everyone an equal right to speak and be heard and where **win/win solutions** can take place. A circular seating arrangement serves best. Ask students for suggestions about forming the circle, listen to them, and write their ideas on the board. Make decisions based on their suggestions.

Building Block 2: Practice Compliments and Appreciations
It is important to begin class meetings on a positive note, which can be accomplished by having students and teacher say complimentary things to each other. Students have difficulty giving and receiving compliments. Practice helps. Ask them to recall when someone said something that made them feel good about themselves. Let them share their examples with the group. Then ask them to think about something they would like to thank others for, such as thanking a classmate for lending a pencil or eating lunch together. See if they can put their feelings into words.

Receiving compliments is often as difficult as giving them. Probably the best response to a compliment is a simple "Thank you." The notion of giving and receiving compliments seems embarrassing to some middle school students. When that is the case, use the term *show appreciation* instead of compliment.

Building Block 3: Create an Agenda
All class meetings begin with a specific agenda. When students and teachers experience concerns, they jot them down in a special notebook, at a designated time such as when leaving the room. The class meeting will address only the concerns that appear in the notebook.

Building Block 4: Develop Communication Skills
Nelsen, Lott, and Glenn suggest a number of activities for developing communication skills such as taking turns speaking (begin by going around the circle and letting each person speak), listening attentively to what others say, learning to use **I-statements** (saying I think, I feel, and so forth), seeking solutions to problems rather than placing blame on others, showing respect for others by never humiliating or making judgments about them, learning how to seek and find win/win solutions to problems, and framing conclusions in the form of "we decided," showing it was a group effort and conclusion.

Building Block 5: Learn about Separate Realities
In this building block, teachers focus on helping students understand that not everyone is the same or thinks the same way. Nelsen, Lott, and Glenn describe an approach to this skill segment that poses situations involving turtles, lions, eagles, and chameleons, showing that each has special talents as well as limitations. This activity should be made appropriate to the age level of students.

Building Block 6: Recognize the Four Reasons People Do What They Do
Ask students if they have ever wondered why people do what they do. Ask for their ideas, acknowledge them, and then ask if they have ever heard of the four mistaken goals of misbehavior. Proceed by using examples to illustrate the mistaken goals of undue attention, power, revenge, and giving up (see Dreikurs, Chapter 2).

Building Block 7: Practice Role Playing and Brainstorming
By the third class meeting, students are usually ready to begin considering problems and seeking solutions to them. Suggestions for exploring problems in a tactful manner involve discussions about the problem, role playing in which students act out roles involved in the problem, brainstorming in which a number of possible solutions are sought for the difficulty, and allowing students to select a solution that will work to solve the problem.

Building Block 8: Focus on Nonpunitive Solutions
Ask students the following and write their answers on the board: "What do you want to do when someone bosses you? What do you want to do when someone calls you names or puts you down? When others do these things to you, does it help you behave

better?" Then ask them how their behavior is affected when someone is kind to them, helps them, or provides stimulation and encouragement. Have them compare their answers, which you have written on the board. Use the comparison to draw attention to the value of encouragement versus punishment.

Tell the students that you intend never to punish them, and that when they do something wrong you will try to help them behave more appropriately. Explain that what you will do to help will always be *related* to what they have done wrong, *respectful* of them as persons, and *reasonable*. These are what Nelsen, Lott, and Glenn (1993, p. 81) call the **Three R's of Solutions.** They explain the concept this way:

> If students don't do their homework, sending them to the office is not related to missed homework. A *related* solution might be to have them make up the homework or not get points for that assignment. *Respectful* means supporting the solution with dignity and respect: "Would you like to make up the homework assignment at home or right after school?" *Reasonable* means you don't add punishment such as, "Now you'll have to do twice as much."

Beyond Consequences

Nelsen, Lott, and Glenn caution that it is easy to misuse logical consequences, pointing out that well-meaning teachers often perpetuate the use of punishment, giving it the new label of logical consequences. They urge teachers always to think in terms of solutions rather than consequences. The following illustrates their point (Nelsen, 1997, p. 8):

> During a class meeting, students in a fifth grade class were asked to brainstorm logical consequences for two students who didn't hear the recess bell and were late for class. Following is their list of consequences:
>
> 1. Make them write their names on the board.
> 2. Make them stay after school that many minutes.
> 3. Take away that many minutes from tomorrow's recess.
> 4. No recess tomorrow.
> 5. The teacher could yell at them.
>
> The students were then asked to forget about consequences and brainstorm for solutions that would help the students be on time. The following is their list of solutions:
>
> 1. Someone could tap them on the shoulder when the bell rings.
> 2. Everyone could yell together, "Bell!"
> 3. They could play closer to the bell.
> 4. They could watch others to see when they are going in.
> 5. Adjust the bell so it is louder.
> 6. They could choose a buddy to remind them that it is time to come in.

The difference between these two lists is profound. The first looks and sounds like punishment. It focuses on the past and making kids "pay" for their mistake. The second list looks and sounds like solutions that focus on helping the kids do better in the future. It focuses on seeing problems as opportunities for learning. In other words, the first list is designed to hurt; the second is designed to help.

Among Nelsen, Lott, and Glenn's other suggestions for moving beyond consequences are:

1. *Involve students in the solutions.* When students participate in finding solutions to behavioral problems, they strengthen communication and problem-solving skills. They are also more likely to abide by agreements they have helped plan. Because they are made to feel part of the classroom community, they have less reason to misbehave and are more willing to work on solutions to problems.

2. *Focus on the future instead of the past.* When teachers apply logical consequences, they often are likely to be focusing on the past, on the behavior the student has already committed. Rather than that, teachers should ask students to look to the future, thinking of solutions that will improve conditions in days to come.

3. *Make connections between opportunity, responsibility, and consequence.* Nelsen, Lott, and Glenn do not say that students should never experience logical consequences. Students need to learn that every new opportunity they encounter brings with it a related responsibility. If students are unwilling to take on the responsibility, they should not be allowed the opportunity. Nelsen, Lott, and Glenn (1997) illustrate this point as follows: Elementary students have the opportunity to use the playground during recess. Their related responsibility is to treat the equipment and other people with respect. If they treat things or people disrespectfully, the logical consequence is losing the opportunity of using the playground. A way to instill a sense of responsibility in students who have been given a consequence is to say, "You decide how much time you think you need to cool off and calm down. Let me know when you are ready to use the playground respectfully." Nelsen, Lott, and Glenn remind us that consequences are effective only if they are enforced respectfully and students are given another opportunity as soon as they are ready for the responsibility.

4. *Be sure you don't piggyback.* To piggyback is to add something to a consequence that isn't necessary and may actually be hurtful, such as, "Maybe this will teach you!" or, "You can just sit there and think about what you did!" Teachers who use piggybacking make punishment out of what would otherwise be a solution, or even a respectful consequence.

5. *Plan solutions carefully in advance.* A good way to prevent punishment's creeping into solutions is to plan out the solution in advance, with student collaboration. During a class meeting, ask students to think about what sort of solutions would actually help them learn. Make the questions specific, such as, "What kind of solution do you think would help any of us to remember to use the school equipment respectfully?" "What do you think a helpful solution would be when we return books late to the library?"

Standard Format for Class Meetings

This is the format that class meetings should follow:

1. *Express compliments and appreciations.* Each session begins in this way as a means of setting a positive tone.
2. *Follow-up on earlier solutions applied to problems.* Any suggested solution is to be tried only for a week, so it is important to determine if the solution has been working. If it hasn't, the class may wish to put the issue back on the agenda for future problem solving.
3. *Go through agenda items.* When an agenda item is read, ask the person (student or teacher) with the issue if he or she still wants help with it. If so, ask that person what a satisfactory solution could be. If he or she can't think of any, go around the circle giving every student an opportunity to offer a suggestion. Ask the student to select the most helpful solution from the suggestions offered.
4. *Make future plans for class activities.* End the class meeting by discussing a fun activity for the entire class at a future date. For example, the class might decide to set aside some time on Friday to discuss an upcoming event, view a videotape, or complete homework assignments with a friend.

Remember That the Process Takes Time

When new procedures are implemented, it often takes some time for them to function smoothly. Nelsen, Lott, and Glenn say that if students do not respond to class meetings with the enthusiasm one had hoped for, don't be discouraged. Trust in the procedure; it will eventually come together. Although class meetings seem difficult at first, they will get better with practice, just like any academic skill.

Respectful Classroom Management

Nelsen, Lott, and Glenn continually emphasize mutual respect. They make suggestions such as:

1. *Limit the choices you give to students.* Teachers should provide students with choices that are appropriate and acceptable. **Appropriate choices** are those that further the educational program. Instead of saying, "What do you want to do first this morning?" teachers should say "We can begin with our directed work or our group discussion—which do you prefer?" An **acceptable choice** is one that you, the teacher, deem worthwhile, no matter which alternative the students choose. Do not provide unacceptable choice options to students.
2. *Ask students to use a problem-solving process to settle disputes.* A **four-step problem-solving process** should be introduced for this purpose and its steps posted in the room:
   a. Ignore the situation.

   b. Talk it over respectfully with the other student.

   c. Find a win/win solution.

   d. (If no solution is agreed to) Put it on the class meeting agenda.

   Nelsen, Lott, and Glenn (1993, p. 111) explain the steps as follows:

> Step 1 encourages students to avoid involvement or to leave the area of conflict for a cooling-off period. Step 2 is an opportunity for students to tell each other how they feel, to listen to and respect their own feelings, to figure out what they did to contribute to the problem, and to tell the other person what they are willing to do differently. Step 3 could involve brainstorming for solutions or simply apologizing. Step 4 lets students know it's okay to ask for help.
>
> When students come to you with a problem, refer them to the Four Problem-Solving Steps chart, and ask if they have tried any of the steps. If they haven't tried any, ask which one they would like to try. This keeps you out of the "fix-it" role.

3. *When you cannot wait for a class meeting, follow through immediately.* At times, kind and firm action is called for. In ten words or less, identify the issue and redirect the student's behavior. "I need your help to keep the noise down."

4. *When conflict occurs, ask students about it rather than telling them what to do.* Teachers tend to tell students what happened, why it happened, how they should feel about it, and what they should do. Instead of telling, they should ask students their perception of why it happened, how they feel about it, and how they could use that information next time. This encourages students to use judgment and be accountable for their actions. Nelsen, Lott, and Glenn say whenever you feel like telling students, stop yourself and *ask.* This is usually enough to get students to think about their behavior and decide what ought to be done.

5. *Use questions that redirect behavior.* Certain questions cause students to think about what they are doing and decide on better behavior. For example, the teacher might say, "How many of you think it is too noisy in here for people to concentrate? How many do not?"

6. *Be willing to say no with dignity and respect.* It is all right to say no. Many teachers don't think they have the right to say no without giving a lengthy explanation, but often a kind and succinct No is all that is required.

7. *Act more, but talk less.* Most teachers would be amazed if they could hear the number of useless words they speak. It is better to let one's behavior do the talking. Use hand signals, body posture, and facial expressions.

8. *Put everyone in the same boat.* It is almost impossible to identify the culprit and judge behavior correctly in every situation that arises. When some students are talking and others are not, say, "It is too noisy in here." If someone says, "It wasn't me; I wasn't doing anything wrong," simply say, "I'm not interested in finding fault or pointing fingers but in getting the problem resolved."

Putting It All Together

Teachers who wish to replace authoritarian methods with democratic ones must realize that it will be some time before the process runs efficiently. These efforts are for long-term quality, not short-term convenience. Have faith that students and teachers can cooperate happily with each other. When putting class meetings into practice, be willing to give up *control over* students in favor of gaining *cooperation with* students. Forego lecturing in favor of asking questions about students' thoughts and opinions. When students are encouraged to express themselves and are given choices, they are better able to use group problem solving, cooperation, and collaboration.

STRENGTHS OF *POSITIVE DISCIPLINE IN THE CLASSROOM*

Nelsen, Lott, and Glenn provide a discipline program intended to help students behave responsibly and realize that they have positive control over their own lives. They do not believe that either punishment or praise serves to develop self-directed people. They do believe that each problem is an opportunity for learning and that students learn important life skills when they help each other find positive solutions to problems. As the major device through which to implement their suggestions, they advocate regular and frequent use of class meetings, which they feel afford the best opportunity for group discussions, identification of problems, and pursuit of solutions. They give many suggestions for making the meetings work effectively within the daily class program.

Although Nelsen, Lott, and Glenn provide lists of suggestions and cautions, the discipline system they advocate is not highly structured. Much leeway remains for teachers to adapt it to their needs and realities. This will be seen as a strength by teachers who like the ideas but want to incorporate them in their own preferred ways. It may be seen as a weakness by other teachers who are looking for a structure they can put into place quickly and that will bring immediate results. The Nelsen, Lott, and Glenn system will require some time for organizing and for student acclimatization. Therefore, its results may be somewhat slow in coming, but will probably be more permanent than those achieved in discipline systems based on reward and punishment.

INITIATING *POSITIVE DISCIPLINE IN THE CLASSROOM*

The Nelsen, Lott, and Glynn model of discipline depends largely on the implementation of effective class meetings, included as an integral part of the instructional program. Those meetings make it possible to involve students in discussions about curriculum and behavior and to secure their input in making decisions about behavior and solutions. They also furnish a venue for practicing many of the skills of communication, problem-solving, and conflict resolution that Nelsen, Lott, and Glynn advocate. Therefore, a teacher wishing to implement *Positive Discipline in the Classroom* must at least give serious thought to setting up class meetings and using the typical agenda suggested for them. This is best introduced at the beginning of the year or semester, but can be done at any time not too near the end of the year or class. Implementing this plan will take time, but will help students develop skills of getting along with others that will last their entire lives. And it may be that any lost academic time will be regained once students begin behaving helpfully so that instruction is not disrupted.

REVIEW OF SELECTED TERMINOLOGY

The following terms are central to understanding the Nelsen, Lott, and Glenn model of discipline.

acceptable choice

accountability mentality

appropriate choices

barriers

builders

class meetings

eight building blocks

four essential skills

four-step problem solving

I-statements

interpersonal skills

intrapersonal skills

judgmental skills

significant seven

strategic skills

three R's of solutions

three perceptions

victim mentality

win/win solutions

APPLICATION EXERCISES

CONCEPT CASES

Case 1: Kristina Will Not Work

Kristina, a student in Mr. Jake's class, is quite docile. She socializes little with other students and never disrupts lessons. However, despite Mr. Jake's best efforts, Kristina will not do her work. She rarely completes an assignment. She is simply there, putting forth no effort at all.

How would Nelsen, Lott, and Glenn deal with Kristina? They would advise Mr. Jake to do the following: In a regular class meeting, go around the circle and ask students to brainstorm solutions to help students who do not complete their work. Write down every suggestion. When finished, ask a volunteer to read the suggestions. Allow students to choose the best solution, such as working with a buddy. Ask Kristina to try the solution for a week and report back in a class meeting how it is working. If she begins to do her work, give her a compliment in the class meeting. If she does not, ask her at the end of the week if she would like to put the problem on the agenda again to receive more suggestions from the class. It is rare that students do not follow through on suggestions they choose.

Case 2: Sara Cannot Stop Talking

Sara is a pleasant girl who participates in class activities and does most, though not all, of her assigned work. She cannot seem to refrain from talking to classmates, however.

Her teacher, Mr. Gonzales, has to speak to her repeatedly during lessons, to the point that he often becomes exasperated and loses his temper.

What suggestions would Nelsen, Lott, and Glenn give Mr. Gonzales for dealing with Sara?

Case 3: Joshua Clowns and Intimidates

Joshua, larger and louder than his classmates, always wants to be the center of attention, which he accomplishes through a combination of clowning and intimidation. He makes wise remarks, talks back (smilingly) to the teacher, utters a variety of sound-effect noises such as automobile crashes and gunshots, and makes limitless sarcastic comments and put-downs of his classmates. Other students will not stand up to him, apparently fearing his size and verbal aggression. His teacher, Miss Pearl, has come to her wit's end.

Would Joshua's behavior be likely to improve if Nelsen, Lott, and Glenn's techniques were used in Miss Pearl's classroom? Explain.

Case 4: Tom Is Hostile and Defiant

Tom has appeared to be in his usual foul mood ever since arriving in class. On his way to sharpen his pencil, he bumps into Frank, who complains. Tom tells him loudly to shut up. Miss Baines, the teacher, says, "Tom, go back to your seat." Tom wheels around, swears loudly, and says heatedly, "I'll go when I'm damned good and ready!"

How would Nelsen, Lott, and Glenn have Miss Baines deal with Tom?

QUESTIONS AND ACTIVITIES

1. Each of the following exemplifies an important point in the Nelsen, Lott, and Glenn model of discipline. Identify the point illustrated by each.
   a. Miss Sterling, when Jacob interrupts her for the fifth time, says angrily, "Jacob, you go sit at the back table by yourself and stay there until you figure out how to act like a gentleman!"
   b. "If I catch you talking again during the class, you will have to stay an extra five minutes."
   c. "I am concerned about the lack of neatness in the work being turned in. I'd like to know your thoughts about neatness and what we might want to do, if anything, to improve.
   d. Teacher: "You are simply not working up to the standards I have for this class. You will need to put in more effort, or else I will have to increase the homework assignments."
2. Examine Scenarios 4 and 9 in the Appendix. How could *Positive Discipline in the Classroom* be used to improve behavior in (1) Mrs. Desmond's second grade? (2) Mr. Wong's American literature class?
3. For a grade level and/or subject you select, outline in one page what you would do if you wished to implement Nelsen, Lott, and Glenn's ideas in your classroom.

REFERENCES AND RECOMMENDED READINGS

Adler, A. 1958. *What life should mean to you.* New York: Capricorn.

Glenn, H. 1989. *Developing capable people.* (Audiotape Set). Fair Oaks, Calif.: Sunrise Productions.

———. 1989. *Empowering others: Ten keys to affirming and validating people.* (Videotape). Fair Oaks, Calif.: Sunrise Productions.

———. 1989. *Six steps to developing responsibility.* (Videotape). Fair Oaks, Calif.: Sunrise Productions.

———. 1989. *Teachers who make a difference.* (Videotape). Fair Oaks, Calif.: Sunrise Productions.

Glenn, H., and J. Nelsen. 1988. *Raising self-reliant children in a self-indulgent world.* Rocklin, Calif.: Prima.

Nelsen, J. 1987, 1996. *Positive discipline.* New York: Ballantine.

———. 1997. No more logical consequences—At least hardly ever! Focus on solutions. *Empowering People Catalog,* Winter/Spring, 8.

Nelsen, J., R. Duffy, L. Escobar, K. Ortolano, and D. Owen-Sohocki. (1996). *Positive discipline: A teacher's A–Z guide.* Rocklin, Calif.: Prima.

Nelsen, J., L. Lott, and H. Glenn. 1993, 1997. *Positive discipline in the classroom.* Rocklin, Calif.: Prima.

Positive discipline in the classroom. 1997. *The Video Journal of Education,* 6(7). Issue.

CHAPTER 9

William Glasser's
Noncoercive Discipline

*William
Glasser*

PREVIEW OF GLASSER'S WORK

Focus

■ Increasing student satisfaction with school as a deterrent to misbehavior.

■ Teachers' changing themselves from boss teachers to lead teachers.

■ Emphasizing quality in curriculum, teaching, and learning.

Logic

■ Most misbehavior occurs because students are bored or frustrated by school expectations.

■ Students whose basic needs are being met show comparatively little misbehavior.

■ The best curriculum concentrates on what students consider important in their lives.

■ The most effective teaching is done in a leading manner rather than a bossing manner.

Contributions

■ The concept and practice of classroom meetings as a regular part of the curriculum.

■ The focus on meeting students' basic needs as the key element in good discipline.

■ The concepts and practices of quality curriculum, quality teaching, and quality learning.

Glasser's Suggestions

■ To the extent possible, help meet students' needs for belonging, freedom, power, and fun.

■ Establish quality as the prime ingredient in all aspects of teaching, learning, and curriculum.

■ Seek to work with students in a role of lead teacher, rather than boss teacher.

■ Learn nonpunitive, noncoercive techniques for motivating students to work and participate.

ABOUT WILLIAM GLASSER

William Glasser, a psychiatrist and educational consultant, has for many years written and spoken extensively on issues related to education and discipline. Born in Cleveland, Ohio, in 1925, he was first trained as a chemical engineer but later turned to psychology and then to psychiatry. He first achieved national acclaim in psychiatry for the theories expressed in his book *Reality Therapy: A New Approach to Psychiatry* (1965), which shifted the focus in treating behavior problems from past events to present reality. Glasser later extended reality therapy to the school arena. His work with juvenile offenders convinced him that teachers could help students make better choices about their school behavior. He explained how to do that in his book *Schools without Failure* (1969), acclaimed as one of the century's most influential books in education. In 1986, Glasser published *Control Theory in the Classroom*, which gave a new and different emphasis to his contentions concerning discipline, as encapsulated in his pronouncement that if students are to continue working and behaving properly, they must "believe that if they do some work, they will be able to satisfy their needs enough so that it makes sense to keep working" (p. 15). Since the publication of that book, Glasser has emphasized the school's role in meeting basic needs as the primary means of encouraging participation and desirable behavior. This theme is furthered in his 1992 book *The Quality School: Managing Students Without Coercion*. Because of its historical importance, a synopsis of Glasser's earlier work is presented in this chapter. Major emphasis is given, however, to his more recent work. Glasser can be contacted through the Institute for Reality Therapy, 7301 Medical Center Drive, Suite 104, Canoga Park, CA 91307; telephone 818-888-0688; fax 818-888-3023.

GLASSER'S CONTRIBUTIONS TO DISCIPLINE

Glasser has greatly influenced thought and practice in school discipline. He was the first to say unreservedly that students are in control of their behavior, that no unseen factors are forcing them to do this or that, and that in fact they actually choose to behave as they do. He claimed that it should be recognized that good choices result in good behavior, while bad choices result in bad behavior. He insisted, further, that teachers have the power and the obligation to help students make better behavioral choices, and he provided numerous suggestions about how to interact with students to help them succeed. He set forth the concept of **classroom meetings,** now universally acclaimed, in which teacher and students jointly discuss, and find solutions to, problems of behavior and other class matters. These contributions were all made in Glasser's earlier work.

Since 1985, Glasser has made many new contributions to thought and practice in discipline. His contention that discipline depends upon meeting students' basic needs for belonging, freedom, fun, and power, is revolutionary. Furthering that theme, he has contributed the concepts of quality curriculum, quality learning, and quality teaching, depicting all of them as important, if not essential, in discipline.

GLASSER'S CENTRAL FOCUS

Prior to 1985, Glasser's main focus, as we have seen, was on helping students make good **behavior choices** that would lead to personal success in the classroom and elsewhere. That early work had great impact on school discipline, and you will probably recognize several of his teachings incorporated into the Canter, Jones, and Albert models of discipline (Chapters 4, 5, and 6, respectively).

Since 1985, Glasser's views on discipline have changed markedly. Previously he depicted the school as a benevolent place that provides unbounded opportunities for students, and he placed responsibility on students for taking advantage of those opportunities. Now, given the fact that student effort has declined and behavior has steadily grown worse, Glasser has concluded that improvement in education and student behavior can only be accomplished by changing the way classrooms function. Consequently, his present work focuses on strategies that motivate students to participate willingly in the school program. He says this approach is essential because it is now evident that attempts to force students to behave properly will not succeed.

Glasser also maintains that if schools are to survive, they must be redesigned to emphasize quality in all student work. They must no longer attempt to coerce students, a tactic that is clearly ineffective. Instead, teachers must lead students deeply into learning that addresses what is important in students' lives. Glasser therefore urges teachers to make sure that curricular activities work to satisfy students' **basic needs** for survival, belonging, power, fun, and freedom. Glasser has moved away from tactics he advocated in earlier work for confronting student misbehavior, feeling that if students cannot be enticed willingly into learning, it is fruitless to try to make them behave in an orderly manner; they will simply drop out of learning, figuratively if not literally.

GLASSER'S PRINCIPAL TEACHINGS

Prior to 1985

Students are rational beings who can control their behavior. They choose to act the way they do. Their behavior, though influenced by societal or familial conditions, is not outside their control.

Good choices equal good behavior, while bad choices equal bad behavior. Behavior is almost always a matter of choice.

Teachers must always try to help students make good choices throughout each day. Teachers must strive continually to show the relationship of choice to behavior, and to help students learn to make good choices.

Teachers who truly care about their students accept no excuses for bad behavior. Students who misbehave usually make excuses or blame outside conditions for how they have acted. Teachers should not accept these excuses but, rather, help offending students to make better choices.

Teachers must see to it that reasonable consequences always follow student behavior, good or bad. When students choose to behave properly, they should be acknowledged for doing so. When they choose to misbehave, they should suffer reasonable consequences.

It is essential that every class have a workable list of rules to govern behavior and that those rules be consistently enforced. Teachers should involve students in formulating rules and consequences, but it is the teacher's responsibility to enforce compliance with the rules.

Classroom meetings are effective vehicles for addressing matters of class rules, behavior, and consequences. Such meetings of the entire class should be conducted regularly, with teacher and students sitting together in a closed circle, an arrangement that has come to be known as the Glasser circle. The purpose of classroom meetings is never to find fault or assign blame but only to seek solutions to problems that concern the class.

Since 1985

All of our behavior is our best attempt to control ourselves to meet five basic needs. Those basic needs are continually to satisfy survival, belonging, power, fun, and freedom. The school experience is intimately associated with all but survival, and not infrequently with survival as well.

Students feel pleasure when their basic needs are met and frustration when they are not. Students are usually contented and well-behaved when their needs are being met, but discontented and often misbehaving when their needs are not being met.

At least half of today's students will not commit themselves to learning if they find their school experience boring, frustrating, or otherwise dissatisfying. Furthermore, there is no way that teachers can make students commit to learning, though they can often force compliance with directions temporarily.

Few students in today's schools do their best work. The overwhelming majority is apathetic about schoolwork. Many do none at all.

Today's schools must create quality conditions in which fewer students and teachers are frustrated. Students must feel they belong, enjoy a certain amount of power, have some fun in learning, and experience a sense of freedom in the process.

What schools require is a new commitment to quality education. Quality education occurs in quality schools, where students are encouraged, supported, and helped by the teacher.

The school curriculum should be limited to learnings that have usefulness or other relevance in students' lives. This usefulness or relevance is the hallmark of quality curriculum, which is delivered through activities that attract student interest, involve students actively, provide enjoyment, and lead to meaningful accomplishments.

Students should be allowed to acquire in-depth information about topics they recognize as being useful or relevant in their lives. This results in quality learning.

Students show that quality learning has occurred when able to demonstrate or explain how, why, and where their learnings are valuable. The opportunity for making such explanations should be made a part of daily classroom activities.

Teachers, instead of scolding, coercing, or punishing, should try to befriend their students, provide encouragement and stimulation, and show an unending willingness to help. Their ability to do so is a mark of quality teaching.

Teachers who dictate procedures, order students to work, and berate them when they do not, are increasingly ineffective with today's students. These are known as boss teachers.

Teachers who provide a stimulating learning environment, encourage students, and help them as much as possible are most effective with today's learners. These are known as lead teachers.

ANALYSIS OF GLASSER'S *NONCOERCIVE DISCIPLINE*

What School Offers

In his earlier views on discipline, Glasser contended that school offered students an excellent opportunity to encounter success and be recognized. Indeed, he said, for many students school afforded the only real possibility for meeting those needs. Success in school produced a sense of self-worth and an identity of being successful, both of which mitigate deviant behavior. The road to this identity begins with good relationships with people who care. For students who come from atrocious backgrounds, school may be the only place where they will find adults who are genuinely interested in their well-being. Yet students often resist entering into quality relationships with their teachers. They may fear teachers, distrust adults in general, or obtain peer rewards by disdaining teachers. Teachers must therefore be very persistent, never waning in their efforts to help students make better **behavior choices.** Glasser maintained that students cannot begin to make better, more responsible choices until they become involved emotionally with people who regularly make such choices in their own lives—people such as teachers.

In keeping with these views, Glasser (1978) said teachers should do the following:

- Stress **student responsibility** in making good choices, showing that students must live with the choices they make.
- Establish **class rules** that lead to success. Glasser considered class rules essential and wrote disparagingly of teachers who tried to function without them in the mistaken belief that rules stifle initiative, self-direction, and responsibility. Rules should be formulated jointly by teacher and students and should always emphasize that students are in school to study and learn.
- Accept no **excuses.** A teacher who accepts an excuse says, in effect, that it is all right to break a commitment, that it is all right for students to harm themselves. Teachers who care about their students accept no excuses.
- Call for **value judgments.** When students misbehave, they should be required to make judgments about their actions.

- Suggest suitable alternatives. If a student is unable to think of alternatives to the inappropriate behavior, the teacher should suggest two or three possibilities and encourage the student to select one of them.
- Invoke reasonable **consequences** following student behavior. Glasser stressed that reasonable consequences should follow any behavior the student chooses. Consequences should be desirable to the student when good behavior is chosen and undesirable when poor behavior is chosen. The knowledge that behavior always brings consequences, desirable or undesirable, helps students take charge of their lives and control their own behavior.
- Be persistent. Caring teachers work toward one major goal: getting students to commit themselves to desirable courses of behavior. They must always help students make choices and have them make value judgments about their bad choices.
- Continually review the discipline system. Glasser said that any discipline system should be reviewed periodically and revised as necessary.

You can see that in Glasser's earlier work, he depicted the school in a very positive light. While acknowledging that students encounter problems there, he maintained that schools afford students the best—often the only—opportunity to associate with quality adults who genuinely care about them. He believed that it is in school that students enjoy the best opportunity many will ever have for finding belonging, success, and positive self-identity. In order to help students take advantage of this crucial opportunity, teachers should continually ask them to make value judgments about their misbehavior and urge students to make choices and plans that improve their chances for success. At the same time, teachers should see to it that students receive the consequences of whatever behavior they choose, good or bad.

Glasser's Views Today

Today, Glasser remains concerned about student behavior in the classroom, but his focus has moved away from tactics for maintaining discipline and toward **quality education,** in which students engage themselves willingly in the curriculum and therefore have little reason to misbehave. These new views have grown from his realization that the majority of students at this time are quite satisfied to do low-quality work or even no work at all in school. He states (Glasser 1986) that "No more than half of our secondary school students are willing to make an effort to learn, and therefore cannot be taught," (p. 3) and further, "I believe [in light of student apathy] that we have gone as far as we can go with the traditional structure of our secondary schools" (p. 6). What we must find, he says, is a way to improve instruction. He earlier determined that ". . . no more than 15 percent of high school students do quality work." (Glasser 1990, p. 5). He insists that this situation must be changed ". . . so that a substantial majority do high-quality schoolwork: Nothing less will solve the problems of our schools." (Glasser 1990, p. 1).

The solution that Glasser proposes involves stimulating students to work while providing encouragement and assistance that helps meet students' needs. This requires only modest changes in curricula, materials, and physical facilities but a significant change in the way teachers work with students. Glasser (1990) contends that teaching effectively is the hardest job in the world and expresses sympathy for beleaguered secondary teachers who yearn to work with dedicated, high-achieving students but who are continually frustrated by the majority who make little effort to learn. Those teachers report that their main discipline problems are not defiance or disruption but, rather, students' overwhelming apathy and resigned unwillingness to participate in classroom activities and assignments. Students, for their part, tell Glasser that the problem with schoolwork is not its difficulty; the problem is that it is too boring (Glasser 1990). For Glasser, this means that schoolwork does not meet students' primary psychological needs. He has a remedy for this problem, which he puts forth in three fundamental propositions:

1. The school curriculum must be organized to meet **students' needs** for survival, belonging, power, fun, and freedom.
2. **Quality schoolwork** and **self-evaluation** (of quality) by students must replace the fragmented and boring requirements on which students are typically tested and evaluated.
3. Teachers must abandon traditional teaching practices and move toward **quality teaching.** Let us examine what Glasser means by these three points.

Students' Needs

All human beings have genetic needs for (1) survival (food, shelter, freedom from harm); (2) belonging (security, comfort, legitimate membership in the group); (3) power (sense of importance, of stature, of being considered by others); (4) fun (having a good time, emotionally and intellectually); and (5) freedom (exercise of choice, self-direction, and responsibility). Glasser is adamant in his contention that education which does not give priority to belonging, power, fun, and freedom is bound to fail. Teachers do not have to be psychologists in order to attend to students' basic needs. Glasser points out that students sense **belonging** when they are involved in class matters, receive attention from the teacher and others, and are brought into discussions of matters that concern the class. Students sense **power** when the teacher asks them to participate in decisions about topics to be studied and procedures for working in the class. A sense of power comes, too, from being assigned responsibility for class duties, such as helping take attendance, caring for class animals, helping distribute and take care of materials, being in charge of audiovisual equipment, and so forth. Students experience **fun** when they are able to work and talk with others, engage in interesting activities, and share their accomplishments. And they sense **freedom** when the teacher allows them to make responsible choices concerning what they will study, how they will do so, and how they will demonstrate their accomplishments. Glasser frequently mentions the value of cooperative learning groups in helping students meet their basic needs.

Curriculum and Quality Work

Glasser (1990, p. 22) says that present-day education is defined in terms of how many fragments of information students can retain long enough to be measured on standardized achievement tests. Students agree, and they resist education of that sort.

Glasser finds much fault with the curriculum, the way it is presented, and how student learning is evaluated. School, he says, should be a place where students learn useful information well. To make that possible, a **quality curriculum** is necessary. The old curriculum should be revised so that it consists only of learnings that students find enjoyable and useful; the rest should be discarded as "nonsense" (Glasser 1992). When teachers introduce new segments of learning, they should hold discussions with students and, if the students are old enough, ask them to identify what they would like to explore in depth. Adequate time should then be spent so that those topics can be learned well. Learning a smaller number of topics very well is always preferable to learning many topics superficially, says Glasser, who calls this type of learning quality learning. Evaluation of learning should call upon students to explain why the material they have learned is valuable and how and where it can be used. Students should regularly assess the quality of their own efforts as well.

Quality Teaching

Even teachers who are committed intellectually to quality teaching may find it difficult to identify and make needed changes. It is not easy to change one's teaching style, but Glasser (1993, p. 22 ff) says it can be done by striving for the following, which lead toward **quality teaching** and **quality learning.**

1. *Provide a warm, supportive classroom climate.* This is done by helping students know and like you. Use natural occasions over time to tell students who you are, what you stand for, what you will ask them to do, what you will not ask them to do, what you will do for them, and what you will not do for them. Show that you are always willing to help.
2. *Ask students to do only work that is useful.* **Useful work** consists of skills, as distinct from information, that students see as valuable in their lives. Not infrequently, teachers have to point out the value of new skills, but students must ultimately recognize that value before they will make a sustained effort to learn. Students should be required to memorize no information except that which is essential to the skill being learned. However, information should be taught and learned provided it meets one or more of the following criteria (1993, p. 48):
   • The information is directly related to an important skill.
   • The information is something that students express a desire to learn.
   • The information is something the teacher believes especially useful.
   • The information is required for college entrance exams.
3. *Always ask students to do the best they can.* Quality work by students must be nurtured slowly. Glasser (1993, p. 77) suggests that a focus on quality can be initiated as follows:
   • Discuss quality work enough so that students understand what you mean.
   • Begin with an assignment that is clearly important enough to do well.
   • Ask students to do their best work on the assignment; do not grade it, because grades suggest to students that the work is finished. Then,

4. *Ask students to evaluate work they have done and improve it.* Quality comes from improvements that result from continued effort. Glasser suggests that when students have done a piece of work on a topic they consider important, the teacher should help them make **value judgments** about it, as follows:
   - Ask students how they think they might improve their work further.
   - Ask students to explain why they feel their work has high quality. As students see the value of improving their work, higher quality will result naturally.
   - Progressively help students begin to use **SIR,** a process of self-evaluation, improvement, and repetition, until quality is achieved.
5. *Help students see that quality work makes them feel good.* This effect will occur naturally as students learn to do quality work. As Glasser (1993, p. 25) says,
   > There is no better human feeling than that which comes from the satisfaction of doing something useful that you believe is the very best you can do and finding that others agree.

   As students begin to sense this feeling, they will want more of it.
6. *Help students see that quality work is never destructive to oneself, others, or the environment.* Teachers should help students realize that it is not possible to achieve the good feeling of quality work by harming people, property, the environment, or other creatures.

Boss Teachers and Lead Teachers

The preceding framework for quality directs one away from what Glasser calls boss teaching and toward what he calls lead teaching. Teachers typically function as bosses, Glasser contends, because they do not realize that motivation cannot be furnished to students but must come from within. **Boss teachers,** as Glasser describes them, do the following:

- Set the tasks and standards.
- Talk rather than demonstrate and rarely ask for student input.
- Grade the work without involving students in the evaluation.
- Use coercion when students resist.

To illustrate how a boss teacher functions, consider the example of Mr. Márquez, who introduces his unit of study on South American geography in the following way:

Class, today we are going to begin our study of the geography of South America. You are expected to do the following things:

1. Learn the names of the South American countries.
2. Locate those countries on a blank map.
3. Describe the types of terrain typical of each country.

4. Name two products associated with each country.
5. Describe the population of each country in terms of ethnic origin and economic well-being.
6. Name and locate the most important rivers that drain to the north, east, and southeast. We will learn this information from our textbooks and encyclopedias. You will have two tests, one at . . .

Mr. Márquez's boss approach limits both productivity and quality of work. Most students will probably find the work boring and will do only enough, and only well enough, to get by.

Glasser would have teachers forgo Mr. Márquez's style and function not as boss teachers but as **lead teachers.** Lead teachers realize that genuine motivation to learn must arise within students. They also realize that their task in teaching is to use any tactic they can to help students learn. Glasser says teachers should spend most of their time on two things: organizing interesting activities and providing assistance to students. Such lead teachers would do the following:

- Discuss the curriculum with the class in such a way that many topics of interest are identified.
- Encourage students to identify topics they would like to explore in depth.
- Discuss with students the nature of the schoolwork that might ensue, emphasizing quality and asking for input on criteria of quality.
- Explore with students resources that might be needed for quality work and the amount of time such work might require.
- Demonstrate ways in which the work can be done, using models that reflect quality.
- Emphasize the importance of students' continually inspecting and evaluating their own work in terms of quality.
- Make evident to students that everything possible will be done to provide them with good tools and a good workplace that is noncoercive and non-adversarial.

To illustrate how lead teaching might proceed, consider the example of Mr. Garcia's introduction to a unit of study on the geography of South America:

Class, have any of you ever lived in South America? You did, Samuel? Which country? Peru? Fantastic! What an interesting country! I used to live in Brazil. I traveled in the Amazon quite a bit and lived for a while with Indians. Supposedly they were headhunters at one time. But not now. Tomorrow I'll show you a bow and arrow I brought from that tribe. Samuel, did you ever eat monkey when you were in Peru? I think Peru and Brazil are very alike in some ways but very different in others. What was Peru like compared to here? Did you get up into the Andes? They have fabulous ruins all over Peru, I hear, and those fantastic Chariots of the Gods lines and drawings on the landscape. Do you have any photographs or slides you could bring for us to see? What a resource you could be for us! You could teach us a lot!

Class, Samuel lived in Peru and traveled in the Andes. If we could get him to teach us about that country, what do you think you would most like to learn? (The class discusses this option and identifies topics.)

We have the opportunity in our class to learn a great deal about South America, its mountains and grasslands, its dense rain forests and huge rivers, and its interesting people and strange animals. Did you know there are groups of English, Welsh, Italians, and Germans living in many parts of South America, especially in Argentina? Did you know there are still thought to be tribes of Indians in the jungles that have no contact with the outside world? Did you know that almost half of all the river water in the world is in the Amazon basin, and that in some places the Amazon River is so wide that from the middle you can't see either shore?

Speaking of the Amazon, I swam in a lake there that contained piranhas, and look, I still have my legs and arms. Surprised about that? If you wanted to learn more about living in the Amazon jungle, what would you be interested in knowing? (Discussion ensues.)

How about people of the high Andes? Those Incas, for example, who in some mysterious way cut and placed enormous boulders into gigantic, perfectly fitting fortress walls? Samuel knows about them. The Incas were very civilized and powerful, with an empire that stretched for three thousand miles. Yet they were conquered by a few Spaniards on horseback. How in the world could that have happened? If you could learn more about those amazing people, what would you like to know? (Discussion continues in this manner. Students identify topics about which they would be willing to make an effort to learn.)

Now let me see what you think of this idea: I have written down the topics you said you were interested in, and I can help you with resources and materials. I have lots of my own, including slides, South American music, and many artifacts I have collected. I know two other people who lived in Argentina and Colombia that we could invite to talk with us. We can concentrate on what you have said you would like to learn about. But if we decide to do so, I want to see if we can make this deal: We explore what interests you; I help you all I can; and you, for your part, agree to do the best work you are capable of. We would need to discuss that to get some ideas of what you might do that would show the quality of your learning. In addition, I hope I can persuade each of you regularly to evaluate yourselves as to how well you believe you are doing. Understand, this would not be me evaluating you, it would be you evaluating yourself—not for a grade but for you to decide what you are doing very well and what you think you might be able to do better. What do you think of that idea? Want to give it a try?

The Relation of Quality Teaching to Discipline

Glasser believes that teachers who learn to function as leaders of quality classrooms avoid the trap of becoming adversaries of their students, a trap that destroys incentive to learn and pleasure in teaching. When teachers stay out of that trap, they not only foster quality learning but at the same time reduce discipline problems to a minimum. Glasser does admit that no approach to teaching can eliminate all behavior problems. He acknowledges that it is necessary to work with students to establish standards of conduct in the classroom. He makes the following suggestions.

The teacher should begin with a discussion of the importance of quality work, which is to be given priority in the class, and of how the teacher will do everything possible to help students without forcing them. That discussion should lead naturally into asking students about class rules they believe will help them get their work done and truly help them learn. Glasser says that if teachers can get students to see the importance of courtesy, no other rules may be necessary. Mrs. Bentley's second graders decided they needed only two rules in order to do their work well.

1. Be kind to others.
2. Do our best work.

Mr. Jason's physical education class decided on these rules:

1. Be on time.
2. Play safely.
3. Show good sportsmanship.
4. Take care of the equipment.

Teachers should also solicit student advice on what should happen when rules are broken. Glasser says students will suggest punishment, though they know punishment is not effective. If asked further, they will agree that behavior problems are best solved by looking for ways to remedy whatever is causing the rule to be broken. Glasser urges teachers to ask, "What could I do to help?" and to hold classroom meetings to explore alternatives to inappropriate behavior. Once the rules and consequences are agreed to, they should be written down. All students sign, attesting that they understand the rules and that, if they break those rules, they will try—with the teacher's help—to correct the underlying problem. Rules established and dealt with in this way, says Glasser, show that the teacher's main concern lies in quality, not power, and that the teacher recognizes that power struggles are the main enemy of quality education.

When Rules Are Broken

Every teacher knows that rules will invariably be broken, even in the best classes. Glasser (1990) acknowledges that fact and provides specific guidance for teacher intervention, in the form of nonpunitive steps that stop the misbehavior and refocus the student's mind on class work. Suppose that Jonathan has come into the room obviously upset. As the lesson begins, he turns heatedly and throws something at Michael. Glasser would suggest that the teacher do the following:

TEACHER: It looks like you have a problem, Jonathan. How can I help you solve it? [Jonathan frowns, still obviously upset.]

TEACHER: If you will calm down, I will discuss it with you in a little while. I think we can work something out.

Glasser says you should make it clear that you will not help Jonathan until he calms down. You are to speak without emotion, recognizing that your anger will only put Jonathan on the defensive. If Jonathan doesn't calm down, there is no good way to deal with the problem. Glasser (1990) says to allow him 20 seconds, and if he isn't calm by then, admit that there is no way to solve the problem at that time. Give Jonathan time out from the lesson, but don't threaten or warn him.

TEACHER: Jonathan, I want to help you work this out. I am not interested in punishing you. Whatever the problem is, let's solve it. But for now you must go sit at the table. When you are calm, come back to your seat.

Later, at an opportune time, the teacher discusses the situation with Jonathan, approximately as follows:

TEACHER: What were you doing when the problem started? Was it against the rules? Can we work things out so it won't happen again? What could you and I do to keep it from happening?

If the problem involves hostilities between Jonathan and Michael, the discussion should involve both boys and proceed along these lines:

TEACHER: What were you doing, Jonathan? What were you doing, Michael? How can the three of us work things out so this won't happen anymore?

It is important to note that no blame is assigned to either Jonathan or Michael. No time is spent trying to find out whose fault it was. You remind the boys that all you are looking for is a solution so that the problem won't occur again. Glasser contends that if you treat Jonathan and Michael with respect and courtesy, if you show you don't want to punish them or throw your weight around, and if you talk to them as a problem solver, both their classroom behavior and the quality of their work will gradually improve.

INITIATING GLASSER'S *NONCOERCIVE DISCIPLINE*

Suppose you find Glasser's current views on schooling and discipline so persuasive that you want to use them in your classroom. How do you go about putting them into practice? The general framework suggested by Glasser for moving toward quality teaching was presented earlier in the chapter. But for immediate use of his ideas, the implication seems to be that you would begin with class discussions about how they think school could be made more interesting. In doing so, you would do the following:

- Involve students in discussions about topics to be pursued, ways of working, procedures for reporting or demonstrating accomplishment, establishment of class rules, and decisions about steps to be taken when misbehavior occurs. You would offer your opinions but give serious attention to student suggestions as well.
- Make plain to students that you will try to arrange activities they might have suggested and that you will do all in your power to help them learn and succeed.

Meanwhile, you would also take the following steps:

- Learn how to be a lead teacher rather than a boss teacher. (The scenario given earlier showing Mr. Garcia's introduction of his unit on South America illustrates lead teaching.)
- Hold regular class meetings to discuss curriculum, procedures, behavior, and other educational topics. These meetings should always be conducted with an eye to improving learning conditions for students, never as a venue for finding fault, blaming, or criticizing.
- When students misbehave, discuss their behavior and why it was inappropriate for the class. Ask them what they feel you could do in order to be more helpful to them. If the misbehavior is serious or chronic, talk with the involved student privately at an appropriate time.

Arranging times and places for these talks can be awkward. Here is how it is done by Maureen Lewnes, who teaches a fourth- and fifth-grade combination class.

For conferencing with students I use a consultation corner, which in my room is not a corner at all but rather four feet of wall space to the rear of my desk between a table and file cabinet. A small kindergarten chair is there for students to sit in, which they love to do as I bend down low to converse with them, out of sight of the rest of the class, which creates an impression of closeness between the two of us.

I introduce the consultation corner at the beginning of the year, telling my students I may request them to join me there to discuss matters of class work or behavior or to tell them how much I appreciate their help and good work, which I make sure to emphasize. Several benefits have come from use of the corner. When the need arises, I say to the student, "May I see you in the consultation corner at study time?" The chat there gives me insights into matters that might be troubling the students, and it encourages shy students to share feelings, interests, and problems.

Most students react well to the talks, appreciating the privacy, and I find that problems of misbehavior are more easily resolved there. When I ask their opinions, my students say that every room should have a consultation corner because it makes them more comfortable about talking with the teacher.

STRENGTHS OF GLASSER'S *NONCOERCIVE DISCIPLINE*

Glasser points out that schools traditionally expect students to do boring work while sitting and waiting, which goes strongly against their inherent nature. Glasser wrote that expecting students to do boring work in school "is like asking someone who is sitting on a hot stove to sit still and stop complaining" (1986, p. 53). Glasser insisted that "Teachers should not depend on any discipline program that demands that they do something to or for students to get them to stop behaving badly in unsatisfying classes. Only a discipline program that is also concerned with classroom satisfaction will work." (1986, p. 56)

Glasser expanded on that theme in his 1990 work *The Quality School* by describing how schools can emphasize quality work. This depends on teachers' functioning as lead teachers who provide great support and encouragement but do not coerce, throw their weight around, or punish. In such environments, students find their genetic needs met sufficiently that they will stay in school and do better quality work. Glasser now gives discipline per se much less attention than before, insisting that if schools and classes are conducted in keeping with his quality concept, discipline problems will be few and relatively easily resolved. The difficulty for teachers is that schools are not likely to change their curriculum in accordance with the scheme Glasser proposes. Though such a change may well occur over time, for the present it is to be expected that most schools will continue to cover textbook material as broadly as possible, thus enabling students to perform better on achievement tests. Can teachers, then, make any significant use of Glasser's newest suggestions about discipline? No doubt they can. Like Jones's model, Glasser's does not have to be taken as a total system and set into place lock, stock, and barrel. His suggestions for teachers' acting as problem solvers without arguing or punishing should be seriously considered. His procedures can be practiced, allowing teachers to evaluate for themselves the effect on classroom climate and morale. Glasser didn't imply that his quality school would wipe out all discipline problems. Students are human beings, and even the best intentioned sometimes violate established rules, producing conflict with others, including teachers. When such behavior occurs, teachers can practice calmly trying to identify the problem and then, without assigning blame, enlist students' help in correcting its cause. Glasser's suggestions, while time consuming, offer a good procedure for helping students learn well while becoming self-directing and responsible.

REVIEW OF SELECTED TERMINOLOGY

The following terms are central to Glasser's suggestions regarding education and discipline.

basic needs	quality curriculum
behavior choices	quality education
belonging	quality learning
boss teacher	quality schoolwork
class rules	quality teaching
classroom meetings	self-evaluation
consequences	SIR
excuses	student needs
freedom	student responsibility
fun	useful work
lead teacher	value judgments
power	

APPLICATION EXERCISES

CONCEPT CASES

Case 1: Kristina Will Not Work

Kristina, a student in Mr. Jake's class, is quite docile. She socializes little with other students and never disrupts class. However, despite Mr. Jake's best efforts, Kristina never does her work. She rarely completes an assignment. She is simply there, putting forth no effort.

How would Glasser deal with Kristina? Glasser would first suggest that Mr. Jake think carefully about the classroom and the program to try to determine whether they contain obstacles that prevent Kristina from meeting her needs for belonging, power, fun, and freedom. He would then have Mr. Jake discuss the matter with Kristina, not blaming her but noting the problem of nonproductivity and asking what the problem is and what he might be able to do to help. In that discussion, Mr. Jake might ask Kristina questions such as the following:

- You have a problem with this work, don't you? Is there anything I can do to help you with it?
- Is there anything I could do to make the class more interesting for you?
- Is there anything in this class that you especially enjoy doing?
- Do you think that, for a while, you might like to do only those things?

- Is there anything we have discussed in class that you would like to learn very, very well?
- How could I help you do that?
- What could I do differently that would help you want to learn?

Mr. Jake would not punish Kristina, nor would he use a disapproving tone of voice. Meanwhile, every day he would make a point of talking with her in a friendly and courteous way about nonschool matters such as trips, pets, and movies. He would do this casually and frequently, showing he is interested in her and willing to be her friend. Glasser would remind Mr. Jake that there is no magic formula for success with all students. Mr. Jake can only encourage and support Kristina. Scolding and coercion are likely to make matters worse, but as Mr. Jake befriends Kristina she is likely to begin to do more work and of better quality.

Case 2: Sara Cannot Stop Talking

Sara is a pleasant girl who participates in class activities and does most, though not all, of her assigned work. She cannot seem to refrain from talking to classmates, however. Her teacher, Mr. Gonzales, has to speak to her repeatedly during lessons, to the point that he often becomes exasperated and loses his temper.

What suggestions would Glasser give Mr. Gonzales for dealing with Sara?

Case 3: Joshua Clowns and Intimidates

Joshua, larger and louder than his classmates, always wants to be the center of attention, which he accomplishes through a combination of clowning and intimidation. He makes wise remarks, talks back (smilingly) to the teacher, utters a variety of sound-effect noises such as automobile crashes and gunshots, and makes limitless sarcastic comments and put-downs of his classmates. Other students will not stand up to him, apparently fearing his size and verbal aggression. His teacher, Miss Pearl, has come to her wit's end.

How do you think Glasser would have Miss Pearl deal with Joshua?

Case 4: Tom Is Hostile and Defiant

Tom has appeared to be in his usual foul mood ever since arriving in class. On his way to sharpen his pencil, he bumps into Frank, who complains. Tom tells him loudly to shut up. Miss Baines, the teacher, says, "Tom, go back to your seat." Tom wheels around, swears loudly, and says heatedly, "I'll go when I'm damned good and ready!"

How would Glasser have Miss Baines deal with Tom?

QUESTIONS AND ACTIVITIES

1. Select a preferred grade level and/or subject. As the teacher, outline what you would consider and do, along the lines of Glasser's suggestions, concerning the following:
    a. Organizing the classroom, class, curriculum, and activities to better meet your students' needs for belonging, fun, power, and freedom
    b. Your continual efforts to help students improve the quality of their work
2. Do a comparative analysis of Glasser's system with that of either Canter, Jones, Albert, Gordon, or Nelsen, Lott, and Glenn. Explain your conclusions concerning the following:
    a. Effectiveness in suppressing inappropriate behavior
    b. Effectiveness in improving long-term behavior
    c. Ease of implementation
    d. Effect on student self-concept
    e. Effect on bonds of trust between teacher and student
    f. The degree to which each model accurately depicts realities of student attitude and behavior.
3. Examine Scenario 9 or 10 in the Appendix. What advice would Glasser give Mr. Wong or Miss Thorpe to help improve learning conditions in the classroom?

REFERENCES AND RECOMMENDED READINGS

Glasser, W. 1965. *Reality therapy: A new approach to psychiatry.* New York: Harper & Row.

———. 1969. *Schools without failure.* New York: Harper & Row.

———. 1977. 10 steps to good discipline. *Today's Education, 66,* 60–63.

———. 1978. Disorders in our schools: Causes and remedies. *Phi Delta Kappan, 59,* 331–333.

———. 1986. *Control theory in the classroom.* New York: Harper & Row.

———. 1990. *The quality school: Managing students without coercion.* New York: Harper & Row. (Reissued with additional material in 1992)

———. 1992. The quality school curriculum. *Phi Delta Kappan, 73*(9), 690–694.

———. 1993. *The quality school teacher.* New York: Harper Perennial.

CHAPTER **10**

Richard Curwin
and Allen Mendler's
Discipline with Dignity

Richard
Curwin

Allen
Mendler

PREVIEW OF CURWIN AND MENDLER'S WORK

Focus

- Building classroom discipline upon a basis of dignity and hope.

- Reclaiming students destined to fail in school because of their misbehavior.

- Finding long-term solutions to problems of misbehavior.

Logic

- Schools exist primarily for the benefit of students, not teachers or others.

- By solving misbehavior problems, we can salvage students who otherwise fail in school.

- Most students behave acceptably when their sense of dignity is kept intact.

- It is essential to restore a sense of hope in students who chronically misbehave.

Contributions

- The concept of student dignity as the cornerstone of effective classroom discipline.

- The understanding that most chronically misbehaving students have no sense of hope.

- A systematic approach to discipline based on preserving dignity and restoring hope.

Curwin and Mendler's Suggestions

- Accept that helping students learn to behave acceptably is an integral part of teaching.

- Always, in all circumstances, interact with students in a manner that preserves their dignity.

- Do all you can to reinstill hope of success in students who chronically misbehave.

- Make sure that discipline techniques you use never interfere with motivation to learn.

ABOUT RICHARD CURWIN AND ALLEN MENDLER

Richard Curwin, born in 1944, began his teaching career in a seventh-grade class of boys whose behavior was seriously out of control. This experience led to a career specialization in school discipline, first as a classroom teacher and later as a university professor and private consultant and writer. He earned a doctorate in education from the University of Massachusetts in 1972.

Allen Mendler, born in 1949, earned a doctorate in psychology at Union Institute in 1981. His career has been devoted to serving as school psychologist and psychoeducational consultant. He has worked extensively with students and teachers at all levels.

Curwin and Mendler attracted national attention through the book they coauthored in 1983, *Taking Charge in the Classroom.* They revised and republished that work in 1988 as *Discipline with Dignity,* a title that more accurately reflects the central concept of their approach. They also coauthored *The Discipline Book: A Complete Guide to School and Classroom Management* (1980) and several journal articles. In 1992 Curwin published *Rediscovering Hope: Our Greatest Teaching Strategy,* a book devoted to helping teachers improve the behavior of difficult-to-control students who are otherwise likely to fail in school.

Curwin and Mendler regularly conduct training seminars across the nation. They can be contacted through Discipline Associates, P.O. Box 20481, Rochester, NY 14602; telephone 800-772-5227.

CURWIN AND MENDLER'S CONTRIBUTIONS TO DISCIPLINE

Curwin and Mendler's major contributions to school discipline have been strategies for improving classroom behavior through maximizing student dignity and hope. Their ideas have been especially useful to teachers who work with chronically misbehaving students. Those students—about five percent of the student population, Curwin and Mendler say—are the ones who disrupt instruction, interfere with learning, and make life miserable for teachers. Described by Curwin and Mendler as "without hope," such students will almost certainly fail unless treated with special consideration and care. Curwin and Mendler explain what without-hope students need if they are to have a chance for success in school, and they provide strategies to help teachers reclaim those students.

CURWIN AND MENDLER'S CENTRAL FOCUS

The central focus of Curwin and Mendler's work is on building students' sense of dignity and providing them a sense of hope in school. They describe techniques that encourage students, in a dignified manner, to behave acceptably in school, and they provide a number of explicit suggestions for interacting with students, motivating them, ensuring success, and developing responsible behavior.

CURWIN AND MENDLER'S PRINCIPAL TEACHINGS

The number of students whose chronic classroom misbehavior puts them in imminent danger of failing in school is on the increase. These students are referred to as behaviorally at risk.

Most of these chronically misbehaving students have lost all hope of encountering anything worthwhile in school. A crucial responsibility of teachers is to help those students believe that school can be of benefit and that they have some control over their lives.

Students do all they can to prevent damage to their dignity, to their sense of self-value. Much serious misbehavior occurs as students attempt to avoid such damage.

Schools exist for students, not for teachers. Teachers are the professionals placed in schools for the benefit of their clients, the students. The teacher's role is basically simple: to do everything possible to help students learn and behave responsibly.

Five underlying principles of effective discipline should always be kept in mind. Those principles are that (1) discipline is a very important part of teaching, (2) short-term solutions are rarely effective, (3) students must always be treated with dignity, (4) discipline must not interfere with motivation to learn, and (5) responsibility is more important than obedience.

Short-term solutions to discipline problems, such as writing offending students' names on the board, often turn into long-term disasters. Damaging student dignity reduces motivation, increases resistance, and promotes desire for revenge.

Responsibility, not obedience, is the goal of discipline. Responsibility, which involves making enlightened decisions, almost always produces better long-term behavior changes than does obedience to teacher demands.

A thorough approach to classroom discipline has three dimensions. They are: (1) prevention (steps taken to forestall misbehavior), (2) action (steps taken when class rules are broken), and (3) resolution (special arrangements for improving the misbehavior of out-of-control students).

Consequences, which are preplanned actions invoked when class rules are broken, are necessary in discipline. Consequences are best when planned by teacher and students working together.

The Insubordination Rule is a bottom-line rule to be included in the discipline plan, or social contract. It states that whenever a student refuses to accept the consequence for breaking a rule, that student will not be allowed back into the class until he or she accepts the consequence. This rule requires the support of the school administrator.

Creative responses are unexpected responses to misbehavior that teachers can occasionally use effectively. Examples include exchanging roles with the student, taping the class's behavior, and throwing an occasional tantrum.

Wise teachers de-escalate potential confrontations by actively listening to the student, using I-messages, and keeping the discussion private. In typical confrontations between teacher and student, both try to "win" the argument. The resulting struggle often escalates to a more serious level.

The behavior of difficult-to-manage students can be improved through providing interesting lessons on topics of personal relevance that permit active involvement and lead to competencies students value. Students who are very difficult to manage usually have little or no motivation to learn what is ordinarily taught in school.

ANALYSIS OF CURWIN AND MENDLER'S *DISCIPLINE WITH DIGNITY*

Students Who Are Behaviorally At-Risk

Behaviorally at-risk is a label given to students whose behavior prevents their learning and puts them in serious danger of failing in school. Like most labels, *at-risk* is often misinterpreted and misapplied. The label is useful for communication about students but is not helpful in remediating their misbehavior. Curwin and Mendler therefore make plain that they use the term to refer solely to behavior, not to the nature of the student: "It is what students do under the conditions they are in, not who they are, that puts them at risk" (Curwin 1992, p. xiii).

The students Curwin and Mendler refer to are those whom teachers consider to be out of control—students often referred to as lazy, turned off, angry, hostile, irresponsible, disruptive, or withdrawn. They are commonly said to have "attitude problems." They make no effort to learn, disregard teacher requests and directions, and provoke trouble in the classroom. Because they behave in these ways, they are unlikely to be successful in school. Curwin and Mendler (1992) describe them as follows:

- They are failing.
- They have received, and do not respond to, most of the punishments and/or consequences offered by the school.
- They have low self-concepts in relation to school.
- They have little or no hope of finding success in school.
- They associate with and are reinforced by similar students.

The number of behaviorally at-risk students is increasing steadily. The reasons for this increase are many: failure of the family unit to provide emotional, social, and intellectual security; increased violence in society; birth of infants addicted to alcohol or drugs; reemergence of racial tensions; lack of admirable models for children to emulate; replacement of a sense of right and wrong by personal gratification. These conditions contribute to loss of hope in the young. Many can see no role for themselves in the mainstream. Many do not expect to live very long. Increasingly, adolescents experience depression and contemplate suicide, which accounts for almost one quarter of all adolescent deaths (Curwin 1992). Students without hope do not care how they behave in the classroom. It does not worry them if they fail, bother the teacher, or disrupt the class.

Helping Students Regain Hope

Teachers can do little about the depressing conditions in society, but they can do a good deal to help students regain a **sense of hope.** Hope is what inspires us. We require it in order to live meaningfully. It provides courage and the incentive to overcome barriers. When hope is lost, there is no reason to try. Students who are behaviorally at risk have, for the most part, lost hope. Curwin and Mendler contend that such students can be helped to regain hope and, further, that as they do so their behavior will improve. This can be accomplished, they say, by making learning much more attractive. If they are to get involved in the learning process, students

> need something to hope for, something to be gained to make their risk worthwhile. . . . Learning activities can succeed when they promise students competence in doing what is important to them. (Curwin 1992, p. 25)

Learning must not only be made attractive but must provide student success as well. At-risk students will not persevere unless successful, despite the attractiveness of the topic. To ensure success, teachers can explore ways to redesign the curriculum, encourage different ways of thinking, provide for various learning styles and sensory modalities, allow for creativity and artistic expression, and use grading systems that provide encouraging feedback without damaging the students' willingness to try. In Curwin's (1992) words,

> For students who are alienated, are fearful, or believe that school offers them nothing of importance, we must alter conditions to create hope. (p. 28)

Dignity

Although interesting activities and success are crucial to restoring hope among the behaviorally at risk, an equally important consideration has to do with their sense of dignity. **Dignity** refers to respect for life and self, and it has long been at the center of Curwin and Mendler's work. In their book *Discipline with Dignity* (1988a), they point out that students with chronic behavior problems see themselves as losers and have stopped trying to gain acceptance in normal ways, telling themselves it is better not to try than to fail yet again, that it is better to be recognized as a troublemaker than to be seen as stupid.

Dignity cannot be disregarded. Chronically misbehaving students try to protect their dignity at all costs, even with their lives if they are pushed hard enough (Curwin and Mendler 1988a). Teachers must take pains, therefore, to keep dignity intact and bolster it when possible. Curwin (1992) advises:

> We must . . . welcome high risk students as human beings. They come to school as whole people, not simply as brains waiting to be trained. Our assumptions about their social behavior need to include the understanding that their negative behaviors are based on protection and escape. They do the

best they can with the skills they have under the adverse conditions they face. . . . When they are malicious, they believe, rightly or wrongly, that they are justified in defending themselves from attacks on their dignity. (p. 27)

For most teachers, a posture of understanding helpfulness is not easy to maintain, especially when students behave disdainfully and use abominable language. Given a steady diet of defiant hostility, many teachers become cynical and give up on students. Many leave teaching because they don't feel its rewards are commensurate with the turmoil they must endure.

While very supportive of teachers, Curwin and Mendler make a telling point in their writings: School exists for students, not for teachers. As **professionals,** teachers are there to help their **clients,** the students; they should enter the profession with that understanding. When teachers are able to see their role as supportive of student dignity, rather than confrontive, they can more easily retain their sense of purpose. They must expect to encounter student behavior that reflects society's ills, but they need to accept, as a matter of faith, that they can and will make a difference in their students' lives, even though that difference may not become apparent for a long time.

Why Students Break Rules

All students misbehave at times. They talk without permission, call each other sarcastic names, and laugh when they shouldn't. Some misbehave out of boredom, some because they find certain misbehaviors (such as talking) irresistible. Some break rules simply for expedience's sake. These kinds of misbehavior are relatively benign. They irritate teachers, but they do not place students in danger of failing. In contrast, students who are behaviorally at risk break rules for more serious reasons, such as "gaining a measure of control over a system that has damaged their sense of dignity." (Curwin 1992, p. 49) They exert their control by refusing to comply with teacher requests, arguing and talking back to the teacher, tapping pencils and dropping books, or withdrawing from class activities. These students have found they can't be very good at learning but that they can be very good at being bad and, by doing so, can meet their needs for attention and power. Although such students are relatively few in number, they are not isolated. They find others like themselves with whom to bond, which further encourages misbehavior.

Why At-Risk Students Are Difficult to Discipline

Behaviorally at-risk students are difficult to control for several reasons. To begin with, they usually, though not always, have a history of academic failure. Unable to maintain dignity through achievement, they protect themselves by withdrawing or acting as if they don't care. They have learned that it feels better to misbehave than to follow rules that lead nowhere. Curwin (1992) illustrates this point.

Ask yourself, if you got a 56 on an important test, what would make you feel better about failing? Telling your friends, "I studied hard and was just too stupid to pass." Or, "It was a stupid test anyway, and besides I hate that dumb class and that boring teacher." (p. 49)

When students' dignity has been repeatedly damaged in school, it makes them feel good to lash back at others. As they continue to misbehave, they find themselves systematically removed from opportunities to act responsibly. When they misbehave in class, they are made to sit by themselves in isolation. When they fight, they are told to resolve the dispute and make amends. In such cases they are taken out of the very situations in which they might learn to behave responsibly. Curwin (1992) makes the point as follows:

> No one would tell a batter who was struggling at the plate that he could not participate in batting practice until he improved. No one would tell a poor reader that he could not look at any books until his reading improved. In the same way, no student can learn how to play in a playground by being removed from the playground, or how to learn time-management skills by being told when to schedule everything. Learning responsibility requires participation. (p. 50)

Students who are behaviorally at risk know and accept that they are labeled "discipline problems." They know that they can't do academic work as expected and that they are considered bothersome and irritating. Wherever they turn, they receive negative messages about themselves. They have become, in their own eyes, bad persons. How can teachers help students who see themselves as bad persons and whose only gratification in school comes from causing trouble?

Discipline Methods That Do Not Work

It should be recognized that traditional methods of discipline are ineffective with students who are behaviorally at risk. These students have grown immune to scolding, lecturing, sarcasm, detention, extra writing assignments, isolation, names on the chalkboard, or trips to the principal's office. It does no good to tell them what they did wrong; they already know. Nor does it help to grill them about their ability to do class work or follow rules. They already doubt their ability, and they know they don't want to follow rules. Sarcastic teacher remarks, because they attack students' dignity, almost always make matters worse. At-risk students need no further humiliation. Punishment destroys their motivation to cooperate. They see no reason to commit to better ways of behaving and therefore cannot achieve the results teachers hope for.

Disciplining Difficult-to-Control Students

If traditional methods of discipline are ineffective in working with students who are difficult to control, what would be an effective set of methods? What degree of success might the new methods have? And if the entire process is so difficult, is it worth teachers' time to try to help these resistant students?

Curwin and Mendler set forth principles and approaches that, if not effective with all recalcitrant learners, are in their opinion significantly better than the discipline approaches normally used. They acknowledge that dealing with the chronic rule breaker is never easy and admit that the success rate is far from perfect, but they claim it is possible to produce positive changes in 25 to 50 percent of students considered to be out of control (Curwin and Mendler 1992).

Underlying Principles of Effective Discipline

Curwin (1992, pp. 51–54) would have teachers base their discipline efforts upon the following **principles of effective discipline:**

1. *Dealing with student behavior is an important part of teaching.* Most teachers do not want to deal with behavior problems, but being a professional means doing whatever one can to help the client. Teachers should therefore look upon misbehavior as an ideal opportunity for teaching responsibility. They should put as much effort into teaching good behavior as they put into teaching content.

2. *Short-term solutions often become long-term disasters.* The discipline techniques that most teachers use are **short-term solutions** that stifle misbehavior in order for the teacher to continue teaching. However, such quick solutions as writing names on boards, scolding, sarcasm, and detention often turn into long-term disasters because they assault students' self-image and thus further reduce desire to learn while provoking additional disobedience.

3. *Always treat students with dignity.* Dignity is a basic need that is essential for healthy life; its importance cannot be overrated. To treat students with dignity is to respect them as individuals, to be concerned about their needs and understanding of their viewpoints. Effective discipline does not attack student dignity but instead offers students hope. Curwin and Mendler advise teachers to ask themselves this question when reacting to student misbehavior: "How would this strategy affect my dignity if a teacher did it to me?"

4. *Good discipline must not interfere with student motivation.* Any discipline technique is self-defeating if it reduces student motivation to learn. Students who are motivated cause few discipline problems. Poorly behaved students are usually unmotivated and badly in need of reason and encouragement to learn. Curwin suggests that teachers, when about to deal with misbehavior, ask themselves this question: "What will this technique do to motivation?"

5. *Responsibility is more important than obedience.* Curwin differentiates between obedience and responsibility as follows: **Obedience** means "do as you are told." **Responsibility** means "make the best decision possible." Obedience is desirable in matters of health and safety, but when applied to most misbehavior it is a short-term solution against which students rebel. Responsibility grows, although slowly, as students have the opportunity to sort out facts and make decisions. Teachers should regularly provide such opportunities.

Contents of a General Discipline Plan

Curwin and Mendler (1988a) maintain that, to be effective, discipline plans should address three **dimensions of discipline** (1) a prevention dimension, (2) an action dimension, and (3) a resolution dimension. The **prevention dimension** focuses on what can be done to prevent discipline problems. The **action dimension** describes what teachers should do when discipline problems occur. The **resolution dimension** helps chronically misbehaving students learn to make and abide by decisions that serve their needs. All three dimensions are important for discipline in general and especially for students who are behaviorally at risk.

The Prevention Dimension

In prevention, the teacher gives attention to motivation and to establishing a social contract, that is, to formulating class rules and consequences. Rules help specify behaviors that are acceptable, or unacceptable, in the classroom. When carefully planned, rules help meet everyone's needs. Curwin and Mendler (1992) say that a good rule should state in behavioral terms what is required, be brief, be clear, and make sense to everyone. The teacher must be willing to enforce rules appropriately when they are broken.

Consequences are steps taken by the teacher when a rule is violated. Curwin and Mendler (1988a) advise that a list of possible consequences be established in advance. From that list the teacher can select an appropriate consequence when a rule is broken. For example, Susan continually fails to turn in homework on schedule. Miss Martin invokes a consequence selected from a list that might include a reminder, a warning, or a conference with Susan and her parents. Unlike other authorities in discipline, Curwin and Mendler do not tie specific consequences to rule violations. They believe it is better to provide teachers with a range of possibilities. The result is what they call "fair is not always equal." Students have different needs, behave differently, and react differently. They may therefore need to be treated differently.

Curwin and Mendler warn that consequences should not be seen as punishment. Consequences should be logical, which usually involves doing correctly what was done wrong. For example, when James throws wadded paper and fills the corner with clutter, his consequence may be to clean up the mess. It is important that consequences preserve student dignity and allow students the opportunity to make responsible decisions.

One particular rule—**the insubordination rule**—should be made plain to students and enforced when broken. This rule states that if a student does not accept the consequence after breaking a class rule, then he or she will not be allowed to remain in the class until the consequence is accepted. This is a bottom-line rule that prevents students from defying the teacher with impunity. The insubordination rule must, of course, be agreed to by the principal.

When students and teacher have selected, through group discussions, the rules and consequences that they believe are best for the class, their agreements (which should be written and posted in the room) become the **social contract** for behavior in the classroom. Curwin and Mendler (1992, p. 79) suggest that a **Classroom Social Contract Test** also be used to prevent students from using the excuse that they didn't understand the rules. This test is comprised of items on class rules and consequences, of which the following might be typical:

- When must homework be handed in?
- Name three things you must always bring to class.
- When someone else is speaking and you want to speak, you should first . . . .

The Action Dimension

Taking action refers to what teachers do when rules are broken. Curwin and Mendler advise teachers to select and apply, from alternatives previously identified, the consequence that best fits the situation. They see this not as a mechanical process of fitting consequence to offense but as an opportunity to interact productively with the student. They say that the method of implementation is at least as important as the consequence itself, and they remind teachers to avoid power struggles while remaining positive and mindful of student dignity.

The Resolution Dimension

The **resolution** dimension is used to formulate plans of positive action for students who misbehave chronically. As noted, such students have given up hope and have grown immune, through repeated exposure, to the discipline tactics teachers normally use. As teachers interact with noncooperative students, they should attempt to find out what is needed to prevent the problem's occurring again, work out a mutually agreeable plan with the student, implement and monitor the plan, and use creative approaches as necessary—approaches that will be explained later in the chapter.

More about Consequences

Curwin and Mendler give considerable attention to the nature of consequences and how they should be invoked. They maintain that students must have a very accurate idea of what is likely to happen if they break rules. Consequences should therefore be stated clearly and specifically and must always protect and maintain the student's dignity. There is no reason ever to use a consequence that is humiliating or dehumanizing.

If teachers apply consequences as Curwin suggests, they are certain to treat individual students differently from each other. Students and parents may complain about this inequality, but it is fair, Curwin and Mendler say. Curwin (1992) suggests that teachers say the following to parents who might complain about **unequal treatment** their child has received:

> Thank you for coming in, Mr. and Mrs. Blake. I am glad you are here to talk about your daughter. It is true that I have treated your daughter differently. . . . My goal is to teach her how to behave responsibly, and I will do anything to help her learn. If you think my method is not appropriate in this case, I will be glad to listen to any suggestions you have. . . . However, . . . please do not ask me to treat your child just like everybody else. Your child deserves a lot better than that. (pp. 74–75, abridged)

Curwin and Mendler differentiate between four types of consequences: (1) logical, (2) conventional, (3) generic, and (4) instructional.

Logical Consequences

Logical consequences are those in which students must make right what they have done wrong. If they make a mess, they must clean it up. If they willfully damage material, they must replace it. If they speak hurtfully to others, they must practice speaking in ways that are not hurtful.

Conventional Consequences

Conventional consequences are those that are commonly in practice, such as time out, removal from the room, and suspension from school. Curwin and Mendler suggest modifying conventional consequences so as to increase student commitment. For time out, they suggest that instead of banning the student for a specified length of time, teachers should say something like "You have chosen time out. You may return to the group when you are ready to learn."

When students must be removed from the room, they should not be embarrassed or humiliated. They may be sent to another teacher's room, where they sit in the back but do not participate. For suspension, sending students home is counterproductive. In-school suspension is preferable, in which students go to a designated room and complete assignments. Students are readmitted to their class only after they have made a plan for working and learning.

Generic Consequences

Generic consequences are reminders, warnings, choosing, and planning that are invoked for almost all misbehavior. Often, simple reminders are enough to stop misbehavior: "We need to get this work completed." Warnings are very firm reminders: "This is the second time I have asked you to get to work. If I have to ask you again, you will need time out." Choosing allows students to select from three or four options a plan for improving their behavior. Planning, which Curwin (1992) calls "the most effective consequence that can be used for all rule violations" (p. 78), requires that students plan their own solution to a recurring behavior problem. Planning conveys that the teacher has faith in the student's competence. That faith often engenders a degree of commitment. The plan should name specific steps the student will follow and should be written, dated, and signed.

Instructional Consequences

Instructional consequences teach students how to behave properly. Simply knowing what one ought to do does not ensure correct behavior. Some behaviors, such as raising one's hand or speaking courteously, are learned more easily when taught and practiced.

Invoking Consequences

Curwin (1992, pp. 79–80) makes a number of suggestions for helping teachers use consequences. They include the following:

- Always implement a consequence when a rule is broken.
- Select the most appropriate consequence from the list of alternatives, taking into account the offense, situation, student involved, and the best means of helping that student.
- State the rule and consequence to the offending student. Nothing more need be said.
- Be private. Only the student(s) involved should hear.
- Do not embarrass the student.

- Do not think of the situation as win–lose. This is not a contest. Do not get involved in a power struggle.
- Control your anger. Be calm and speak quietly, but accept no excuses from the student.
- Sometimes it is best to let the student choose the consequence.
- The professional always looks for ways to help the client.

Creative Responses to Chronic Misbehavior

Curwin and Mendler (1988a, pp. 151–155) suggest that when normal consequences are no longer effective with behaviorally at-risk students, teachers may wish to try creative responses. **Creative responses,** of which there are seven, include (1) role reversal, (2) humor and nonsense, (3) agreement with put-downs, (4) improbable answers, (5) paradoxical behavior, (6) teacher tantrums, and (7) taping classroom behavior.

Reverse Roles

With role reversal, you give the student the responsibility of teaching the class for a time, a quarter hour for primary students, a bit longer for middle-grade students, and entire periods for secondary students. You take the student's place and behave as the student usually does. Afterward, discuss the situation in a private conference in which the student retains the teacher role and you the student role.

Use Humor and Nonsense

Make a list of sayings you find humorous and/or nonsensical. When a chronically misbehaving student commits another rule violation, surprise him or her with one of the sayings. Curwin and Mendler give this example: When Jack comes into the class late for the third day in a row, say, "Jack! Did you know that Peter Piper picked a peck of pickled peppers?" While Curwin and Mendler acknowledge that this tactic will not produce long-term behavior change, humor and nonsense may ease tensions and provide an opportunity for better communication.

Agree with Put-downs

Agreement with put-downs works this way: When a student makes a nasty comment about you, you defuse the situation by acknowledging that the comment may have some truth, and then return to the matter of concern. For example, if a student says, "This assignment is stupid and so are you!" you might say, "Well, you may be right. I haven't had my IQ checked lately. But the assignment still needs to be completed."

Answer Improbably

Sometimes when a student defies you, you can defuse the situation by giving an improbable answer. For example, if when you tell the student to go to the in-school suspension room, the student says, "I'm not going. What are you going to do about it?" then in reply you might say, "Well, I think maybe I'll pack my bags and catch the next plane for a long vacation. But before I do, I hope you will help us both by honoring my request that you go to the suspension room."

Use Paradoxical Behavior

Teachers behave paradoxically by sending messages that ask students to behave in an undesirable manner. Curwin and Mendler (1988), who feel paradoxical behavior is an especially effective way of dealing with chronically misbehaving students, provide the following contrast between typical teacher behavior and paradoxical behavior:

> Typical: "This is the third day that you have not done your homework. The consequence is that you will have to remain after school."
>
> Paradoxical: "This is the third day that you have not done your homework. Your assignment for tonight is to try your best to forget to do tomorrow's homework." [This statement is made sincerely, not sarcastically or jokingly.] (p. 153)

Naturally, one must be cautious about using paradoxical behavior. You would not want to use it for misbehaviors that damage property, hurt students, or interfere drastically with teaching.

Throw an Occasional Tantrum

Very occasionally, when highly provoked, you may find it helpful to throw a temper tantrum for the class's benefit. With teacher tantrums you may shout, slam books, show great exasperation, and carry on about discourtesy or lack of effort. While doing so, you must make sure that you do not attack individual students. You can use I-messages such as: "I am so furious I can barely speak!" "Am I ever going to get this message across?!" and "My Lord, I am dumbfounded!" Curwin and Mendler say that if you throw a tantrum more than three or four times a year, the tactic loses its impact.

Audio- or Videotape the Class

Behavior usually improves markedly when students know they are being taped. If when taping classroom behavior you happen to record bothersome disruptions, meet with the offending student privately to consider the misbehaviors. Discuss with the student how he or she feels about the behavior. See if you can jointly come up with a specific plan for change. Keep track for a week to see whether improvement has occurred, and again discuss the result with the student. For especially troublesome behaviors, particularly those that the student denies committing, Curwin and Mendler (1988a, p. 155) suggest that you say to the student, "Beginning today, I will keep the tape recorder on 'record.' Since I think it important that you and your parents understand the problem we have here, I will make the tape available to your parents when we get together to discuss your progress. Good luck!"

Preventing Escalation

When teachers respond to student misbehavior, students often dig in their heels and a contest of wills ensues, from which neither teacher nor students will back down. Curwin and Mendler remind teachers that their duty is not to win such contests but to do what they can to help the student. The way to help is to keep channels open for rational discussion of problem behavior. That cannot be done if the teacher humiliates, angers, embarrasses, or demeans the student. This point is critical for high-risk students, who are predisposed to responding negatively. Curwin (1992) suggests that teachers do the following toward **preventing escalation** of incipient conflicts:

- Use active listening. Teachers acknowledge and/or paraphrase what students say without agreeing, disagreeing, or expressing value judgment.
- Arrange to speak with the student later. Allow a time for cooling off. It is much easier to have positive discussions after anger has dissipated.
- Keep all communication as private as possible. Students do not want to lose face in front of their peers and so are unlikely to comply with public demands. Nor do teachers like to appear weak in front of the class. When communication is kept private, the chances for productive discussion are much better because egos are not so strongly on the line.
- If a student refuses to accept a consequence, invoke the insubordination rule.

Motivating Difficult-to-Manage Students

Rules, consequences, and enforcement are necessary in all classrooms, but the key to better student behavior lies elsewhere—in motivation to learn. Most students are somewhat motivated to learn and behave properly in school, whether because they find school interesting, like to please the teacher, or simply want to avoid failure. Such is not the case for students behaviorally at risk, who have exceptionally low levels of motivation.

It would be foolish to suggest that a magical set of techniques exists for helping such students. But teachers do know what motivates students in general. Students who are behaviorally at risk have the same general needs and interests as other students, but they have encountered so much failure that they have turned to resistance and misbehavior to bolster their egos. Curwin (1992, pp. 130–144) makes the following suggestions for increasing motivation among students who are behaviorally at risk:

- Select for your lessons as many topics as you can that have personal importance and relevance to the students.
- Set up learning goals that are real—goals that lead to genuine competence that students can display and be proud of.
- Help students interact with the topics in ways that are congruent with their interests and values.
- Involve students actively in lessons. Allow them to use their senses, move about, and talk. Make the lessons as much fun as possible. The lessons don't need to be easy if they are important and enjoyable.
- Give students numerous opportunities to take risks and make decisions without fear of failure.
- Show your own genuine energy and interest in the topics being studied. Show that you enjoy working with students. Try to connect personally with them as individuals.

- Each day, do at least one activity that you love. Show pride in your knowledge and ability to convey it to your students. Don't be reluctant to ham it up.
- Make your class activities events that students look forward to. Make them wonder what might happen next.

INITIATING CURWIN AND MENDLER'S *DISCIPLINE WITH DIGNITY*

Suppose you teach a class that contains several chronically misbehaving students, and you decide that the Curwin and Mendler model might help you deal with them more effectively. How do you put the model in place?

Principles You Must Accept

Before using the approaches Curwin and Mendler propose, you must subscribe to certain principles that undergird their model, as described earlier in this chapter. A primary principle is that student dignity must be preserved. You must understand that students will do all in their power to protect their dignity against threat. They don't want to appear stupid. They don't want to feel incapable. They don't want to be denigrated, especially in front of their peers. When faced with threat, students, especially the chronically misbehaved, use antisocial behavior to deflect it. You must be willing to guard against threatening students' dignity, even when they threaten yours.

A second principle is that dealing with misbehavior is an important part of teaching. You are in the classroom to help your students. Those whose behavior puts them at risk of failure especially need your help, though their behavior may suggest that they want nothing to do with you. The best thing you can do for them is to find ways to encourage prosocial behavior.

A third principle is that lasting results are achieved only over time. There are no quick-fix solutions to chronic misbehavior, but by finding ways to motivate students and help them learn, you will enable many to make genuine improvement.

A fourth principle is that responsibility is more important than obedience. The ability to weigh facts and make good decisions is far more valuable in students' lives than is obedience to demands. You must be willing to put students into situations where they can make decisions about matters that concern them, be willing to allow them to fail, and then help them try again. Progressively, they will learn to behave in ways that are best for themselves and others.

The Social Contract

You will have given much thought to the kind of classroom you want and how you want your students to behave. When you first meet the students, spend as much time as necessary discussing goals for the class, activities that might be helpful, and class behavior that will improve enjoyment and accomplishment. In those discussions, class rules and consequences should be agreed to. It is important that students contribute heavily to those decisions and that you obtain their agreement to abide by them. The rules and consequences should be written out, dated, and signed by teacher and students. The document should be posted in the room and copies sent to parents and administrators.

Motivation and Helpfulness

From the outset you must seek to structure lessons to help students be active and successful. It is far more important that students engage in activities of interest than that they be dragged perfunctorily through the standard curriculum. Your own energy, enjoyment of learning, and pride in teaching will affect students positively, while your willingness to help without confrontation will slowly win them over.

STRENGTHS OF CURWIN AND MENDLER'S *DISCIPLINE WITH DIGNITY*

All teachers experience misbehavior in their classrooms. Most have found ways to deal with minor infractions such as talking, speaking out, chewing gum, and failing to complete homework. But all teachers dread dealing with students whose behavior is so chronically poor that they not only disrupt learning but are likely to fail in school. Dealing with such students makes teachers feel trapped and overwhelmed. The Curwin and Mendler model seems to provide realistic help for working with chronically misbehaving students. They say that school is for students. Like that of all good professionals, teachers' primary responsibility is to help their clients, the students, learn and behave in socially acceptable ways.

Curwin and Mendler point out the ineffectiveness of traditional methods of discipline, the damage that school has done to student dignity, and the self-defeating nature of power struggles between teacher and student. They do not pretend that all out-of-control students can be reformed by the teaching approach they advocate, but they insist that many can and that they are worth saving from failure.

Can teachers make the adjustments Curwin and Mendler advocate? Can they calmly accept being called nasty names, acknowledge that slanderous expletives leveled at them may be partially correct, and all the while keep trying to help students who spurn their every effort? Can they wait weeks or months to see their efforts bear fruit, if indeed they ever do? Human nature does not seem attuned to what Curwin and Mendler ask of teachers. Yet, there is strength in their argument that teachers are professionals and that their job is to help students however they can. If teachers accept that premise, they can also accept that student misbehavior comes from defense of dignity, not from maladaptive pleasure in defying the teacher. And teachers know that Curwin and Mendler's warning about slowly emerging effects is true, even though they always hope for instant success. The way for teachers ultimately to appraise Curwin and Mendler's approach is to try it in the classroom. They have little to lose and potentially a good deal to gain.

REVIEW OF SELECTED TERMINOLOGY

The following terms are central to the Curwin and Mendler model of discipline.

action dimension	logical consequences
behaviorally at-risk	obedience
classroom social contract test	preventing escalation
clients	prevention dimension
consequences	principles of effective discipline
conventional consequences	professionals
creative responses	resolution dimension
dignity	responsibility
dimensions of discipline	sense of hope
generic consequences	short-term solutions
instructional consequences	social contract
insubordination rule	unequal treatment

APPLICATION EXERCISES

CONCEPT CASES

Case 1: Kristina Will Not Work

Kristina, in Mr. Jake's class, is quite docile. She never disrupts class and does little socializing with other students. But despite Mr. Jake's best efforts, Kristina rarely completes an assignment. She doesn't seem to care. She is simply there, putting forth virtually no effort.

How would Curwin and Mendler deal with Kristina? They would suggest the following sequence of interventions: Consider that Kristina's behavior might be due to severe feelings of incapability. She may be protecting herself by not trying. Relate to Kristina as an individual. Chat with her informally about her life and interests. Find topics that interest Kristina. Build class lessons around them. Assign Kristina individual work that helps her become more competent in her areas of special interest. Have a private conversation with Kristina. Ask for her thoughts about how you could make school more interesting for her. Show her you are interested and willing to help. As Kristina begins to work and participate, continue private chats that help her see herself as successful.

Case 2: Sara Cannot Stop Talking

Sara is a pleasant girl who participates in class activities and does most, though not all, of her assigned work. She cannot seem to refrain from talking to classmates, however. Her teacher, Mr. Gonzales, has to speak to her repeatedly during lessons, to the point that he often becomes exasperated and loses his temper.

What suggestions would Curwin and Mendler give Mr. Gonzales to help with Sara's misbehavior?

Case 3: Joshua Clowns and Intimidates

Joshua, larger and louder than his classmates, always wants to be the center of attention, which he accomplishes through a combination of clowning and intimidation. He makes wise remarks, talks back (smilingly) to the teacher, utters a variety of sound-effect noises such as automobile crashes and gunshots, and makes limitless sarcastic comments and put-downs of his classmates. Other students will not stand up to him, apparently fearing his verbal and physical aggression. His teacher, Miss Pearl, has come to her wit's end.

What do you find in Curwin and Mendler's work that might help Miss Pearl deal with Joshua?

Case 4: Tom Is Hostile and Defiant

Tom has appeared to be in his usual foul mood ever since arriving in class. On his way to sharpen his pencil, he bumps into Frank, who complains. Tom tells him loudly to shut up. Miss Baines, the teacher, says, "Tom, go back to your seat." Tom wheels around and says heatedly, "I'll go when I'm damned good and ready!"

How would Curwin and Mendler have Miss Baines deal with Tom?

QUESTIONS AND ACTIVITIES

1. In small groups, conduct practice situations in which classmates act as students who make hurtful comments to you, the teacher. Begin with the examples given here and explore new ones you have seen or think might occur. Take turns being the teacher and responding to the comments in some of the ways Curwin and Mendler suggest.

Example 1

Teacher: "Jonathan, I'd like to see that work finished before the period ends today."

Jonathan: [Sourly] "Fine. Why don't you take it and finish it yourself if that's what you want?"

Teacher:

Example 2

Teacher: "Desirée, that's the second time you've broken our rule about profanity. I'd like to speak with you after class."

Desirée: "No thanks. I've seen enough of your scrawny butt for one day."

Teacher:

Example 3

TEACHER: "Marshall, I'd like for you to get back to work, please."

MARSHALL: [Says nothing but nonchalantly makes a finger signal at the teacher. Other students see it and snicker.]

TEACHER:

Compose additional occurrences. Practice de-escalating the confrontations without becoming defensive, fighting back, or withdrawing your request.

2. Explore Scenario 1 or 2 in the Appendix. Discuss how Curwin and Mendler would have Mrs. Miller or Mr. Platt respond to the situation encountered.
3. One of the suggestions given for motivating students who are difficult to motivate was "Make your class activities events that students look forward to. Make them wonder what might happen next." For a selected grade level, brainstorm ways of complying with this suggestion.

REFERENCES AND RECOMMENDED READINGS

Curwin, R. 1980. Are your students addicted to praise? *Instructor, 90,* 61–62.

———. 1992. *Rediscovering hope: Our greatest teaching strategy.* Bloomington, Ind.: National Educational Service.

———. 1993. The healing power of altruism. *Educational Leadership, 51*(3), 36–39.

———. 1995. A humane approach to reducing violence in schools. *Educational Leadership, 52*(5), 72–75.

Curwin, R., and A. Mendler. 1980. *The discipline book: A complete guide to school and classroom management.* Reston, Va.: Reston Publishing.

———. 1984. High standards for effective discipline. *Educational Leadership, 41*(8), 75–76.

———. 1988a. *Discipline with dignity.* Alexandria, Va.: Association for Supervision and Curriculum Development.

———. 1988b. Packaged discipline programs: Let the buyer beware. *Educational Leadership, 46*(2), 68–71.

———. 1992. Discipline with dignity [Workshop participants handout]. Rochester, N.Y.: Discipline Associates.

Mendler, A., and R. Curwin. 1983. *Taking charge in the classroom.* Reston, Va.: Reston Publishing.

CHAPTER 11

Two Emerging Views on Classroom Discipline

Barbara Coloroso's *Inner Discipline* and Alfie Kohn's *Beyond Discipline*

Barbara Coloroso

Alfie Kohn

PART 1. BARBARA COLOROSO'S *INNER DISCIPLINE*

PREVIEW OF COLOROSO'S WORK

Focus

- Treating students with respect; giving them power and responsibility to make decisions.

- Teachers functioning as guides and supporters to help students manage their own discipline.

Logic

- Students, when helped by teachers, have the ability to develop the quality of inner discipline.

- Decision making is best taught by letting students make decisions and learn from the results.

- Consequences should not punish; they should invite constructive responses from students.

Contributions

- A vision of classrooms as places for learning problem solving and developing inner discipline.

- Clarification of the differential effects of consequences, rewards, bribery, and punishment.

- Creation of the RSVP test as a checklist to evaluate consequences established for students.

Coloroso's Suggestions

- Believe that students are worth every effort, then treat them as adults want to be treated.

- Give students opportunity to solve their problems. "You have a problem: What is your plan?"

- Use natural or reasonable consequences to problems, rather than bribes, rewards, or threats.

- Apply the RSVP checklist to test the value and practicality of consequences.

ABOUT BARBARA COLOROSO

Barbara Coloroso is a former Franciscan nun, now a parent, teacher, workshop leader, author, and affiliate instructor at the University of Northern Colorado. She contends that the climate for a responsibility-oriented school is based upon trust that is cultivated by teachers and administrators from the grassroots level throughout the system. Her ideas are set forth in her books *Kids Are Worth It!: Giving Your Child the Gift of Inner Discipline* (1994) and *Parenting With Wit and Wisdom in Times of Chaos and Confusion* (1998). She has also made numerous contributions to educational publications on topics such as strategies for working with troubled students, creative media for students with special needs and talents, winning at teaching without beating your kids, and assertive confrontations and negotiations. Her 1994 "Kids are worth it!" series includes videos, audiotapes, and workbooks to assist educators in developing a discipline system that creates trust, respect, and success in school. The materials are available from *Kids Are Worth It!,* Post Office Box 621108, Littleton, CO 80162; telephone 800-729-1588; fax 303-972-1204; e-mail bcoloroso@aol.com

COLOROSO'S CENTRAL FOCUS

Coloroso puts major emphasis on guiding students to make their own decisions and take responsibility for their choices. She believes that in order to have good discipline, teachers must do three things: treat students with respect and dignity, give them a sense of positive power in their own lives, and give them opportunities to make decisions, take responsibility for their actions, and learn from their successes and mistakes. She believes that children, with adult help, have the ability to develop inner discipline and manage problems they encounter. She says that with adult guidance and support students can grow to like themselves, think for themselves, and believe there is no problem so great it can't be solved.

COLOROSO'S PRINCIPAL TEACHINGS

Students are worth all the effort teachers can expend on them. They are worth it not just when they are bright, good looking, or well behaved, but always.

School should be neither adult dominated nor student controlled. Rather, it should be a place where joint efforts are made to learn, relate, grow, and create community.

Teachers should never treat students in ways they, the teachers, wouldn't want to be treated. Children have dignity and innate worth, and they deserve treatment accordingly.

If a discipline tactic works, and leaves student and teacher's dignity intact, use it. Self-worth and dignity are to be maintained; anything that damages them is to be avoided.

Proper discipline does four things that punishment cannot do: shows students what they have done wrong, gives them ownership of the problems created, gives them ways to solve the problems, and leaves their dignity intact.

In order to develop inner discipline, children must learn how to think, not just what to think. To this end, teachers must give students responsibility and allow them to make mistakes.

Students have the right to be in school, but they have the responsibility to respect the rights of those around them. This right and responsibility go hand in hand.

Teachers fall into three categories. "Brickwall teachers" are rigid, use power and coercion to control others, and teach what instead of how to think. "Jellyfish teachers" provide little structure, consistency, or guidance, and rely on putdowns, threats, and bribery to control students. "Backbone teachers" provide the support and structure necessary for students to behave creatively, cooperatively, and responsibly, which lead to inner discipline.

Disputes and problems are best resolved with win–win solutions. Rather than rescuing students or lecturing them, teachers can give students opportunities to solve their problems, but in ways that do not depict any disputants as "losers."

Consequences, natural and reasonable, are associated with rules, and are to be allowed or invoked consistently when rules are violated.

Natural consequences are events that happen naturally in the real world. You kick a chair; the consequence is that your toe gets hurt. Teachers should allow students to experience natural consequences so long as the consequences are not physically dangerous, immoral, or unhealthy.

Reasonable consequences are events imposed by the teacher that are related to a violation of rules. If you damage material on loan from a museum, you need to write a letter of apology to the museum indicating how you will avoid a similar accident in the future.

The RSVP test is used to check on consequences the teacher imposes. It reminds teachers that consequences must be reasonable, simple, valuable, and practical.

Students who experience consistent, logical, realistic consequences learn that they themselves have positive control over their lives. On the other hand, students who are constantly bribed, rewarded, and punished learn to be dependent on others for approval, work only to please the teacher, and figure out how to avoid getting caught.

When reasonable consequences are invoked, students frequently try to get teachers to change their minds. To accomplish this, they use "con games" such as crying and begging, arguing angrily and aggressively, and sulking, but teachers must not give in.

ANALYSIS OF COLOROSO'S *INNER DISCIPLINE*

Coloroso's views on discipline are in concert with recent trends that assign students a more active role in taking responsibility for their own behavior. She believes that educators should work with students to help them develop **inner discipline,** the ability to behave creatively, constructively, cooperatively, and responsibly.

Coloroso firmly contends that teachers must believe in the value of their students, that those students are worth all effort expended in their behalf, and that the students can learn to be responsible for their own behavior, make their own decisions, and resolve their own problems. Of course, they require help in developing the ability to do so. The best way for teachers to help is to allow students to make decisions and grow from the results of those decisions, whatever they may be. Teachers have the responsibility to make sure that student decisions do not lead to situations that are life threatening, morally threatening, or unhealthy.

Otherwise, the role of teachers is to bring students to situations that require decisions and, without making judgments, let them proceed through the process. What students then do will sometimes make teachers and students uncomfortable: The discomfort disappears when students resolve the problem constructively. This experience builds the power to deal with problem situations and keeps students' self-esteem intact because it leaves responsibility and power to them. Teachers must trust students with this responsibility and power.

Coloroso believes that responsibility and decision making are essential ingredients in helping students develop inner discipline. She advises teachers to help students confront problem situations, make plans for resolving the situations, and take action on the decision. All the while, students must be allowed to make mistakes and the dignity of everyone involved must be maintained.

Tenets of Inner Discipline

Coloroso bases her work on two fundamental tenets. The first is that students are worth all the time, energy, and effort it takes to help them become resourceful, responsible, resilient, compassionate human beings. She believes that because they are children, and for no other reason, students have dignity and worth. She calls on teachers to make an unconditional commitment to their students.

The second tenet reflects the Golden Rule. Coloroso words it this way: "I will not treat a student in a way I myself would not want to be treated." (1994, p. 11) Discipline based on this proposition places limits on power and control, while making preservation of dignity and self-worth paramount.

Discipline, Not Punishment

Everybody knows that misbehavior has reached serious levels in today's schools. In order to deal successfully with misbehavior, teachers must distinguish clearly between punishment and discipline. Coloroso describes **punishment** as treatment that is psychologically hurtful and unjust to students and likely to provoke anger, resentment, and additional conflict. She goes on to describe punishment as adult-oriented, with power imposed that arouses anger and resentment, which invites more conflict. Students typically respond to punishment with the "three F's"—fear, fighting back, and fleeing, either into themselves or out the door. They become afraid to make a mistake. Students rarely know for sure that a given act will bring punishment. They see it as depending on who the student is and how the teacher feels at the time.

Discipline, on the other hand, shows students what they have done wrong and gives them ownership of the problem. It provides options and opportunities to solve the problems and in so doing leaves students' dignity intact. It uses reasonable, simple, practical, and valuable consequences to help students see that they are responsible for and in control of themselves. Those consequences either occur naturally or are provided by the teacher, but are always related to decisions students have made. By making clear the connections between behavior and consequence, teachers help students better understand whether their behavior has been responsible or irresponsible. Discomfort that arises from irresponsible behavior only goes away after students work together to resolve the problem constructively.

Effective Classroom Discipline Leads to Inner Discipline

The purpose of classroom discipline is ultimately to enable students to take charge of their own decisions. They must also learn to accept the consequences of their decisions. Recognizing the relationship between decisions and their consequences teaches students that they have control over their lives, a requisite for the development of inner discipline.

Coloroso assigns teachers a key role in bringing about inner discipline. She believes teachers can best help by bringing students face to face with their problems and providing them tactics for resolution. She says that before teachers can see themselves in this role, rather than that to which they are accustomed, they must ask themselves two questions and answer them honestly: "What is my goal in teaching?" and "What is my teaching philosophy?" The first has to do with what they hope to achieve with learners, and the second with how they think they should approach the task. Coloroso says that because teachers act in accordance with their beliefs, it is important for them to clarify those beliefs: "Do I want to empower students to take care of themselves, or do I want to make them wait for teachers to tell them what to do and think?" Teachers who feel they must control students turn to bribes, rewards, threats, and punishment to restrict and coerce behavior. On the other hand, teachers who want to empower students to make decisions and resolve their own problems will give students opportunities to think, act, and take responsibility.

Students will make mistakes in the process; therefore they must be provided a safe and nurturing environment in which to learn and deal with consequences. Teachers should allow and respect student decisions, even when they are clearly in error, and must let students experience the consequences of their decisions. Regardless of whether consequences are unpleasant, students learn from them and at the same time learn that they have control over their lives by means of the decisions they make. This process makes it unnecessary for teachers to nag, warn, and constantly remind students of what they ought to be doing.

Teaching Decision Making

Coloroso says that the best way to teach students how to make good decisions is to bring them to situations that call for decisions, ask them to make the decision (while the teacher provides guidance without judgment), and let them experience the results of their decision. This may seem inefficient, but it produces rapid growth in problem solving. Mistakes and poor choices are now the students' responsibility. If they experience discomfort, they have the power to correct the situation in the future.

Coloroso believes that teachers should never rescue students by solving thorny problems for them. Doing so sends the message that students don't have power in their own lives and that some other person (the teacher) must take care of them. When students make mistakes, as they will do, teachers must not lecture them: "If you had studied more, you wouldn't have failed the test." Students already know this. What they now need is opportunity to correct the situation they have created. Coloroso suggests saying the following to them: "You have a problem . . . What is your plan?"

When students are given ownership of problems and situations, they know it is up to them to make matters better. There is no one else to blame. Teachers are there to offer advice and support—options, but not solutions. This allows students to take responsibility for their mistakes, rather than rationalizing them away.

Three Types of Schools and Teachers

Coloroso says there are three basic types of schools and teachers. They have very different effects on students. She calls them the *brickwalls,* the *jellyfish,* and the *backbones.*

Brickwall schools and teachers are rigid, use power and coercion to control. They demand that students follow rules without question and use punishment, humiliation, threats, and bribes to make them do so. When Greg tries to explain that his homework is not completed because he had to stay late to close up the store, Mr. Brickwall replies, "That's really too bad, but I'm not interested in excuses. You know that homework is due on Thursdays. I won't accept it now."

Two types of **jellyfish** schools and teachers exist, but the effect on students is the same. Generally, jellyfish schools and teachers have little or no recognizable structure, consistency, or guidelines. Punishments and rewards are arbitrary and inconsistent, and teachers use lecturing, putdowns, threats, and bribes for control. These teachers only know how to act and react according to rules, and they don't know how to change their behavior. These jellyfish teachers are lax in discipline, set few limits, and more or less let students have their way. As the fourth graders finish their messy art project, Ms. A. Jellyfish is laughing and having fun with them. Later, when the period is ending and the students have not begun to clean up, she says, "Oh my, look at this mess! Clean it up immediately or we'll have to stay after school while you do it."

Other jellyfish teachers are focused almost completely on themselves and don't believe in students' capabilities. They often believe that if anything is to get done, they must do it themselves. Consequently, their remarks to students are often destructive and unsupportive. Ms. B. Jellyfish would say: "I spent an hour in class today explaining how to do these problems, and you still don't get it. If you haven't figured it out yet . . ." She shakes her head.

Backbone schools and teachers provide support and structure necessary for children to act responsibly by reasoning through problems. They use rules that are clear and simple, with consequences that are reasonable, simple, valuable, and purposeful. Children get opportunities to correct mistakes they make or solve problems they have, with full support from the teacher. Because the teacher neither tells them what to do nor does the work for them, students learn how to think. When Greg explains that he had to stay late to close up the store, Ms. Backbone says: "I understand why your homework would not be finished. Give me your plan to get it done."

The Three Cons

When students violate class rules, consequences come into play. But even when the consequences are expected and reasonable, many students will try to get out of them. Coloroso describes three ploys students typically use in hopes of escaping consequences. She calls them the **three cons.** They are:

Con 1: Students beg, bribe, weep, and wail ("Oh, please, oh, please"). Some teachers give in and admonish students, saying "All right this once, but you better never do that again." Coloroso says that the message teachers are really sending by giving in is: "I don't believe in you or trust in you. . . . I'll have to take care of you." This is counterproductive in developing students' sense of inner discipline. If Con 1 fails, students often follow with . . .

Con 2: Students respond with anger and aggression: "I hate this stupid class." Because Con 2 affects teachers' emotions, they tend either to lash back or become passive. Passivity invites aggression, and lashing back tends to produce counter-attack. Teachers must be calm and say, "I'm sorry you do, but this is the consequence we have agreed to."

Con 3: Students sulk. Sulking is the most powerful of the three cons: Students' actions say, "I'm not gonna do what you say. You can't make me." Teachers cannot make students do anything they choose not to do. But it is counterproductive to say something like "That's right! Go ahead and pout!" This statement almost certainly will make the sulking worse. The best course is calmly to invoke the consequence in a matter-of-fact way.

Coloroso says that teachers lose positive power in students' lives when they give in to pleas or bribes, become angry at students in response to the student's anger, and reinforce sulking. To retain their positive power, teachers encourage students to own both the problem and the solution. By not giving in to con games, teachers also preserve more energy for teaching.

Problem Solving

Problem solving is one of the most important skills students can learn. They will learn better and more quickly if they know that it is all right to make mistakes. They must also learn to distinguish between *reality* and *problem,* with reality being an accurate appraisal of what has occurred in a situation and problem being the discomfort being caused by the reality. Coloroso says that in learning to solve problems, "We accept (the) realities; (then) we solve the problems that come from them." (p. 31) Coloroso contends that as students make this distinction they begin to see that there is no problem so great it cannot be solved. But when experiencing a problem, students need a way of attacking it. The approach they use should culminate in a plan, not an excuse. Coloroso suggests a problem-solving strategy that consists of six steps:

Identify and Define the Problem

Accurate identification and definition of the problem is a necessary first step in problem solving. Josh asks for the book he lent Melissa. He needs it for a report due on Friday. Melissa can't find the book, but remembers she left it on the kitchen table near the books her mother was donating to the library. Both Josh and Melissa experience a problem—discomfort for Josh regarding the assigned report, and pressure on Melissa for not returning the book. Let us look at the problem from Melissa's perspective. How is it to be resolved?

List Possible Solutions

Melissa's first thoughts are to (1) say she left the book on Josh's desk, or (2) avoid Josh. With more thought, Melissa adds three more options: 3) see if she can find the book at the library, 4) buy a new book for Josh, or (5) borrow Randy's book for Josh to use.

Evaluate the Options

Melissa now evaluates the options and finds one that might work for her. The option she first identified isn't satisfactory. Though the thought crossed her mind, Melissa decides she is unwilling to lie. The second cannot work either: Josh is her neighbor and they usually do homework together after school. The third is a possibility: The book may have been delivered to the library and can be found there. The fourth is an option but not a desirable one: Melissa borrowed the book in the first place because she didn't want to pay what a new book cost. The fifth would be only a temporary solution and, besides, Randy needs his book for himself.

As Melissa attempts to decide which of the options to use, she has learned to ask herself four questions about each of the options:

1. Is it unkind?
2. Is it hurtful?
3. Is it unfair?
4. Is it dishonest?

Melissa recognizes that the first option would be dishonest, the second hurtful, and the fifth unfair to both Randy and Josh. That leaves her two possible options.

Choose One Option

Melissa decides that she must go to the public library and see if the book can be found. If the book is located, she will explain the circumstances and get the book back.

Make a Plan and DO IT

Admitting to and owning a problem, making a plan, and following through are difficult things to do, for adults as well as students. It means that excuses are not acceptable, and it means one must accept responsibility for mistakes and consequences. If the plan does not work, then a new option must be tried. If Melissa cannot find the book at the library, she will have to borrow money from her parents to replace the book. That will mean taking on extra chores to repay them, but it is a responsibility she knows she must accept.

Re-evaluate the Problem and the Solution
Most people skip this step, but it is important for learning. Three questions should be asked:

1. What caused the problem in the first place?
2. How can a similar problem be avoided in the future?
3. Was the problem solution satisfactory?

In this instance the problem was probably caused accidentally. However, if Melissa is often careless in misplacing things she needs, a change in her behavior is called for. She might improve by designating a special place in which to put borrowed items. In this process of solving the problem, Melissa's self-esteem has remained intact and her sense of ability to solve problems has been reinforced. No one told her what to do. She maintained positive control over her own decisions.

Natural Consequences

When students are allowed to solve their own problems, their decisions will produce consequences that they may or may not anticipate. Coloroso believes in allowing consequences to occur without adult intervention, provided the consequences are not harmful. For example, if Jacob walks to the gym without his coat, he will get cold. Being cold is a **natural consequence** to dressing improperly for weather and temperature. If Fazilat borrows crayons but returns them broken, her table mates will stop lending her their crayons.

Physically Dangerous
Adults must intervene whenever students' decisions place them in undue physical danger. If Jose and Zachary are fighting on the playground and Zachary produces a knife, it is no time for teachers to stand aside so the boys can work out the situation between them. The teacher must intervene. Zachary will experience the consequences of having a knife at school.

Immoral
When students make decisions that are unlawful or unethical, the teacher must intervene. These are excellent times for discussions about behavior that is right and wrong, but teachers must not allow students to commit immoral acts just so they can learn from the consequences.

Reasonable Consequences and RSVP

At times, natural consequences do not help students learn. This is especially the case when students decide to break rules that have been established for the good of the class, as when they shout out during instruction. To deal with cases such as this, teacher and students should jointly agree to a set of **reasonable consequences** that will be invoked for transgressions of rules. Coloroso proposes a checklist she calls **RSVP** to use in assessing the quality of reasonable consequences. RSVP stands for reasonable, simple, valuable, and practical, traits that should characterize all consequences established for violations of class rules. These consequences do not punish, but instead call upon the student to take positive steps to improve behavior. They do so by helping students see what they have done wrong, giving them ownership of the problems created, and helping them find ways to solve the problems, all while leaving their dignity intact.

COLOROSO'S BELIEFS IN REVIEW

As you can see, Coloroso believes in students' ability to accept ownership of their problems, resolve the problems, and live by the consequences of their decisions. She believes that dealing with problems and accepting consequences help students take charge of their lives.

Coloroso doesn't limit her suggestions to individual classrooms. She sees discipline as a school-wide concern and would have schools establish an overarching positive climate that permits students and teachers to solve problems, make mistakes, and profit from the mistakes. Every adult in such a school would provide safe choices for helping students become more responsible.

Within this broad climate, students would understand that they have a rightful place in school, but that they also have the responsibilities to respect the rights of others and to be actively involved in their own behavior and learning. They learn they must take ownership of their decisions and not try to rationalize mistakes. While active in making choices and problem-solving, students maintain their dignity.

Coloroso provides teachers a tangible philosophy of discipline. Her beliefs are humanistic and focused on preserving dignity and sense of self-worth. It is through experiences with these qualities that Coloroso believes students develop inner discipline.

REVIEW OF SELECTED TERMINOLOGY

The following terms are central to understanding Coloroso's work.

backbone teachers and schools	natural consequences
brickwall teachers and schools	punishment
discipline	reasonable consequences
inner discipline	RSVP
jellyfish teachers and schools	three cons

PART 2. ALFIE KOHN'S *BEYOND DISCIPLINE*

PREVIEW OF KOHN'S WORK

Focus

- Classrooms that promote thinking, decision-making, and consideration for others.
- Replacing coercive controls with student involvement in resolving classroom problems.

Logic

- Students develop self-control and responsibility when teachers show trust and allow initiative.
- The most effective teachers use collaborative problem-solving instead of coercive control.

Contributions

- Pointed out how coercive discipline is detrimental to the development of caring human beings.
- Popularized the concept of classroom as community, where everyone participates equally.
- Provided operating principles to help teachers transform their classrooms into communities.

Kohn's Suggestions

- Relinquish traditional discipline in favor of truly participative classroom management.
- Do all that is possible to develop bonds of trust between teacher and students.
- Involve students seriously in discussions about curriculum, procedures, and class problems.
- Always ask the question: How can I bring my students into helping decide on this matter?

ABOUT ALFIE KOHN

Formerly a teacher, Alfie Kohn is now a full-time writer and lecturer. He has five influential books to his credit: *The Brighter Side of Human Nature: Altruism and Empathy in Everyday Life* (1990), *You Know What They Say . . . : The Truth About Popular Beliefs* (1990), *No Contest: The Case Against Competition* (1986, 1992), *Punished By Rewards: The Trouble with Gold Stars, Incentive Plans, A's, Praise, and Other Bribes* (1993), and his most recent, *Beyond Discipline: From Compliance to Community* (1996). He has also published a number of articles in prestigious journals related to motivation, grading, discipline, and developing caring people. Now recognized as one of the most original thinkers in education, Kohn has appeared on over 200 radio and television programs, including "Oprah" and "The Today Show," and his work has received mention in scores of national newspapers and magazines. He speaks frequently at major conferences and conducts workshops across the nation. He can be reached at 242 School St., Belmont, MA 02178.

KOHN'S CENTRAL FOCUS

Kohn's work in school discipline has been focused mainly on developing caring, supportive classrooms in which students participate fully in solving problems, including problems of behavior. He has roundly criticized discipline programs that do things *to* students rather than *involving* students as partners in resolving problems. His attacks on discipline schemes that involve reward and punishment—which most of them do— have been particularly scathing. He says that "consequence" is just another word teachers use for "punishment," and contends that nothing valuable comes from reward and punishment—that they are actually counterproductive in that they cause students to mistrust their own judgment and stunt their becoming caring and self-reliant. In the place of discipline based on reward and punishment, he advises teachers to work toward developing a sense of community in their classes, where students feel safe but are continually brought into making judgments, expressing their opinions, and working cooperatively toward solutions that benefit the class.

KOHN'S CONTRIBUTIONS TO DISCIPLINE

Kohn has made two significant contributions to discourse on classroom discipline. The first is his persuasive dismantling of programs based on reward and punishment, which most of them are, he contends, though humanistic-sounding language may be used by their originators. The second contribution is his rationale and prescription for sense of community in the classroom, which he judges essential for developing students who are caring and responsible.

KOHN'S PRINCIPAL CONTENTIONS

Educators must look beyond the techniques of discipline and ask the question: What are we attempting to accomplish with discipline? Doing this, he says, will make evident that most teachers are thinking in terms of making students compliant and quiet, conditions that do not develop the kinds of people we'd like students to become over the long term.

Virtually all popular discipline programs are based on threat, reward, and punishment, used to gain student compliance. Essentially, discipline programs differ only in how kindly and respectfully the teacher speaks to students while using threat, reward, and punishment.

When students are rewarded (or punished) into compliance, they usually feel no commitment to what they are doing. They have no real understanding of why they are doing the act and are not becoming people who *want* to act this way in the future.

Rules are of no practical value in the classroom. This is because students learn how best to behave not from being told, but from having the opportunity to behave responsibly.

Some teachers—and most authorities in discipline—have an unrealistically negative view of students' basic motives. They consider students to be predisposed to disobedience and trouble-making. They seem also to ignore that the curriculum powerfully influences student interest and involvement.

Student growth toward kindness, happiness, and self-fulfillment depends on working closely with fellow students. This includes students' disagreeing and arguing with each other.

There is something a little suspicious about classrooms that operate too smoothly and cleanly. Healthy conflict may have been conveniently pushed aside or suppressed.

When concerns arise, the teacher should always ask students "What do you think we can do to solve this problem?"

Class meetings offer the best forum for addressing questions that affect the class.

Education must be reformed so that classrooms take on the nature of communities. A classroom community is a place where students are cared about and care about others, are valued and respected, and think in terms of *we* instead of *I.*

Teachers who wish to move beyond discipline must do three things: provide an engaging curriculum, develop a sense of community, and draw students into meaningful decision-making.

ANALYSIS OF KOHN'S *BEYOND DISCIPLINE*

What Is Discipline For?

It is time, Kohn says (1996, p. 54), to decide just what it is we hope to accomplish with discipline. That is, we should take a serious look beyond the *methods* of discipline to the *goals* of discipline. This statement gives pause. Most people have taken for granted that the goal of discipline is to control student behavior (or enable students to control their own behavior in accordance with adult expectations) so that teaching and learning may proceed as intended. But Kohn persists in putting the question: "Just what is it we are trying to do here?"

This question presents an issue, he says, that people who write about and do research in discipline never address. They expound on "effective discipline," but effective in regard to what? The obvious answer is that discipline is effective when it causes students to behave as teachers wish them to. Therein lies the rub, in Kohn's view. All approaches to discipline, when analyzed, reveal a clear set of assumptions about students, learning, and the role of the teacher. While these assumptions are never made explicit, even in the writings of the most respected authorities, they directly suggest that (1) students are by nature predisposed to disrupt the learning program and deal misery to teachers, (2) learning occurs best in an atmosphere of structure, quiet, and order, and (3) the teacher's role in discipline is to make students obedient, compliant, and above all, quiet.

Kohn contends that these three assumptions are ill-founded, and therefore he finds fault with virtually all the popular approaches to classroom discipline. He points, for example, to the work of Jacob Kounin (see Chapter 2), one of the first writers to attempt a scientific analysis of classroom behavior related to discipline. Preeminent among several teacher traits that Kounin found helpful in discipline is one called "withitness." Teachers display this trait when they are attentive to what all students are doing in the classroom at all times, and makes sure the students are aware of it. Such teachers are shown to be more effective than their "withoutit" colleagues, to use Kohn's words. But to what does the word "effective" refer? Kohn points out that Kounin used it to mean getting student conformity and obedience. In other words, it means that students keep busy at their assigned work and don't do anything the teacher considers inappropriate. Kohn says:

> Now, if a good classroom is one where students simply do what they're told, we shouldn't be surprised that a teacher is more likely to have such a classroom when students are aware that she can quickly spot noncompliance. (p. 55).

Kohn goes on to note that subsequent researchers have found that classroom management is most effective when the teacher controls pacing and does not allow long periods of student talk. Kohn adds that effective teachers are depicted as those who retain control over just about everything, closely direct and monitor students, and provide highly structured tasks. Kohn says:

> Again, these results are perfectly logical if we accept the premises; the techniques follow naturally from the objective. The objective is not to promote depth of understanding, or continuing motivation to learn, or concern for others. It is to maximize time on task and obedience to authority. (p. 55).

Kohn levels some of his sharpest criticisms against the Canters' *Assertive Discipline,* citing passages from the Canters' (1992, p. 180) work such as:

> Remember, what you really want is for the student to comply with your request. Whether or not the student does it in an angry manner is not the issue. The student is still complying with your expectations.

But Kohn plays no favorites: He is troubled by the similar contentions in the works of Dreikurs (see Chapter 2), Albert (see Chapter 6), and Curwin and Mendler (see Chapter 10). He alludes to what he calls the rhetoric that accompanies the newer, supposedly more humane discipline systems, but says:

> What really counts, however, is what goes on in a classroom where such a program is in operation. What would be inferred by a visitor who had never read the rhetoric? What philosophy is implied by the specific practical recommendations? The answer, I have reluctantly concluded, is that the New Disciplines are just as much about getting compliance as is the more traditional approach. The overriding goal is to get students to do what they are supposed to be doing . . . (and) to learn what's acceptable to the teacher and what's not. (Kohn 1996, p. 59)

After reviewing a number of popular discipline systems, Kohn concludes that all are based on threat, reward, and punishment, as ways to obtain student compliance. Essentially, they differ only in how kindly and respectfully the teacher speaks to students. The real problem with all the popular discipline systems, he says, is that they are designed to control people, which in turn reflects the schools' view that the teacher should base teaching on a strategy that gets students to comply.

The Trouble with Compliance

Clearly, Kohn is deeply troubled by the notion that schooling is structured to force, or at least entice, compliant behavior from students. Most teachers are delighted when students comply with their expectations, so what is wrong with compliance? Kohn describes how he often begins workshops with teachers by asking the question: "What are your long-terms goals for the students you work with? What would you like them to be—to be like—long after they've left you?" (p. 60).

The answers, he says, describe a kind of person. Teachers want their students to be caring, happy, responsible, curious, and creative. This exercise, Kohn (1996, p. 61) contends,

> is unsettling because it exposes a yawning chasm between what we want and what we are doing, between how we would like students to turn out and how our classrooms and schools actually work. We want children to continue reading and thinking after school has ended, yet we focus their attention on grades, which have been shown to reduce interest in learning. We want them to be critical thinkers, yet we feed them predigested facts and discrete skills—partly because of pressure from various constituencies to pump up standardized test scores. We act as though our goal is short-term retention of right answers rather than genuine understanding.

Many teachers rely heavily on rewarding students who behave or respond as teachers want. But Kohn points out that even when students are rewarded into compliance, they usually feel no commitment to what they are doing, no genuine understanding of the act or why they are doing it, and no sense that they are becoming people who *want* to act this way in the future.

> The more we "manage" students' behavior and try to make them do what we say, the more difficult it is for them to become morally sophisticated people who think for themselves and care about others. (Kohn 1996, p. 62)

Kohn says that if compliance is *not* what teachers are looking for in the long run, then we are faced with a basic conflict between our ultimate goals for learners and the methods we are using to achieve those goals. Something, Kohn asserts, has got to give.

The Trouble with Rules

Virtually every discipline system suggests that a set of rules be constructed to govern behavior in the classroom. These rules are not entirely arbitrary. Usually, students and teachers collaborate in developing them. The result is a list of rule statements for everyone to follow that will ensure the conditions they desire. The great majority of teachers have such rules for their classrooms, and they often write them out and post them in the room.

Kohn doesn't think rules are such a good idea. While acknowledging that many teachers when making rules have a more laudable goal in mind than just getting kids to obey, they err, Kohn contends, when they try to reach their objectives by drilling students in the right way to act. This is because students learn best not from being told, but from having the opportunity to reflect on the proper way to conduct themselves. This has nothing to do with what teacher-made rules may tell students to do (respect other people's feelings, for example). The problem is that rules blind teachers to what students can achieve when allowed to function more autonomously. Kohn cites Lewis (1995, p. 144) who writes that we ought to be concerned even when "very reasonable rules [are] . . . imposed and enforced from above, with little opportunity for students to develop an understanding of or personal commitment to them." Kohn says that we see this "imposed from above" approach every time a teacher uses public praise to re-inforce behavior.

But there are deeper reasons for staying away from class rules. *First,* there is something about rules that makes all of us, certainly including students, look for lim-its and loopholes. When a discussion about behavior occurs, students have already pre-pared a list of technicalities they can present to show that their behavior was within limits. This process obviously runs contrary to the intended purpose of rules and cre-ates a disturbing mindset in students: How can I gain by hedging on the rules, and will the gain of violations be worth the pain of getting caught? Thus the rules do nothing to develop moral judgment, nor do they define the kind of community in which the student can flourish. They exist merely to enforce a predetermined code of conduct that remains the same for various situations and problems.

Second, rules cause teachers to function as police officers, whether they want to or not, a role greatly at odds with their serving as facilitators of learning and caring al-lies. Upon becoming a teacher, one immediately feels duty-bound to uphold order, ac-cepting that whenever students are present one must always be on guard for violations. And students, for their part, avoid the presence of adults for fear that they will be con-trolled or chastised for what they would otherwise do naturally. This taking-on of ad-versarial roles is ruinous to creating a caring community.

Third, rules by definition carry the concept of punitive consequences for viola-tions. This, says Kohn, throws teachers back into believing they must do something *to* students rather than working *with* them to solve problems. The more hard and fast the rule, the more likely it is that this will happen.

Doing without classroom rules does not mean that students and teacher are to do whatever they personally feel like doing. Rather, it means that teacher and students work together to try to identify how they want their classroom to be and how that can be made to happen. There is a vast difference between a classroom's being guided by a set of behavioral rules and a considered reflection about how teacher and students prefer to live and learn together. Kohn likens the difference to spending a lifetime doing what one is told, as contrasted with taking an active role in helping construct the sort of society in which one would prefer to live.

The Changes That Are Needed

If we do away with reward and punishment to coerce behavior, indeed if we move away from compliance entirely as the goal of discipline, then what are we left with? Most people ask, "Aren't there times when we simply need students to do what we tell them?" Kohn begins his reply to that question with the suggestion that teachers think carefully about the number of occasions when "students need to do what the teacher tells them." He notes that the number of such occasions varies widely from one teacher to another, which suggests that the need for student compliance is seated in the teacher's personality and background, rather than in an objective feature of the situa-tion. Teachers ought to examine their preferences and bring them to their conscious level: If one teacher needs students to be more compliant than another, is that teacher then entitled to use a coercive discipline program to meet his or her particular needs?

Kohn suggests that it is far preferable for that teacher to examine the source of his or her need for student compliance.

Upon considering this point, many teachers are inclined to ask whether this means that anything goes, that students don't have to comply with expectations that they participate and learn, that they can ignore assignments, shout obscenities, and create havoc.

This concern, Kohn explains, misses the point. The question isn't whether it's all right for students to act in those ways, but rather, are they likely to do so if their teacher does not demand control and compliance, but instead emphasizes a curriculum that appeals to students. Teachers do not have to choose between chaos on the one hand and being a strong boss on the other. There is another, and better, approach for teachers, which is to work with students in creating a democratic community where the teacher is not much concerned with personal status and only rarely with demanding compliance.

Kohn contends that students in such classrooms are likely to comply with teacher expectations when it is truly necessary for them to do so, and he admits that there will be such times. But students are more apt to comply willingly when bonds of trust have been built between teacher and students. Just as the teacher has made a habit of trusting students, students come to trust and respect the teacher in return.

The Value of Conflict

Student growth toward kindness, happiness, and self-fulfillment depends more on working closely with fellow students, including disagreeing and arguing with them, than with following rules and learning discrete bits of information. Kohn says that it is more important for students to wrestle with dilemmas, clash with others' ideas, and take others' needs into account than to follow sets of rules. The sound of children arguing (at least in many circumstances) should be music to teachers' ears. True, conflict can become destructive, in which case it must be stopped. But disagreement presents golden opportunities for learning and, hence, should not be suppressed. Even hurtful forms of conflict need to be resolved rather than pushed aside. (Kohn notes that teachers should be wary of various versions of "conflict resolution" that do not examine the deeper issues involved, including people's motives and the possibility that something valuable may be gained from dealing with the conflict.) Kohn expresses suspicion about classrooms that operate too smoothly and cleanly: To him, they suggest that conflict may have been conveniently suppressed by the teacher. He quotes Eric Schaps (1990, p. 8), who expressed concern about a classroom where cooperative learning was proceeding with students saying all the right things. "Deeper learning would look somewhat messier than what I am seeing," Schaps remarked, adding that the teacher was typical of many who seem "satisfied with easy or predictable answers. Their questions do not often probe or challenge; their comments are often routine and formulaic." If teachers and students were really exploring ideas wholeheartedly, there would be more conflict, more frustration.

Teachers question the practicality of stopping planned lessons in favor of lessons about resolving conflict. Certainly many situations do not permit an extended discussion at the time they occur. When that is the case, the teacher may wish to ask for a conversation about the matter later on. The enlightened point of view, hard though it may be to accept at first, is that teachers should expect and welcome students' arguments about the rules. Students become thinkers when they try to make sense of things in their own minds. Students who cannot voice their opinions find ways of expressing them in ways far less productive than rational argument. Kohn says that discipline writers are wrong in suggesting that teachers should do everything possible to keep classroom misbehavior from occurring. He suggests instead that

> the real quantum leap in thinking is not from after-the-fact to prevention, where problems are concerned. It involves getting to the point that we ask, "What exactly is construed as a problem here—and why?" It means shifting from eliciting conformity and ending conflict to helping students become active participants in their own social and ethical development. (1996, p. 77)

Regarding Structure and Limits

Most teachers feel structure and limits on student behavior are essential. Is their belief justified? Kohn presents criteria for determining how defensible a structure or limit is, that is, how much it resembles plain teacher control. Here are some of his criteria:

- *Purpose.* A restriction is legitimate to the extent its objective is to protect students from harm, as opposed to imposing order for its own sake.
- *Restrictiveness.* The less restrictive a structure or limit, the better. Kohn says that it is harder, for example, to justify a demand for silence than for quiet voices.
- *Flexibility.* While some structure is helpful, one must always be ready to modify the structure in accordance with student needs.
- *Developmental appropriateness.* Kohn uses the example that while we need to make sure that young children are dressed for winter weather, it is better to let older students decide on such matters for themselves.
- *Presentation style.* The way in which restrictions are presented to a class makes a big difference in their acceptance. Kohn cites a study that found no negative effects when guidelines for using art supplies were presented respectfully to students. But when the identical rules were presented to another group in a tone that ordered them to comply, the students showed less interest and did less creative work.
- *Student involvement.* Most importantly, it is student input that makes structure acceptable. When concerns arise, the teacher can ask students "What do you think we can do to solve this problem?"

Class Meetings

Kohn agrees with many other authorities that class meetings offer the best forum for addressing questions that affect the class. He makes these points about class meetings:

- *Sharing.* Class meetings are a place to talk about interesting events. Students decide whether or not they want to speak up.

- *Deciding.* Class meetings are ideal places for deciding on matters that affect the class, such as furniture arrangement and procedures for working on projects.
- *Planning.* Class meetings are places where planning should be done for field trips, raising money, inviting chaperons, and so forth. Teachers should always be asking themselves "Wait a minute: How can I bring the students in on this?"
- *Reflecting.* Class meetings are good places to think about progress, what has been learned, what might have worked better, and what changes might help the class.

Holding good class meetings is not as easy as it sounds, Kohn cautions. Sometimes participants can't agree on a solution. Sometimes students don't participate. Sometimes students behave in an unkindly manner to someone's idea, or don't pay attention. Sometimes one or two students dominate the meeting. Kohn reminds us that these are not problems for the teacher to solve alone. They are to be brought up for consideration and dealt with by the group.

Many teachers say they like the idea of class meetings, but there simply isn't time in their schedules to include them. Kohn gives a simple response to that concern: You make the time. Class meetings are too important to leave by the wayside. They bring social and ethical benefits, foster intellectual development, motivate students to become more effective learners, and greatly cut down on the need to deal with discipline problems. Kohn tells of a secondary math teacher who regularly devotes time to class meetings even though the class is limited to a total of 45 minutes per day. In their meetings the students reflect on how the class is going, exchange ideas on their independent projects, decide when the next test should be scheduled, and decide when it would be appropriate to work in small groups.

Making Decisions

The process of making decisions produces many benefits for students, such as helping them be more self-reliant, causing them to think issues through, and encouraging them to buy-in to the school program. This is not a matter to be reserved for older students alone. As Kohn says, it is experience with decisions that helps children become capable of handling them.

But students long accustomed to being told what to do may need time to get used to deciding on things for themselves. Kohn cautions that students may respond to increased freedom in several different ways—ways that can be discouraging to educators who aren't prepared for reactions such as:

- *Acting out.* As students adjust to greater freedom, teachers may see a lot more behavior of every kind, including negative behavior. This is not especially pleasant, Kohn says, but he urges teachers to keep thinking, "Bring the kids in on it." In class meetings ask them if they can figure out what's going on and what to do about it.
- *Testing.* Students may test teachers in several ways in order to see whether the teacher means what he or she says about wanting students to express

themselves. They may be trying to see whether the teacher really means it when saying "This is *our* classroom!"

- *Outright resistance.* Students may simply refuse to do what the teacher asks. That is a good time to discuss with them questions such as "What is the teacher's job? And what about yours? Are you old enough to participate in such decisions? Do you learn better in a classroom where someone is always telling you what to do?"
- *Silence.* Some students will not participate in class discussions, even when asked for their opinion. The teacher should reflect on why this is happening. It might be that the student has nothing to say for the moment, or doesn't feel safe with the teacher or classmates, or is chronically shy, or has trouble handling new responsibility.
- *Parroting.* Some students will make glib remarks in discussions, hoping to say what the teacher wants to hear. When that occurs, the teacher might want to invite deeper reflection rather than taking that response at face value. In so doing, one should be careful not to criticize the individual student.

School as a Community

Kohn writes at length about the importance of transforming schools and classrooms into **communities.** By *community* Kohn means

> a place in which students feel cared about and are encouraged to care about each other. They experience a sense of being valued and respected; the children matter to one another and to the teacher. They have come to think in the plural: they feel connected to each other; they are part of an "us." And, as a result of all this, they feel safe in their classes, not only physically but emotionally. (1996, pp. 101–102)

Kohn suggests various strategies teachers and schools can use in moving toward a greater sense of community. Among them are the following:

Building Relationships between Teachers and Students
Students come to behave more respectfully when important adults in their lives behave respectfully toward *them.* They are more likely to care about others if they know *they* are cared about. If their emotional needs are met, they show a tendency to help meet other people's needs rather than remaining preoccupied with themselves.

Enhancing Connections among Students
Connections among students are established and enhanced through activities that involve interdependence. Familiar activities for accomplishing this objective include cooperative learning, getting-to-know-you activities such as interviewing fellow students and introducing them to the class, and finding a partner to check opinions with on whatever is being discussed at the moment. Kohn also suggests using activities that promote "perspective taking," in which students try to see situations from another person's point of view.

Undertaking Classwide and Schoolwide Activities

To develop a sense of community, students need plenty of opportunity for the whole class to collaborate on group endeavors. This might involve producing a class mural, producing a class newsletter or magazine, staging a verse choir performance, or doing some community service activity as a class. Kohn contends that the overall best activity for involving the entire group is a class meeting, as discussed earlier. Such meetings at the beginning of the year can be particularly helpful in establishing a sense of community. Kohn suggests posing questions at these first meetings, such as: What makes school awful sometimes? Try to remember an experience during a previous year when you hated school, when you felt bad about yourself, or about everyone else, and you couldn't wait for it to be over. What exactly was going on when you were feeling that way? How was the class set up?"

Kohn says that not enough teachers encourage this sort of rumination, particularly in elementary schools where an aggressively sunny outlook pervades. Feelings of anger or self-doubt do not vanish when their expression is forbidden.

Using Academic Instruction

The quest for community is not separate from academic learning. Class meetings can be devoted to talking about how the next unit in history might be approached, or what the students thought was best and worst about the math test. Academic study pursued in cooperative groups enables students to make connections while learning from each other. And units in language arts and literature can be organized to promote reflection on helpfulness, fairness, and compassion.

Moving beyond Discipline

Teachers who wish to move beyond discipline must do three things: provide an engaging curriculum, develop a caring community, and provide students latitude in making choices. When this is accomplished, Kohn says, the result can be properly called a democracy. In this kind of classroom, the teacher's point of departure when problems occur is to ask: *How can I work with students to solve this problem? How can I turn this into a chance to help them learn?*

Kohn offers ten suggestions that he believes will be helpful to teachers who wish to move beyond discipline but find that their efforts do not produce the desired results:

1. Work on establishing a trusting, caring relationship with your students. It's hard to work with a student to solve a problem unless the two of you already have a relationship on which to build.
2. Work diligently toward acquiring in yourself, and developing in your students, skills of listening carefully, remaining calm, generating suggestions, and imagining someone else's point of view.
3. When an unpleasant situation occurs, your first effort should be to diagnose what has happened and why. If you have a trusting relationship with students, you can gently ask them to speculate about why they hurt someone else's feelings, or why they keep coming to class late.

4. To figure out what is really going on, be willing to look beyond the concrete situation. Do not immediately identify the student as the sole source of the problem while letting one's self off the hook. We should ask ourselves, or the student or the class, what is really going on here? Can we do anything to help? Try sitting down in a friendly way and see if a plan can be made that will resolve the problem.

5. Maximize student involvement in making decisions and resolving problems. Individual students should be asked, "What do you think we can do to solve this problem?" Involving students is far more likely to lead to a meaningful, lasting solution than having the teacher decide unilaterally what must be done.

6. Work with students on coming up with authentic solutions to problems. This requires not easy responses but an open-ended exploration of possibilities and reflection on motive.

7. When students do something cruel, our first priority is to help them understand that what they did is wrong, and why it is wrong, to deter it from happening again. Then, an examination should be made of ways to make restitution or reparation, such as trying to restore, replace, repair, clean up, or apologize. Making amends is important and should be viewed as an essential part of the process, but more importantly, students must construct meaning for themselves around concepts of fairness and responsibility, just as they would around concepts in mathematics and literature.

8. When new plans or strategies are put into effect, be sure to review them later to see how they have worked.

9. Remain flexible and use judgment concerning when you need to talk with a student about a problem. Sometimes it is better to delay the talk for a while so the student will feel more inclined to discuss it.

10. On the rare occasions when you must use control, do so in a way that minimizes its punitive impact. Sometimes, despite your every effort, you will have to control misbehavior. A student may be disrupting the class, despite repeated requests not to do so. In that case you may have to isolate the student or send him or her from the room. But even then your tone should be warm and regretful and you should express confidence that the two of you will eventually solve the problem together.

APPLICATION EXERCISES

QUESTIONS AND ACTIVITIES

1. In what ways are Coloroso's and Kohn's ideas on discipline similar? In what ways do they differ?

2. Examine Scenario 1 in the Appendix. Explain (a) how you believe Coloroso would advise dealing with the class and (b) how you believe Kohn would advise doing so.

REFERENCES AND RECOMMENDED READINGS

Coloroso, B. 1994. *Kids are worth it!: Giving your child the gift of inner discipline.* New York: William Morrow.

———. 1989. *Winning at parenting . . . without beating your kids.* Booklet; video; audio. Littleton, Colo.: Kids are worth it!

———. 1990. *Winning at teaching . . . without beating your kids.* Booklet; video; audio. Littleton, Colo.: Kids are worth it!

———. 1990. *Discipline: Creating a Positive School Climate.* Booklet; video; audio. Littleton, Colo.: Kids are worth it!

———. 1998. *Parenting with wit and wisdom in times of chaos and confusion.* Littleton, Colo.: Kids are worth it!

Kohn, A. 1990. *The brighter side of human nature: Altruism and empathy in everyday life.* New York: Basic.

———. 1990. *You know what they say . . . : The truth about popular beliefs.* New York: HarperCollins.

———. 1992. *No contest: The case against competition.* Boston: Houghton Mifflin.

———. 1993. *Punished by rewards: The trouble with gold stars, incentive plans, A's, praise, and other bribes.* Boston: Houghton Mifflin.

———. 1994. Bribes for behaving: Why behaviorism doesn't help children become good people. *NAMTA Journal, 19*(2), 71-94.

———. 1995. Discipline is the problem-not the solution. *Learning 1995, 24*(2): 34.

———. 1996. *Beyond discipline: From compliance to community.* Alexandria, Va.: Association for Supervision and Curriculum Development.

Schaps, E. 1990. Cooperative learning: The challenge in the '90s. *Cooperative Learning Magazine,* June, 5-8.

PART III Toward Building a Personal System of Discipline

The overriding purpose of this book has been to help individual readers put together their own personal systems of discipline. As emphasized, teachers differ in personalities and philosophies of teaching. The settings in which they work are different, as are the students they teach. A discipline plan that works for one teacher may therefore be entirely inappropriate for another. That is why individual teachers always personalize their approaches to classroom discipline and why this book urges them to do so. But they should proceed from a basis of sound knowledge, as provided by the authorities whose work is distilled in the preceding chapters. From that basis, they can assemble a set of practical techniques that produce the overall effect they desire.

Chapter 12, Classrooms That Encourage Good Behavior, presents information concerning how one establishes and maintains a productive classroom climate—one that enhances student self-concept through encouragement, support, and commitment. And finally, Chapter 13, Building a Personal System of Discipline, provides guidance to help teachers construct their own systems of discipline, attuned to their personalities, philosophies, and realities of their teaching situation.

CHAPTER **12**

Classrooms That Encourage Good Behavior

PREVIEW OF THE CHAPTER

Three components contribute to classrooms that promote considerate, responsible behavior:

The Person Component concerns how teachers and students interact and treat each other.

- Teacher gives each student regular personal attention.
- All students experience genuine success in learning.
- Students interact cooperatively, considerately, and responsibly.
- Students receive recognition for their accomplishments.

The Management Component concerns productive classroom climate and efficient routines.

- The classroom climate is made warm, nurturing, supportive, and caring.
- Class routines are managed efficiently; students help by assuming some of the duties.
- Communication with parents is regular and informative.

The Teacher Component concerns what teachers do to promote learning and positive attitude.

- Well-liked Teachers: Classes are fun, warm, supportive; learning results are uncertain.
- Efficient Teachers: Classes are efficiently run; learning is good but may not be enjoyable.
- Expert Teachers: Classes combine warmth, fun, and efficiency; learning and enjoyment are high.

The most valuable tactic in classroom discipline is to do everything possible beforehand to prevent misbehavior. Once misbehavior has occurred, even the best corrective techniques disrupt teaching and may erode relationships. It would be unrealistic to suggest that misbehavior can be eliminated entirely, but it can be kept to a minimum by organizing classes in ways known to support good behavior. Such classes are warm and nurturing. They present activities of high interest to students and are efficiently run. Student input is sought and valued. Those qualities usually lead to overall good behavior and high achievement. A number of strategies for establishing such classrooms are examined in this chapter, within three broad categories referred to as the *person component,* the *management component,* and the *teacher component.*

THE PERSON COMPONENT

The **person component** has to do with students and teachers, and with how they treat each other. A number of authorities emphasize the importance of helping students feel they belong in the class. Given a sense of belonging, students do not misbehave much, except for talking and laughing when they shouldn't. But a great many of today's students feel no sense of belonging to class or school. Those students typically have low self-image and show little interest in school achievement. Their behavior—or misbehavior—reflects their attempts to protect or bolster their sense of self. A primary concern in any discipline system is therefore to take steps to enhance students' self-concept and sense of belonging.

Enhancing Student Self-Concept and Sense of Belonging

Teachers can do much to enhance student self-concept and sense of belonging. Specifically, they can (1) give each student regular personal attention, (2) make sure that each student experiences success in learning, (3) solicit student input concerning curriculum, procedures, and problems, and (4) help students receive recognition for their accomplishments. Simultaneously, failure, rejection, and humiliation are eliminated from the classroom. Let us examine these tactics in greater detail.

Personal Attention from the Teacher

Most of us, when thinking back on teachers we liked best, recall that those teachers gave us much **personal attention.** They acknowledged us, spoke with us, encouraged us, sometimes pushed us, and enjoyed the improvements we made. After a while, we began to see ourselves as worthwhile, even important. We felt we belonged in the class, were growing more capable, and that someone important cared about us. As a result, we came to believe more strongly in our ability to accept responsibility and succeed. What those fine teachers did was not especially difficult. They merely treated us as *all students want to be treated,* with attention, encouragement, and support. They also taught us that it was not acceptable to be second-rate learners or second-rate people. They did this by continually encouraging us to improve in all we did.

Experiencing Genuine Success

Students can be made to think they are successful when truthfully they are not. One often hears teachers tell students they are "really learning" or "behaving great" when it is simply not true. Teachers say such things hoping to motivate students, but any sense of success coming from inaccurate praise is short-lived, for sooner or later students learn the truth. That is why **genuine success** is necessary for students—success based on true accomplishment. Teachers can help students experience success regularly, by providing the following:

Clear Goals as Targets

Students have a better chance of experiencing genuine success when they clearly understand the goals for which they are striving. They must see these goals as worthwhile and attainable, and are likely to do so if brought into cooperative discussions about them. When goals and activities are not understood or accepted by students, they must be clarified or changed. **Time lines** and **checkpoints** can be established to monitor progress toward goals. Evidence of continual progress encourages students to keep trying.

Curriculum Aimed at Competence

An interesting and well-organized curriculum encourages students to acquire knowledge and skills they consider important in their lives. While hit-and-miss activities can be fun for students, they often lead nowhere. In contrast, a sound curriculum enables students to see that they are becoming steadily more competent. Students should note their progress regularly and should be acknowledged for effort and improvement.

Direction, Urging, and Help

Many students have never become self-directed nor self-controlled and may have trouble doing their work even in the best activities. In such cases teachers must monitor, guide, urge, help, and otherwise encourage quality work. This helping role is very important. Most students need a considerate, persistent teacher if they are to learn well in school.

Effective Instructional Materials

Good instructional materials enliven learning by making subjects interesting and understandable. They allow students to explore far afield and help them apply new learnings. There is no way most students can visit the Amazon jungle, the Pyramids, Antarctica, or Lapland. They cannot see molecules, solar systems, or the inner workings of nuclear reactors. Good instructional materials help them comprehend what they cannot observe.

Teaching Students How to Behave

Teachers, particularly of older students, often take for granted that students know how to behave properly. While that is usually true, student behavior improves when teachers demonstrate how they expect students to behave in the classroom, academically and socially, and when students practice and role-play those behaviors.

Recognition for Student Success

There are a number of ways teachers can bring recognition to students for success:

Public Recognition. Motivation and group spirit burgeon when students prepare for public exhibitions or performances. When the kindergarten class invites parents to its annual Thanksgiving feast, the children work eagerly to make costumes, complete artwork for decorations, and learn songs about Thanksgiving to sing to their parents. When the middle school general science classes prepare for the science fair, students work enthusiastically on projects which they will display. When the high school physical education department presents its recreational sports night for the public, students work to perfect rhythmic exercises, collaborative games, and tumbling. Events such as these are often reported in the local media. As students anticipate public recognition, their behavior becomes more purposeful and responsible.

Of course, only a small portion of a semester's or year's work can be shown in exhibitions, but recognition can also be furnished in the classroom. The following are how some teachers provide recognition for their students.

Chart Group Gains. Gains and other improvements shown by the class as a whole can be depicted graphically. Many elementary classes demonstrate progress through time lines set up in the room. Some make murals that illustrate activities and accomplishments. Elementary and secondary classes can keep class diaries that provide a documented history of class activities and accomplishments, which students enjoy reading later in the year.

Chart Personal Gains. Charts showing individual progress also motivate student effort. These charts are not to be displayed in the classroom if they show any student in a derogatory light, but all students may keep them in personal folders to be seen by teacher and parents. Such charts can indicate attainment of objectives, amount of work attempted and completed, percentage of correct responses, and the like. Parents react well to this documentation, which demonstrates the teacher's plans and efforts on behalf of their child.

Inform Parents. Student motivation usually rises when the teacher informs parents regularly about their child's success, not just the lack thereof. This information can be provided through student communication with parents, teacher communication with parents, and other materials that show student progress. In order to help students better report to parents, at the end of the day for elementary students and the end of the week for secondary students, teachers should take a few minutes to review what the class has accomplished. Students can then relay this information to their parents.

Systematic communication from teacher to parents is also excellent for publicizing group and individual success. This takes time but pays good dividends. Teachers can send notes home with students, prepare occasional newsletters, and make very brief telephone calls. In all cases, the purpose is to convey accomplishment and success, not to speak of problems. Of course, problems must be dealt with, too, but in separate communications.

Parents are always eager to see samples of their child's work, including creative efforts, written work, and test results. Teachers should carefully check all work sent home because errors or omissions they make are almost certain to be noticed by parents. One small mistake can erode respect for the teacher.

Share in the Classroom. Students are motivated by having peers recognize their accomplishments. Attention for every student can come from oral presentations, demonstrations, and displays of work. Some students are hesitant to participate, but with gentle encouragement most overcome their reticence.

Produce a Class Newsletter. Many classes enjoy producing a monthly or quarterly newsletter that explains projects, contains creative work, and presents announcements of displays and performances. The tone of the newsletter is best when kept businesslike. All students' names should be included, and the newsletters sent to administrators, parents, other community members, and even organizations and businesses. Local newspapers usually show interest in them.

Esprit de Corps and How It Is Built

Esprit de corps, or group spirit, strengthens students' desire to learn, participate, and work for the benefit of the group. Unfortunately, no precise formula exists for building esprit de corps, though it is known to be affected by teacher enthusiasm, personal attention to students, an exciting curriculum, inclusion of students in making decisions, and a sense of group purpose. Often, classes acquire esprit de corps when they undertake a major project, such as a public performance or a contest against another class. Esprit de corps may or may not occur automatically, but teachers can do several things to encourage it, as the following paragraphs indicate.

Sense of Togetherness

It is helpful to hold discussions about how the class resembles a family that lives and works together, in which all members work to accomplish goals they share in common. All members contribute and benefit from helping each other. All lose something when any member is unsuccessful, and all can take justifiable pride in the accomplishments of the group. That picture contrasts with classrooms where the successful student is prized and rewarded while the unsuccessful is slighted. To bolster a sense of togetherness, the teacher should regularly solicit advice from the class about how they will deal with the problems and how they will work together to enjoy the best achievement for everyone.

Purpose in Class Activities

Sense of purpose grows when students understand what they are to do. Specific short-range goals are helpful, such as completing a class mural by Friday, having every student get at least 90 percent correct on the vocabulary test, or getting the six math problems completed correctly by the end of the class period. Short-term specific goals are vastly preferable to vague, long-range goals such as enjoying life more, passing the final test at the end of the year, or making a better living later in life. Sense of purpose is not dependent simply on enjoyable activities, but on recognizing the value of new learnings. Students resent what they consider to be busy work.

THE MANAGEMENT COMPONENT

The **management component** refers to how students are treated and how the instructional program is organized, delivered, and monitored. In well-managed classrooms students work responsibly without being cajoled by the teacher. Disruptions are minimal, and little conflict occurs. Students learn, and teachers feel successful and rewarded. Poorly managed classrooms, on the other hand, are often in turmoil. Unproductive noise abounds. Students are dissatisfied, and they misbehave. Teachers labor under stress and continual frustration. The following aspects of management help teachers and students enjoy more rewarding educational experiences.

Managing the Classroom Climate

Classroom climate refers to the feeling or tone that prevails in the classroom, a composite of attitudes, emotions, values, and relationships. All teachers are aware of its existence and, when visiting a classroom, can almost always tell whether the climate is good or bad.

A poor classroom climate tends to be chaotic and disorganized, and possibly cold, unfriendly, and threatening. Little humor is in evidence, but much sarcasm and animosity. Such climates depress learning. Although a threatening environment may cause students to work under duress, it results in their disliking both teacher and school. They obey rules not because they consider it proper to do so, but to prevent teachers taking reprisal against them.

In contrast, a good classroom climate is warm, supportive, pleasant, friendly, and filled with good nature and acceptance. It is encouraging, helpful, and nonthreatening. Such a climate encourages productive work and promotes a sense of enjoyment and accomplishment.

Cynthia, a second-grade teacher, describes how she attempts to set the tone in her classroom.

I begin the year with a discussion about my expectations for the year. I tell the children that I consider them my "school family." I explain that just as in any family we might not always agree on everything, nonetheless I will always care about them. I say that each and every one of them is very special and important to me and that I want them to have the best possible school year.

Because they are so important to me, I will not tolerate any cruelty or unkindness to each other. I expect them to be the best behaved and well-mannered class in the entire school, both in the classroom and on the playground. I tell them that good behavior is really just good manners, because it shows respect for others, whether children or adults. I also go over the Golden Rule, and I make a bulletin board on that theme. I refer to the Golden Rule as our class motto. That is the only rule we have in the class, and I discuss with them how it covers everything. If you don't want to be called names, then don't call other people names. If you want people to listen to you, then be sure to listen to others. And most important, if you want to have friends, then be a friend.

The children seem to understand and accept all of this very well. They see it as a fair and sensible way to do things, and I think it helps them know they have a teacher who cares about them.

Human Relations Skills and Classroom Climate

Human relations skills improve the quality of classroom interactions, thereby contributing to a positive atmosphere. Three groups of human relations skills merit understanding and implementation: (1) general human relations skills, (2) human relations skills with students, and (3) human relations skills with parents.

General Human Relations Skills

Four general human relations skills serve well in almost all situations. They are (1) friendliness, (2) positive attitude, (3) ability to listen, and (4) ability to compliment genuinely.

Friendliness is a trait everyone admires, yet many of us have difficulty displaying it, especially when we are threatened or in the company of people we dislike. Yet with small effort we can show friendliness even toward people who displease us, by smiling, speaking gently, addressing them by name, asking how they are, asking about their family and work, and so on. When we behave in this way, we find that others begin to respond similarly.

Having a *positive attitude* means that we focus on the brighter side of things. When dealing with problems, we look for solutions rather than lamenting obstacles or finding fault in others. We refrain from complaining, backbiting, and gossiping. When we speak positively, others begin to do so as well.

Ability to listen is a trait we admire in others but often find lacking in ourselves, as most of us would rather talk than listen. Yet listening produces many desirable outcomes. It communicates genuine interest in the other person, an essential first step in establishing good relationships. It shows that we value the other person's opinions, and it improves the quality of communication by permitting a true exchange of ideas.

The ability to *compliment genuinely* is a behavior that receives relatively little attention in human relations. It nevertheless has considerable power. Many of us, having seen compliments used falsely, find ourselves hesitant to compliment others. Yet we all like to receive compliments. Do you prefer being around people who compliment you, or around those who do not (or who give you unsolicited "constructive criticism")?

As you give compliments, however, you must make sure they are genuine. It helps if you make your compliment explicit. Rather than say, "Your ideas are brilliant," you might say, "Your explanation of the Mesopotamian lifestyle was very clear." On a more personal level, rather than saying, "Hey, you're looking great today!" you might say, "That color surely suits you."

Human Relations Skills with Students

The general skills of human relations apply to everyone in all situations. When working with students, however, there are four additional skills that teachers should employ:

Giving regular attention to students does much to build trust and enlist cooperation. Attention should be given to all students equally, not just to favorites and those who misbehave.

Continual willingness to help is a trait much appreciated in teachers. Students gravitate to helpful teachers, tend to admire them, and usually remember them with respect years later. You hear students say, "Yeah, Miss Smith expected a lot, but she really tried to help every one of us."

In regular class meetings, teachers should *invite student input* about curriculum, procedures, activities, and the resolution of problems. When students are thus listened to and see their opinions valued, they become more inclined to assume responsibility for doing their part to further the work of the class.

In their own behavior, teachers should *model the courtesy and good manners* they hope to see in their students. Teachers should be genteel, even on those occasions when students are boorish, and always show good manners. If students are to live by the Golden Rule, teachers' behavior must exemplify the Golden Rule in practice.

Human Relations Skills with Parents

Teachers have a responsibility to communicate with parents. Many teachers use this responsibility to advantage while others avoid it, believing it not worth the effort. Yet good communication usually brings increased parental support. For building stronger relationships with parents, teachers should employ the general skills of human relations described earlier as well as the following:

Communicating regularly with parents is accomplished through notes, telephone calls, and newsletters. It shows respect for parents and interest in their child, and it causes parents to hold teachers in high regard.

Communicating clearly is accomplished by bearing in mind that most parents do not understand educational jargon such as "critical thinking" or "cognitive levels," nor do they recognize acronyms such as SAT, IEP, or GATE. It is also wise to avoid involved sentence structure and the use of big words where little ones suffice. In short, make sure your messages to parents are clear, simple, and to the point.

Describing expectations is accomplished by outlining for the parent what your program is and explaining what their child is involved in and supposed to do, how you will evaluate, what you require concerning homework, and what their role at home is to be. Most parents like to know this information.

Always remember one thing: Parents don't like to hear their child criticized, but they do want to know *how their child is progressing.* Criticism is a sure way to alienate parents. Emphasizing progress is a better approach. Where shortcomings exist, call them "new learnings" that you and the child are working on.

All teachers must *conference with parents,* routinely or when difficulties arise. Such conferences produce anxiety on both sides. Teachers fear criticism of their program, judgment, ways of teaching, or means of dealing with students. Parents fear hearing about faults in their children, which they internalize as faults in themselves. It helps to remember that the purpose of parent conferencing is to improve the overall success of the child. If you keep that essential point in mind, and if you prepare adequately for the conference, you will find that most meetings with parents are pleasant and productive.

Careful *preparation* is important to the success of the conference. Remember to do these things:

1. Have the student's strengths and needs clearly in mind.
2. Prepare an attractive folder with the student's name on it.
3. Include in the folder a summary of your program, showing work completed and work yet to be done.

4. Include samples of the student's work.
5. Have available grades, tests, and other assessments that back up your evaluation.
6. Anticipate questions parents are most likely to ask.
   - How does my child get along with others?
   - Does my child cause problems?
   - Is my child progressing as well as expected?
   - What are my child's specific needs?
   - Is there anything you want me to do to help?

Once you have made your preparation, free your mind to concentrate on conducting the conference professionally. It helps if you do the following:

1. Put yourself in the parent's place. Be tactful and polite.
2. Greet the parent in a friendly, relaxed manner.
3. Sit side by side with the parent at a table rather than on opposite sides of a desk.
4. Begin by chatting about the student as a worthwhile person. Reassure the parent by mentioning good traits.
5. Guide the parent through the student's file, commenting on samples of work included. Refer to tests and grades if appropriate.
6. Encourage the parent to talk. Listen carefully and be accepting. Do not argue or criticize; this causes resentment. Parents cannot be objective about their child.
7. Throughout the conference, make sure the parent sees that you want the best education for the child.
8. End the conference by describing your plans for the student's future progress. Earnestly request the parent's support. Thank the parent for meeting with you to talk about the child.

Be careful about *giving parents advice* on matters in which you have no expertise. Limit advice to academics and normal behaviors that affect learning. If parents ask you about matters outside of what you are trained to do, refer them to the school nurse, psychologist, or other expert. If they ask you about study time at home, suggest that they stipulate a specific place for doing homework with no distractions and that they talk with the child about schoolwork. If they ask about how to control misbehavior at home, tell them only what you insist on in school—such as sticking to a few important rules, invoking reasonable consequences when the rules are followed and broken, maintaining open communication, and showing that the child is wanted, loved, and respected.

Managing Classroom Routines

Generally speaking, effective teachers use classroom routines that minimize disruption while maximizing productive work. Keith, a secondary math teacher, describes an opening routine he uses to good advantage and shares some related views.

It is important to me for things to run smoothly. I begin the period with a one-minute timed exercise. The students know I will quickly say, "Go," and if they don't have their pencils, scratch paper, and test sheet ready they are out of luck—they can try again the next day.

The subject matter is very important to me. Assignments are to be completed. If they are not, a note goes home, filled out by the student, stating what was not completed and why. The work must be made up on their own time. I go over all the assignments ahead of time so students know exactly what is expected. They know the schedule of tests and what they have to do to earn their grades. This makes them responsible for their own grades.

Occasionally, I receive a call from a parent whose child has received a failing grade for the first time ever. Their anger quickly subsides when I remind them that the child knew exactly what work was required for a good grade, and I explain how little the child did.

This may sound harsh, but I treat the students with great respect and courtesy. I always say, "Please" and "Thank you" and "Excuse me." I admit my mistakes and tell the students I am sorry. They reflect my example. We are courteous, we are considerate, we have an enjoyable time, and best of all, we get our work done.

Routines, the commonplace procedures and chores inherent in day-to-day activities, are far more important to discipline than is generally recognized. Well-managed routines permit students to know exactly what they are supposed to do and thus reduce dead time that fosters misbehavior. The following are routines teachers should consider:

Opening and Closing Activities

In many classrooms students waste several minutes before starting work. They come into the classroom talking, are slow to take their seats, continue talking once seated, and do not stop until the teacher's insistent voice is heard above the noise. This condition is corrected by establishing routine procedures to follow upon entering the room.

Generally, it is best to have students begin work immediately. This can be established as one of the class rules. Secondary teachers may write an assignment on the board. Students enter, sit down, and begin work within one minute after the bell. Elementary teachers may have students write in journals, read silently from library books, or do math or vocabulary exercises while roll is taken. Very young children may begin by playing with instructional toys or sitting quietly while the teacher or aide reads a story. In all cases, students are helped to begin schoolwork at once rather than talk and fool around.

It is equally important to establish routine procedures for ending class activities. In classes such as art, shop, and physical education, a cleanup time is required. In practically all classes, materials are to be re-stored, completed work is to be filed, and everything is to be readied for dismissal. Students should be taught to follow established routines on cue.

Using Materials

Inefficient classrooms permit wasted time while students obtain materials and re-place them after use. Procedures should be established for quickly obtaining needed materials. If materials are distributed, several students should help, each distributing materials to five or six other students. If students are to get their own materials, they should be able to go to convenient shelves or cupboards without crowding or waiting in line. Pencil sharpening can be especially distracting. Many teachers permit pencil sharpening only before class begins. Others keep containers of sharpened pencils at hand; students can exchange their dull pencils for sharp ones when necessary. At the end of the period, materials should be replaced as efficiently as they were obtained. Students are taught exactly what to do and are allowed a minimum of time to replace the materials.

Handling Completed Work

Clear procedures should spell out what students are to do with completed work. If they are allowed to come individually to the teacher and hand in their work, there is likelihood of noise, wasted time, and disturbance to students still working. For that reason, many teachers have students place completed work on the corner of their desks or tables or in conveniently located baskets. The work is then collected by a teacher, aide, or student assistant.

Using Student Assistants

It is strongly recommended that class members be assigned duties to help with routine procedures. Not only does this assist teachers, but it also improves student attitude. At the secondary level, student assistants are most useful for distributing and collecting materials and for replenishing and taking care of supplies. They are frequently used as well for simple checking of papers, keeping records, typing, and duplicating. At the elementary level, teachers often assign tasks to every student in the class—president, flag salute leader, lights monitor, window monitor, news and weather reporter, messenger, line monitor, group or table leader, plant and pet caretaker, materials monitor, audiovisual assistant, visitor greeter, and so on. There are plenty of jobs for all students, and all should participate.

Providing Assistance to Students at Work

As you recall from the Jones model (Chapter 5), teachers tend to be inefficient in providing help to students doing seatwork. In particular, they spend too much time with each student who raises a hand, thus allowing other students to sit for several minutes doing nothing or getting into trouble. Jones has provided excellent advice on how to give help efficiently, such as:

1. Make sure students know what they are supposed to do and how they are supposed to do it.
2. Provide a written model to which students can refer.
3. Circulate among students to check for progress and errors.

4. When students raise their hands, give them direct help and then move away quickly, preferably in 20 seconds or less. Do not let students become psychologically dependent on your presence before they will do their work.

5. Do not succumb to the temptation to reteach individual students or take them through question-and-answer tutorials. If several students are having the same difficulty, reteach the concept or process to the entire class.

THE TEACHER COMPONENT

Although most teachers can ultimately develop good discipline techniques, some do so only through considerable effort. Others seem to give discipline little attention, yet their classes run smoothly with few difficulties. Such teachers are often called "naturals," though they may vary considerably in the way they teach. One thing they have in common is that they seem to anticipate problems and take steps to prevent them.

The **teacher component** of classroom management focuses on these teachers with good preventive discipline. They seem to be of three rather distinct types, which we will call (1) well-liked teachers, (2) efficient teachers, and (3) expert teachers. The three types are certainly not exclusive. Not only is there overlap, but some teachers vacillate between types from day to day, especially with regard to efficiency.

Well-liked teachers are sought out by students because they provide individual attention, interesting activities, a relaxed atmosphere, and an abiding sense of humor. Good academic learning can occur in their classes, but can also be mediocre or poor. Students tend to behave well because they want to please the teacher and want the teacher to like them.

Efficient teachers plan, organize, instruct, and manage well, leaving nothing to chance. Achievement tends to be high in their classes, but those teachers are not necessarily well liked, especially when efficiency takes precedence over stimulation and caring. As students are often uncomfortable in classrooms that contain little personal warmth, they do not enjoy their educational experience. They usually behave well because there is little opportunity to do otherwise in tightly structured programs backed by strong rules and consequences.

Expert teachers display the best qualities of the other two types. These teachers are efficient yet flexible. They show that they care about students and do what they can to make learning interesting, exciting, and satisfying (Ramsay and Oliver 1995; Lowman 1996). Their students learn well, admire and respect them, and usually like them personally. Good behavior occurs because of reasonable standards and the teacher's personal concern for students, which makes students want to please the teacher in return.

How to Become an Expert Teacher

If you see yourself as well-liked but feel you need to be more efficient, work on procedures that keep students on task. Ask students for their ideas. You may wish to add more structure to your lessons and concentrate on keeping instruction free from disruption. But remember that while expert teachers organize well, they are not slaves to efficiency. They remain flexible in accord with circumstances.

As much as anything else, expert teachers provide stimulating lessons. They add mystery, suspense, and drama to their teaching. They regularly invite students' active involvement. While doing so, they use communication skills to build human relations, which contribute to that most desirable of all classroom qualities, esprit de corps.

REVIEW OF SELECTED TERMINOLOGY

The following terms were used with particular meanings in the chapter.

checkpoints	management component
classroom climate	person component
efficient teacher	personal attention
esprit de corps	teacher component
expert teacher	time lines
genuine success	well-liked teacher

APPLICATION EXERCISES

QUESTIONS AND ACTIVITIES

1. Examine this contribution from teacher Colleen Meagher, and identify management that has to do with physical environment, classroom climate, and routines.

   "I arrange things so that the daily schedule flows more smoothly and I don't have to give unnecessary directions. Transitions are timed with a kitchen timer, and the class is challenged to see if they can quietly clean up and prepare for the next activity before it rings. I allow the students to work in cooperative groups and at times allow them to talk quietly and move about the room. Traffic patterns are clearly defined. Desks are arranged in a U-shape facing the chalkboard, so I have eye contact and easy access to all students."

2. Mr. Tales has prepared the following note to send to parents describing his goals for the class:

   "We will be working to maximize self-image through both traditional and newer affective approaches. Intended learnings will be stated in terms of experiences rather than behaviorally. Assessment of progress will be accomplished observationally. Your input into this process will be valued."

   Mr. Tales asks you to look over the note and make suggestions before he sends it out. What do you suggest to him?

3. For a grade, subject, and topic you select, describe how you would manage materials distribution and collection, work routines, and assistance for students during independent or group work.

4. For a grade or subject you select, describe what you would want to communicate to parents at the beginning of school and how you would communicate with them. Be realistic in terms of time and effort required.

5. You are preparing for a conference with the father of James, a delightfully humorous and well-intentioned boy who is barely passing his course work. His study habits are poor in school and, you suspect, nonexistent at home. The principal has informed you that James's father requires that James work in their upholstery shop after school. How will you approach the father? What will you say?

6. Examine Scenario 1 or 2 in the Appendix. From what you can see in the scenario you select, what changes would you make so that better behavior might be encouraged, as opposed to enforced?

REFERENCES AND RECOMMENDED READINGS

Angell, A. 1991. Democratic climates in elementary classrooms: A review of theory and research. *Theory and Research in Social Education, 19,* 241–266.

Augustine, D., K. Gruber, and L. Hanson. 1990. Cooperation works! *Educational Leadership, 47,* 4–7.

Banbury, M., and C. Hebert. 1992. Do you see what I mean? Language in classroom interactions. *Teaching Exceptional Children, 24,* 24–28.

Bartell, J. 1992. Starting from scratch. *Principal, 72,* 13–14.

Brophy, J. 1987. Synthesis on strategies for motivating students to learn. *Educational Leadership, 45,* 40–48.

Brophy, J., and J. Putnam. 1979. Classroom management in the elementary school. In D. L. Duke (ed.), *Classroom management: The seventy-eighth yearbook of the National Society for the Study of Education* (pp. 182–216). Chicago: University of Chicago Press.

Cangelosi, J. 1993. *Classroom management strategies: Gaining and maintaining students' cooperation.* 2d ed. White Plains, N.Y.: Longman.

Canter, L., and M. Canter. 1992. *Assertive Discipline: Positive behavior management for today's classroom.* 2d ed. Santa Monica, Calif.: Canter & Associates.

Cawthorne, B. 1981. *Instant success for classroom teachers, new and substitute teachers in grades K through 8.* Scottsdale, Ariz.: Greenfield.

Charles, C., and G. Senter. 1995. *Elementary classroom management.* 2d ed. White Plains, N.Y.: Longman.

Charney, R. 1991. *Teaching children to care: Management in the responsive classroom.* Greenfield, Mass.: Northeast Foundation for Children.

Corno, L. 1992. Encouraging students to take responsibility for learning and performance. *Elementary School Journal, 93,* 69–83.

Edwards, C. 1997. *Classroom discipline and management.* Upper Saddle River, N.J.: Prentice-Hall.

Emmer, E., C. Evertson, and L. Anderson. 1980. Effective classroom management at the beginning of the school year. *Elementary School Journal, 80,* 219–231.

Evertson, C. 1989. Classroom organization and management. In M. Reynolds (ed.), *Knowledge base for the beginning teacher.* Oxford: Pergamon Press.

————. 1989. Improving elementary classroom management: A school-based training program for beginning the year. *Journal of Educational Research, 83,* 82–90.

Evertson, C., E. Emmer, B. Clements, J. Sanford, and M. Worsham. 1989. *Classroom management for elementary teachers.* Englewood Cliffs, N.J.: Prentice-Hall.

Evertson, C., and A. Harris. 1992. What we know about managing classrooms. *Educational Leadership, 49*(7), 74–78.

Fraser, B., and P. O'Brien. 1985. Student and teacher perceptions of the environment of elementary school classrooms. *Elementary School Journal, 85*(5), 567-580.

Hoover, R., and R. Kindsvatter. 1997. *Democratic discipline: Foundation and practice.* Upper Saddle River, N.J.: Prentice-Hall.

Jones, V., and L. Jones. 1990. *Comprehensive classroom management: Motivating and managing students.* Needham Heights, Mass.: Allyn & Bacon.

Kohn, A. 1996. *Beyond discipline: From compliance to community.* Alexandria, Va.: Association for Supervision and Curriculum Development.

Kramer, P. 1992. Fostering self-esteem can keep kids safe and sound. *PTA Today, 17*(6), 10–11.

Latham, G. 1993. Managing the classroom environment to facilitate effective instruction [Six-part videotape in-service training program]. Logan, Utah: P & T Ink.

Lowman, J. 1996. Characteristics of exemplary teachers. *New Directions for Teaching and Learning, 65,* 33–40.

Markoff, A. 1992. *Within reach: Academic achievement through parent-teacher communication.* Novato, Calif.: Academic Therapy Publications.

Novelli, J. 1990. Design a classroom that works. *Instructor, 100*(1), 24–27.

Queen, J., B. Blackwelder, and L. Mallen. 1997. *Responsible classroom management for teachers and students.* Upper Saddle River, N.J.: Prentice-Hall.

Ramsay, P., and D. Oliver. 1995. Capacities and behaviour of quality classroom teachers. *School Effectiveness and School Improvement, 4*(4), 332–366.

Ruot, C. 1994. *Discipline strategies for the bored, belligerent and ballistic in your classroom.* Captiva, Fla.: Sanibel Sanddollar Publications.

Schell, L., and P. Burden. 1992. *Countdown to the first day of school: A 60-day get-ready checklist for first-time teachers, teacher transfers, student teachers, teacher mentors, induction-program administrators, teacher educators* (NEA Checklist series). Washington, D.C.: National Education Association.

Sidman, M. 1989. *Coercion and its fallout.* Boston: Authors Cooperative.

Slavin, R. 1991. Synthesis of research on cooperative learning. *Educational Leadership, 48,* 71–82.

Weade, R., and C. Evertson. 1988. The construction of lessons in effective and less effective classrooms. *Teaching and Teacher Education, 4*(3), 189–213.

Weinstein, C. 1992. Designing the instructional environment: Focus on seating. In *Proceedings of selected research and development presentations at the Convention of the Association for Educational Communications and Technology.* ERIC Document Reproduction Service.

Wong, H., and R. Wong. 1991. *The first days of school: How to be an effective teacher.* Sunnyvale, Calif.: Harry K. Wong.

CHAPTER 13

Building a Personal System of Discipline

PREVIEW OF THE CHAPTER

Focus

On helping teachers prepare discipline systems that

- Teach students how to behave responsibly.
- Keep the classroom safe and conducive to learning.

Logic

- Effective discipline systems teach students how to behave properly while curtailing misbehavior.
- In order to be effective, any discipline system must meet the needs of students involved.
- To be used successfully, the discipline system must meet the needs of the teacher.

- The most effective discipline systems are those constructed by teachers of particular classes.

Structure

When teachers construct high-quality discipline systems, they give attention to:

Preventive Discipline: Teachers make the curriculum fun and enjoyable and teach good behavior.

Supportive Discipline: Teachers show interest in students, provide help, and keep them on track.

Corrective Discipline: Teachers stop misbehavior, reteach correct behavior, and preserve dignity.

TOWARD BUILDING A PERSONAL SYSTEM OF DISCIPLINE

The ultimate purpose of this book is to help you build an effective system of discipline that attends to the traits and needs of your students while remaining consonant with your own personality and philosophy. Traditionally, teachers and students have been pitted as adversaries in discipline, but that no longer need be the case. Preceding chapters have shown how noncoercive techniques can ensure classroom behavior that preserves student dignity, conserves energy and instructional time, and enhances personal relationships. The primary question for teachers today is not whether they can foster responsible classroom behavior but rather how they might do so while meeting the needs of students. One might think the best approach would be to implement the most desirable of the models presented in this book. But as many teachers have discovered, prepackaged systems seldom serve as well as anticipated. None of the established models, despite their marvelous attributes, interfaces well with all groups and situations. Students differ in backgrounds and values, and they react differently according to their age. Teachers differ, too. Any five at random are likely to have five distinct personalities, philosophies, sets of preferences, styles of communication, and ways of teaching. Given the range of differences among environments, schools, students, and teachers, it is understandable that preorganized discipline programs seldom accomplish all that a teacher might hope. Usually, teachers end up better satisfied when they build personal systems of discipline tailored to their students, situations, and preferences.

What Teachers Want

Teachers want students to be well behaved and keenly interested in learning. But since they rarely encounter such ideal groups, teachers search for a discipline system that accomplishes the following:

- Prevents most misbehavior
- Redirects misbehavior positively
- Promotes trusting relationships between teacher and students
- Is accepted as fair by students
- Secures parental support
- Is efficient and easy to use

Does this list describe what you want in your discipline system? If you need to modify the list, do so. You can use it as a checklist while building your system.

What Teachers Know, and Don't Know, about Students

In order to serve as intended, a system of discipline must take student traits into account. Many of those traits are genetically controlled and are fairly well understood. Others are culturally determined and elusive. This is a time of rapid social change. Drug use has devastated a significant portion of the population. Poverty is increasing—it now affects one student in every four. The homeless are seen in almost every city. Tens of thousands of children live in single-parent homes, often with no parental supervision during the day. Inadequate nutrition and lack of health care are common. Some years ago, Grant and Sleeter (1989, pp. 1–2) reported the following characteristics of students entering public schools in the United States:

25% were from families living in poverty

14% were children of teenage mothers

15% were non-English-speaking immigrants

almost 30% were of color

40% would live in a single-parent home before age 18

25%–30% were latchkey children

The 1990 United States census revealed the following about American public school students (Population Reference Bureau 1992):

25% were born to unmarried parents

25% had no health insurance

82% had working mothers

20% were living in a single-parent home

9% (5.7 million children) lived in a home not headed by either parent

Among African American families, single-parent homes outnumbered two-parent homes. Trends predicted by Sobol (1990) indicated that by the year 2020 one person of every three in the United States will be what we now call a minority. Most of those people will exhibit cultural, social, and linguistic traits associated with lower school achievement, possibly exacerbating the "achievement gap" that exists between certain groups (Hernandez 1989). Poverty, which also depresses school achievement, exists in differing degrees. In 1987 it was reported that 48 percent of African Americans lived in poverty, compared to 42 percent for Latinos, 29 percent for other nonwhite groups, and 13 percent for whites (Slavin, Karweit, and Madden 1989). On a numerical basis, twice as many white children live in poverty as all nonwhite groups combined (Hernandez 1989, p. 15). Accompanying the changes in social conditions is the disquieting fact that Americans no longer seem to place as much value on education as they once did. Community support for schools has declined, as has parental insistence that children do well in school. Students now drop out in alarming numbers, while many of those who remain make little effort to learn.

All this is not to suggest that teachers know nothing about their students. To the contrary, they know a great deal, especially about human traits that cut across social and economic groups, as indicated in the following paragraphs.

Primary Grades (Ages 4 to 9)

Kindergarten children come to school at the age of 4 or 5. They parallel play, talk to themselves, tire easily, get fussy, cry, and require frequent rest. They fall, sprawl, and crawl about the floor. They make little distinction between work and play, and they require close supervision. Some play well together; others expect to have their own way.

Teachers at this level usually establish two or three rules for behavior, knowing that those rules will be broken regularly. They spend much time reminding students of rules and proper behavior. This pattern continues into grades 1 and 2, with students gradually becoming socialized to school, learning to raise hands, stand in lines, and wait patiently. At the primary level, students accept adult authority without question though they often try to circumvent it. They respond well to affection and personal attention.

Intermediate Grades (Ages 9 to 12)

As students move into grade 4 they are becoming much more independent, though they still want attention and affection from their teachers. Hugging may no longer be eagerly sought; holding hands with the teacher may take its place. These students now recognize the need for rules and rule enforcement. They accept reasonable consequences for breaking rules, especially when others break them. They can help establish rules and consequences and are usually eager to discuss procedures of enforcement. No longer is teacher authority blindly accepted. Students may argue, talk back, and drag their heels. But they are sure to complain if rules and consequences are not administered consistently and impartially to others.

Middle School Grades (Ages 12 to 14)

Behavior becomes more diverse among students at the middle school level, and their teachers must have exceptional skill if they are to maintain control, teach well, build supportive relationships, and retain their own sanity. Teaching these students is difficult for many reasons. Their bodily changes worry, perplex, excite, and dismay. New realities of an opposite sex stir and baffle. Psychological weaning from parents leaves them feeling lost and cut off, yet the emerging need for independence produces conflict with adults. If that were not enough to contend with, students at this age are required to adjust to new school organization, curriculum, and styles of teaching. These factors provide serious distractions to learning. Meanwhile, students are becoming increasingly rebellious and disposed to probing at outer boundaries of rules and customs. Their awe of the teacher has waned, but awe can be replaced with respect and affection for those who provide encouragement and support.

High School Grades (Ages 15 to 18)

The high school years mark a time of settling down, as most students begin to find themselves and reach a truce with their bodies and emotions. Some develop ideas of what they hope to do in the future. Others, lamentably, become further alienated from the educational mainstream. A new level of relationship with adults becomes evident. For most students, the love–hate attitude of earlier years fades, while respect for adults grows as students recognize their own interdependence with the larger community. Teachers should now deal with students on an adult-to-adult basis. This does not imply equal authority. The teacher is still in charge, but students assume greater responsibility for their own learning and behavior while looking upon teachers as guides and role models.

BUILDING YOUR SYSTEM OF DISCIPLINE

Three Faces of Discipline

It is helpful to think of discipline as having three faces: (1) preventive, (2) supportive, and (3) corrective. The labels suggest the different but equally important aspects of classroom discipline to which you must give attention.

Preventive Discipline

Preventing misbehavior is greatly preferable to having to deal with it after it has occurred. Most authorities contend that the best way to prevent classroom misbehavior is to provide a very interesting curriculum that involves students so deeply that they never think of misbehaving. As you plan your discipline system, emphasize preventive discipline by giving strong attention to the following:

- Make your curriculum as worthwhile and enjoyable as possible.
- Remember that students crave fun, belonging, freedom, power, and dignity.
- Be pleasant and helpful. Ask your students for input and help.
- With your students, reach clear understandings about appropriate class conduct.
- Discuss and practice the behaviors to which you have jointly agreed.
- Continually emphasize good manners and abidance by the Golden Rule.
- Be the best model you can by showing concern, etiquette, courtesy, and helpfulness.
- Discuss manners frequently and call attention to student improvements.

Supportive Discipline

All students at times become restive and subject to temptation. When signs of incipient misbehavior appear, bring supportive discipline into play. This facet of discipline assists students with self-control by helping them get back on task. Often only the student involved knows it has been used. The following tactics are suggested for supportive discipline:

- Use signals directed to a student needing support.
- Learn to catch students' eyes and use head shakes, frowns, and hand signals.
- Use physical proximity when signals are ineffective.
- Show interest in student work. Ask cheerful questions or make favorable comments.
- Sometimes provide a light challenge: "Can you complete five more before we stop?"
- Restructure difficult work by changing the activity or providing help.
- Give hints, clues, or suggestions to help students get going.
- Inject humor into lessons that have become tiring. Students appreciate it.

- Remove seductive objects such as toys, comics, notes, and the like. Return them later.
- Acknowledge good behavior in appropriate ways at appropriate times.
- Use suggestions, hints, and I-messages as students begin to drift toward misbehavior.
- Show that you recognize students' discomfort: ask for a few minutes more work.

Corrective Discipline

Even the best efforts in preventive and supportive discipline cannot eliminate all misbehavior. When students violate rules, you must deal with the misbehavior expeditiously. Corrective discipline should neither intimidate students nor prompt power struggles but rather should proceed as follows:

- Stop disruptive misbehavior. It is usually best not to ignore it.
- Talk with the offending student or invoke a consequence appropriate to the misbehavior, in accordance with class rules.
- Remain calm and speak in a matter-of-fact manner.
- Follow through consistently, the same way each day.
- Redirect misbehavior in positive directions.
- If necessary, talk with students privately about misbehavior. Ask how you can help.
- Be ready to invoke an insubordination rule for students who refuse to stop misbehaving.

Eight Steps to Personalized Discipline

Your preventive, supportive, and corrective techniques can provide a balanced approach that serves everyone comfortably. What remains is to tailor the system so it allows you to function naturally. You can accomplish this final task through eight steps.

1. *Clarify student and teacher needs and tentatively set limits.* Make a list of your students' predominant traits and needs, then make a list of your own traits and needs. Envision behavior limits (what students should and/or should not do) that allow both sets of needs to be met. Consider matters such as talk, movement, noise, manners, self-control, effort, and beginning and completing work. If you have an especially strong need, such as for quiet or order, be up front about it and willing to ask for cooperation.
2. *On the first day, discuss with students behavior that will serve the class best.* Ask older students how they would prefer to work so that they can learn well under pleasant circumstances. Share your needs and explore procedures students find comfortable. Show that you are flexible and willing to compromise, but retain the right to veto suggestions if you are certain they are not in the students' best interest.

3. *Together with students, write out agreements and consequences for governing behavior in the classroom.* Make sure students understand the agreements, consider them fair, and express their willingness to abide by them.
4. *Establish a support system.* Inform your principal about your discipline plan and ask for support. Ask one or more fellow teachers if you can turn to them for assistance, should it be needed. Write out a description of your system and send it to parents. Tell them that the system is intended to provide the best learning opportunity for their children. Request their support. Ask them to sign and return a copy to indicate they understand and support your system.
5. *Decide what you will do regarding preventive and supportive discipline.* List ideas for building a positive classroom climate that will help students maintain self-control as they learn. Talk possibilities over with students, if they are old enough to participate. Select activities that students consider interesting and valuable. Include topics about which you are excited and knowledgeable. Establish procedures for smooth flow between activities so that dead spots and confusion do not occur.
6. *List what you will do in trying to be the best possible model for your students.* Act as you would like them to act. Speak as you would like them to speak. Talk with them and show interest not only in their work but in them personally.
7. *Determine what you will say and do when students violate class agreements.* Practice your responses in private or with a colleague. Set up arrangements for talking with students privately. Always remember to ask students how they think you might help them learn better and enjoy school more. Resolve to continue trying to provide a quality learning opportunity, even when students don't seem to appreciate your efforts.
8. *Implement, evaluate, and modify your system.* Continually assess your system in terms of its contribution to a positive, enjoyable climate, its ease of implementation, and its effectiveness in controlling misbehavior. If you teach third grade or higher, discuss your observations with students and ask for their input. Remain open to modifying your system when necessary.

SCHOOLWIDE SYSTEMS OF DISCIPLINE

Increasingly, schools are developing schoolwide discipline programs which all teachers use in more or less the same way. This movement, intended to make discipline more consistent and effective, emerged in the middle 1980s, prompted in part by the nationwide push for schools to provide a safe and orderly environment for learning, high standards and expectations, opportunities for student involvement and responsibility, and emphasis on positive behavior and preventive discipline.

Schoolwide systems typically have three main components: (1) a policy concerning discipline established by the school board and then disseminated to the school and community, (2) rules or agreements about desirable student conduct, and (3) enforcement procedures, consequences, or other types of follow-up, such as conferences with offending students.

Component one, the school board policy, might explain (1) the district's philosophy concerning the relationship of discipline to education; (2) the students' responsibilities at school and in the educational program; (3) the teachers' responsibilities for communicating clear standards and consequences and consistently implementing them; (4) the administrators' responsibilities in communicating and enforcing discipline; (5) a list of prohibited behaviors, such as use of drugs and alcohol, destruction of property, fighting, and so forth; and (6) the consequences that will be invoked for violations of rules.

Component two in the schoolwide system consists of rules or agreements about how students are expected to behave, such as:

- Always be on time and ready to work.
- Treat all people and property with respect.
- Cooperate with people in positions of authority.
- Do not disrupt the teaching-learning process.

In some schools, all school personnel, including librarians, secretaries, bus drivers, cafeteria workers, custodians, and others are empowered to enforce the rules.

Component three, enforcement, consequences, and follow-through, might include measures similar to the following:

- All students are carefully made aware of the agreements, consequences, and enforcement procedures. Charts displaying the agreements are posted in classrooms and elsewhere in the school.
- When a student violates an agreement, a verbal warning is given. This warning carries no penalty. If the student misbehaves again, the person in authority makes a notation on a special form in triplicate—one copy goes to the student, a second to the office, and the third is kept by the person writing the complaint.
- School counselors keep a conduct card for all students assigned to them. When the counselor receives a note indicating misbehavior, that infraction is entered on the student's conduct card.
- Consequences are imposed on the student. Depending on the system, consequences might include making a plan for appropriate behavior in the future, making some kind of restitution, in-school detention, conferences with the teacher, referral to the counselor, calls to the parent, referral to the vice principal, and loss of normal privileges. Many keep a severe clause in effect that calls for immediate referral to the principal.

Appraisal of Schoolwide Systems

While many teachers see benefit in schoolwide systems, many others, especially those who have been successful in discipline, don't support a standardized approach. They claim that overall student behavior is no better than when teachers take care of problems in their own way, and they resent giving up effective approaches in favor of systems they can't wholeheartedly support. Teachers also strongly resist anything that carries the stigma of "still more extra work." They feel they already have too much to do and too little time. It is fair to say that while schoolwide systems do not improve class control for stronger teachers, they do benefit teachers who have difficulty with control. They seem to improve behavior significantly in difficult to manage areas such as library, shops, cafeteria, grounds, and buses. Community and parents especially seem to appreciate schoolwide systems.

EXEMPLARS: PERSONAL SYSTEMS OF DISCIPLINE

Presented here are discipline systems organized and used by real teachers at different grade levels who have graciously agreed to share their work. The plans reflect in varying degrees the guidelines given earlier in the chapter.

1. Kindergarten

TEACHER: LINDA POHLENZ The discipline system I use with my kindergarten children revolves around win–win conflict resolution. The conflicts may be between students or between a student and myself. Young children learn the process easily, and by using it they learn to solve their own problems and situations. I also help them learn how to evaluate their behavior. As they become more proficient in doing so, they become more self-directed.

Learning the Win–Win Process
To introduce the win–win process to my children, I help them understand something of how the mind works and then have them apply what they have learned to a problem situation that does not involve conflict. I begin like this:

TEACHER: Do you have a big toe?
STUDENT: Yes.
TEACHER: How do you know? We can't see it through your shoes.
STUDENT: I know because it's there.
TEACHER: Wiggle your toe. *[Pause]* Did you wiggle it?
STUDENT: Yes.
TEACHER: I couldn't see it. How do you know your toe wiggled?
STUDENT: I could feel it.
TEACHER: You know that inside your head you have a brain to think with. The brain is part of your body, just as your big toe is. You cannot see your brain inside your head, but you can make it work.

I move ahead to three special terms to describe thinking. I teach students the term *mud mind* to describe thinking that is bogged down, where there is a problem but the person can't think of a solution. I teach them the term *air mind* to describe thinking that is calm and has no problems to worry about. I teach them the term *twinkler mind* to describe thinking that helps find solutions to problems. I go on to show how twinkler minds can find answers to a number of problems that students encounter every day. I begin this process by pretending I have lost my green marker:

TEACHER: Oh me! I can't find my green marker to write on the chart. I guess I can't teach. We'll just have to stop everything. Oh dear, we can't do that during school time. Oh, what can I do? I'm really in my mud mind. I guess I can throw a tantrum. Or can somebody help me find a solution?

FIRST STUDENT: I can go look for it.

TEACHER: You used your twinkler mind for that good idea. Does anyone have a different idea?

SECOND STUDENT: You could use a different color marker.

TEACHER: Another good idea from a twinkler mind. Those are both good suggestions. Now that my mud mind is gone, I can choose. I'll try writing with a different color first. Thank you for using your twinkler mind.

Applying the Win–Win Process

After I have modeled several such examples, I introduce children to the terms *I-messages* and *active listening*. Then, I show how the process is applied in resolving personal conflict. I use a role-playing scenario where Jonathan and Aliseah are arguing over a crayon. I walk students through the process as follows:

TEACHER: Aliseah, did you take Jonathan's crayon?

ALISEAH: I needed a red crayon to do my work.

TEACHER: Why didn't you use your own red crayon instead of taking Jonathan's?

ALISEAH: I don't have a red crayon. I had to use his.

TEACHER: I see. The problem is that you need a red crayon, but Jonathan needs his. Is there a different way we could solve the problem?

ALISEAH: I don't know.

TEACHER: I believe you. Let's take a minute to get out of our mud minds and see if a twinkler mind can find another idea. *[Pause]* Is there a place in this room where spare crayons are kept?

ALISEAH: In the crayon can on the shelf?

TEACHER: The problem is that you need a red crayon. How can you solve your problem?

ALISEAH: I can get a red crayon from the crayon can.

TEACHER: I hear you using your twinkler mind to solve this problem. Can you think of still another way to solve it?

ALISEAH: Ask Jonathan to share his red crayon?

TEACHER: Your twinkler mind is really working now. Which solution would you like to try?

ALISEAH: I'll go get a crayon from the can.

TEACHER: Okay. Try your plan. Let's talk at recess. I want to hear about how you took care of your problem.

Continual follow-up is necessary as students learn this process. It helps if they receive feedback in the form of a smile, nod, or thumbs-up signal when they resolve conflicts and personal problems.

2. Grade 3

TEACHER: DEBORAH SUND

My Students' Needs

1. To learn interesting and useful information, especially that which promotes skills in reading, math, and language.
2. A learning environment that is attractive, stimulating, free from threat, and conducive to productive work.
3. A teacher who is attentive, helpful, and kind.
4. The opportunity to work and interact cooperatively with other students.
5. To be accepted and feel part of the group.
6. To learn how to relate to others humanely and helpfully.
7. To have the opportunity to excel.

My Needs

1. Orderly classroom appearance: good room arrangement; materials neatly stored; interesting, well-thought-out displays.
2. Structure and routines: a set schedule that is flexible and allows for improvisation when needed.
3. Attention: student attention given for directions and to all speakers and instructional activities.
4. Situationally appropriate behaviors: quiet attention during instruction, considerate interaction during group activities.
5. Enthusiasm from me and my students.
6. Warmth as reflected in mutual regard among all members of the class.
7. Positive, relaxed classroom environment reflecting self-control, mutual helpfulness, and assumption of responsibility.

My Dislikes

1. Inattention to speaker, teacher, other adult, or class member.
2. Excessive noise: loud voices, inappropriate talking, and laughing.
3. Distractions: toys, unnecessary movement, poking, teasing, and so on.
4. Abuse of property: misusing, wasting, or destroying instructional materials.
5. Unkind and rude conduct: ridicule, sarcasm, bad manners, and physical abuse.

Classroom Rules

The following are classroom rules that have emerged from discussions with my students, who agree to abide by them.

1. Be considerate of others at all times. (Speak kindly. Be helpful. Don't bother others.)

2. Do your best work. (Get as much done as you can. Do your work neatly so that you can be proud of it. Don't waste time.)
3. Use quiet voices in the classroom. (Use regular speaking voices during class discussions. Speak quietly during cooperative work groups. Whisper at other times if you need help.)
4. Use signals to request permission or receive help. (I explain the signal systems for assistance, movement, restroom pass.)

I ask students on the first day of school to tell me how they would like to be treated by others in the room. I ask them what they especially dislike. We discuss their contributions at length, making sure through examples that we have a clear understanding of their wishes. By the next day, I have written out some statements that summarize what they have said. I ask them if these ideas seem good ones to live by in the room. They invariably agree, and we call the statements our class rules. We spend some time practicing how we will behave and speak, in accordance with the rules. In the days that follow, I show students prompts, cues, hints, and other assistance I will give to help them internalize the behaviors we have agreed on.

Negative Consequences

As we discuss the rules, I ask students what they think should happen when someone breaks a rule. They usually suggest punishments. I tell them that because I want them always to be as happy as possible, I don't want to punish them. I say that instead of punishment, I will do the following:

1. I will give them "pirate eyes": I show them a stern glance, accompanied by a disappointed and puzzled expression.
2. If necessary, I will remind them of what rule is being transgressed: "I hear noise." "Some people are not listening."
3. If necessary, I will tell them exactly what they are doing wrong: "Gordon, you did not use the signal. Please use the signal."
4. If they can't control themselves, I will separate them from the group until they can.
5. If nothing else works, I will contact their parents to see what we can do to help.

Positive Consequences

I emphasize that I will always try to show how pleased I am when students follow the rules we have agreed to. I tell them:

1. Mostly I will give them smiles, winks, nods, and pats when they are behaving well.
2. Sometimes I will say out loud how pleased I am with the way they are working or behaving toward each other.

3. Once in a while, when the whole class has behaved especially well, I will give them a special privilege (go early to recess, do one of their favorite activities, see a videotape).
4. From time to time I will send a complimentary note to their parents, or call their parent to comment on how well they are doing.

My Preventive Discipline Measures

I take the following steps to minimize the occurrence of behavior problems in my classroom:

1. Involve students in establishing class rules and assuming responsibility. In discussions I ask questions such as "How do you like others to treat you when you are (working, speaking to the class, playing outside, etc.)" and "What do you think happens when everyone tries to talk at the same time? What could we do instead?"
2. Organize a classroom environment for best temperature, light, and comfort and with traffic patterns for efficient movement within the room.
3. Emphasize, model, and hold practice sessions on good manners, courtesy, and responsibility.
4. Provide a varied, active curriculum with opportunities for physical movement, singing, interaction, and times of quiet.
5. Provide a sense of consistency, familiarity, and security through structure and routines.
6. Make contact with parents as follows:
   - Send letters outlining expectations and discipline system.
   - Make short, positive phone calls to parents.
   - Send home with children notes concerning good work and behavior.

My Supportive Discipline Measures

To help my students support their own self-control, I use the following supportive measures:

1. Eye contact; facial expressions.
2. Physical proximity.
3. Reference to classroom rules.
4. Interest in individual students' work.
5. Modification of the lesson or routine if needed to increase interest or reduce anxiety.

My Corrective Discipline Measures

When my students misbehave, I use the negative consequences I explained to them, and to which they agreed when we formulated the class rules.

My Way of Maintaining a Positive Classroom Climate

I have found that a positive climate results in better feelings, more enjoyment, and ultimately better self-control for both the students and myself.

The following are some of the things I do to maintain such a climate:

1. Show respect for each child as an individual who is entitled to a good education.
2. Look for the good or likable qualities in each child.
3. Acknowledge appropriate behavior, good work, effort, and improvement.
4. Take time to get to know each student better.
5. Give out as many nonverbal positive responses as possible—winks, nods, and smiles.
6. Take time each day to assess student feelings and discuss them if necessary.
7. Talk with students in ways that imply their own competence, such as "Okay, you know what to do next."
8. Provide interesting and fun activities that are challenging but in which students can succeed.
9. End each day on a positive note, with a fond good-bye and hope for a happy and productive tomorrow.

3. Grade 5

TEACHER: MICHAEL BRUS I base my discipline system on the Golden Rule and find I need to spell out only three rules, which I prepare calligraphically in gold Gothic lettering and display prominently in the room. My rules read as follows:

- Teachers have a right to teach!
- Students have a right to learn!

Therefore:

1. We agree to treat fellow students and teachers as we ourselves would like to be treated.
2. We agree to be on time, to be prepared to work, and to stay on task.
3. We agree to have no unauthorized food, gum, or drink.

I believe in treating my students very much like adults, letting them know they are responsible for how they behave. I define the behavior boundaries within my three rules and discuss gray areas around them. I invite my students to add a fourth rule, if there is one in which they believe strongly.

I use much positive reinforcement. Whenever I see a student behaving especially well, I make a notation on my clipboard. The student receiving the most marks in a month is named citizen of the month. Having been a professional portrait artist, I honor the student by drawing a color pastel portrait of him or her.

The points accumulated by other students may be used at an end-of-the-month auction to bid for prizes I furnish, such as inexpensive toys, books, erasers, pieces of chalk, and stickers. In order to emphasize good group behavior, I keep a separate tally of points earned by the class as a whole for being quiet and orderly at lunch, library, auditorium, and especially for helping us all have an unusually pleasant day at school. These points accumulate toward free minutes on Fridays, extra physical education, or time for playing with computers and games.

By my own demeanor in the classroom, I try to show my sincere belief that there is much good in every person. I try to find in all my students something they do especially well and help instill in them a sense of pride and achievement.

When my students break class rules, I remind them of the rule they are breaking. If they do so again, I make a mark on my clipboard, indicating that I am doing so. The consequences associated with these negative marks are as follows:

First mark: I give a short verbal desist, referring again to the rule that is broken.

Second mark: I remove the student from the activity until he or she indicates to me readiness to return.

Third mark: I send the student to a fellow teacher's room with an assignment to complete. (This is arranged in advance, reciprocally, with the other teacher.)

Fourth mark: The student is sent to the principal's office. The principal knows and supports my system and takes further appropriate action.

When the consequences for more serious misbehavior are invoked, I follow up with the student, insisting that a plan for proper behavior be made that is acceptable to both the student and me. At appropriately private times, I talk openly and honestly with the student about his or her success in living up to the plan and what must be done next when the plan does not work.

4. Grade 7 (Humanities Core)

TEACHER: DEBORAH TRIVOLI When school begins, I use a four-day sequence to establish rules of behavior for the class, as follows:

Day 1: Students' Needs, My Needs, and Rules

Students' Needs. When I first meet the students, I spend as much time as necessary—usually about an hour—discussing how we would like our class to function. I tell them I want the class to be worthwhile and enjoyable, for them as well as for me, and that if we work together we can make it so. I then ask them to tell me, without mentioning any names, some of the things they have *not* liked about school in the past, things we would like to avoid. Their comments usually include the following:

- Stupid (irrelevant, meaningless, boring) work
- Mean (inconsiderate, demanding, unreasonable, unfriendly) teachers
- Put-downs (sarcasm, remarks) by teachers and other students
- Not being listened to by teachers
- Not being allowed to discuss or express their own opinions

I list their comments on the board and assure them I don't want those things in our class. But, I say, we will need to work together if we are to keep them out.

My Needs. I move on to say that sometimes there are things in classes that I don't like either and that just as I will try to make the class good for the students, I need them to help make it good for me. I don't list my concerns as dissatisfactions; rather, I list them as my needs, which I write on the board alongside their concerns:

- Considerate behavior (students and teacher being kind and helpful)
- High-quality work (work to be proud of)
- Student responsibility in learning (attention, participation, completing assignments)
- Low level of noise (just one of my personal needs, I explain)
- Clean, orderly classroom

For each of my needs, I give a positive and negative example to help explain what I mean.

Rules. I ask them if they can help come up with some rules for the class that will meet their needs as well as mine. We compare the lists and before long decide that one rule could have to do with respectful behavior for everyone, teacher and students alike. Another rule could have to do with important learnings done well. The students express other rules, but after discussion usually decide that only two rules are needed.

1. Every person in the class—teacher and student alike—shows consideration and respect for everyone else.
2. Every person in the class—teacher and student alike—shows responsibility for doing high-quality work on important learnings.

We discuss these two rules. I relate example scenarios and ask the class whether in those scenarios our rules are being followed or violated.

I end the first day's session by thanking them for their excellent thinking and by asking this question: "Do you ever see drivers speeding—driving well over the speed limit?" They all say they do. I then say, "The speed limits are rules that most people consider wise and important. And yet those rules are sometimes broken. In our class, I know you consider our rules wise and important, yet there may be times when they are broken. For your homework tonight, I'd like you to write out four suggestions concerning how we can remember to follow our rules."

Day 2: Suggestions for Rules Enforcement
Next day, students make many suggestions for enforcing our rules. Most of their suggestions are unrealistic or counterproductive, such as the following:

- Make them (rule breakers) stay in after school.
- Send them to the principal's office.
- Make them do extra work.

- Make them sit in the back of the room.
- Make them apologize.

I remind the students of our rule 1, showing consideration and respect for everyone. I ask what we might do, or what I might do, that would be helpful and respectful to students who violate our rules. This question really causes students to think. It is hard for them to come up with much besides the following:

- You could warn us that we are breaking a rule and need to stop.
- You could talk with students who break rules.
- Maybe you could tell the parents and get them to help.
- Maybe we could remind each other.

I end the second day's session by saying, "I need to think about your suggestions. You think some more about them, too. Tomorrow let's see what we come up with."

Day 3: Enforcement
On the third day I tell students I have thought a good deal about their excellent suggestions for helping us follow rules. I ask them if they have had new thoughts. I lead them into a discussion in which I give them credit for guiding us to the following:

1. Post the two rules on a chart on the front wall.
   Rule 1: Be considerate of everyone.
   Rule 2: Do our best work.
2. Have some sessions in which we practice showing consideration and working responsibly.
3. Refer to the rules occasionally, evaluate how well we are abiding by them, and compliment ourselves when we deserve it.
4. For students who continue to break rules, the teacher talks with them privately and tries to find ways to help them follow the rules.
5. For students who continue to break rules after private conferences with the teacher, a discussion meeting will be set up that involves student, teacher, parent, and principal, who together will try to decide how best to help.

We discuss these ideas and sometimes modify them a bit. When finished with the third day's session, I say that by tomorrow I will have the rules and agreements printed for them to sign and have their parent sign to show agreement and support.

Day 4: Forward
I have students take agreements home for parents to read and sign. They bring them back and I keep them on file. We continue to refer to our rules regularly. When I see minor violations, I take the opportunity to explore with the class whether the rules are working. I conduct occasional practice activities in which we role-play abiding by or violating the rules. In some of these, I have the teacher violate a rule and ask students

what they think should be done. These practices clarify and serve as reminders to do the following:

1. Use considerate behavior.
2. Take responsibility for learning.
3. Keep the classroom pleasant and orderly.
4. Resolve difficulties without causing hurt feelings.

The activities also help me remember to do the following:

1. Treat all students with dignity and respect.
2. Provide worthwhile learnings through interesting activities.
3. Use verbal and physical cues to help students follow rules.
4. Maintain positive interactions with all my students.
5. Have fun and pat myself on the back at the end of each day.

5. Grade 8 (English)

TEACHER: GAIL CHARLES I have been teaching for 20 years. Most of that time I tried to control student misbehavior with scowls, reprimands, lectures, threats, and detentions. My students grudgingly behaved well enough and they learned, but I'm sure they felt under siege. I know I did, and the effort left me continually frustrated and exhausted.

In recent years I have begun to understand that I am more effective and enjoy my work more when I organize the curriculum to accommodate, even embrace, the needs of my adolescent students. While I still provide a strong and challenging curriculum, I have switched from a coercive to a collaborative way of teaching. I now try to guide, encourage, and support my students' efforts rather than push and prod. The result has been fewer power struggles, more success, and happier students and teacher.

Winning My Students Over

My students want to feel part of the group. They want to feel accepted and valued by each other and especially by me. They want to feel safe, so I forbid all ridicule and sarcasm. I've never ridiculed a student, but sorry to say, I have spoken sarcastically many times when struggling against students who defied my rules. I no longer use sarcasm nor allow students to belittle each other in any way.

I give my students a voice in classroom matters and listen to them sincerely. I allow them to make decisions about where they sit and with whom they wish to work. I do this as part of trying to make learning enjoyable. They like to work with each other, participate, talk, and cooperate.

Meeting My Needs

We discuss the importance of making classwork enjoyable, and I tell my students that the class needs to be enjoyable for me, too. I tell them up front what I need in order to feel good about the class—that I want the tone to be positive, with everyone showing patience, tolerance, good manners, and mutual respect. I tell them that I want them to show enthusiasm and do the best work they can. I say I need their attention and that I want them to help care for materials and keep the room clean. I promise to treat them with respect, and they usually want to reciprocate.

Rules and Student Input
My new style of discipline has required me to make changes in my curriculum and ways of establishing rules. I have learned to request and make use of student input concerning expectations, operating procedures, and codes of conduct. Formerly, I greeted new students with a printed set of rules and consequences, but they always saw them as impositions rather than as cooperative agreements they wanted to support. Now when I meet a new class, I discuss their needs and mine and focus on how we can meet those needs and make our class productive. I give students power to make many decisions and show that I respect what they say.

Together we write a plan for how we will work and behave in the class. Because I want them to make thoughtful suggestions, I ask them, for their first homework assignment, to think back on previous years in school and write brief responses to the following:

1. When have you felt most successful in school?
2. What did the teacher do to help you feel successful?
3. What kinds of class activities have you found most helpful and enjoyable?
4. What suggestions do you have for creating a classroom in which all can work, learn, and do their best?

The next day, I organize students into small groups to share and discuss what they have written. Volunteers present each group's responses, which I list on the overhead projector. Occasionally I may add a suggestion of my own. We then streamline, combine, reword, and sometimes negotiate until we reach a set of agreements we think best. Before the next class, I type up the agreements and ask each student and his or her parent to sign, indicating their support. I do this for each of my five classes. The agreements turn out to be quite similar from class to class.

Enforcement
With the collaborative plan in place, I have few discipline problems and little difficulty dealing with those that occur. Most often, a simple reminder is all that is needed to get students back on track. For the occasional student who repeatedly misbehaves despite our agreement, I ask the counselor to set up a meeting with the student's parents and, sometimes, other teachers. We discuss the problem and how it can be resolved. Very occasionally, a student may behave in a dangerous manner or prevent my teaching. When that happens, I call on the vice-principal for immediate intervention.

Prevention
In classes of 35 adolescents, there exists an endless supply of distractions. It is up to me to keep students engaged successfully in activities they enjoy and find rewarding. I have had considerable success using reading and writing activities in which students

choose books to read and respond to them in writing. I present mini-lessons that address common needs I see in the class. Students evaluate their own work and make it the best possible for inclusion in their Showcase Portfolios, which are displayed for parents, teachers, administrators, and others at a Writers' Tea. In addition, students complete at least one project per quarter. They have choices on what they will pursue in their projects and how they will show what they have learned. Always there is a high emphasis on quality.

During these efforts, I try to interact personally with every student. It is not easy to forge relationships with 160+ students, but I do so in order to show them I "see" and like them. At the beginning of the year I write a letter to my students introducing myself and telling a bit about my family, hobbies, interests, and goals. I ask them to do the same so I can know them better. I keep a birthday calendar to remember student birthdays. I try to comment on new hairstyles, new outfits, or how great a now brace-free set of teeth looks. I chaperon field trips and dances, supervise the computer writing lab after school, and make myself available for conversation before and after school. These little things mean a lot to students.

For their part, many students like to involve themselves in the workings of the classroom. I assign them tasks such as classroom librarian, bulletin board designer, plant caretaker, and class secretary. Their involvement makes them feel important and useful.

More than anything else, I have found that if I want respect from my students, I must show them respect. I want writers, so I write along with them. I want them involved, so I get involved with them. I want them to show good manners, humor, and kindness, so I exemplify those qualities the best I can. I make mistakes in these efforts and lots of them, but the more sincerely I try, the more forgiving my students become.

6. Grade 10 (English Language Development)

TEACHER: LINDA BLACKLOCK Over the years, I have developed my discipline style by incorporating good ideas from many different sources. I have learned the importance of laying groundwork before school begins, which helps bring about a low-stress, successful, and fun year for my students and me. I never leave the discipline structure to chance, because I know I will pay for it if I do. My discipline system always precedes my instructional program.

My discipline plan emphasizes four areas, all of which allow me to approach discipline in a positive way: (1) classroom environment and seating, to facilitate learning and physical proximity to students, (2) limit setting, to ensure that students understand how we are to conduct ourselves in the classroom; (3) responding to misbehavior by disciplining with body movements instead of my mouth, and (4) training for responsibility through preferred activity time.

Classroom Environment and Seating
In this area of discipline, I try to arrange every aspect of the classroom environment so that learning is more likely to occur and student fooling around is less likely to happen. I arrange student seating close to the board with rows moving across the room instead of front to back. I put my desk at the side and leave two aisles from front to back. This arrangement allows me to circulate easily within the group.

Limit Setting
We do not have rules, as such, for the class. Instead, we have what I call *understandings.* We understand that our purpose is to get our work done in a responsible manner, that I will try to make the work interesting so students will enjoy it, and that none of us will interfere with student learning in any way. This requires essentially that we treat others the way we wish to be treated. We discuss these ideas at length to ensure understanding and acceptance.

Responding to Misbehavior
When it is necessary to react to student misbehavior, I have trained myself to remain cool, calm, and collected so that I can rely on experience and diagnosis rather than act on the heat of the moment. I remind myself that I cannot control students if I cannot first control myself.

My Body Language
I emphasize body language and timing, as follows:

1. I turn in a slow and regal fashion to face the disruptive student(s).
2. I point my toes toward the student, thus committing myself to discipline. I give no mixed messages.
3. I focus on the student's face and look only at that student.
4. I keep my hands down so that I won't appear agitated.
5. I show no expression on my face. I do not smile, which would give ambivalent messages and appear submissive.
6. I keep my breathing slow and deep, remain relaxed, and move slowly.

Students' Body Language
All the while, I am reading the students' body language as well. I look under the desk at their knees and feet. If they are talking and don't come all the way around with their bodies turned to work, I know they are likely to begin talking again. I have learned that students use their upper bodies for faking and their lower bodies for commitment.

Dealing with Back Talk
I have learned that when students talk back, it triggers a strong reaction in me. But I have also learned that I'm better off ignoring it. When a student talks back, I stay calm and relaxed and keep my mouth shut, which causes the student's show to fizzle out.

Training for Responsibility
I use preferred activity time (PAT) as an incentive to encourage students to behave responsibly. I include discussions of PAT on the first day of school, and I implement it beginning on the second day. Students enjoy PAT, which leads to good relations and good behavior. I use it as follows:

1. I explain the meaning of preferred activity time, what it can consist of, what students can do to earn it, and what they can do to lose it.
2. I use a wall chart for each class and a stopwatch.

3. I award bonuses (minutes of time) to the class for being in the right place at the right time, for smooth class transitions, and for contests between classes.
4. When students misbehave or waste time, I record the amount of lost time on the chart with a minus sign and continue class instruction. I never have to do any nagging.
5. When students have earned enough minutes to fill a complete class period, I let them decide which day they prefer to use it and what they prefer doing that day. They may select from test reviews, skill drills, homework, team games, or enrichment activities.

I have found that this system of discipline gives me a variety of nonadversarial procedures for encouraging good behavior and intervening when necessary to stop misbehavior.

7. Grade 11 (Physical Science)

TEACHER: LESLIE HAYES My personal belief is that every one of my students can behave appropriately in my classroom every day. My personal goal is to be an effective teacher for them. I try to accomplish this through clarity, firmness, and a human touch. It is very important to me to establish a sense of class belonging and unity marked by shared objectives and goals. Toward that end I try to inject humor and fun, and I find that student participation follows naturally. At the same time I concentrate on preventive and supportive discipline by doing extensive planning and by constantly monitoring each of my students. This frees me from having to deal continually with misbehavior. I communicate with parents by note and telephone, and most of them are so thankful that I have called them to talk about their child that they become my allies in class control.

My students range from remedial (almost always considered behavior problems) to advanced. With all levels, my discipline plan works best for me with a very structured approach that communicates my standards and requirements.

My plan goes into effect within the first five minutes of class each September. Students are given a class behavior contract, which must be taken home, signed by their parents, and returned to me the next day. If they bring it back when due, I give them points; if they are a day late, they get no points; and if it doesn't come back the third day, I call the parents at home. The contract outlines my philosophy and behavior guidelines (Figure 13.1).

After reviewing the rules with the students, I have them fill out a behavior card that becomes part of my system for recording behavior problems. This is yet another way of telling the students that discipline is an important part of my classroom organization. I begin by seating students according to a seating chart, then explain procedures concerning homework, grading, and required materials. Textbooks are distributed and we go over the plans for the semester. After that, we begin the first lesson. By the end of the first class, all students have the feeling that I am in control and have a well-organized plan.

Over years of trying various discipline approaches, I have found that students react positively to my system. As the year progresses, occasional gentle reminders are

Figure 13.1
Class behavior contract

Dear Student and Parent:
 In order to guarantee all the students in my classroom the excellent learning climate they deserve, I use the following discipline plan.
 Attendance: Attendance is essential to the learning process. You cannot expect to succeed if you do not participate in the daily activity of the classroom. Therefore, after a student's fourth absence, the parent will be notified. After 15 absences, the student will be subject to failure in the class.
 Tardies: Students are expected to be in their assigned seat and ready to begin work when the final bell rings. A warning is issued after two tardies, and the parent will be informed. Citizenship grades will be lowered one grade for every two tardies. After four tardies a letter will be sent home describing the situation. Following the seventh tardy, the student is subject to being dropped from the class with an F.
 Class Behavior: I believe that all my students can behave appropriately in my classroom. I will not permit a student to stop me from teaching or to keep other students from learning.
 Class Rules:
 1. Bring your science book, notebook, and pencil every day. *I don't lend anything.*
 2. Be attentive while the teacher, or a student who is called on, is talking.
 3. Bring no food, drink, candy, gum, hats, or sunglasses to the class.
 4. Handle all equipment properly.
 5. Profanity and verbal abuse are not tolerated.
 6. Remain in your seat at the end of the period until dismissed by the teacher.
 Consequences: High citizenship and conduct grades will be awarded to those students who contribute positively to the daily activities of the classroom. If, on the other hand, a student chooses to interfere with the learning process, the following consequences will be invoked:
 First time: Warning; mark on discipline card.
 Second time: Notify parent of behavior problem.
 Third time: Refer student to counselor.
 Fourth time: Refer student to vice-principal for disciplinary action.
 Students who write on desks or throw trash around the room will be assigned immediate after-school detention to clean the desktops and remove all the trash.
 Note: More serious problems such as defiance, fighting, theft, abuse of equipment, or violation of laboratory safety rules will result in immediate referral to the vice-principal.
 It is in the student's best interest that student, teacher, and parent work together. I will therefore be in close contact with parents regarding students' progress. Parents, please sign the tear-off signature portion of this contract and have the student return it to me tomorrow. If you have any questions or comments, please call me or write them on the tear-off.

usually enough to maintain good behavior. I also use eye contact, hand signals, and physical proximity to assist. When more serious disruptions do occasionally occur, students know the rules and consequences, and it thus becomes easier to invoke the consequences without emotional upheavals and confrontations that I find personally offensive.

A Schoolwide Discipline Plan

 PROVIDED BY KRIS HALVERSON, ASSISTANT PRINCIPAL, DRY CREEK ELEMENTARY SCHOOL Dry Creek School is just completing a five-year restructuring project that emphasizes brain-based education. One of our most important tasks in this effort is implementing a positive learning environment in which everyone feels safe yet excited about learning.

Toward this end, we have put into schoolwide practice Cooperative Discipline, which has helped us build quality relationships between students and staff. The strategies in Cooperative Discipline are made specific to individual students' needs through five steps.

1. Pinpoint and describe the student's behavior.
2. Identify the goal of the misbehavior.
3. Select and apply appropriate intervention techniques.
4. Apply encouragement strategies to build self-esteem.
5. Involve the parents as partners in the process.

Prior to using Cooperative Discipline, our staff had made use of a more forceful type of class discipline. As we have moved into Cooperative Discipline, we have been challenged to rethink, redefine, and rework our former ways of dealing with children.

The Critter Code

In order to provide uniformity and continuity in behavior management, our staff developed what we call the Dry Creek Critter Code. This code of behavior, used by everyone in the school, aims at Cooperative Discipline's Three C's: Capable, Connect, and Contribute. We have designed a logo in the form of an umbrella with CAPABLE, CONNECT, CONTRIBUTE written on the umbrella. Just beneath the umbrella are these four statements:

I will respect myself, others, and property.

I will be responsible for my behavior.

I will be punctual and prepared.

I will be safe.

We make a constant effort to help everyone live by these code statements.

Life Skills

In connection with the Critter Code and Cooperative Discipline, we provide our students systematic instruction in life skills of teamwork, perseverance, responsibility, caring, and cooperation. This is aimed at helping our students become more effective citizens. In this effort we make use of Dorothy Rich's *Megaskills* and Susan Lovalik's *Integrated Thematic Instruction Model.* We devote a month to each of the major skills; at the end of each month, we hold a ceremony to recognize students who have demonstrated the skill in exemplary fashion.

The Citation Program

When students misbehave seriously, they are given citations. But rather than carry a punitive connotation, the citations provide a positive opportunity for us to help students understand why they are misbehaving, to assist them with problem-solving skills, and to support them as they learn to connect effectively with school. The following are some of the key elements of our citation program:

1. Manners and Safety Class. Any student receiving a citation must attend manners and safety class during the last recess to make a problem-solving map with a teacher. This allows the child to connect with a caring adult and to learn problem-solving skills that support better behavior choices.

2. Action Plan Meetings. These meetings are held once a week. Student referrals are made by classroom teachers on the basis of accumulated citations or social, emotional, or academic needs. These meetings are attended by teacher, student, parent, principal, and action plan coordinator, and their purpose is to develop a plan to positively reconnect the student to the school.

3. Critter Activities. On Friday afternoons, we provide Critter Activities for students who have lived by our code. These activities, used as incentives for good behavior, tap into the seven intelligences. [H. Gardner's (*Frames of mind: The theory of multiple intelligences,* New York: Basic Books, 1983) seven intelligences are: (1) logical-mathematical, (2) linguistic-verbal, (3) musical, (4) spatial, (5) bodily-kinesthetic, (6) interpersonal, and (7) intrapersonal.] The activities are characterized by meaningful content, student choice, multiage groupings, and adequate time for goal accomplishment. Activity groups include landscape architects, dance troupes, newsletter editors, culinary academicians, artists in residence, clay masters, musicians, athletes, jewelers, math masters, and technologists.

4. Citation Clinic. This is a weekly counterpart of Critter Activities. The clinic is conducted by the Student Success Team, comprised of sixth-grade students who have been trained to work, under adult supervision, with peers and younger students who have received serious citations, such as those for fighting or repeated use of profanity. Problems are discussed and worked out, strategies that lead to good behavior are reviewed, and supportive connections are established between students. The Success Team also helps in other leadership roles, such as schoolwide decision making. As school leaders, their self-esteem grows and they become models of responsibility.

5. The Newcomer Club. This club of sixth-grade students creates and extends a warm, welcoming environment for new students. Each new student at Dry Creek School is invited to a luncheon to meet club members and other new students. At the luncheon, they receive folders with supplies and special correspondence welcoming them.

All of these programs at Dry Creek School focus on making students feel that they are capable, connected, and contributing members of our school. We believe these programs are helping greatly to cultivate good citizenship, enhance self-esteem, and raise academic achievement.

APPLICATION EXERCISES

QUESTIONS AND ACTIVITIES

1. Clarify what you as a teacher consider acceptable with regard to noise, talk, movement, and courtesy. Formulate your ideas into questions or topics that you could discuss with your class.
2. Outline your personal system of discipline to include as many of the eight steps to personalized discipline as possible.

3. Select, from classroom scenarios presented in the Appendix, one that is most similar to the grade, subject, or type of students that interests you. Test your system against the scenario. Ask yourself whether your system will
   - stop the misbehavior
   - keep students working productively
   - reduce the cause(s) of misbehavior
   - preserve student dignity and build positive relationships
   - engender support from parents and administrators.

REFERENCES AND RECOMMENDED READINGS

Albert, L. 1996. *Cooperative discipline.* Circle Pines, Minn.: American Guidance Service.

Gaustad, J. 1992. *School discipline* (ERIC Digest No. 78). Eugene, Oreg.: ERIC Clearinghouse on Educational Management.

Grant, C., and C. Sleeter. 1989. *Turning on learning: Five approaches for multicultural teaching plans for race, class, gender, and disability.* Columbus, Ohio: Merrill.

Hernandez, H. 1989. *Multicultural education: A teacher's guide to content and process.* Columbus, Ohio: Merrill.

Knapp, M., B. Turnbull, and P. Shields. 1990. New directions for educating the children of poverty. *Educational Leadership, 48*(4), 1–8.

Population Reference Bureau for the Center for the Study of Social Policy. 1992. *Challenge of change: What the 1990 census tells us about children.* Washington, D.C.: Author.

Schaps, E., and D. Solomon. 1990. Schools and classrooms as caring communities. *Educational Leadership, 48*(3), 38–42.

Schulman, J. 1989. Blue freeways: Traveling the alternate route with big-city teacher trainees. *Journal of Teacher Education, 40*(5), 2–8.

Slavin, R., N. Karweit, and N. Madden. 1989. *Effective programs for students at risk.* Needham Heights, Mass.: Allyn & Bacon.

Sobol, T. 1990. Understanding diversity. *Educational Leadership, 48*(3), 27–30.

Classroom Scenarios for Analysis and Practice

Presented here are descriptions of 10 classrooms exhibiting misbehaviors typical of those teachers might encounter. The scenarios can be used for behavior analysis, application of concepts and strategies, and testing of personal systems of discipline. Each scenario consists of a general description of the class followed by one or more typical occurrences. It is suggested that when analyzing the scenarios, you ask yourself the following questions:

1. What is the problem behavior, if any, and why is it a problem?
2. If it is a genuine problem, what seems to be causing it?
3. What should the teacher do to stop the misbehavior?
4. Should the teacher involve the other students in resolving the situation, and if so, how?
5. How can the misbehaving students be put back on a positive course?
6. What can be done when resolving the situation to maintain student dignity and good personal relations?

SCENARIO 1: FIFTH GRADE

The Class

Mrs. Miller's fifth grade enrolls students from a small, stable community. Because the transiency rate is low, many of her students have been together since first grade, and during those years they have developed certain patterns of interacting and role playing. Unfortunately, many of those behaviors interfere with teaching and learning. During the first week of school Mrs. Miller noticed that four or five students enjoyed making smart-aleck remarks about most things she wanted them to do. When such remarks were made, the other students laughed and sometimes joined in. Even when Mrs. Miller attempts to hold class discussions about serious issues, many of the students make light of the problems and refuse to enter genuinely into a search for solutions. Instead of obtaining the productive discussion she had hoped for, Mrs. Miller finds the class degenerating into flippancy and horseplay.

Typical Occurrences

Mrs. Miller has begun a history lesson that contains a reference to Julius Caesar. She asks if anyone has ever heard of Julius Caesar. Ben shouts out, "Yeah, they named a salad after him!" The class laughs and calls out encouraging remarks such as "Good one, Ben!" Mrs. Miller tells Ben she does not appreciate such contributions. She waits for some semblance of order, then says, "Let us go on." "Lettuce, continue!" cries Jeremy from the back of the room. The class falls into a chaos of laughter and talk. After waiting a while, Mrs. Miller slams a book down on the desk and demands quiet. "Any more such comments and you will go straight to the office!" she says loudly. For the remainder of the lesson, no more students call out remarks, but most continue to smirk and whisper comments about Caesar salad. A great deal of giggling goes on. Mrs. Miller tries to ignore the display, but because of the disruptions she is not able to complete the lesson on time or to get the results she hoped for.

SCENARIO 2: HIGH SCHOOL BIOLOGY

The Class

Mr. Platt teaches advanced placement classes in biology to students from middle- to upper-income families. Most of the students have already made plans for attending college. When the students enter the classroom, they know they are to go to their assigned seats and write out answers to the questions of the day that Mr. Platt has written on the board. After that, Mr. Platt lectures on text material that he assigned students to read before coming to class. During the lecture, he calls randomly on students to answer questions and requires that they support their answers with reference to the assigned reading. Following the lecture, students engage in lab activity for the remainder of the period.

Typical Occurrences

Mr. Platt has begun his lecture on the process of photosynthesis. He asks Arlene what the word photosynthesis means. She pushes her long hair aside and replies, "I don't get it." This is a comment Mr. Platt hears frequently from Arlene. "What is it you don't understand?" "None of it," she says. Mr. Platt retorts, "Be more specific! I've only asked for the definition!" Arlene is not intimidated. "I mean, I don't get any of it. I don't understand why plants are green. Why aren't they blue or some other color? Why don't they grow on Mercury? The book says plants make food. How? Do they make Twinkies? That's ridiculous. I don't understand this business about photosynthesis." Mr. Platt stares at Arlene for a while, and she back at him. He asks, "Are you finished?" Arlene shrugs. "I guess so." She hears some of the boys whistle under their breath; she enjoys their obvious admiration. Mr. Platt says to her, "Arlene, I hope some day you will understand that this is not a place for you to show off." "I hope so, too," Arlene says. "I know I should be more serious." She stares out the window. For the remainder of the lecture, delivered in an icy tone of voice, Mr. Platt calls only on students he knows will give correct answers. His lecture completed, Mr. Platt begins to give instructions for lab activity. He notices that Nick is turning the valve of the gas jet on and off. He says to Nick, "Mr. Turner, would you please repeat the rule about the use of lab equipment?" Nick drops his head and mumbles something about waiting for directions. Arlene says calmly, "Knock it off, Nick. This is serious business." She smiles at Mr. Platt. Mr. Platt stares at the class for a moment, then completes his directions and tells them to begin. He walks around the room, monitoring their work. He stands behind lab partners Sherry and Dawn, who are having a difficult time. He does not offer them help, believing that advanced placement students should be able to work things out for themselves. But as they blunder through the activity, he shakes his head in disbelief, leaving the strong impression that he hopes the two girls will drop the class.

SCENARIO 3: MIDDLE SCHOOL LIBRARY

Setting and Students

Mrs. Daniels is a media specialist in charge of the middle school library. She sees her job as serving as resource person to students who are seeking information and is always eager to give help to those who request it. The students in her school would be characterized as lower middle class. About half are white, the remainder African American, Latino, and Southeast Asian. Each period of the day differs as to the number and type of students who come under Mrs. Daniels's direction. Usually, small groups have been sent there to do cooperative research. Always some unexpected students appear who have been excused from physical education for medical reasons but who hate to be sent to the library, or else they bear special passes from their teachers for a variety of purposes.

Typical Occurrences

Mrs. Daniels has succeeded in getting students settled and working when Tara appears at her side, needing a book to read as makeup work for missing class. Mrs. Daniels asks Tara what kinds of books interest her. Tara sullenly shrugs her shoulders. Mrs. Daniels takes her to a shelf of newly published books. "I read this one last night," she says. "I think you might like it. It's a good story and fast reading." Tara only glances at it. "That looks stupid," she says. "Don't you have any good books?" She glances down the shelf. "These are all stupid!" Another student, James, is tugging at Mrs. Daniels's elbow, with a note from his history teacher, who wants the source of a particular quotation. Mrs. Daniels asks Tara to look at the books for a moment while she takes James to the reference books. As Mrs. Daniels passes a table of students supposedly doing research, she notices that the group is watching Walter and Tim have a friendly pencil fight, hitting pencils together until one of them breaks. She admonishes Walter, who appears to be the more willing participant. Walter answers hotly, "Tim started it! It wasn't me!" "Well," Mrs. Daniels replies, "if you can't behave yourself, just go back to your class." The other students laugh at Walter, who feels he has been treated unjustly. He sits down and pouts. Meanwhile, Tara has gone to the large globe and is twirling it. Mrs. Daniels starts to speak to her but realizes that James is still waiting at her shoulder with the request for his teacher. Somehow, before the period ends, Tara leaves with a book she doesn't want and James takes a citation back to his teacher. The research groups have been too noisy. Mrs. Daniels knows they have done little work and wonders if she should speak to their teacher about the students' manners and courtesy. After the period finally ends, Mrs. Daniels notices that profane remarks have been written on the table where Walter was sitting.

SCENARIO 4: SECOND GRADE

The Class

Mrs. Desmond teaches second graders in a highly transient neighborhood. She receives an average of one new student each week, and those students typically remain in her class for fairly short lengths of time before moving elsewhere. Most are from single-parent, dysfunctional homes, and their poor behavior, including aggression, boisterousness, and crying, seems to reflect many emotional problems.

Typical Occurrences

The morning bell rings, and students who have been lined up outside by an aide enter the classroom noisily. Mrs. Desmond is speaking with a parent who is complaining that her son is being picked on by others in the class. When finally able to give attention to the class, Mrs. Desmond sees that Ricky and Raymond have crawled underneath the reading table, while a group of excited children is clustered around Shawon who has brought his new hamster to share with the class. Two girls are pulling at Mrs. Desmond's sleeves, trying to give her a note and lunch money. Mrs. Desmond has to shout above the din before she can finally get everyone seated. Several minutes have passed since the bell rang. Mrs. Desmond, having lost much of her composure, finally gets the reading groups started when she realizes that the assembly scheduled for that morning has slipped her mind. She suddenly stands up from her reading group and exclaims, "We have an assembly this morning! Put down your books and get lined up quickly! We are almost late!" Thirty-one students make a burst for the door, pushing and arguing. Rachael, a big, strong girl, shoves Amy and shouts, "Hey, get out of the way, stupid!" Amy, meek and retiring, begins to cry. Mrs. Desmond tries to comfort Amy while Rachael pushes her way to the front of the line. During the assembly, Ricky and Raymond sit together. They have brought some baseball cards and are entertaining the students seated around them. When the first part of the assembly performance is over, they boo loudly and laugh instead of applaud. Under the school principal's disapproving eye, Mrs. Desmond separates Ricky and Raymond, but for the rest of the performance they make silly faces and gestures to each other, causing other students to laugh. Upon returning to the classroom, Mrs. Desmond, certain that the principal will speak to her about her class's behavior, tries to talk with them about the impropriety of their actions. She attempts to elicit positive comments about the assembly, but several students say it was dumb and boring. The discussion has made little progress before time for recess. Mrs. Desmond sighs and directs the students to line up, ordering them sternly to use their best manners. As they wait at the door, Rachael is once again shoving her way to the head of the line.

SCENARIO 5: HIGH SCHOOL SPECIAL EDUCATION

The Class

Mrs. Reed teaches special education English to high school students, all of whom have a history of poor academic performance, though some seem to her to have at least average intelligence. Some of the students have been diagnosed as learning disabled. For others, no specific learning difficulties have been identified. Several live in foster homes. About one-third are Latinos bused from a distant neighborhood. Some of the students are known to be affiliated with gangs.

Typical Occurrences

The students enter the classroom lethargically, find their seats, and as directed, most of them begin copying an assignment from the board. Something is going on between Lisa and Jill, who shoot hateful glances at each other. Neither begins work. When the students are settled, Mrs. Reed reviews the previous day's lesson and then begins instruction on how to write a business letter. She asks the class to turn to an example in their textbooks. Five of the fourteen students do not have their books with them, though this is a requirement that is reemphasized almost daily. Students without books are penalized points that detract from their course grade. Mrs. Reed sees that Lisa has her book and asks her to open it to the correct page. Lisa shakes her head and puts her head down on the desk. Mrs. Reed gives her the option of time out. Lisa leaves the room and sits by herself at a table outside the door. Mrs. Reed goes on with the lesson. She asks the students to work in pairs to write a letter canceling a magazine subscription and request-ing a refund. She lets them pick their own partners but finds after a while that several students have formed no partnerships. Lisa's absence leaves an odd number of students. Jill asks if she can work by herself. Mrs. Reed grants her request, but Jill spends most of her time glancing back at Lisa. Two other girls, Marcia and Connie, have taken out mirrors and are applying makeup in-stead of working on their assignment. Mrs. Reed informs them that she intends to call on them first to share their letter with the class. After the allotted work time, Mrs. Reed asks for volun-teers to read their letters. With prodding, a pair of boys is first to share. Mrs. Reed then calls on Marcia and Connie. They complain that they didn't understand how to do the assignment. Mrs. Reed tells them they must complete the letter for homework. They agree, but Mrs. Reed knows they will not comply and expects them to be absent the next day. Other students read their let-ters. Some are good; others contain many mistakes. The students do not seem to differentiate between correct and incorrect business letter forms. Mrs. Reed tries to point out strengths and weaknesses in the work, but the class applauds and makes smart-aleck remarks impartially. At the end of the period, Mrs. Reed, intending that the students refine their work the next day, asks the students to turn in their letters. She finds that two papers are missing and that Juan and Marco have written on theirs numerous A+ symbols and gang-related graffiti.

SCENARIO 6: CONTINUATION HIGH SCHOOL PHOTOGRAPHY LAB

The Class

Mr. Carnett teaches photography lab, an elective class, in a continuation high school attended by students who have been unsuccessful for behavioral reasons in regular high school settings. Many of the students want to attend this particular school, as it is located in what they consider their turf. Some of the students are chemically dependent and/or come from dysfunctional homes. The photography lab class enrolls 18 students, all of whom are on individual study con-tracts.

Typical Occurrences

As students begin work, Mr. Carnett busies himself with a number of different tasks: setting out needed materials, giving advice on procedures, handing out quizzes for students who have com-pleted contracts, examining photographs, and so forth. He sees Tony sitting and staring into space. He asks Tony if he needs help. Tony shrugs. Mr. Carnett asks if Tony has brought his ma-terials to work on. Tony shakes his head. Mr. Carnett tells Tony he can start on a new part of his contract. Tony doesn't answer. Mr. Carnett asks what's the matter. When Tony doesn't respond, Mike mutters, "He's blasted out of his head, man." At that moment, Mr. Carnett hears heated words coming from the darkroom. He enters and finds two students squaring off, trying to stare each other down. He asks what the problem is but gets no reply. He tells the boys to leave the darkroom and go back to their seats. They ignore him. As tension grows, another student in-tervenes and says, "Come on, we can settle it later. Be cool." Mr. Carnett calls the office and in-forms the counselor of the incident. The boys involved hear him do so and gaze at him insolently. The class settles back to work, and for the remainder of the period Mr. Carnett circulates among them, providing assistance, stifling horseplay, urging that they move ahead in their contracts, and reminding everyone that they only have a limited amount of time in which to get their work done. From time to time he glances at Tony, who does no work during the period. He asks Tony if something is bothering him. Tony shakes his head. Mr. Carnett asks Tony if he wants to trans-fer out of the class, since it is elective. Tony says, "No, man, I like it here." "That's fine," Mr.

Carnett says. "But this is not dream time. You do your work, or else we will find you another class. You understand?" "Sure, man. I understand." Mr. Carnett turns away, but from the corner of his eye he is sure that he sees Tony's middle finger aimed in his direction.

SCENARIO 7: SHELTERED ENGLISH KINDERGARTEN

The Class

Mrs. Bates teaches a sheltered English kindergarten class comprised of 30 students, only seven of whom speak English at home. The ethnic/racial makeup of the class is a mixture of Vietnamese, Laotian, Chinese, Samoan, Iranian, Latino, Filipino, African American, and Caucasian. The emphasis of the class is rapid English language development. For the most part, the students work in small groups, each of which is directed by a teacher, aide, or parent volunteer. The groups rotate every half hour so as to have a variety of experiences.

Typical Occurrences

Shortly before school begins, a new girl, Mei, is brought into the class. She speaks very little English and is crying. She tries to run out of the classroom but is stopped by the aide. When Mrs. Bates rings her bell, the students know they are to sit on the rug, but those already at the play area do not want to do so. Mrs. Bates calls them three or four times, but finally she has to get up and physically bring two of them to the rug. As the opening activities proceed, Mrs. Bates repeatedly asks students to sit up. (They have begun rolling around on the floor.) Kinney is pestering the girl seated next to him. Twice Mrs. Bates asks him to stop. Finally, she sends him to sit in a chair outside the group. He has to sit there until the opening activities are finished, then he can rejoin his group for the first rotation at the art table. As soon as the groups get under way, Mrs. Bates hears a ruckus at the art table, which is under the guidance of Mrs. García, a parent volunteer. She sees that Kinney has scooped up finger paint and is making motions as if to paint one of the girls, who runs away from him. Mrs. García tells him to put the paint down. Kinney, who speaks English, replies, "Shut up, you big fat rat's ass!" Mrs. Bates leaves her group and goes to Kinney. She tells him, "You need time out in Mrs. Sayres's room (a first-grade next door to Mrs. Bates's kindergarten)." Kinney, his hand covered with blue paint, drops to the floor and refuses to move. He calls Mrs. Bates foul names. Mrs. Bates leaves him there, goes to the phone, and calls the office for assistance. Kinney gets up, wipes his hand first on a desk and then on himself, and runs out the door. He stops beside the entrance to Mrs. Sayres's room, and when Mrs. Bates follows he goes inside and sits at a designated table without further resistance. Mrs. Bates returns to her group, comprised mostly of Asian students. They sit quietly and attentively but do not speak. Mrs. Bates is using a Big Book on an easel, trying to get the students to repeat the words she says, but she has little success. When it is time for the next rotation, Mrs. Bates goes quickly to Mrs. Sayres's room and brings Kinney back to the class. He rejoins his group. As Mrs. Bates begins work with her new group, she sees Ryan and Duy at the measuring table pouring birdseed on each other's heads. Meanwhile, the new girl, Mei, continues sobbing audibly.

SCENARIO 8: JUNIOR HIGH WORLD HISTORY

The Class

Mr. Jaramillo's third-period world history class is attended by students whose achievement levels are average to below average. He paces his work slowly and keeps it simple. For the most part he enjoys the class, finding the students interesting and energetic. Mr. Jaramillo's lessons follow a consistent pattern. For the first part of the period, students take turns reading aloud from the textbook. Mr. Jaramillo selects the student readers at random from cards with students' names on them. If a student who is called on has lost the place in the textbook or is unable to answer a question about material read by the previous reader, the student loses a point, which affects the final grade. For the second part of the period, the class is divided into work groups. Each group selects a portion from the text reading and uses the information it contains as the basis for making something creative, such as group posters, to be shared at the end of the class if time allows.

Typical Occurrences

During oral reading, Mr. Jaramillo calls on Hillary to read. Although she has been following along, she shakes her head. This has happened several times before. Mr. Jaramillo, not wanting to hurt Hillary's feelings, simply says, "That costs you a point, Hillary," and he calls on someone else. Unfortunately, Hillary's reluctance carries over into group work as well, in which she refuses to participate. The other students ignore her and complete the work without her involvement. Occasionally, Clarisse refuses to involve herself in group work as well. When Mr. Jaramillo speaks to her about it, she replies, "You don't make Hillary do it." Mr. Jaramillo answers, "Look, we are talking about you, not about Hillary." However, he lets the matter lie there and says no more if Clarisse doesn't participate. On this particular day, Deonne has come into the classroom looking very angry. He slams his pack down on his desk and sits without opening his textbook for reading. Although Mr. Jaramillo picks Deonne's card from the deck, he recognizes Deonne's mood and decides not to call on him. Will is in an opposite mood. Throughout the oral reading portion of the class, he continually giggles at every mispronounced word and at every reply students give to Mr. Jaramillo's questions. Will sits in the front row and turns around to laugh, seeing if he can get anyone else to laugh with him. Although most students either ignore him or give him disgusted looks, he keeps laughing. Mr. Jaramillo finally asks him what is so funny. Will replies, "Nothing," and looks back at the class and laughs. At the end of the period, there is time for sharing three posters. Will makes comments and giggles about each of them. Clarisse, who has not participated, says, "Will, how about shutting up!" As the students leave the room, Mr. Jaramillo takes Deonne aside. "What's the matter with you, Deonne?" he asks. "Nothing," Deonne replies. His jaws are clenched as he strides past Mr. Jaramillo.

SCENARIO 9: HIGH SCHOOL AMERICAN LITERATURE

The Class

Mr. Wong teaches an 11th-grade one-semester course in American literature. The course is required for graduation. Among Mr. Wong's 33 students are eight seniors who failed the course previously and are retaking it. The students at Mr. Wong's school are from middle-class affluent families, and many of them are highly motivated academically. At the same time, there is also a significant number who have little interest in school aside from the opportunity to be with their friends. Mr. Wong's teaching routine proceeds as follows: First, he begins the period with a three-question quiz over assigned reading. The quiz items focus on facts such as names, places, and description of plot. Second, when the quiz papers are collected, Mr. Wong conducts a question-and-discussion session about the assigned reading. He calls on individual students, many of whom answer, "I don't know." Third, Mr. Wong has the class begin reading a new chapter in the work under study. They take turns reading orally until the end of the period. The remainder of the assignment not read orally is to be completed as homework.

A Typical Occurrence

The students enter Mr. Wong's classroom lethargically and begin taking the quiz from questions written on the board. Mr. Wong notices that many of the answers are obvious guesses. He notices Brian in particular, who has already failed the class and must pass it now in order to graduate. Mr. Wong says, "Didn't any of you read your assignment?" When oral reading begins, Mr. Wong notices that Brian does not have his copy of *Huckleberry Finn,* the work being studied. This is nothing new. Mr. Wong lends Brian a copy. Brian follows along in the reading for a while, then begins doodling on a sheet of paper. Mr. Wong calls on Brian to read. Brian cannot find the place. Mr. Wong says, "Brian, this is simply unacceptable. You have failed the class once; fail it again now and you know you don't graduate."

Brian does not look up but says, "Want to make a bet on that?"

"What?"

"I guarantee you I'll graduate."

"Not without summer school, you won't!"

"That's okay by me. That will be better. This class is too boring, and the assignments are too long. I've got other things to do besides read this stupid story. Who cares about this anyway? Why can't we read something that has to do with real life?"

Mr. Wong, offended, replies, "You couldn't be more wrong! Other students enjoy this work, and it is one of the greatest books in American literature! There is nothing wrong with the book! What's wrong, Brian, is your attitude!"

Brian's eyes are hot, but he says nothing further. His book remains closed. Mr. Wong struggles through the final 10 minutes of class. Brian is first out of the room when the bell rings.

SCENARIO 10: SIXTH GRADE, STUDENT TEACHER

The Class

Denise Thorpe is a student teacher in an inner-city magnet school that emphasizes academics. Half of her students are African American, and the other half, of various ethnic groups, have been bused in to take advantage of the instructional program and rich resources. All are academically talented, and none has what would be called a bad attitude toward school. Mrs. Warde, the regular teacher of the class, does not seem to rely on any particular scheme of discipline, at least none obvious to Miss Thorpe. Mrs. Warde simply tells the students what to do and they comply. For the first few lessons that Miss Thorpe teaches, Mrs. Warde remains in the room, acting the role of aide to Miss Thorpe. The students work well, and Miss Thorpe feels happy and successful.

When Mrs. Warde Leaves the Room

Mrs. Warde tells Miss Thorpe that she will leave the room during the math lesson so that Miss Thorpe can begin getting the feel of directing the class on her own. Mrs. Warde warns her that the class might test her with a bit of naughtiness, though nothing serious is likely to occur. Just be in charge, Mrs. Warde counsels. The math lesson begins well, without incident. The lesson has to do with beginning algebra concepts, which Miss Thorpe approaches through a discovery mode. She tells the class, "I want you to work independently on this. Think your way through the following equations and decide if they are true for all numbers."

$$a + 0 = a$$
$$a + b = b + a$$

$$a(b + c) = ab + c$$
$$a + 1 = 1$$
$$a \times 0 = a$$

The students begin work, but within two minutes hands are shooting up. Miss Thorpe goes to help Alicia, who is stuck on the third equation. "What's the matter?" Miss Thorpe whispers.

"I don't understand what this means."

"It was like what I showed you on the board. The same."

"Those were numbers. I don't understand it with these letters."

"They are the same as the numbers. They take the place of the numbers. I showed you how they were interchangeable, remember? Go ahead, let me see. Tell me what you are doing, step-by-step."

Miss Thorpe does not realize it, but she spends almost five minutes with Alicia. Meanwhile, a few of the students have finished and are waiting, but most are holding tired arms limply in the air. Miss Thorpe rushes to the next student and repeats her questioning tutorial. Meanwhile, Matt and Alonzo have dropped their hands and are looking at each other's papers. They begin to talk, then laugh. Others follow, and soon all work has stopped and the classroom has become quite noisy. Miss Thorpe repeatedly says, "Shhh, shhh!" but with little effect. At last she goes to the front of the room, demands attention, and tells the class how disappointed she is in their rude behavior.

Glossary
Discipline Terms with Indication of Origin

Acceptable choice (Nelsen, Lott, and Glenn): An option made available to students that the teacher considers worthwhile, whether students choose it or not.

Accountability (Kounin): Holding each student responsible for active involvement in what is being taught.

Accountability mentality (Nelsen, Lott, and Glenn): Student predisposition to accept responsibility for his or her own shortcomings. Contrasts with victim mentality.

Acknowledgment responses (Gordon): Teacher behavior that shows interest and attention when students are speaking.

Action dimension (Curwin and Mendler): Concerns what teachers should do when discipline problems occur.

Active listening (Gordon): Mirroring back what another person is saying, or otherwise confirming that one is attentive, interested, and nonjudgmental.

Activity movement (Kounin): The psychological and physical progression of lessons.

Activity reinforcers (Skinner's followers): Activities that students prefer in school: They can be used as reinforcing stimuli.

Appraising reality (Redl and Wattenberg): Helping students examine their behavior, note what is occurring, and anticipate the probable consequences.

Appreciative praise (Ginott): Praise that expresses gratitude or admiration for student effort.

Appropriate choices (Nelsen, Lott, and Glenn): Options that teachers make available to students, which further the educational program.

Assertive response style (the Canters): Responding to student behavior in a helpful manner while enforcing class rules.

Assertive teachers (the Canters): Teachers who clearly, confidently, and consistently express class expectations and attempt to build trust with students.

Authority (Gordon): A condition that allows a person to exert influence or control over others.

Authority P (Gordon): Authority manifested in a person's power to control others.

Authority C (Gordon): Authority that comes from commitments, agreements, or contracts.

Authority J (Gordon): Authority that comes with one's job description.

Authority E (Gordon): Authority based on expertise such as special knowledge, experience, training, skill, wisdom, or education.

Autocratic teachers (Dreikurs): Teachers who boss students, command, demand cooperation, dominate, and criticize.

Aversive discipline (Dreikurs): Control on behavior that uses unreasonable constraints coupled with harsh consequences when rules are broken.

Backbone teachers and schools (Coloroso): Teachers and schools that have in place clear expectations and standards of conduct.

Backup system (Jones): The planned action teachers take when students misbehave seriously and refuse to comply with positive teacher requests—usually means being sent to the principal's office.

Barriers (Nelsen, Lott, and Glenn): Teacher behaviors that are disrespectful and discouraging to students.

Behavior: Whatever one does, whether good or bad, right or wrong, helpful or useless, productive or wasteful. (Compare with misbehavior.)

Behavior contracts (Skinner's followers): Written agreements between teacher and students indicating what students are to do and what they will receive when they comply.

Behavior journal (the Canters): A log book in which students write accounts of their own misbehavior, why they broke a rule, and what a better behavior choice would have been.

Behavior modification (Skinner's followers): The use of Skinnerian principles of reinforcement to control or shape student behavior.

Behavior shaping (Skinner): The process of gradually modifying behavior through reinforcement.

Behavior window (Gordon): A graphic device used to determine the existence of a problem and indicate who owns it.

Behaviorally at-risk (Curwin and Mendler): Those students whose behavior prevents their learning and puts them in serious danger of failing in school.

Bell work (Jones): Work students do to begin a class period and that does not require active instruction from the teacher, such as reading, journal writing, and completion of warm-up activities.

Belonging (Glasser): A basic student need that is met when students are brought into discussions of topics that concern the class and receive acknowledgment from the teacher and others.

Body carriage (Jones): Posture and movement can indicate to students whether the teacher is well, ill, in charge, tired, disinterested, or intimidated.

Body language (Jones): Nonverbal communication transmitted through posture and facial expressions.

Boss teachers (Glasser): Teachers who set tasks, direct the learning activities, ask for little student input, and grade student work.

Brickwalls (Coloroso): Schools and teachers that rigidly use power and coercion to control students.

Builders (Nelsen, Lott, and Glenn): Teacher behaviors that show respect and encouragement to students.

Catch 'em being good (Skinner's followers): A behavior modification plan that involves rewarding students who are seen doing what is expected of them.

Challenge (Kounin): Teachers' giving puzzles, problems, or dares as a means of delaying satiation (boredom).

Checkpoints: Devices used in classrooms to monitor progress made toward stated goals.

Choose their behavior (Dreikurs, Glasser, Albert): The belief that students choose to behave as they do, rather than being forced to do so by background or other conditions.

Class meetings (Glasser; Nelsen, Lott, and Glenn): Meetings held in the classroom for addressing and solving problems.

Class rules: Written code of conduct for classroom behavior.

Classroom structure (Jones): Classroom organization, including room arrangement, class rules, class routines, chores, and the like.

Clients (Curwin and Mendler): The students in school, there to be helped by professionals, the teachers.

Climate: The feeling or tone that prevails in the classroom.

Collaborative rule-setting (Gordon): A procedure in which teachers and students work together to establish rules for making the classroom safe, efficient, and harmonious.

Community (Kohn): Classrooms and schools where students feel cared about and care about each other, are valued and respected, are involved in decision making, and have a sense of "we" rather than "I."

Conferring dignity (Ginott): Respecting students by putting aside their past history and being concerned only with the present situation.

Confrontive I-message (Gordon): An I-message used to ask students for input about a problem perceived by the teacher. "I need your help on this matter."

Confrontive skills (Gordon): A cluster of skills teachers can employ when they own a problem, used in such a way that they do not make students want to fight back or withdraw.

Congruent communication (Ginott): A style of communication in which teachers acknowledge and accept students' feelings about situations and themselves.

Consequences (Curwin and Mendler): Categories of interventions for misbehavior, such as reminders, warnings, and choosing.

(the Canters): Penalties invoked by teachers when students interfere with others' right to learn.

(Glasser): Students' agreement that when they break rules, they will try, with the teacher's help, to correct the underlying problem.

(most authorities): Steps to be taken when rules are violated, or complied with.

Contagious behavior (Redl and Wattenberg): Undesirable behavior that is attractive and is imitated by other students.

Conventional consequences (Curwin and Mendler): Consequences commonly seen in practice, such as time out, removal from the room, and suspension from school.

Correcting by directing (Ginott): Teachers correcting student misbehavior simply by telling students respectfully what they should be doing, instead of what they are doing wrong.

Creative responses (Curwin and Mendler): Unusual responses to student behavior such as role reversal, humor and nonsense, agreement with put-downs, improbable answers, paradoxical behavior, teacher tantrums, and taping classroom behavior.

Democratic teachers (Dreikurs): Teachers who show friendly guidance and encourage students to take on responsibility, cooperate, and participate in making decisions.

Dependency syndrome (Jones): A condition in which a student will not work unless the teacher is hovering nearby.

Desists (Kounin): Remarks and reprimands made to stop misbehavior.

Diagnostic thinking (Redl and Wattenberg): How teachers should analyze misbehavior, by forming a first hunch, gathering facts, exploring hidden factors, taking action, and remaining flexible.

Dignity (Curwin and Mendler): Respect for life and self.

Directions (the Canters): Statements that apply only to a given activity, in contrast to *rules* which are always in effect.

Discipline: What teachers do to help students behave acceptably in school.

(Jones): Teacher efforts to engage students in learning in the most positive, unobtrusive fashion possible.

(Coloroso): What teachers do to help students become aware of their behavior and accept its consequences.

Discipline hierarchy (the Canters): A list of consequences and the order in which they will be imposed within the period or day.

Displaying inadequacy (Dreikurs): Student withdrawal and failure to try.

Door openers (Gordon): Invitations to students to discuss their problems, as when the teacher, sensing that a student is troubled, asks quietly, "Would you like to talk about what's bothering you?"

Educational value (Jones): A quality of work that promotes academic learning, instead of merely keeping students occupied.

Effective discipline, principles of (Curwin and Mendler): Five fundamental notions concerning the duty to deal with misbehavior, the ineffectiveness of short-term solutions, the need to treat students with dignity, the maintenance of student motivation, and the importance of responsibility rather than obedience.

Efficient help (Jones): Help given to students, in 20 seconds or less, that returns them to productive work.

Encouragement (Dreikurs): Showing belief in students and stimulating them to try, as distinct from praising students for their accomplishments.

Esprit de corps: Group spirit, characterized by enthusiasm, sense of purpose, and desire to work for the benefit of the group.

Evaluative praise (Ginott): Praise that expresses judgment about students' character or quality of work, considered to be detrimental by Ginott and various other authorities.

Excuses (Glasser): Reasons students give for not behaving properly; should not be accepted by teachers.

Extinction (Skinner): The gradual removal of a given behavior accomplished by withholding reinforcement.

Eye contact (Jones): The teacher's looking at students' eyes or faces.

Facial expressions (Jones): Nonverbal communication through winks, frowns, smiles, and the like.

Four essential skills (Nelsen, Lott, and Glenn): Intrapersonal, interpersonal, strategic, and judgmental skills that students need for success in life.

Four-step problem-solving process (Nelsen, Lott, and Glenn): A problem-solving strategy for students to use in resolving their disputes: (1) Ignore the situation, (2) Talk it over respectfully with the other student, (3) Agree with the other student on a solution, (4) If no solution is found, put the matter on the class meeting agenda.

Freedom (Glasser): A basic student need that is met when students are allowed to make responsible choices concerning what they will study, how they will do so, and how they will demonstrate their accomplishments.

Fun (Glasser): A basic student need that is met when students are permitted to pursue activities they find intriguing and that allow them to interact with others.

General rules (Jones): Classroom rules that define the teacher's broad guidelines, standards, and expectations for work and behavior.

Genuine goal of belonging (Dreikurs): A fundamental desire to acquire sense of place and value in a group.

Genuine incentives (Jones): Incentives that motivate all members of the class rather than just a few.

Genuine success: Student success based on true accomplishment.

Getting attention (Dreikurs): Student behavior, such as disruption and showing off, intended to gain recognition from the teacher and other students.

Graceful exits (Albert): Steps teachers can take to distance themselves from confrontations with students who are very upset.

Grandma's rule (Jones): "First eat your vegetables, then you can have your dessert," or, "Finish your work first, then you can do something you especially enjoy."

Graphic reinforcers (Skinner's followers): Marks such as numerals, check marks, stars, and so forth that serve as reinforcing stimuli.

Group alerting (Kounin): Getting students' attention and quickly letting them know what they are supposed to do.

Group concern (Jones): A condition in which every student has a stake in the behavior that permits the group to earn a promised incentive.

Group disintegration (Redl and Wattenberg): A loss of cohesiveness that ultimately occurs in most groups.

Group dynamics (Redl and Wattenberg): Psychological forces that occur within groups and subsequently influence the behavior of group members.

Helping skills (Gordon): A cluster of helpful skills teachers can employ when the student owns the problem.

Hidden asset (Ginott): The following teacher question, when sincerely addressed to students: "How can I help you?"

Hope, sense of (Curwin and Mendler): Anticipation of success and well-being, which inspires us, enables us to live meaningfully, and provides courage and incentive to overcome barriers.

Hostile response style (the Canters): Bossing, putting-down, and ordering students about.

Hostile teachers (the Canters): Teachers who are openly disrespectful to students.

Hurdle help (Redl and Wattenberg): Assistance given to misbehaving students that helps them know what to do.

Identifying mistaken goals (Dreikurs): Ascertaining mistaken goals by noting the teacher's response to the misbehavior, such as annoyance, feeling threatened, and feeling hurt.

I-messages (Ginott, Gordon): Teachers' expressing their personal feelings and reactions to situations, such as "I have trouble teaching when there is so much noise in the room."

I-statements (Nelsen, Lott, and Glenn): Statements that begin with "I" and tell how the speaker feels. The same as I-messages.

Incentive (Jones): Something outside of the individual that entices the individual to act.

Influence techniques (Redl and Wattenberg): Steps teachers take to maintain class control.

Inner discipline (Coloroso): The ability to control one's own behavior and make responsible decisions.

Instructional consequences (Curwin and Mendler): Consequences that teach students how to behave properly.

Insubordination rule (Curwin and Mendler): If a student does not accept the consequence after breaking a class rule, then he or she will not be allowed to participate with the class until the consequence is accepted.

Interior loop (Jones): A classroom seating arrangement that allows teachers to move easily among students at work.

Interpersonal skills (Nelsen, Lott, and Glenn): Dialogue, sharing, listening, empathizing, cooperating, negotiating, and resolving conflicts—skills needed for working cooperatively with others.

Intrapersonal skill (Nelsen, Lott, and Glenn): Self-discipline and self-control, brought about by making distinctions between feelings, which are always acceptable, and resultant actions, which are not always acceptable.

Invasion of privacy (Ginott): Teachers attempting to discuss students' personal matters, making the students uncomfortable, embarrassed, or resentful.

Invite cooperation (Ginott): Encouraging and enticing students into activities and giving them choices, rather than demanding their participation.

Jellyfish teachers and schools (Coloroso): Teachers and schools that are wishy-washy, with unclear expectations or standards of conduct.

Judgmental skills (Nelsen, Lott, and Glenn): The ability to evaluate situations and make good choices.

Labeling is disabling (Ginott): Ginott's warning about the effects of teachers' labeling students in what they say.

Laconic language (Ginott): Brevity and succinctness of teacher's comments about misbehavior, such as "This is work time."

Lead teachers (Glasser): Teachers who discuss with students what the students wish to learn and how, provide necessary help, and encourage students to do quality work.

Logical consequences (Dreikurs): Conditions invoked by the teacher that are logically related to behavior that students choose.

   (Curwin and Mendler): Consequences in which students make right what they have done wrong.

   (Coloroso): Positive behavior of students in response to breaking rules: The behavior is to be responsible and related to the rule broken.

Management component: Aspect of classroom management that refers to how students are treated and how the instructional program is organized, delivered, and monitored.

Massive time wasting (Jones): The great amount of instructional time that is lost because of student misbehavior, mainly talking and goofing off.

Misbehavior: Behavior that is considered inappropriate for the setting or situation in which it occurs.

   (Gordon): An adult concept in which a student's behavior causes a consequence that is unpleasant to the teacher.

Mistaken goals (Dreikurs): Conditions students try to achieve in the mistaken belief they will bring the recognition students desire.

Modifying the environment (Gordon): A way of dealing with student misbehavior that involves changing the room or eliminating distractors.

Momentum (Kounin): Refers to teachers' getting activities started promptly, keeping them moving ahead, and bringing them to efficient closure or transition.

Need for extra attention (the Canters): A need evident in students who disrupt and call unnecessarily for the teacher's attention.

Need for extra motivation (the Canters): A need evident in students who do not engage in activities or complete work.

Need for firmer limits (the Canters): A need evident in students who disregard class rules.

Negative reinforcement (Skinner): Removing aversive stimuli in order to strengthen behavior.

No-lose method of conflict resolution (Gordon): An approach that enables both sides to find a mutually acceptable solution to their disagreement, so that neither is made to feel a loser.

Nonassertive response style (the Canters): Letting students get by with misbehavior in the classroom.

Nonassertive teachers (the Canters): Teachers who take a passive, hands-off approach to students.

Noncongruent communication (Ginott): Teacher communication that is not harmonious with students' feelings about situations and themselves.

Obedience (Curwin and Mendler): Not the goal of discipline: Responsibility is the true goal.

Omission training (Jones): An incentive plan for an individual student who, by cutting down on undesired behavior, can earn preferred activity time for the entire class.

Operant conditioning (Skinner): The process of shaping operant behavior through reinforcement.

Operant behavior (Skinner): Any behavior that an organism produces voluntarily.

Overdwelling (Ginott): Teachers' spending a long time needlessly explaining, warning, or reacting to misbehavior.

Overlapping (Kounin): Refers to teachers' attending to two or more issues at the same time.

Participative classroom management (Gordon): An operating procedure in which teachers share power and decision making with their students.

Passive listening (Gordon): A helping technique teachers use with students; includes attention, eye contact, and alertness as the student speaks.

Permissive teachers (Dreikurs): Teachers who put few if any limits on student behavior and do not invoke consequences for disruptive behavior.

Person component: An aspect of classroom practice having to do with how everyone treats each other in the classroom.

Physical proximity (Redl and Wattenberg; the Canters; Jones): The teacher's moving close to a student who is misbehaving.

Pleasure–pain principle (Redl and Wattenberg): Synonymous with reward and punishment.

Positive recognition (the Canters): Giving sincere personal attention to students who behave in keeping with class expectations.

Positive reinforcement (Skinner): Supplying reinforcing stimuli as a means of strengthening behavior.

Positive repetition (the Canters): Correcting a misbehaving student by commenting on what another student is doing properly—used in primary grades.

Power (Glasser): A basic student need that is met when students are given significant duties to discharge in class and are allowed to participate in decisions about topics and procedures.

Praise (the Canters; Albert): Laudatory comments, which the Canters maintain to be the most effective technique teachers have for encouraging responsible behavior.

(Dreikurs, Ginott): Approval given to students for effort and accomplishment: It is ineffective; encouragement should be used instead.

Preferred activity time (Jones): Time allocated for students to engage in activities of their preference; used as an incentive to encourage responsible behavior.

Preventing escalation of conflicts (Curwin and Mendler): Employing tactics such as allowing a cool-off period or rescheduling the work for a more appropriate time.

Prevention dimension (Curwin and Mendler): The aspect of discipline that attends to preventing the occurrence of misbehavior.

Preventive I-messages (Gordon): I-messages teachers use to help prevent misbehavior.

Preventive skills (Gordon): A cluster of skills teachers can employ to prevent behavior problems.

Preventive you-messages (Gordon): Messages directed at student misbehavior and intended to prevent its recurrence, such as, "You behaved very badly on our last field trip. I certainly hope you do better this time." (Should not be used.)

Primary feelings (Gordon): Emotions such as fear, worry, or disappointment that accompany problems; can give way later to secondary feelings such as anger or hostility.

Proactive teacher behavior (the Canters): Preplanned reactions to student misbehavior which, when practiced, can help teachers remain calm and effective.

Problem ownership (Gordon): A term used to indicate who is troubled by a situation: The troubled person is said to "own the problem."

Problem solving (Redl and Wattenberg; Gordon; Coloroso): A process, to be taught in the classroom, for collaboratively resolving concerns.

Professionals (Curwin and Mendler): Refers to teachers, emphasizing that their primary purpose is to do what they can to help students.

Promises (Redl and Wattenberg): Assurances made to students that unpleasant consequences will be invoked when rules are broken.

Proper breathing (Jones): Breathing technique, slow and deep, that helps teachers remain calm when facing student misbehavior.

Proximity praise (the Canters): Giving praise to a properly behaving student who is seated near a misbehaving student.

Punishment (Dreikurs): Action taken by the teacher to get back at misbehaving students and show them who is boss.

(Gordon): Aversive treatment of students; has overall negative effects.

(Redl and Wattenberg): Planned, unpleasant consequences, not physical, the purpose of which is to change behavior in positive directions.

(Skinner): Supplying aversive stimuli, a process that may or may not result in behavior change.

(Coloroso): Psychologically harmful consequences applied by teachers to students; likely to provoke resentment and retaliation.

Quality curriculum (Glasser): Characteristic of a program of study that emphasizes excellence in learnings that students consider useful.

Quality education (Glasser): Education in which students acquire knowledge and skills that the students themselves see as valuable.

Quality learning (Glasser): Learning in which students attain high competency in knowledge and skills they judge to be important in their lives.

Quality school work (Glasser): Learning activities centered around knowledge and skills that students find important and engaging.

Quality teaching (Glasser): Instruction in which teachers help students become proficient in knowledge and skills the students consider important.

Reactive teacher behavior (the Canters): Reactions to student behavior, not thought out in advance: They are frequently counterproductive.

Reasonable consequences (Coloroso): Consequences arranged by teacher and students that make sense and are appropriate to the violation of a given rule.

Reinforcement (Skinner): Supplying (or in some cases, removing) stimuli in such a manner that the organism becomes more likely to repeat a given act.

Reinforcing stimuli (Skinner): Stimuli received by an organism immediately following a behavior that increase the likelihood that the behavior will be repeated.

Resolution dimension (Curwin and Mendler): Focuses on helping chronically misbehaving students learn to make and abide by decisions that serve their needs.

Responsibility (Curwin and Mendler): A condition of self-control and good decision making, which are the primary goals of discipline.

Restructuring activities (Redl and Wattenberg): Changing activities when misbehavior occurs, such as by giving a brief rest or providing direct help.

Rewards (Gordon): Pay-offs used to control student behavior; considered ineffective in the long run.

Ripple effect (Kounin): The spread of effects to other students when a particular student is reprimanded.

Roadblocks to communication (Gordon): Things teachers say that inadvertently shut off student willingness to talk, such as preaching, advising, and analyzing.

RSVP (Coloroso): Qualities of consequences: reasonable, simple, valuable, and practical.

Rules (most authorities): Statements that indicate clearly how students are to behave.

Rules-ignore-praise (RIP) (Skinner's followers): A behavior modification plan that involves ignoring inappropriate behavior while reinforcing appropriate behavior.

Rules-reward-punishment (RRP) (Skinner's followers): A behavior modification plan that reinforces appropriate behavior while punishing inappropriate behavior.

Sane messages (Ginott): Teacher messages that address situations rather than students' character.

Satiation (Kounin): Getting too much exposure to an activity, resulting in one's becoming bored and listless.

Scapegoating (Redl and Wattenberg): A phenomenon in which the group seeks to displace its hostility onto an unpopular individual or subgroup.

Secondary feelings (Gordon): Manufactured feelings that arise as a consequence of the primary feeling: For example, the primary feeling of fear, resulting from a student being injured, is replaced by anger at the student's breaking rules, once the student is found to be all right.

Seeking power (Dreikurs): Student behavior that attempts to gain control over teachers through arguing, lying, throwing temper tantrums, and refusing to follow directions.

Seeking revenge (Dreikurs): Student behavior intended to hurt the teacher or other students.

Self-discipline (Dreikurs): Self-control, which grows out of living with reasonable limits on behavior while recognizing that all behavior produces consequences.

Self-evaluation (Glasser): Students appraising the quality of their own work; a key step leading to improvement and quality work.

Series of little victories (Ginott): Ginott's depiction of how teachers gradually develop good discipline in the classroom, through encouraging self-direction and responsibility while showing concern and helpfulness.

Setting limits (most authorities): Clarifying with the class exactly what is expected of them.

Severe clause (the Canters): Invoking the most severe penalty in the discipline hierarchy when extreme behaviors such as fighting occur: usually means being sent to the principal.

Shifting gears (Gordon): A change teachers make—from an assertive posture to a listening posture.

Short-term solutions (Curwin and Mendler): Steps to stop misbehavior, such as scolding, lecturing, or detention: They are not likely to have lasting positive effect.

Signals (Redl and Wattenberg): Physical gestures, eye contact, and the like, that indicate to students what they should, or should not, be doing.

Significant seven (Nelsen, Lott, and Glenn): Three self-perceptions and four sets of skills that successful students develop.

SIR (Glasser): An acronym standing for the process of self-evaluation, improvement, and repetition, used until quality is achieved.

Situational assistance (Redl and Wattenberg): Steps teachers take to help students regain self-control, such as restructuring the activity, taking a break, or using humor.

Smoothness (Kounin): Teachers' avoidance of abrupt changes that interfere with students' activities or thought processes.

Social contract (Curwin and Mendler): The agreement concerning rules and consequences that teacher and students have decided should govern behavior in the classroom.

Social contract test (Curwin and Mendler): A test to prevent students' using the excuse that they didn't understand the rules. This test deals with class rules and consequences.

Social reinforcers (Skinner's followers): Words and behaviors such as comments, gestures, and facial expressions that serve as reinforcing stimuli.

Specific rules (Jones): Classroom rules that detail specifically what students are to do and how they are to do it.

Strategic skills (Nelsen, Lott, and Glenn): Responding to the limits and consequences of everyday life with responsibility, adaptability, flexibility, and integrity.

Student responsibility (Glasser): An earlier Glasser contention that students have the obligation to consider their behavior choices and live with the consequences.

Students' needs (Glasser): A group of five basic needs—for survival, belonging, power, fun, and freedom—upon which curriculum and teaching should be based.

Supporting self-control (Redl and Wattenberg): Low-key steps teachers take to help students control their own behavior, such as using signals and physical proximity.

Tangible reinforcers (Skinner's followers): Real objects given to students when they behave appropriately.

Teacher component: A component of teaching that refers to teachers' skills in preventing misbehavior.

Teacher enthusiasm (Kounin): A trait Kounin found to be positively correlated with student motivation and learning.

Teacher roles (Redl and Wattenberg): Roles that students assign to their teachers, such as representatives of society, referees, and judges of quality.

Teachers at their best (Ginott): Teachers, when using congruent communication that addresses situations rather than students' character, invites student cooperation, and accepts students as they are.

Teachers at their worst (Ginott): Teachers, when they name-call, label students, ask rhetorical "why" questions, give long moralistic lectures, and make caustic remarks to their students.

Teacher's own self-discipline (Ginott): One of the most important factors in class discipline, where teachers only rarely lose their composure and always treat students with respect.

Threats (Redl and Wattenberg): Emotional statements that make students anxious and fearful, given in the form of "If you don't . . . I will . . . !"

Three perceptions (Nelsen, Lott, and Glenn): Perceptions of personal capability, significance in primary relationships, and personal power to influence one's own life.

Three R's of solutions (Nelsen, Lott, and Glenn): Solutions for correcting misbehavior that are *related* to what was done wrong, *respectful* of the persons involved, and *reasonable.*

Time lines: Devices used in classrooms to monitor progress over periods of time.

Token economies (Skinner's followers): Elaborate behavior modification systems that involve giving students graphic or tangible reinforcers that they can save and trade later for other items.

Types of classroom misbehavior: In descending order of seriousness, as judged by social scientists, they are aggression, immorality, defiance of authority, class disruption, and goofing-off.

Unequal treatment (Curwin and Mendler): The best discipline systems cannot treat students equally, but must treat them differently in accordance with individual needs.

Useful work (Glasser): Schoolwork that deals with skills and information that students deem valuable in their lives.

Value judgments (Glasser): In Glasser's earlier work, the contention that when students misbehave, they should be required to make judgments about their actions. Now refers to Glasser's insistence that students appraise the quality of their own work.

Variety (Kounin): Varying instructional activities so that students have movement, use their senses, and employ different thought modalities.

Victim mentality (Nelsen, Lott, and Glenn): A predisposition to blame others for one's own shortcomings. Contrasts with accountability mentality.

Why questions (Ginott): Counterproductive questions that teachers put to students, asking them to explain or justify their behavior.

Win–lose conflict resolution (Gordon): A method of resolving conflict in which one person emerges as "winner" and the other as "loser." This method is to be avoided in favor of "no-lose conflict resolution."

Win–win solutions (Nelsen, Lott, and Glenn): Solutions to problems that are found acceptable by all sides.

Withitness (Kounin): The teacher's knowing what is going on in all parts of the classroom at all times.

You-messages (Ginott, Gordon, and others): Teacher messages that attack students' character, such as "You are acting like barbarians." These messages carry heavy blame and putdowns.

Bibliography

A place for problem students: Separate school proposed for disruptive teenagers. 1994. *Washington Post*, VAW, 1:5. January 13.

A handbook of alternatives to corporal punishment. Fourth edition. 1994. Oklahoma City, Okla: Oklahoma State Department of Education.

Adler, A. 1958. *What life should mean to you.* New York: Capricorn.

Agne, J., G. Greenwood, and L. Miller. 1994. Relationships between teacher belief systems and teacher effectiveness. *Journal of research and development in education, 27*(3), 141-152.

Albert, L. 1985. *Coping with kids and school.* New York: Ballantine.

———. 1992. *An administrator's guide to cooperative discipline.* Circle Pines, Minn.: American Guidance Service.

———. 1993. *Coping with kids.* Tampa, Fla.: Alkorn House.

———. 1994. *Bringing home cooperative discipline.* Circle Pines, Minn.: American Guidance Service.

———. 1994. *Responsible kids at school and at home: The cooperative discipline way.* (Videotape series). Circle Pines, Minn.: American Guidance Service.

———. 1996. *A teacher's guide to cooperative discipline.* Rev. ed. Circle Pines, Minn.: American Guidance Service.

———. 1996. *Cooperative discipline.* Circle Pines, Minn.: American Guidance Service.

———. 1996. *Cooperative discipline implementation guide.* Circle Pines, Minn.: American Guidance Service.

———. 1996. *Cooperative discipline staff development.* (Videotape series). Circle Pines, Minn.: American Guidance Service.

Albert, L., and M. Popkin. 1989. *Quality parenting.* New York: Ballantine.

Angell, A. 1991. Democratic climates in elementary classrooms: A review of theory and research. *Theory and Research in Social Education, 19,* 241-266.

Augustine, D., K. Gruber, and L. Hanson. 1990. Cooperation works! *Educational Leadership, 47,* 4-7.

Banbury, M., and C. Hebert. 1992. Do you see what I mean? Body language in classroom interactions. *Teaching Exceptional Children, 24,* 24-28.

Bartell, J. 1992. Starting from scratch. *Principal, 72,* 13-14.

Berne, E. 1964. *Games people play.* New York: Grove.

Black, S. 1994. Throw away the hickory stick. *Executive Educator, 16*(4), 44-47.

Blank, M., and C. Kershaw. 1993. Perceptions of educators about classroom management demands when using interactive strategies. Paper presented at the annual meeting of the American Educational Research Association (Atlanta, Ga., April 12-16).

Blendinger, J. 1996. *QLM: Quality Leading & Managing. A Practical Guide for Improving Schools.* Dubuque, Iowa: Kendall Hunt.

Boothe, J., L. Bradley, and T. Flick. 1993. The violence at your door. *Executive Educator 15*(1), 16-22.

Bozzone, M. 1994. Spend less time refereeing and more time teaching. *Instructor, 104*(1), 88-93.

Brophy, J. 1987. Synthesis on strategies for motivating students to learn. *Educational Leadership, 45,* 40-48.

Brophy, J., and J. Putnam. 1979. Classroom management in the elementary school in D. L. Duke (ed.), *Classroom management: The seventy-eighth yearbook of the National Society for the Study of Education* (pp. 182-216). Chicago: University of Chicago Press.

Burke, K. 1992. *What to do with the kid who . . . : Developing cooperation, self-discipline, and responsibility in the classroom.* Palatine, Ill.: IRI/Skylight.

Cangelosi, J. 1993. *Classroom management strategies. Gaining and maintaining students' co-operation.* 2d ed. White Plains, N.Y.: Longman.

Canter, L. 1976. *Assertive Discipline: A take-charge approach for today's educator.* Seal Beach, Calif.: Canter & Associates.

———. 1978. Be an assertive teacher. *Instructor, 88*(1), 60.

———. 1988. Let the educator beware: A response to Curwin and Mendler. *Educational Leadership, 46*(2), 71-73.

———. 1996. First, the rapport—then, the rules. *Learning, 24*(5), 12,14.

Canter, L., and M. Canter. 1986. *Assertive Discipline Phase 2 in-service media package* [Videotapes and manuals]. Santa Monica, Calif.: Canter & Associates.

———. 1989. *Assertive Discipline for secondary school educators. In-service video package and leader's manual.* Santa Monica, Calif.: Canter & Associates.

———. 1992. *Assertive Discipline: Positive behavior management for today's classroom.* 2d ed. Santa Monica, Calif.: Canter & Associates.

———. 1993. *Succeeding with difficult students: New strategies for reaching your most challenging students.* Santa Monica, Calif.: Canter & Associates.

Castle, K., and K. Rogers. 1993. Rule-creating in a constructivist classroom community. *Childhood Education, 70*(2), 77-80.

Cawthorne, B. 1981. *Instant success for classroom teachers, new and substitute teachers in grades K through 8.* Scottsdale, Ariz.: Greenfield.

Charles, C., and G. Senter. 1995. *Elementary classroom management.* 2d ed. White Plains, N.Y.: Longman.

Charney, R. 1991. *Teaching children to care: Management in the responsive classroom.* Greenfield, Mass.: Northeast Foundation for Children.

Classroom discipline and lessons in social values. 1990. *New York Times,* B, 7:3, January 31.

Clawson, P. 1995. Hispanic parents demonstrate to protest students' expulsions. *Chicago Tribune,* 2NW, 2:4, October 24.

Collins, R. 1995. Dover takes action. *Boston Globe,* NH, 1:1, November 12.

Coloroso, B. 1994. *Kids are worth it! Giving your child the gift of inner discipline.* New York: William Morrow.

———. 1998. *Parenting with wit and wisdom in times of chaos and confusion.* Littleton, Colo.: Kids are worth it!

Corno, L. 1992. Encouraging students to take responsibility for learning and performance. *Elementary School Journal, 93,* 69-83.

Curwin, R. 1980. Are your students addicted to praise? *Instructor, 90,* 61-62.

———. 1992. *Rediscovering hope: Our greatest teaching strategy.* Bloomington, Ind.: National Educational Service.

———. 1993. The healing power of altruism. *Educational Leadership, 51*(3), 36–39.

———. 1995. A humane approach to reducing violence in schools. *Educational Leadership, 52*(5), 72–75.

Curwin, R., and A. Mendler. 1980. *The discipline book: A complete guide to school and classroom management.* Reston, Va.: Reston Publishing.

———. 1984. High standards for effective discipline. *Educational Leadership, 41*(8), 75–76.

———. 1988. *Discipline with dignity.* Alexandria, Va.: Association for Supervision and Curriculum Development.

———. 1988. Packaged discipline programs: Let the buyer beware. *Educational Leadership, 46*(2), 68–71.

———. 1989. We repeat, let the buyer beware: A response to Canter. *Educational Leadership, 46*(6), 83.

———. 1992. *Discipline with dignity* [Workshop participants handout]. Rochester, N.Y.: Discipline Associates.

Dao, J. 1995. Suspension now required for taking gun to school. *New York Times,* B, 4:5, August 1.

Dewey, J. 1938. *Logic: The theory of inquiry.* New York: Holt, Rinehart & Winston.

Dowdy, Z. 1995. School officers to merge with Boston police force. *Boston Globe,* 33:4, March 16.

Dreikurs, R. 1957. *Psychology in the classroom.* New York: Harper and Row.

———. 1968. *Psychology in the classroom.* 2d ed. New York: Harper & Row.

Dreikurs, R., and P. Cassel. 1972. *Discipline without tears.* New York: Hawthorn.

Dreikurs, R., B. Grunwald, and E. Pepper. 1982. *Maintaining sanity in the classroom.* New York: Harper & Row.

Eccles, J., A. Wigfield, and C. Midgley. 1993. Negative effects of traditional middle schools on students' motivation. *Elementary School Journal, 93*(5), 553–574.

Edwards, C. 1997. *Classroom discipline and management.* Upper Saddle River, N.J.: Prentice-Hall.

Ehrgott, et al. 1992. A study of the marginal teacher in California. Paper presented at the annual meeting of the California Educational Research Association (San Francisco, November, 1992).

Elam, S. 1989. The second Gallup/Phi Delta Kappa poll of teachers' attitudes toward the public schools. *Phi Delta Kappan, 70*(10), 785–798.

Elam, S., L. Rose, and A. Gallup. 1996. The 28th annual Phi Delta Kappa/Gallup poll of the public's attitudes toward the public schools. *Phi Delta Kappan, 78*(1), 41–59.

Ellis, D., and P. Karr-Kidwell. 1995. A study of assertive discipline and recommendations for effective classroom management methods. Paper 26 p. Washington, D.C.: U.S. Department of Education. ERIC Clearinghouse #35596.

Emmer, E., C. Evertson, and L. Anderson. 1980. Effective classroom management at the beginning of the school year. *Elementary School Journal, 80,* 219–231.

Evertson, C. 1989. Classroom organization and management. In M. Reynolds (ed.), *Knowledge base for the beginning teacher.* Oxford: Pergamon Press.

———. 1989. Improving elementary classroom management: A school-based training program for beginning the year. *Journal of Educational Research, 83,* 82–90.

Evertson, C., E. Emmer, B. Clements, J. Sanford, and M. Worsham. 1989. *Classroom management for elementary teachers.* Englewood Cliffs, N.J.: Prentice-Hall.

Evertson, C., and A. Harris. 1992. What we know about managing classrooms. *Educational Leadership, 49*(7), 74–78.

Feldman, D. 1994. The effect of assertive discipline procedures on preschool children in segregated and integrated settings: A longitudinal study. *Education and Training in Mental Retardation and Developmental Disabilities, 24*(9), 291–306.

Fighting violence with values. 1993. *Atlanta Journal,* A, 12:1, December 23.

Firth, G. 1985. *Behavior management in the schools: A primer for parents.* New York: Charles C. Thomas.

Fraser, B., and P. O'Brien. 1985. Student and teacher perceptions of the environment of elementary school classrooms. *Elementary School Journal, 85*(5), 567–580.

Fuhr, D. 1993. Effective classroom discipline: Advice for educators. *NASSP Bulletin, 76*(549), 82–86.

Gardner, H. 1983. *Frames of mind: The theory of multiple intelligences.* New York: Harper and Row.

Gaustad, J. 1992. *School discipline* (ERIC Digest No. 78). Eugene, Oreg.: ERIC Clearinghouse on Educational Management.

Gibbons, L., and L. Jones. 1994. Novice teachers' reflectivity upon their classroom management. Paper, 13 p. Washington, D.C.: U.S. Department of Education. ERIC Clearinghouse #SP036198.

Ginott, H. 1965. *Between parent and child.* New York: Avon.

———. 1969. *Between parent and teenager.* New York: Macmillan.

———. 1971. *Teacher and child.* New York: Macmillan.

———. 1972. I am angry! I am appalled! I am furious! *Today's Education, 61,* 23–24.

———. 1973. Driving children sane. *Today's Education, 62,* 20–25.

Glasser, W. 1965. *Reality therapy: A new approach to psychiatry.* New York: Harper & Row.

———. 1969. *Schools without failure.* New York: Harper & Row.

———. 1977. 10 steps to good discipline. *Today's Education, 66,* 60–63.

———. 1978. Disorders in our schools: Causes and remedies. *Phi Delta Kappan, 59,* 331–333.

———. 1985. *Control theory: A new explanation of how we control our lives.* New York: Perennial Library.

———. 1986. *Control theory in the classroom.* New York: Harper & Row.

———. 1990. *The quality school: Managing students without coercion.* New York: Harper & Row. (Reissued with additional material in 1992)

———. 1992. The quality school curriculum. *Phi Delta Kappan, 73*(9), 690–694.

———. 1993. *The quality school teacher.* New York: Harper Perennial.

Glenn, H. 1989. *Developing capable people.* (Audio Cassette Tape Series). Fair Oaks, Calif.: Sunshine Press.

———. 1989. *Empowering others: Ten keys to affirming and validating people.* (Videotape). Fair Oaks, Calif.: Sunshine Press.

———. 1989. *Six steps to developing responsibility.* (Videotape). Fair Oaks, Calif.: Sunshine Press.

———. 1989. *Teachers who make a difference.* (Videotape). Fair Oaks, Calif.: Sunshine Press.

Glenn, H., and J. Nelsen. 1987. *Raising children for success.* Fair Oaks, Calif.: Sunshine Press.

———. 1988. *Raising self-reliant children in a self-indulgent world.* Rocklin, Calif.: Prima.

Gordon, T. 1970. *Parent Effectiveness Training: A tested new way to raise responsible children.* New York: New American Library.

———. 1974. *T.E.T.: Teacher Effectiveness Training.* New York: David McKay.

———. 1976. *P.E.T. in action.* New York: Bantam Books.

———. 1989. *Discipline that works: Promoting self-discipline in children.* New York: Random House.

Gottfredson, D., G. Gottfredson, and L. Hybl. 1993. Managing adolescent behavior: A multiyear, multischool study. *American Educational Research Journal, 30*(1), 179–215.

Grant, C., and C. Sleeter. 1989. *Turning on learning: Five approaches for multicultural teaching plans for race, class, gender, and disability.* Columbus, Ohio.: Merrill.

Greenlee, A., and E. Ogletree. 1993. Teachers' attitudes toward student discipline problems and classroom management strategies. Washington, D.C.: U.S. Department of Education. ERIC Clearinghouse # PS021851.

Hakim, L. 1993. *Conflict resolution in the schools.* San Rafael, Calif.: Human Rights Resource Center.

Hartzell, G., and T. Petrie. 1992. The principal and discipline: Working with school structures, teachers, and students. *Clearing House, 65*(6), 376–380.

Hernandez, H. 1989. *Multicultural education: A teacher's guide to content and process.* Columbus, Ohio: Merrill.

Hill, D. 1990. Order in the classroom. *Teacher Magazine, 1*(7), 70–77.

Hindle, D. 1994. Coping proactively with middle years students. *Middle School Journal, 25*(3), 31–34.

Hoover, R., and R. Kindsvatter. 1997. *Democratic discipline: Foundation and practice.* Upper Saddle River, N.J.: Prentice Hall.

Horne, A. 1994. Teaching children with behavior problems takes understanding, tools, and courage. *Contemporary Education, 65*(3), 122–127.

Hughes, H. 1994. *From fistfights to gunfights: Preparing teachers and administrators to cope with violence in school.* Paper presented at the annual meeting of the American Association of Colleges for Teacher Education, Chicago, February.

Johnson, D., K. Acikogz, and R. Johnson. 1994. Effects of conflict resolution training on elementary school students. *Journal of Social Psychology, 134*(6), 803–817.

Johnson, V. 1994. Student teachers' conceptions of classroom control. *Journal of Educational Research, 88*(2), 109–117.

Jones, F. 1979. The gentle art of classroom discipline. *National Elementary Principal, 58,* 26–32.

———. 1987. *Positive classroom discipline.* New York: McGraw-Hill.

———. 1987. *Positive classroom instruction.* New York: McGraw-Hill.

———. 1996. Did not! Did, too! *Learning, 24*(6), 24–26.

Jones, J. 1993. *Instructor's guide: Positive classroom discipline—a video course of study.* Santa Cruz, Calif.: Fredric H. Jones & Associates.

Jones, V., and L. Jones. 1990. *Comprehensive classroom management: Motivating and managing students.* Needham Heights, Mass.: Allyn & Bacon.

Knapp, M., B. Turnbull, and P. Shields. 1990. New directions for educating the children of poverty. *Educational Leadership, 48*(4), 1–8.

Kohn, A. 1990. *The brighter side of human nature: Altruism and empathy in everyday life.* New York: Basic.

———. 1990. *You know what they say . . . : The truth about popular beliefs.* New York: HarperCollins.

———. 1992. *No contest: The case against competition.* Boston: Houghton Mifflin.

———. 1993. *Punished by rewards: The trouble with gold stars, incentive plans, A's, praise, and other bribes.* Boston: Houghton Mifflin.

———. 1994. Bribes for behaving: Why behaviorism doesn't help children become good people. *NAMTA Journal, 19*(2), 71–94.

———. 1995. Discipline is the problem—not the solution. *Learning 1995, 24*(2): 34.

———. 1996. *Beyond discipline: From compliance to community.* Alexandria, Va.: Association for Supervision and Curriculum Development.

Kounin, J. 1977. *Discipline and group management in classrooms.* Rev. ed. New York: Holt, Rinehart & Winston. (Original work published 1971)

Kramer, P. 1992. Fostering self-esteem can keep kids safe and sound. *PTA Today, 17*(6), 10–11.

Ladoucer, R., and J. Armstrong. 1983. Evaluation of a behavioral program for the improvement of grades among high school students. *Journal of Counseling Psychology, 30,* 100–103.

La disciplina positive. 1994. ERIC Digest. Urbana, Ill.: ERIC Clearinghouse on Elementary and Early Childhood Education.

Landen, W. 1992. Violence and our schools: What can we do? *Updating School Board Policies, 23,* 1–5.

Latham, G. 1993. *Managing the classroom environment to facilitate effective instruction* [Six-part videotape in-service training program]. Logan, Utah: P & T Ink.

Loucks, H. 1993. Teacher education: A success story. *Principal, 73*(1), 27–29.

Lowman, J. 1996. Characteristics of exemplary teachers. *New Directions for Teaching and Learning, 65,* 33–40.

Macht, J. 1989. *Managing classroom behavior: An ecological approach to academic and social learning.* White Plains, N.Y.: Longman.

Mahoney, M., and C. Thoresen. 1972. Behavioral self-control—Power to the person. *Educational Researcher, 1,* 5–7.

Markoff, A. 1992. *Within reach: Academic achievement through parent–teacher communication.* Novato, Calif.: Academic Therapy Publications.

Martens, B., and S. Kelly. 1993. A behavioral analysis of effective teaching. *School Psychology Quarterly, 8*(1), 10–26.

McCormack, S. 1989. Response to Render, Padilla, and Krank: But practitioners say it works! *Educational Leadership, 46*(6), 77–79.

McIntyre, T. 1989. *The behavior management handbook: Setting up effective behavior management systems.* Boston: Allyn & Bacon.

Mendler, A., and R. Curwin. 1983. *Taking charge in the classroom.* Reston, Va.: Reston Publishing.

Micklo, S. 1993. Perceived problems of public school prekindergarten teachers. *Journal of Research in Childhood Education, 8*(1), 57–68.

Milhollan, F., and B. Forisha. 1972. *From Skinner to Rogers: Contrasting approaches to education.* Lincoln, Nebr: Professional Educators Publications.

Morrison, J., K. Olivos, G. Dominguez, D. Gomez, and D. Lena. 1993. The application of family systems approaches to school behavior problems on a school-level discipline board: An outcome study. *Elementary School Guidance and Counseling, 27*(4), 258–272.

Nealon, P. 1995. *Boston Globe,* 17:2, March 14.

Nelsen, J. 1987. *Positive discipline.* New York: Ballantine.

———. 1988. *Positive Discipline Video* (Videotape). Fair Oaks, Calif.: Sunshine Press.

———. 1997. No more logical consequencs—At least hardly ever! Focus on solutions. *Empowering People Catalog,* Winter/Spring, 8.

Nelsen, J., R. Duffy, L. Escobar, K. Ortolano, and D. Owen-Sohocki. 1996. *Positive discipline: A teacher's A–Z guide.* Rocklin, Calif.: Prima.

Nelsen, J., L. Lott, and H. Glenn. 1997. *Positive discipline in the classroom.* Rocklin, Calif.: Prima.

N.H. schools begin program to teach ethics, values. 1989. *Boston Globe,* 67: 1, August 31.

Newman, M. 1995. 16 city schools are taken over by chancellor. *New York Times., A,* 1:2, October 20.

Novelli, J. 1990. Design a classroom that works. *Instructor, 100*(1), 24–27.

Office of Educational Research and Improvement. 1993. *Reducing school violence: Schools teaching peace.* A joint study (Report No. RP-91002002). Washington, D.C.: Author.

O Harrow, R. 1995. Reading, writing, right and wrong. *Washington Post., D,* 1:1, September 8.

Paradise, R. 1994. Spontaneous cultural compatibility: Mazahua students and their teachers constructing trusting relationships. *Peabody Journal of Education, 69*(2), 60-70.

Peng, S. 1993. Fostering student discipline and effort: Approaches used in Chinese schools. Paper presented at the Annual Meeting of the American Educational Research Association (Atlanta, April 12-16).

Population Reference Bureau for the Center for the Study of Social Policy (1992). *Challenge of change: What the 1990 census tells us about children.* Washington, D.C.: Author.

Positive discipline in the classroom. 1997. *The Video Journal of Education, 6*(7). Issue.

Powell, T., and S. Taylor. 1994. Taking care of risky business. *South Carolina Middle School Journal,* Spring 1994, 5-6.

Precision teaching in perspective: An interview with Ogden R. Lindsley. (1971). *Teaching Exceptional Children, 3,* 114-119.

Queen, J., B. Blackwelder, and L. Mallen. 1997. *Responsible classroom management for teachers and students.* Upper Saddle River, N.J.: Prentice Hall.

Ramsay, P., and D. Oliver. 1995. Capacities and behaviour of quality classroom teachers. *School Effectiveness and School Improvement, 4*(4), 332-366.

Rancifer, J. 1993. Effective classroom management: A teaching strategy for a maturing profession. Paper presented at the annual conference of the Southeastern Regional Association of Teacher Educators (Nashville, October 27-30).

———. 1995. Revolving classroom door: Management strategies to eliminate the quick spin. Paper presented at the annual meeting of the Southern Regional Association of Teacher Educators (Lake Charles, La., November 2-4).

Rardin, R. 1978. Classroom management made easy. *Virginia Journal of Education,* September, 14-17.

Redl, F. 1972. *When we deal with children.* New York: Free Press.

Redl, F., and W. Wattenberg. 1959. *Mental hygiene in teaching.* Rev. ed. New York: Harcourt, Brace & World. (Original work published 1951)

Redl, F., and D. Wineman. 1952. *Controls from within.* Glencoe, Ill.: Free Press.

Render, G., J. Padilla, and H. Krank. 1989. What research really shows about Assertive Discipline. *Educational Leadership, 46*(6), 72-75.

Rich, J. 1992. Predicting and controlling school violence. *Contemporary Education, 64*(1), 35-39.

Richardson, G. 1993. Student teacher journals: Reflective and nonreflective. Paper presented at the annual Mid-South Educational Research Association (New Orleans, November 10-12).

Richardson, R., D. Wilcox, and J. Dunne. 1994. Corporal punishment in schools: Initial progress in the bible belt. *Journal of Humanistic Education and Development, 32*(4), 173-182.

Rosen, L. 1992. *School discipline practices: A manual for school administrators.* Perrysburg, Ohio: School Justice Institute.

Ruot, C. 1994. *Discipline strategies for the bored, belligerent and ballistic in your classroom.* Captiva, Fla.: Sanibel Sanddollar Publications.

Ryan, F. 1994. From rod to reason: Historical perspectives on corporal punishment in the public schools. *Educational Horizons, 72*(2), 70-77.

Schaps, E. June, 1990. Cooperative learning: The challenge in the '90s. *Cooperative Learning Magazine,* June, 5-8.

Schaps, E., and D. Solomon. 1990. Schools and classrooms as caring communities. *Educational Leadership, 48*(3), 38-42.

Schell, L., and P. Burden. 1992. *Countdown to the first day of school: A 60-day get-ready check-list for first-time teachers, teacher transfers, student teachers, teacher mentors, induction-program administrators, teacher educators* (NEA Checklist series). Washington, D.C.: National Education Association.

Schulman, J. 1989. Blue freeways: Traveling the alternate route with big-city teacher trainees. *Journal of Teacher Education, 40*(5), 2–8.

Schmidt, S. 1996. Character in the classroom. *The San Diego Union,* May 19, 1:22.

Schwartz, F. 1981. Supporting or subverting learning: Peer group patterns in four tracked schools. *Anthropology and Education Quarterly, 12*(2), 99–120.

Sharpley, C. 1985. Implicit rewards in the classroom. *Contemporary Educational Psychology, 10,* 349–368.

Shen, F. 1995. Educators get tough on violence. *Washington Post,* MDP, 1:1, August 24.

Sheviakov, G., and F. Redl. 1956. *Discipline for today's children.* Washington, D.C.: Association for Supervision and Curriculum Development.

Shreeve, W. 1993. Evaluating teacher evaluation: Who is responsible for teacher probation? *NASSP Bulletin, 77*(551), 8–19.

Sidman, M. 1989. *Coercion and its fallout.* Boston: Authors Cooperative.

Skinner, B. F. 1948. *Walden two.* New York: Macmillan.

———. 1953. *Science and human behavior.* New York: Macmillan.

———. 1954. The science of learning and the art of teaching. *Harvard Educational Review, 24,* 86–97.

———. 1958. Teaching machines. *Science, 128,* 969–977.

———. 1968. *The technology of teaching.* New York: Appleton-Century-Crofts.

———. 1971. *Beyond freedom and dignity.* New York: Knopf.

———. 1973. The free and happy student. *Phi Delta Kappan, 55,* 13–16.

Slavin, R. 1991. Synthesis of research on cooperative learning. *Educational Leadership, 48,* 71–82.

Slavin, R., N. Karweit, and N. Madden. 1989. *Effective programs for students at risk.* Needham Heights, Mass.: Allyn & Bacon.

Smith, M. 1993. Some school-based violence prevention strategies. *NASSP Bulletin, 77* (557), 70–75.

Sobol, T. 1990. Understanding diversity. *Educational Leadership, 48*(3), 27–30.

Stone, S. 1993. Issues in education: Taking time to teach social skills. *Childhood Education, 69*(4), 194–195.

Study backs induction schools to help new teachers stay teachers. 1987. *ASCD Update, 29*(4), 1.

Taking action against violence. *Instructor, 103*(6), 41–43.

Tauber, R. 1982. Negative reinforcement: A positive strategy in classroom management. *Clearing House, 56,* 64–67.

Teachers fear violence in schools. (1994). *Atlanta Journal Constitution,* E, 12:1, March 20.

Wattenberg, W. 1955. *The adolescent years.* New York: Harcourt Brace.

———. 1967. *All men are created equal.* Detroit: Wayne State University Press.

Weade, R., and C. Evertson. 1988. The construction of lessons in effective and less effective class-rooms. *Teaching and Teacher Education, 4*(3), 189–213.

Weiner, B. 1984. Principles for a theory of student motivation and their application within an attributional framework. In *Research on Motivation in Education: Student Motivation.* R. Ames and C. Ames, eds. Vol. 1. New York: Academic Press.

Weinstein, C. 1992. Designing the instructional environment: Focus on seating. In *Proceedings of selected research and development presentations at the Convention of the Association for Educational Communications and Technology,* p. 7. Resources in Education, Phoenix, Ariz.: Oryx Press. (ERIC Document Reproduction Service No. IR 015 706).

Weinstein, C., A. Woolfolk, and L. Dittmeier. 1994. Protector or prison guard? Using metaphors and media to explore student teachers' thinking about classroom management. *Action in Teacher Education, 16*(1), 41-54.

Weirs, M. 1995. Clayton County adds boot camp to school program. *Atlanta Constitution,* XJI, 1:5, October 19.

Williams, S. 1991. We can work it out. *Teacher Magazine, 3*(2), 22-23.

Wong, H., and R. Wong. 1991. *The first days of school: How to be an effective teacher.* Sunnyvale, Calif.: Harry K. Wong.

Woo, E. 1995. New math: Dividing school day differently. *Los Angeles Times,* A, 1:1, September 29.

Zeller, N., and M. Gutierrez. 1995. Speaking of discipline . . . : An international perspective. *Thresholds in Education, 21*(2), 60-66.

Zirpoli, T., and K. Mellow. 1997. *Behavior management: Applications for teachers and parents.* 2d ed. Upper Saddle River, N.J.: Prentice-Hall.

Index